RITES OF CONQUEST

RITES OF CONQUEST

The History and Culture of
Michigan's Native Americans

Charles E. Cleland

Ann Arbor
THE UNIVERSITY OF MICHIGAN PRESS

Copyright © by the University of Michigan 1992
All rights reserved
Published in the United States of America by
The University of Michigan Press
Manufactured in the United States of America

1995   1994   1993   4   3   2

Library of Congress Cataloging-in-Publication Data

Cleland, Charles E., 1936–
    Rites of conquest : the history and culture of Michigan's Native
Americans / Charles E. Cleland.
       p.   cm.
    Includes bibliographical references and index.
    ISBN 0-472-09447-5 (alk. paper). — ISBN 0-472-06447-9 (pbk. :
alk. paper)
    1. Indians of North American—Michigan—History.   2. Indians of
North America—Great Lakes Region—History.   3. Indians of North
America—Michigan—Social life and customs.   4. Indians of North
America—Great Lakes Region—Social life and customs.   I. Title.
E78.M6C57   1992
977.4'00497—dc20   92-16201
                                                                 CIP

For Nancy, Elena, Kate, Josh, and Lisa

Preface

The large and excellent literature relating to the historical experiences of the native peoples of North America often finds its focus on particular ethnic groups, historical periods, or prominent individuals. This book takes a multiethnic and regional approach, a method of organization actually pioneered in the Great Lakes region over fifty years ago by W. Vernon Kinietz in *The Indians of the Western Great Lakes, 1615–1760*. Like Kinietz's work, this book also focuses on Michigan Indians. It is, of course, true that the political boundaries of Michigan, not set until 1837, did not influence the early histories of the tribes that, incidentally, only partially resided within those boundaries. In this regard, a book on Michigan Indians makes little sense. On the other hand, since the formation of the state, Michigan (as a political entity) has had an increasingly important role in the course of the history of its native people. In order to contend with this reality, I began with a regional perspective and then gave more specific geographic focus through time.

In examining the historic events, people, policies, and ideas that were important in charting the place of Great Lakes Indians in the history of the state and region, an ethnohistorical perspective was chosen for the interpretation of written sources. This mode of documentary critique was first applied to Great Lakes history by Harold Hickerson with the publication of his *The Chippewa and Their Neighbors: A Study of Ethnohistory*, which appeared in 1970. What Hickerson understood, and what some anthropologists and historians have since come to appreciate, is that the "facts" of history recorded by non-Indians likely had an entirely different meaning to the

Ojibwa or Potawatomi who were participants in those same events. Ethnohistory is not the history of ethnics; it is history filtered through a different cultural perspective. Where possible, these other realities have been incorporated.

This book is written for a sophisticated lay reader who is curious about the details of the histories and cultures of Great Lakes Indians. I hope it will only be a starting place for many readers. Of course, I also hope fellow ethnohistorians will find a fresh idea or two and perhaps a perspective worth exploring in these pages. Finally, I hope Indian people will read this book as a way of understanding the trials and triumphs of their forebears.

In truth, I believe the histories of the Ojibwa, Ottawa, and Potawatomi peoples on which this book is focused are vastly misunderstood by the public. Like all historical accounts, the history of Indian groups is the product of the historian who selects and interprets the facts to conform to some preconceived theory or perspective. Too often, Indian history or the role of Indians in American history has been written to either glorify or to vilify Indian participants rather than to gain a perspective on their special place in historical events.

Although I intend this book to present the facts of history objectively, it must be admitted that it does so with a perspective sympathetic to the trials of the Great Lakes Indians in the three hundred years of contact with Europeans and Americans. I will confess to both empathy for their suffering and admiration for their long and decidedly uphill struggle to maintain their cultures, dignity, and pride. I believe the ethnohistorical approach, which centers interpretation on the contemporary cultural context in which events are best understood, transcends my own bias.

Finally, I hope this book makes it apparent that the traditional cultures and histories of Great Lakes Indians are worthy of serious study. Beyond the intrinsic qualities of those cultures, their merit as a point of departure for the study of the cultural dynamics, and as a means of satisfying our curiosity about the complexity of the historical process, is the fact that these cultures reveal a philosophy of some import to modern social life. To wit, the advice of the *mide* priests of old: value the knowledge that comes from study, the wisdom that flows from life, and the power of dreams.

Acknowledgments

In the preparation of this book I have profited a great deal from the opinions and advice of several of my colleagues in anthropology at Michigan State University. They have also taken the time to comment on various chapters of the book while it was in preparation. Dr. William Lovis and Dr. Margaret Holman provided excellent suggestions in regard to the organization of archaeological and ethnographic detail and its interpretation. Dr. James McClurken's tremendous knowledge of Great Lakes ethnohistory and its sources has been of invaluable help on many occasions as have his opinions on the interpretation of historical data. Special thanks goes to Dr. Robert McKinley, whose imaginative insights into the nature of culture and human behavior always kept me focused on broader issues.

Mr. Victor Kishigo of Petoskey and Mr. Harold Thompson of Saginaw, both men with little tolerance for nonsense and with serious interests in Great Lakes history, did me the favor of reading earlier drafts of this book. Their comments have frequently been incorporated. Dr. Carol Mason was kind enough to critically review the manuscript and I am grateful for her many excellent suggestions.

I have also profited much from discussions at various times with James Jannetta, Thor Conway, Dr. Earl Prahl, James Morrison, Dr. Helen Tanner, and Ted Halopa, and I am grateful for their insights into Indian life and history.

The illustrations were prepared by Bernadette Nemeth, who has a good eye for design and color and who made some excellent suggestions to improve the various maps and diagrams.

My wife, Nancy, spent many hours at the word processor and in providing editorial criticisms. Her assistance in the preparation of the book and her skill with the English language are a very substantial part of this project, and I am grateful for her help. Thanks are also due to Gerna Rubenstein for her help in word processing.

Finally I want to extend a most special thanks to Nancy, Elena, and Kate Cleland for their patience while I devoted myself to writing.

Contents

Chapter 1

In the Beginning

In the month of *Manitogizis* (January), when the evenings are cold and Indian people gathered around their fires, it was safe to talk of the spirits. Now, the old ones, skilled in myth and legend, could tell their tales, stories of the time when the earth was new and when the trickster hero *Nanabojo* roamed in high adventure creating plants, animals, and the geography of our modern landscape. These were tales well told, spiced with the irony and humor that can only come from the honing of a thousand retellings.

As the children and their parents listened with fascination, they learned that the world and the creatures around them were not always like they are; indeed, they are not even now like they seem. What is puzzling, they learn, may be apparent and what seems so real may truly be quite mysterious.

As the old people told it, the first world was a world of dreams and mist. It was not clear what was plant and what was animal, and humans, too, had no definite place. In this first world lived two people, an old woman and her daughter.[1]

Each day the daughter went to search for food. She was only able to find a single kind of berry and, as a result, had to travel a great deal. One day a spirit saw her and took a liking to her; it was the wind. Although the air was hot and still, the girl felt a sudden gust of wind. The wind swirled around her only to leave her as suddenly as it had appeared.[2]

Shortly thereafter, the old woman had strange feelings about her daughter and asked her if she had seen anyone while she was out berrying. "No" said the girl, "I'm always by myself." Yet the old woman knew that something was strange. Sure enough, the girl discovered that she was pregnant. Only then did she remember the wind and told her mother. The old woman knew right away that the Sun was the father.

When the time came to give birth, the woman went to the forest where three children were born. The first was a normal baby boy. After this baby was born she held it in her arms. Then she heard a voice that said, "Put the baby on the ground." She didn't do it. After some time, the voice said, "You didn't want to do what I tell you. If you had put the baby down, it would have been able to walk. Now the baby won't walk for a year." This is why human babies, unlike animals, can't walk soon after they are born. This first baby was called *Nanabojo*.

Then another child was born. It didn't have human features, yet it looked like a human baby. This was the second brother. The third child, called *Maskasaswabik*, was then born. This baby was made of stone. The three boys grew up fast. After all, they were *manidog* or spirits.

The oldest son, *Nanabojo*, killed everything in sight, and although his mother told him repeatedly not to kill other creatures he persisted, even trying to kill powerful spirits. The two older brothers traveled far and wide exploring the world, but because the stone brother could not travel, they were obligated to return to camp each day.

One day, *Nanabojo* said to the second brother, "Do you think it would be all right if I killed our brother *Maskasaswabik* so we wouldn't have to return to the same place anymore?" His brother replied, "You're the one that's thinking of what you are going to do." When they returned to the camp, the stone brother (who was magically listening to every word) said to *Nanabojo*, "Why don't you do what you were talking about?" So *Nanabojo* borrowed an ax from the old woman and tried to kill the stone brother. He only dulled the ax. The stone brother said to *Nanabojo*, "You will never kill me unless you heat me red hot and then throw water on me." *Nanabojo* did just that and his brother *Maskasaswabik* cracked and died. Then the two remaining brothers were free to travel widely and they began to explore.

As they traveled, the second brother began to tire more and more easily and finally could not keep up with *Nanabojo*, so *Nanabojo* decided to leave him behind. He dug a hole in the earth and put his brother inside, carefully covering him with earth and marking the spot with a rock. Now *Nanabojo* was happy and could roam freely, but, in his enjoyment, he forgot to return for his brother. When he finally did return to look for him he couldn't find the hole. He did, however, see evidence that his brother's spirit had appeared and *Nanabojo* knew his brother was dead. When he knew that he felt alone and cried and cried. His brother heard him and told *Nanabojo* not to cry, but *Nanabojo* said, "What did you come back for? Why don't you return to the place where you were?" His brother replied, "I will make a road for the people to travel along when they die."

The second brother made the road to the spirit world, a road that led in one direction. Once people take this road they can never return. Once the second brother came to that place, he called back to *Nanabojo* and said, "I'll tell you what the Indians will call me— *Nekajiwegizik*." That name means 'someone who goes down behind the sky.' The second brother did not have a name until he named himself.

Now *Nanabojo* was alone. He'd killed his brothers. Since it was *Nekajiwegizik* who created a place for people to go after death, the third brother, *Maskasaswabik,* could not go to that place because the road did not exist when he died. It is for this reason that he is still on earth.[3] At this time, *Nanabojo* had the bowl that he and his brother had shared. This is the reason Indians give someone who has lost a loved one a mourning dish, *bepagwecinunk,* 'something to take your mind off it.'

As he traveled on, *Nanabojo* befriended a wolf, who became his companion and of whom he became very fond. One night, the wolf did not return and *Nanabojo* discovered it had been drowned by underwater spirits who took the form of huge snakes. To take revenge, *Nanabojo* made a bow and succeeded in wounding two serpents. Later, masquerading as a woman doctor, *Nanabojo* entered the house of the serpents and pretended to perform a cure. Instead, he plunged the arrows in deeper, killing the spirit serpents. In revenge, the underwater creatures caused a huge flood to destroy the world. *Nanabojo* barely managed to save himself by climbing the highest pine tree on the highest hill. Even then his nose was just above the water.

As *Nanabojo* clung to the tree he noticed animals swimming in the water. "Brothers," he said, "could you go down and get some soil?

If you do, I will make an earth for us to live on." The otter, a strong swimmer, said he would try, and dove for the bottom. He didn't make it to the bottom and floated back to the surface where he was revived by *Nanabojo,* who blew life back into the otter's body. Next, the beaver was determined to try, and he dived. The beaver stayed down a long time but soon his body, too, floated to the surface. *Nanabojo* blew life back into the beaver and asked him, "Did you see the bottom?" "Yes," said the beaver, "but I couldn't reach it." Next it was the little muskrat's turn. Since the otter and beaver had failed, it didn't seem to have a chance to succeed. *Nanabojo* waited a long time and at last the little muskrat's body floated up. The muskrat's paw was closed and when *Nanabojo* opened it, there were several grains of soil. He dried these in the sun and then threw them into the water where they became a beautiful island.[4] *Nanabojo* added soil and the island grew into the earth.

It was on this new earth that the world of the Indians was formed. The *manidog* created the four separate strata of the cosmos: the earth, underworld, sky, and sky vault. These domains were populated by the many spirits that gave *Nanabojo* what he needed to live on the earth and created for him the parents that became the original humans, the *Anishnabeg.*

A long series of legends details the marvelous travels of *Nanabojo,* who often appears as a mischievous and foolish being who through various misadventures produces the characteristics that we observe in the plants and animals around us. Not least of all, the legends account for similarities and differences among humans and form the rationale for proper social behavior.

The Birth of a Myth

It is true of Indian mythology that the distant past merges ultimately into the historical present. As events known from historical experience lose the dimension of time and place and as events surrender detail for essence, myths are born. These are different kinds of truth that the Ojibwa clearly recognize in distinguishing between *daebaudjimowin,* a chronicle known from personal experience, and *auwaetchigum,* truths that transcend history, that is, truths of parable and allegory.[5]

In 1842 at La Pointe, Wisconsin, interpreter and Ojibwa historian

William Warren recorded an argument between two venerable chiefs that illustrates the way history becomes legend. It seems that a disagreement arose between members of the Loon and Crane clans as to which would provide the hereditary chief at La Pointe. Loon clan chief *Kitchi-wash-keenh*, Great Buffalo, argued that the very numerous and prominent Loon clan had the right to represent the people of La Pointe. He was answered by the elder chief of the Crane clan, *Tug-waug-aun-ay*, who refers to the migration legend of the Ojibwa that was, in that day, a fundamental tenet of the Grand Medicine Society or the *Midé-wi-win*. This legend tells how the Ojibwa people appeared at the shores of the great salt sea in the east and how, over the generations, they moved continually westward to the Great Lakes.[6]

Tug-waug-aun-ay made his argument using an allegory. According to Warren, he arose to reply to *Kitchi-wash-keenh* and began by pointing to the eastern sky: the Great Spirit once made a bird, and he sent it from the skies to make its abode on earth. The bird came, and when it reached halfway down, among the clouds, it sent forth a loud and far-sounding cry, which was heard by all who resided on the earth, and even by the spirits who make their abode within its bosom. When the bird reached within sight of the earth, it circled, looking for a resting place, till it lit on a hill overlooking *Boweting* (Sault Ste. Marie); here it chose its first resting place, pleased with the numerous whitefish that glanced and swam in the clear waters and sparkling foam of the rapids. Satisfied with its chosen seat, again the bird sent forth its loud but solitary cry; the *No-kaig* (bear clan), *A-waus-e-wug* (catfish), *Ah-auh-wauh-ug* (loon), and *Mois-o-neeg* (moose and martin clan) gathered at its call. A large town soon congregated and the bird, whom the Great Spirit sent, presided over all.

Once again it took flight and the bird flew slowly over the waters of Lake Superior. Pleased with the sand point of *Shaug-ah-waum-ik-ong* (Chequamegon Bay, Wisconsin), it circled over it, and viewed the numerous fish as they swam about in the clear depths of the Great Lake. It lit on *Shaug-ah-waum-ik-ong*, and from thence again it uttered its solitary cry. A voice came from the calm bosom of the lake in answer. The crane, pleased with the musical sound of the voice, again sent forth its cry, and the answering bird made its appearance in the wampum-breasted *Ah-auh-wauh* (loon). The bird spoke to it in a gentle tone, "Is it thou that gives answer to my cry?"

Nanabojo and the Ducks

As he was walking along suddenly he came to a lake, and there in the lake he saw numerous ducks. Immediately he ran back quietly before they could see him and sought out a spot where there was a swamp. From it he gathered a large quantity of reedgrass and made himself a big pack. This he put on his back and carried to the lake. He walked along the shore of the lake carrying it ostentatiously. Soon the ducks saw him and said, "Look, that is Trickster walking over there. I wonder what he is doing? Let us call and ask him." So they called to him. But it was only after the fourth call that he replied and said, "Well, are you calling me?" "What are you carrying on your back?" they asked. "My younger brothers, surely you do not know what it is you are asking. What am I carrying? Why, I am carrying songs. My stomach is full of bad songs. Some of these my stomach could not hold and that is why I am carrying them on my back. It is a long time since I sang any of them. Just now there are a large number in me. I have met no people on my journey who would dance for me and let me sing some for them. And I have, in consequence, not sung any for a long time." Then the ducks spoke to each other and said, "Come, what if we ask him to sing? Then we could dance, couldn't we?" So one of them called out, "Well, let it be so. I enjoy dancing very much and it has been a very long time since I last danced."

So they spoke to Trickster, "Older brother, yes, if you will sing to us we will dance. We have been yearning to dance for some time but could not do so because we had no songs." Thus spoke the ducks. "My younger brothers," replied Trickster, "you have spoken well and you shall have your desire granted. First, however, I will erect a dancing lodge, a grass lodge." Then they made a drum. When this was finished he invited them all to come in and they did so. When he was ready to sing he said, "My younger brothers, this is the way in which you must act. When I sing, when I have people dance for me, the dancers must, from the very beginning, never open their eyes. If you do they will become red." So, as soon as he began to sing, the ducks closed their eyes and danced.

After a while one of the ducks was heard to flap his wings as he came back to the entrance of the lodge, and cry, "Quack!" Again and again this happened. Sometimes it sounded as if the particular duck had somehow tightened its throat. Whenever any of the ducks cried out then Trickster would tell the other ducks to dance faster and faster. Finally, a duck whose name was Little-Red-Eyed-Duck secretly opened its eyes, just the least little bit it opened them. To its surprise, Trickster was wringing the necks of his fellow ducks! He would also bite them as he twisted their necks. It was while he was doing this that the noise which sounded like the tightening of the throat was heard. In this fashion, Trickster killed as many as he could reach.

Little-Red-Eyed-Duck shouted. "Alas! He is killing us! Let those who can save themselves." He himself flew out quickly through the opening above. All the others likewise crowded toward this opening. They struck Trickster with their wings and scratched him with their feet. He went among them with his eyes closed and stuck out his hands to grab them. He grabbed one in each hand and choked them to death. His eyes were closed tightly. Then suddenly all of them escaped except the two he had in his grasp.

When he looked at these, to his annoyance, he was holding in each hand a scabby-mouthed duck. In no way perturbed, however, he shouted, "Ha, ha, this is the way a man acts! Indeed these ducks will make fine soup to drink!" Then he made a fire and cut some sharp-pointed sticks with which to roast them. Some he roasted in this manner, while others he roasted by covering them with ashes. "I will wait for them to be cooked," he said to himself. "I had, however, better go to sleep now. By the time I awake they will unquestionably be thoroughly done. Now, you, my younger brother, must keep watch for me while I go to sleep. If you notice any people, drive them off." He was talking to his anus. Then, turning his anus toward the fire, he went to sleep.

—Paul Radin, *The Trickster:*
A Study in American Indian Mythology.

The loon answered, "It is I." The crane then said to him, "Thy voice is music. It is melody. It sounds sweet to my ear. From henceforth I appoint thee to answer my voice in council." "Thus," continued the chief, "the loon became the first in council, but he who made him chief was *Bus-in-ause* (Echo-maker), or the crane. These are the words of my ancestors, who, from generation to generation, have repeated them into the ears of their children."

As Warren tells us, all the assembled Ojibwa understood the allegory perfectly well and, as they quietly listened, they gave their assent by whispering, "It is true, it is true."[7]

The migration of the Ojibwa as told in the allegory of the flight of the crane has a telling visual counterpart in the nineteenth-century birch bark migration charts that have been preserved in various American and Canadian museums. Charts such as Red Sky's migration chart (now held by the Glenbow-Alberta Institute in Calgary) show the westward migration of the Ojibwa from the great salt sea in the east to Leech Lake in Minnesota.[8] Assuming a historical migration of many, many generations, it would be logical to think that the makers of the charts, relying on the legends of the migration itself, would have more detailed knowledge of the more recent parts of the journey, that is, the western part. Indeed, referring to the left side of Red Sky's chart, we see Lake Superior clearly identifiable by the sand bar that even today separates the western end of the lake from Fond du Lac (Minnesota). On the eastern end of Lake Superior, the falls of the St. Marys River (*Boweting*) are recognizable.

Between Lake Superior and Leech Lake, one familiar with the old canoe routes can trace the Ojibwa migration up the St. Louis River to the east branch of the Savannah River, to Big Sandy Lake and then on to the Mississippi River, to the Leech River, and then to Leech Lake itself. The chart shows the route replete with portages, places sacred to the Ojibwa, and places guarded by dangerous serpents. As near as it can be determined, this route from Lake Superior to Leech Lake was developed in the late eighteenth and early nineteenth centuries as the Pillager bands pushed westward, expelling the Lakota who formerly occupied this region.

As we might expect, the geographic detail of the migration journey from the salt sea to Lake Superior is shown in the vaguest geographic detail. Moving east of Sault Ste. Marie, we see Lake Huron and then

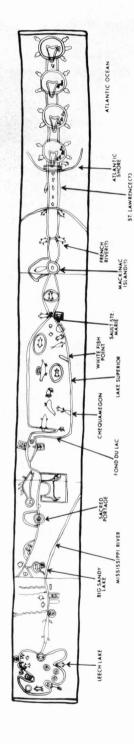

Red Sky's migration chart. (Drawing by B. Nemeth. Courtesy of the University of Toronto Press, Glenbow Museum.)

a series of stylized rivers and portages that have been identified by
chart owners as the French River, the Mattawa, Ottawa, Montreal,
and the St. Lawrence rivers. The salt sea is represented by a shoreline where the first great town of the Ojibwa was established. It was
here that the bear revealed the secrets and ritual of the *Midé-wi-win*
to the Ojibwa people.

Through the migration legends, the use of symbolism and allegory, the distinction between *daebaudjamowin* and *auwaetehigum*
as well as the visual representations of the migration charts, we see
the process of historic truth being transformed into mythological
truth. It is, perhaps, in this reality that we can best understand the
actions of the Indian people of the upper Great Lakes during the
seventeenth, eighteenth, and nineteenth centuries as well as some
actions of their modern descendants.

Science and the Past

There is yet another and distinctly different way to know the origins
of the native peoples of the upper Lakes. Origins not passed on in
words but in material things produced by the minds and hands; objects that, as the truths of mythology, bear witness to the passing of
generation upon generation of Indian people. The interpretation of
these vestiges of the past falls to the domain of archaeologists, scien-
tists learned and skilled in reading evidence from the ground. It is
the archaeologist who, through the study of the villages, camps, burial places, quarries, and workshops of ancient people, sheds scientific
light on origins and developing cultural traditions. As a science, archaeology is based upon objective observation and the formulation
and testing of hypotheses through the use of newly acquired information. In this sense, archaeology is very distinct from mythology; it is
not constructed on faith and belief, but upon healthy skepticism.
Skepticism, it should be mentioned, does not stifle the excitement of
discovery nor still the romance with which most archaeologists perceive their work.

Michigan, her neighboring states, and the province of Ontario,
have, within their boundaries, thousands of archaeological sites.
Each represents at least one episode in the historic occupation of the
region. Each site was formed by people doing the things people do:
cooking food, making tools, giving birth, warming themselves, telling

stories, and dying. In performing many of these activities, people knowingly or unconsciously modified their environments. They left behind broken pots, lost or discarded stone artifacts, fireplaces, remains of meals, and many other telltale signs of their lifeway. These sites are the only "voice" of these ancient people and, unfortunately, they are being destroyed in unprecedented numbers as urban expansion, modern farming techniques, and other earthmoving construction obliterates these precious, nonrenewable resources of our common heritage.

Archaeologists have now been intensively studying the Great Lakes archaeological record for about fifty years. Thanks to the careful excavation of many sites and the use of scientific techniques such as radiocarbon dating and computers for the manipulation of massive amounts of data, a general understanding of the archaeological record has emerged.[9] What a phenomenal record it is!

Archaeological data indicate that Indians have occupied the upper Great Lakes region for about 12,000 years. It is difficult to conceive of such a period of time, even for a people versed in numbers and conditioned to ordering events in continuous time. In contrast to the 350 or so years non-Indian people have lived on the shores of the Great Lakes, such a tenure is immense.

As a way to think about the difference, suppose that we were to produce a home video called "The Human History of Michigan and the Great Lakes," complete with a cast of thousands and accurate in every detail. Suppose our video covered all twelve thousand years and lasted an entire year. It would have to run twenty four hours a day, day in and day out. On that scale, each month would represent one thousand years and each day would show the passing of about thirty-three years. This latter time was about equal to a human life span before the modern era. If we turned on our finished video as the clock struck out the old year on New Year's eve, we would see immense glaciers that would gradually melt, retreating to the north. Behind the waning ice we would see the birth of the first Great Lakes, fed by glacial meltwater. The landscape would at first be stark, with few, if any trees, and the ground would be covered with tundra plants. As the glaciers continued their northward path, the midlatitude tundra would begin to develop patches of conifers, willows, alder, and sedges near watercourses and, as we might imagine, grazing and browsing animals. Our postglacial landscape would be dotted with feeding herds of caribou, musk ox, and mammoth (mastodon), and, perhaps, an occasional giant moose browsing at the margins of ponds.

It is now mid- to late January in our video, and it is into this scene that the first Indian hunters appear. As we watch with fascination through February, March, and then into the spring and summer, we would see generations upon generations of the descendants of these hunters. Each generation would produce changes, inventions, and improvements. We would no doubt also see famines, battles, and human disasters along with progress. Some time during late November, our Indian actors would cultivate corn, beans, and squash, and they would be making pottery and living in substantial villages. Perhaps, most amazing to us, however, is that even by mid-December we have yet to see a non-Indian actor appear in our video. In fact, it would not be until December 21st that a French explorer would make a brief appearance. Only in the few remaining days of the video would non-Indian actors outnumber Indian ones, and only then would the modern cities, towns, and farms of our modern landscape fill the screen. As the curtain closes on our production, which will be notable for its length if not its artistic achievement, we will certainly be impressed with the great cultural journey of the Indian peoples, their endurance as a people, and, most certainly, with their long and close relationship with the land.

What specifically do archaeologists have to say about Indian origins? In sorting through the archaeological record, archaeologists arbitrarily divide the long continuum of cultural development into four episodes. The earliest, the Paleo-Indian, represents the original settlers. This is followed by the long Archaic period, which bears witness to the cultural adaptations made to the formation of the modern natural environments of the region and to other emerging cultures. Beginning in the few centuries preceding the Christian millennia, Great Lakes Indians began to develop skills in horticulture in the southern Great Lakes basin and fishing in the north. Evidence of these events in the archaeological record signals the beginning of the Woodland period. It was these same Woodland people who were encountered by the first visiting European explorers. When artifacts of European materials and manufacture appear on Woodland sites, archaeologists label them as belonging to the Historic era.

Given these major divisions of the archaeological record, we can

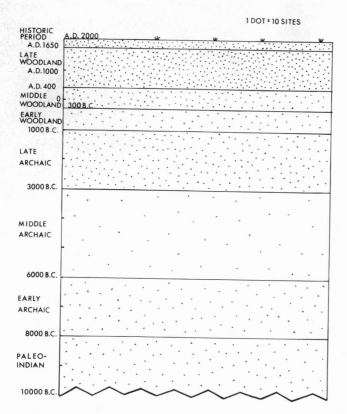

Concentration of known archaeological components (occupations) by period in Michigan. (Drawing by B. Nemeth.)

now proceed with a more detailed recounting of the archaeological story. A visual representation can show a profile of an idealized archaeological site such as might occur if all occupations took place at one locality. The thickness of the deposits and the density of material within them approximately reflects the total archaeological record.

The Paleo-Indians

Few archaeologists, either amateur or professional, have experienced the thrill of finding a fluted spear point. The long, straight-sided chert points with distinct concave grooves on both faces are the hallmark of the Great Lakes country's first residents, the Paleo-Indians. These first Indians were part of the original immigration of people to the

Western hemisphere. As archaeologists have reconstructed it, Paleo-Indians, remote ancestors of modern Indians, reached North America across the land bridge connecting Siberia with Alaska. While some have argued for an earlier date, most prehistorians agree that this event took place at about 14,000 B.P. (years before the present). From sites in western North America, we know these people were big-game hunters who moved rapidly to colonize both North and South America. By about 12,000 B.P. (10,000 B.C.), Paleo-Indians occupied the game-rich zone at the southern margins of the huge continental glaciers that covered the northern part of the Great Lakes basin and the St. Lawrence valley.

As the glacier slowly retreated northward, the newly exposed moraine and till plain country was taken over by tundra vegetation that soon supported herds of grazing animals, particularly caribou.[10] It was into this landscape that Indians first ventured sometime near the middle of the eleventh millennium before the present.

Unfortunately, our knowledge of Paleo-Indians in the Great Lakes region is scant, but, judging from the small, scattered sites occupied by these people, it is assumed they traveled in small groups, camping as they followed game.[11] Presumably, game was hunted with thrusting lances tipped with the distinctive fluted points. They also carried a meager inventory of chert tools that were used for specialized hunting tasks: choppers for dismembering the kill, knives for skinning and cutting, several kinds of scrapers for processing hides, and wood and chert gravers for cutting and working bone and antler.

Most Paleo-Indian sites are located in the southern parts of Wisconsin, Michigan, and Ontario.[12] Most are located on the beaches and knolls associated with glacial Lake Algonquian, one of the earliest lakes from the postglacial lake sequence that leads ultimately to the modern Great Lakes. During the approximately one thousand years between the initial appearance of Paleo-Indian hunters and the last vestige of fluted points, which seem to date from the middle of the tenth millennium before present, Paleo-Indians evolved as they made the adjustments to life in the region. During their tenure, it seems that the environment was rapidly changing. Cultural changes evident in the archaeological record include new techniques for the manufacture of stone tools, new tool forms, and the use of local sources of chert for tool manufacture. Undoubtedly, the nondurable aspect of the cultures of these first inhabitants evolved as well.

The Archaic People

The entire period between 10,000 and 3000 B.P. (8000–1000 B.C.) is known as the Archaic period. More than a period, the Archaic represents a long and poorly known cultural sequence that is perhaps best understood as a reflection of changes in lifeway necessary to accommodate emerging modern landscape and climate.

As the great continental glaciers retreated north of Lake Huron, the weight of ice depressed the land to the extent that the upper Great Lakes drained north, forging a new channel through Lake Nipissing and the Ottawa River to the St. Lawrence.[13] As if a plug had been pulled, the levels of Lakes Michigan and Huron fell until only relatively small bodies of water (called Lakes Chippewa and Stanley) filled the deepest part of their basins. At this time, 10,000 to 8000 B.P. (8000–6000 B.C.), the forests of the Great Lakes region were strongly dominated by pine. Subsequent changes in global weather patterns produced a period of warm, dry weather during the period between about 8000 to 5000 B.P. (6000–3000 B.C.). The climate was thus warmer than it is now and, partially as a result, hardwood species came to dominate Great Lakes forests. As the Archaic period progressed, the land rebounded and the lakes returned to former levels. The weather, too, gradually cooled and with this we see the development of the mixed deciduous and coniferous species in today's Great Lakes forest. It is thus believed that, by about 5000 B.P. (3000 B.C.), Michigan's climate, forests, and shorelines achieved their modern character.

For all intents and purposes, the Archaic can be divided into an early period illustrative of the immediate changes from the late Paleo-Indian and a longer, later phase where we see the long series of adaptive change terminating in specific regional cultural developments.

The earliest Archaic assemblages bear major similarities to the Paleo-Indian culture from which most likely arose. Owing to the scarcity of early Archaic material, much of what we know about their lifeway is conjectural. The long, beautifully made, parallel-sided, stemmed and notched spear points have a wide distribution and are particularly concentrated on the western plains and prairies. These points, which tipped thrusting lances, were used in big-game hunting. Like Paleo-Indian habitation sites, those of the Archaic Period are also widely scattered and concentrated in the southern portion of the Upper Lakes country. This is not to say that early Archaic people did not occupy the cold, northern forest. In fact, a remarkable collection of eighteen whole and fifteen fragmented Early Archaic points were recovered near Deer Lake in Marquette County, Michigan, in the spring of 1987. This locality, called the Gorto site, seems to date to about 9500–9000 B.P. (7500–7000 B.C.).[14] The points, which are made of silicified sandstone, were exposed to intense heat and seem to have been part of a cremation ceremony. This burial form is also known from an early Archaic site in Door County, Wisconsin.[15]

Other early Archaic adaptions are represented by forms very similar to fluted projectiles but without the characteristic flutes. The Hi-lo type of western Lower Michigan as well as small, basally notched Le Croy points are examples.[16]

The appearance of medium-sized notched and barbed points in the archaeological record signals new hunting practices after about 7000 B.P. (5000 B.C.). Presumably, notched and barbed points were designed to penetrate and remain embedded in prey, rather than being withdrawn and plunged in again as in the case of thrusting spears. Thus, the barbed projectiles most likely served as tips for throwing spears. This form of hunting is best used when solitary and secretive animals are being hunted and presumably, the new, mixed deciduous Great Lakes forest was more favorable for moose and woodland caribou in the north and deer and elk in the south. These large animals would best be hunted by stealth and by throwing weapons.

Such forests offered many new opportunities for Archaic people and they responded with new technologies and innovations.[17] Beyond the throwing spear and a new propulsion system, a weighted spear thrower, Archaic Indians also made a variety of tools by pecking and grinding hard granitic stone. This new tool manufacturing technique differs radically from those used in chert knapping and was used to produce axes, adzes, gouges, and spear thrower weights called banner stones. These tools, and those formed by chipping chert, were in turn used to make a wide variety of useful implements from bone, wood, and shell. It is, in fact, probable that Archaic people developed most of the gear we associate with outdoor life even today. Snowshoes, sleds, canoes, fish hooks and spears, traps, snares, and a large number of techniques used to produce basketry, woven bags, and bark implements are likely to have been Archaic inventions. Unfortunately, the archaeological record bears only indirect evidence of these advancements in the form of durable stone tools. What little we know of life during the period around 6000–5000 B.P. (4000–3000 B.C.) comes from the deeply buried Weber 1 site near Frankenmuth in Saginaw County, Michigan, and other sites in the Saginaw River drainage.[18] The picture that emerges is of people living in small hunting and gathering bands that utilized large and small game as well as the nuts, seeds, and berries available in well-established deciduous forests.[19] It is not known how typical the Weber 1 site is, but the strong stylistic similarities of chert projectile points to others recovered in the Midwest indicates a generalized adaptation with newfound specialization as shown by the use of local sources of chert and other raw materials.

The latter part of the Archaic era, the period between about 5000 and 3000 B.P. (3000–1000 B.C.) differed little from the earlier part of the Archaic in that Indians continued to make a living by hunting and gathering. It is true that throughout the Archaic the people of the eastern forests and prairies became increasingly knowledgable about the resources around them; that is, there is evidence of gradual specialization. This appears as increased sedentariness among peoples who were relying more and more on plant resources and the technology required to process plant foods.[20] Also in evidence is increasing specificity in such things as styles of local projectile point forms and the use of more local raw materials. In this sense, the Late Archaic represents the cumulation of a process that began at the end of the glacial period.

There are two primary late Archaic occupations known in archaeological detail from southern Michigan. One is located in the St. Joseph River drainage[21] and the other along the Saginaw River and its tributaries.[22] The fact that these assemblages are quite distinct is evidence of the localization of Late Archaic adaptation. In both cases, however, evidence is preserved for both large-game hunting and the substantial use of nuts including hickory, acorns, butternut, and black walnut. During the Late Archaic period it would seem that people moved from food resource to food resource within established territories, exploiting a wide variety of plant and animal foods.

If the Late Archaic offers evidence of great accomplishment in the specialization of hunting and gathering, it also illustrates the beginning of other trends, such as long distance trade in exotic goods and the appearance of burial ceremonialism that seems linked to this trade.

In many parts of the northeastern United States and Canada, Indians of the era buried their dead in large pits, sometimes singly, sometimes with several bodies included, and often after cremation. These burial sites are often conspicuous in plowed fields because they typically also contained red ocher (or powdered iron oxide), which leaves a bright red stain. Graves also typically included large numbers of artifacts, many made of materials from distant places. Examples include beads, points, knives, and axes made from Lake Superior copper, shell beads and gorgets made from marine conch shell from the Gulf of Mexico, and turkey tail projectile points made from chert from southern Indiana and Illinois, as well as triangular points of Ononadaga chert from New York. Bayport and Norwood chert from Michigan was also used for projectile points that occasionally were deposited with burials, sometimes by the hundreds. Beyond these remarkable artifacts, stone axes, gorgets, and strange birdlike forms beautifully made of local granite also appear in graves. The actual function of the birdstones and gorgets remains a mystery.

Much variation can be found across the Midwest in the use of various burial forms and in the grave goods included. As a result, regional names are in use—Old Copper, Glacial Kame, and Red Ocher culture.[23] It is probably far more accurate to regard these differences in terms of spatial and temporal variations within a widely shared trade network and ceremonial complex than as discrete cultural complexes.

Beyond these remarkable developments, one local Archaic phenomenon that deserves further comment is the mining and working of native copper from the Keewenaw Peninsula and Isle Royale.[24] In both locations, archaeologists have located shallow mine pits where Indians used huge rock hammers to beat copper nuggets from rock matrix. These were pounded into flat sheets, folded, heated and cooled to toughen them, pounded, refolded, and hammered again to produce useful objects. This industry dates as early as 5000 B.P. (3000 B.C.) and reaches its apogee at about 3500 B.P. (1500 B.C.). A truly remarkable variety of heavy copper tools was produced and most were utilitarian rather than decorative. While copper was worked widely in the upper Great Lakes region, the heartland of copper tool production was in the area around Green Bay. Copper mined in northern Michigan and manufactured into tools in eastern Wisconsin appears on Indian sites over much of the eastern United States and Canada. Great Lakes Indians were, therefore, among the earliest people on earth to make metal tools.

Woodland Developments

Sites in the southern Great Lakes region dating from the sixth century before the Christian era (2,500 years ago) contain evidence for two totally new elements: pottery of fired clay and the remains of domesticated plants. While pottery seems to have been an indigenous invention, at least some of the new plants appear to have diffused northward from Mexico where they were first brought under domestication. These developments become both the hallmarks of the Woodland era and the foundation of an agricultural lifeway that replaced hunting and gathering over most of eastern North America. The appearance of ceramics is fortuitous for modern archaeologists because Woodland people decorated the vessels they produced by designs impressed into the wet clay. Since the styles of decoration were different from place to place, migration and trade are detectable among people of neighboring sites. Those with similar pottery designs we assume were in closer communication. Likewise, since decorative style changed in the way modern fads do, it is also possible to trace the continuity of people occupying the same area for long periods of time.

Another general, important characteristic of Great Lakes prehistory that is often overlooked is that the Woodland period features the development of a very distinct northern as opposed to southern tradition. The earliest Woodland cultures develop in the southern part of the region during the five hundred years before the Christian era; at this time it would appear that there is no comparable development in the north. Here we see a persistence of the Archaic hunting and gathering lifeway until about 2,000 years ago. These cultures are generally called the Shield Archaic,[25] which has been defined from sites in eastern Canada.

The Early Woodland cultures in southern Michigan are known from about two dozen widely scattered sites located in the St. Joseph, Kalamazoo, Grand, Muskegon, and Saginaw valleys.[26] Early Wood-

land sites are marked by the presence of square-stemmed points of
the Krammer type and coarse, grit-tempered pottery with distinctive
lug handles. These two characteristics seem to indicate a southern,
if not eastern, origin of the earliest Woodland influences. With this
in mind, it is necessary to remember that Early Woodland lifeway is
highly reminiscent of that of the Late Archaic. Hunting and gathering and the heavy use of nuts, seeds, and berries, supplemented by
the introduction of at least two cultigens, squash and sunflower, provided the basic subsistence for these people.[27]

One of the distinctive characteristics of the earliest Woodland ceramics is cord marking that appears horizontally on the interior upper rim of the vessels and vertically on the exterior. This distinctive
pattern produced in the manufacturing of the pottery by malleating
the unfired pot with a cord-wrapped wooden paddle characterizes the
type known as Marion Thick. In Michigan, Marion Thick is best
known from the Edison and Wymer sites in the St. Joseph valley, the
Elam site in the Kalamazoo valley, Norton Mounds in the Grand
valley, and the Schultz site in the Saginaw valley.[28] The earliest
burial mounds, the Croton-Carrigan Mounds on the Muskegon
River, represent the only known burial locality for the Early Woodland period in Michigan, although elaborate burial ceremonialism is
indicated at this time in the Ohio River valley.[29]

Analysis of the Schultz site indicates seasonal occupation by Early
Woodland hunters and gatherers on the floodplain of the Saginaw
River. Apparently, groups estimated to consist of two to four households camped during both summer and fall and were busy making
stone tools and pottery, cultivating squash, fishing, collecting mussels
and nuts, and hunting deer and other game in the surrounding up-
lands.[30]

At about the beginning of the Christian era, the sites occupied by
Woodland peoples in southern Michigan began to show new artifact
types. Some of these simply evolved from preceding Early Woodland types, while others are the result of a rapid intrusion of cultural
influence and, presumably, people into southwestern Michigan from
the Illinois River valley.[31] This influence is demonstrated by certain
distinctive artifacts and decorative styles associated with the
Hopewellian cultures of Ohio and Illinois. Most notable of the
Hopewell markers are the appearance of well-made ceramics with
dentate, rocker-stamped, and zone-decorated patterns often with

cross-hatched rims. Large corner-notched points of the Snyders type are also typical. The most spectacular evidence of Hopewell influence is the large groups of burial mounds found in the lower reaches of the Grand, Muskegon, and St. Joseph valleys. These mounds represent part of a widespread burial ceremonial complex based upon trade in exotic materials and artifacts. Although not founded on the same beliefs as the Late Archaic burial ceremonialism, it represents a similar pattern and certainly a much more sophisticated version.

While the Hopewell intrusion had a major effect on the people living in the southern part of the Great Lakes basin, it was practically unfelt by the people farther north. Here, on small village sites located on the shores of the Great Lakes, we find the first evidence of pottery making and the first stages in the development of fishing as a major subsistence enterprise. This cultural development, called Laurel, occurs throughout the Lake Superior basin from Manitoba to the eastern Upper Peninsula of Michigan. It is distinct from the southern Middle Woodland although an occasional artifact shows contact between the two. It is thus in Middle Woodland times that the distinction between northerner and southerner is established. The geographic separation of these and subsequent Woodland cultural manifestations is sharply marked by the boundary between the southern oak-hickory forests and the northern conifer-hardwood community often called the northern Lake Forest.[32]

In the hundred years preceding the beginning of the Christian era, the archaeological record seems to reflect a full range of influence from Hopewell. In the lower valleys of the St. Joseph, Grand, and Muskegon rivers there is direct evidence for the appearance of Hopewellian immigrants from Illinois. In the Saginaw valley, local Woodland people seem to have been strongly influenced by Hopewell styles and the growing importance of horticulture. In many other areas, particularly in the Kalamazoo and central Grand valleys and in the Lake Erie drainage, Hopewell influence is barely apparent.

The best-known development of Middle Woodland is in the Saginaw valley, particularly at the Schultz site at the confluence of the Tittabawassee and Shiawassee Rivers.[33] This site was intermittently occupied by small groups of Middle Woodland hunters and gatherers who apparently relied to a great extent on the harvest of the seeds of marsh elder, giant ragweed, and pigweed, plants common to the flood plains of large river valleys.[34] Of course, they were also skilled hunters, fishers, and collectors of nuts, tubers, and berries. It is apparent from the placement of sites of Hopewellian influence in southern Michigan that these Middle Woodland people carefully selected flood plain and wet prairie habitats where this lifeway was most productive.[35]

The western Michigan Middle Woodland culture first known as the Goodall tradition is now called the Norton tradition for the huge burial mound complex near Grand Rapids.[36] Another mound group, the Converse mounds, was destroyed by the construction of the city. These sites give evidence of a complex funerary ritual that included the secondary reburial of skeletal material, the construction of elaborate burial chambers, and the inclusion with the dead of exotic burial goods, presumably as indicators of status. A great deal of effort was devoted to mound construction; Mound M in the Norton group is 17 feet high and 100 feet around the base. It is estimated that over a half million basket loads of dirt were required for its construction.

Grave goods at Norton and the contents of other western Michigan mound groups give evidence for the relationship between these sites and others sharing Hopewell influences. These stretched from western New York to eastern Kansas and from the central Great Lakes to the Deep South. Throughout this vast region, the Hopewell presence is superimposed on local Woodland tradition principally by the common use of exotic artifacts in burial rituals. At Norton, the nearby Spoonville site, and along the lower Muskegon,[37] we see zone-decorated pottery, conch shell beads and containers, engraved turtle shell dishes, copper awls, axes, and rolled copper beads. Copper pan pipes, sheet mica mirrors, beautiful projectile points of exotic chert, carved stone platform pipes, and the teeth and jaws of wolves and bears are noted in association with burial sites.

By about 1500 B.P. (A.D. 500) the trade pattern, burial ceremonial complex, and decorative motifs that gave Hopewell its distinctiveness disappeared, bringing an end to the Middle Woodland era. There is, however, no disruption of the archaeological record. Simple, cord-marked pottery associated with small side- and corner-notched points continues to mark the small village settlements of the major river valleys. These are the earliest sites of the Late Woodland tradition.

While these developments were taking place in the hardwood forests, the northern Lake Forests see the development of the Laurel culture and related North Bay and Saugeen manifestations.[38] These appear at about the same time as Hopewell, 2100 B.P. (100 B.C.) but persist until perhaps 1300 B.P. (A.D. 700). Laurel sites are marked by pottery that is decorated with row upon row of closely spaced impressions made with notched or comblike tools. This pottery, small side-notched points, chert scrapers, small copper awls, toggle-head harpoons, and distinctive end-notched pebble net sinkers are the hallmarks of Laurel sites, which seem to occur most frequently on the Lake Superior shore. Laurel sites do, however, also appear on the northern Lakes Michigan and Huron coasts as far as the southern margin of the Lake Forest.[39]

It would appear that Laurel and related sites represent the first stages in a lake side adaptation that centers on fishing in the Great Lakes proper. Laurel sites are often situated to have access to stream mouths and offshore shallow bays that were used in the spring and summer to take suckers and pan fish, probably with seines.[40] Laurel sites are generally small and show evidence of repeated seasonal occupation of the same sites. It has been suggested that summer fishing sites were occupied by several related families probably constituting in all fewer than a hundred people.[41]

Laurel people seem to have slowly developed an increasingly sophisticated fishery that ultimately led to the Inland Shore Fishing complex of the northern Late Woodland period. Stylistic evidence for this continuum is the Pine River pottery that precedes the Mackinaw phase of the early Late Woodland.[42]

The Late Woodland in the northern Great Lakes appears at about 1200 B.P. (A.D. 800) with the development of the Blackduck and Selkirk ceramic tradition north and west of Lake Superior, the Lakes phase in northern Wisconsin, and the Mackinac phase in the northern parts of Lakes Michigan and Huron. The Mackinac phase, 1200 to 1000 B.P. (A.D. 800–1000), as well as the subsequent Bois Blanc, 1000 to 900 B.P. (A.D. 1000–1200), and Juntunen phases, 800 to 400 B.P. (A.D. 1200–1600), are represented by moderate to large lakeside villages that were occupied during the summer months. The Juntunen site on Bois Blanc Island in the Straits of Mackinac and the Whitefish Island site in the Saint Marys River are typical of the larger villages.[43] These sites are clearly fishing sites that were part of a remarkable fishing adaptation known as the Inland Shore Fishery.[44] This unique fishery was based upon the use of the gill net to capture whitefish and lake trout in the late fall. It is clear from the archaeological record that Mackinac and Juntunen phase sites are very numerous and were intensively occupied (compared to earlier Woodland sites). This seems to also indicate an increase in population.

Northern Late Woodland sites are marked by large, widemouth pottery vessels with round bottoms. These were decorated with the impressions of braided and twisted cords, cord-wrapped sticks, and a variety of objects that were pushed into the wet clay to form punctates and jab-drag designs. It is the sequential popularity of these decorative techniques and the appearance of collared and castellated rim forms that permits archaeologists to recognize and order these cultures in time. Late Woodland sites also contain small, poorly made triangular and notched projectile points, chert scrapers and knives, ground stone axes, and bone tools: awls for punching holes in leather, matting needles, harpoons, and gorges (a primitive, double-pointed fish hook). Small, clay elbow pipes and copper artifacts also occur. Woodland copper artifacts are very different from the earlier Archaic forms. Instead of large, utilitarian implements, Woodland artifacts are mainly decorative and quite small. Beads, hair pipes, tiny awls, and a knife form resembling modern butter knives are typical.

Summer villages probably consisted of 100–200 people who belonged to several related and cooperating families that used common territories. Fishing, gathering, and growing small gardens of corn, beans, and squash as well as hunting were activities of the summer village. Unlike their neighbors to the south, these northern people could not be considered horticulturalists because they depended more on the hunt than their gardens.

The Late Woodland peoples who occupied the deciduous forests south of the Great Lakes were certainly serious farmers. In fact, the distribution of these Late Woodland sites are mostly confined to areas that receive at least 140 frost-free growing days, the minimum to assure a mature corn crop.[45] In fact, it is likely this important feature of their subsistence economy identifies the shift to Late Woodland at about 1500 B.P. (A.D. 500). Theoretically at least, decreased dependence on hunting and gathering as opposed to food produced in gardens led to an abandonment of Middle Woodland territories in favor of isolated farming communities in widely separated river valleys. This trend also led to distinguishable regional traditions with the passage of time.

In looking at the Late Woodland period in general, it is possible to clearly identify four major changes during the period from 1500 to 400 B.P. (A.D. 500–1600). These are: (1) the increasing development of an agricultural base to the subsistence economy as the result of an improved strain of corn adapted to shorter growing seasons and a mixed crop field system, (2) the introduction of the bow and arrow marked by the appearance of small triangular and notched points that is, in turn, linked to more specialized and labor-efficient hunting (incidentally, this improvement also seems to have freed male labor from some aspects of cultivation and led to increased warfare), (3) storable agricultural commodities that could be produced in excess and used in combination with meat protein led to more food and the possibility of better diets, and (4) village life produced greater sedentariness and regional style specialization.

There were three major cultural traditions born in the deciduous woodlands of the Great Lakes. To the west, in southern Wisconsin, the Oneota tradition (often linked historically with Siouan-speaking groups) developed. To the east of Lake Huron and in the Lakes Erie and Ontario basins were the Owasco-Glen Myer and Pickering groups that led to the historic Iroquian-speaking tribes such as the Five Nations Iroquois, Neutral, and Huron. In the middle, from southern Michigan through the Upper Peninsula and in Ontario north of the Lakes, we find the Late Woodland cultures that seem to be the predecessors of Algonquian-speaking groups such as the Ojibwa, Ottawa, Potawatomi, and Miami.[46]

As in the case of the northern region, cultural change in the south is mainly determined from ceramic style changes. Throughout this area, the earliest Late Woodland ceramics are very simple, small, cord-marked vessels. In Lower Michigan, these ceramics are called Wayne ware. These occur with only slight variation over most of southern Michigan.[47] After 1000 B.P. (A.D. 1000) ceramic forms are more complex, often decorated with cord impressions, and collars are added. In Wisconsin, both Heins Creek and Madison wares are related types, while in southwestern Ontario the Glen Meyer and Pickering phases predate 600 B.P. (A.D. 1300). The Oneota tradition of

Wisconsin appears at least by 1000 B.P. (A.D. 1000) and is characterized by smooth surface, shell-tempered vessels that are decorated
with wide-trailed lines and often have strap handles.

The Western Basin tradition of southeastern Michigan is characterized by the Riviere au Vase phase prior to 1000 B.P. (A.D. 1000)
followed by the Young, 1000–900 B.P. (A.D. 1000–1100); Springwells, 900–600 B.P. (A.D. 1100–1300); and finally the Wolf phase,
600–500 B.P. (A.D. 1300–1400).[48] The Western Basin tradition of
southeastern Michigan is closely related to the Glen Myer phase in
adjacent Ontario and shows distinct similarities, including intensive
village occupation, the use of longhouses, and complex reinterment
and multiple reinterment as part of burial ritual.[49] This pattern appears to be well established by the early Middleport phase of the
Ontario sequence.[50]

In southwestern Michigan, the Late Woodland begins at about
1200 B.P. (A.D. 800) with the Brems phase. After about 1000 B.P.
(A.D. 1000) there is evidence of more intense occupation, presumably
associated with increased reliance on agricultural production. This
development is called the Moccasin Bluff phase, 1000 to 700 B.P.
(A.D. 1000–1300).

At about 700 B.P. (A.D. 1300) influence from the Upper Mississippian cultures of the central Mississippi valley appears in the archaeological record of Late Woodland cultures in southern Michigan.

Small, triangular arrow points and the appearance of pottery tempered with crushed mollusk shell rather than granitic rock character-
ize this influence.[51] Shell-tempered pottery appears on sites such as
Moccasin Bluff in Berrien County along with typical Woodland ceramics indicating Upper Mississippian influence rather than immigrants. It is true, however, that the period around 700 B.P. (A.D.
1300) seems to be one of widespread disruption and aggression. Sites
fortified with earthen berms and pallisades appear in the Lower Peninsula of Michigan at this time, and the fortification of sites seems to
become more common in the whole Great Lakes region.

The Berrien phase, dated at 600–400 B.P. (A.D. 1400–1600) in
extreme southwest Michigan is marked by the appearance of shell-
tempered, plain-surface pottery often showing inverted rims and in-
cised line decoration. This ceramic ware is ultimately related to the
Oneota-Huber occupation around the end of Lake Michigan, the
Koshkonong, Grand River, and Lake Winnebago phases of

Oneota,[52] and also to the grit-tempered Dumaw Creek and Traverse Ware occupations along the Lake Michigan coast to the north.[53]

Thus, on the eve of contact with Europeans, the Great Lakes region saw the development of several independent cultural complexes that were the product of direct continuity in lifeway and artifact style from at least 1200 B.P. (A.D. 800). In Ontario, there is the late prehistoric Neutral, Huron, and Iroquois complex of the Lake Erie basin and the region around Georgian Bay. Upper Michigan and adjacent parts of Ontario see the development of a northern, late Juntunen phase around the eastern end of Lake Superior and the northern Lake Michigan and Huron basins. Separate Woodland developments in the southern two-thirds of the Lower Peninsula are thought to be associated with various Algonquian-speaking groups. Around the southern end of Lake Michigan and in northern and central Wisconsin we find the Upper Mississippian Oneota cultures usually linked historically to Siouian-speaking tribes. With the exception of the inhabitants of the northern forests, all of these people were dependent upon the cultivation of corn, beans, and squash for a major part of their subsistence needs. In all cases, their lives centered around one or a few semipermanent village localities. When the first French explorers entered the western Great Lakes country, it was these cultivators and fishing people whose villages they visited.

The Historic Period

The historic phase of the archaeological record is marked by the appearance of artifacts made of iron, glass, and other nonnative materials. In most cases, the goods were actually manufactured by Europeans, but arrow points cut by Indians from copper-kettle fragments or chipped in the traditional method from pieces of bottle glass are also markers for the period of historic contact.

Sites of the historic period are, surprisingly, quite rare in the upper Great Lakes country. While the French presence is well known east of Lake Huron before 350 B.P. (A.D. 1650), most, if not all, historic sites in the western Great Lakes postdate this time. The Rock Island site at the mouth of Green Bay and the Marquette Mission site at St. Ignace both represent late seventeenth-century occupations by Huron and Ottawa refugees. These are also among

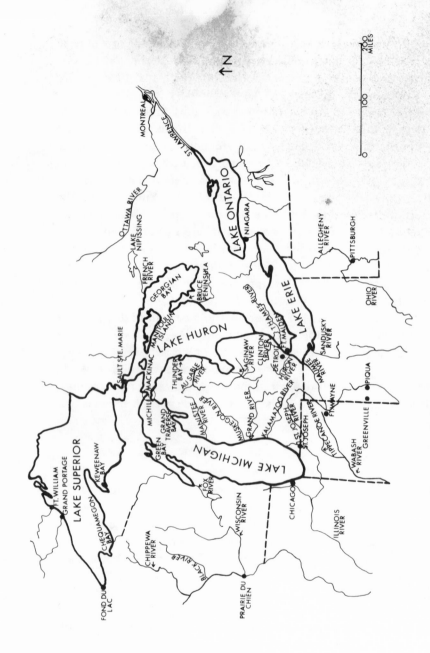

The Great Lakes region. (Drawing by B. Nemeth.)

the very few sites that show continuity over the prehistoric to historic boundary. It is, perhaps, ironic that, while archaeologists can trace the development of specific prehistoric cultural groups for at least a thousand years into the Woodland past, this continuity of artifacts is broken very abruptly with the appearance of European goods and materials. As a result, archaeologists seeking to identify the ethnic affiliation of historic sites or to link historically known groups with prehistoric sites usually must rely on informed speculation. This is because the only sure evidence would be finding a historic document that mentions the specific location of a village of a known group of people, and finding an archaeological site on that very spot attributable to a particular prehistoric sequence. Unfortunately, both conditions are seldom met.

Our best knowledge of the historic period comes from the eighteenth- and early nineteenth-century sites that are mostly large burial sites unearthed by modern construction.[54] An incredibly rich and interesting assemblage of artifacts made of European materials and techniques including glass beads, firearms, iron axes, knives, awls and strike-a-lites, copper and brass kettles, silver gorgets, arm bands, head bands, and earrings, finger rings, and many more types of trade goods have been recovered from historic sites. These artifacts represent materials given to Indians in trade for furs or as presents to try to assure their political loyalties. Thanks to the study of fur trader invoices, we know that the durable commodities represented archaeologically were only a small part of a much larger trade inventory of which cloth and tailored clothing were the most important elements.[55]

Structuring the Past

Beliefs about Indian origins that are drawn from myths and legends that have been passed down by word of mouth from generation to generation contrast sharply with the story that emerges through the examination of artifacts unearthed by archaeologists or documents carefully studied by learned ethnohistorians. One is left to wonder, which version of history is correct? Or, even more to the point, what difference does it make? Can the two positions have any modern relevance? Clearly, the beliefs that underlie these two ways of looking at history involve more than making a relative judgment about

truth. Indeed, our sense of history and the historical process ultimately define the way in which Indians and non-Indians deal with
each other. Here is an example.

For years, Michigan Indians, like those all across North America,
have been concerned with the long-standing archaeological practice
of collecting Indian skeletal material for study. In some cases, archaeologists have excavated mounds and cemeteries, but in many
others these remains have been salvaged from the path of bulldozers
building highways and homes and excavating sand and gravel. Archaeologists and physical anthropologists have used the skeletons to
study the physical condition, sex, and age structure of prehistoric
populations, their diet and nutrition, and their systems of rank and
status and changing cultural relationships, that is, to reconstruct Indian cultural history. After study, the remains have been stored in
museums for future research. In these activities, archaeologists see
themselves as protecting burial material from destruction and adding
to Indian history. Many Indians take a contrary view. The proper
place for these dead ancestors is in the ground, where they had been
consigned by loving relatives. Further, the study of these skeletons
represents a desecration of the grave, a violation of its sanctity, and,
as a matter of decency, all Indian skeletons and associated burial
artifacts should be returned to the ground.

On January 30, 1990, a group of Michigan Indians and archaeologists met to try to hammer out a draft of a new state law to govern
the study of human skeletal material. It was an uncomfortable meeting filled with tension, a meeting that cast old friends as opponents
and where potential understanding often gave way to political pos-
turing and strategy.

The position of the archaeologists was expressed by prominent
archaeologists on the Michigan scene representing their professional
organization as well as various private and public institutions. Dr.
John O'Shea of the University of Michigan spoke eloquently for the
scientific position. "Archaeological sites," he reminded everyone,
"are each unique. Each contains information about the past that can
be gained from no other source. Archaeological sites and data are
nonrenewable resources. Once destroyed they cannot be recreated.
Where no literate tradition exists, the arrowheads, soil strata, skeletons, and pottery are the only means to understand the events of
past history. In asking us to give up skeletal collections and burial

artifacts, you are asking us to give up access to the past. You are asking us to forever surrender the data by which future generations of archaeologists may come to new or different conclusions by reexamining this material" (personal communication). Beyond that, reburying skeletons and artifacts also denies future generations of Indians the right to reinterpret Indian history. Dr. O'Shea then raised a point about the ownership of history. "The past," he said, "does not belong to any particular ethnic or religious group. The past belongs to everyone because, in the end, we all share in the past and profit by understanding it. By denying science the right to examine Indian skeletons or to use them to train students, you will deny everyone the right to understand prehistoric diets, disease, and other factors of population dynamics that may alert us to information important to the future. It can also help us to understand the past in other places and at other times. Science," he said emphatically, "is not static but is constantly discovering new methods to test and retest hypotheses. Unless we preserve our ability to correct our errors, science cannot advance knowledge. If you deny us access to these bones and artifacts, who will bring Indians' history to light?"

Victor Kishigo of Petoskey presented the argument that is shared by most Indian people. "I know," he said, "that you archaeologists have studied Indian customs and Indian history. I know you know a great deal about us as a people but you don't know and can't know what it is to be an Indian. The bones of our dead are not archaeological specimens to be dug up and kept on museum shelves. These bones are the essence of our ancestors. They are the union of our people to the land for which we were created. These burials represent our link with the past. It is our belief that once a body has been committed to the ground in a religious ceremony, it should be respected and left in place by all people. Why should the skeleton of an Indian be treated differently than the skeleton of a non-Indian? No grave should be excavated to satisfy curiosity, and if they are dug up accidentally the bones should be reburied. Would you want your ancestors to be condemned to a cardboard box on a dusty museum shelf?" (personal communication). Mr. Kishigo continued, "You say the skeletons will tell us about our history. That's your history, not our history! Our history comes to us from our grandfathers and grandmothers. We know our history. The history you say is ours has very little meaning for us. You say some skeletons are historic and some are prehistoric. That is a distinction of your history. We deny it. The skeletons we speak of do not belong to you, to your history or to science. They are the bodies of our ancestors. We have the responsibility to see that they are not dug up and that if they are, that they will be reburied."

In these two positions, we see the practical aspects of two very different ways of looking at the past brought into sharp focus. The practical political questions raised by the reburial issue seem to founder on the control of the interpretation of Indian history. No doubt, the question will be resolved by a law that does not please anyone. More important here, however, is that this debate raises deeper questions about the cultural assumptions that form the underpinning of two vastly different kinds of history.

Indian Time and Power

There is a standing joke among Indians when meetings don't start at the appointed hour. "This meeting," the early birds tell each other, "is being run on Indian time." "Indian time" means more than being late. It means that the participants are not obsessed with promptness. It has nothing to do with a lack of efficiency. For many Indians, time is not the main criterion of social interaction. While this seems a small point, "Indian time" is common to Indian meetings. This we can contrast to some segments of American society, which seem to run with amazing chronological accuracy. Our comings and goings are precisely timed and coordinated. Our social interactions are scheduled to order our present and future. Our view of history is, of course, similar. It is a vast continuum from the distant past to the present: people, places, and events are interlocked in a series of unique episodes. History's schedule plays out in its infinite complexity, all organized in time. The fact that the motivations of history's players may be vague to us or that, at some remote time of the past, the identities of the players may fade does not change the way we believe history is constructed.

This, however, is not the only way the past can be arranged. In many non-Western societies, including those of the native people of the Great Lakes prior to the turn of the present century, the actors of history were not bound to human form or to chronological time. As Sahlins reminds us in the case of ancient Hawaii, mythology provides archetypal situations through which mythical protagonists are reexperienced by the living in analogous circumstances. Thus, gods and heroes stand beside ordinary men.[56] History is structured by the past in the sense that modern actors play out expected themes. From this perspective, history not only repeats itself, the present and the past are without distinction.

One of the important expectations of Western history is that change is unavoidable and irreversible; it is a thing of great importance. Again, this expectation was not commonly accepted by Great Lakes natives until very modern times. In fact, it was their expectation that things would not change. Their Creation mythology explained the form and behavior of both living and nonliving things. The legendary adventures of *Nanabojo* and the other cultural heroes provided the metaphors and symbols through which all subsequent events could be interpreted. Even during the period of intense conflict with non-Indians, the power of dreams and visions was evident in the actions of chiefs, shamans, warriors, and men and women. These actions were a reaffirmation of the balance between the past and the present. In the Indian Wars, in the struggles to maintain land, and in the agonies of lost traditions, the Indian hero of old and Indian people of the modern day merge as one, actors in the history of the present.

In the Western view, official and popular, the Indians of the Great Lakes are people without history.[57] Not only did their worldview prize stability over change and then, in turn, attribute change to the repetition of ancient themes, but the "history" and "literature" of these people was not written down! Unfortunately, people with written traditions have had great difficulty applying democratic principles to oral traditions. Perhaps, the struggle to establish literacy has been so intense that we dismiss the fantastically rich oral literature of nonliterate peoples as "quaint" or their history as "interesting but not reliable." Worse, the absence of written documents not only often leads us to dismiss the validity of a people's history, but, in fact, to deny their very existence as a people.

A case in point is the process used by the U.S. government to "recognize" or to "acknowledge" the formal relationship between a specific tribe and the government. The criteria for such recognition is that tribes document their historical existence through the use of written documents (written by non-Indians) and that the documents show historical continuity in relationships with the U.S. government through recent history (chronological time).[58] Obviously, the control of history is power, and power controls the way the past is constructed. From this perspective Indian time is time without reality and history without writing is history without power.

History, Indian and non-Indian, is the product of cultural perceptions. As we will see, the way Americans fit into Indian history and the way Indians were incorporated into U.S. history was a product of the assumptions each society made about the other—a dim reflection in the other's eyes. Perhaps with time an intermediate view will develop that is based upon mutual respect for the different contexts of history. As a start we might listen to the opinion of an Ojibwa elder who observed that "the earth guards the archaeological record, it can be collected from the ground with respect like any other medicine for the benefit of us all."[59]

NOTES

1. While the origin myths of the Great Lakes Algonquian groups are somewhat different in detail, the theme is the same. The myth given here is adapted from one collected by Victor Barnouw at Lac du Flambeau, Wisconsin, in 1944. This myth, as told by Tom Badger, is representative of Ojibwa and Ottawa origin mythology. For origin mythology, see Jones 1916; Brown and Brightman 1988; Schoolcraft 1839; Radin 1956; Barnouw 1977. Johnston (1981); Gringhuis (1970); Walker (1959); and Coleman, Frogner, and Eich (1961) have adapted these stories for children.

2. George Nelson, an early nineteenth-century Anglo-Canadian fur trader familiar with Lake Superior, northern Ojibwa, and Cree symbolism, notes that when the Indians visualized the Sun, it was as a handsome young man who walked on the wind (Brown and Brightman 1988, 37).

3. Ottawa and Ojibwa mythology often place the remains of *Maskasaswabik* at particular geographic locations. Foster Otto of Petoskey once showed the author a limestone rock formation near Norwood in Antrim County, Michigan, that contains chert lenses as the ultimate resting place of the stone brother. This is the same locality called *Pewan-go-ing* ('place of flint') by Andrew Blackbird in his history of the Ottawa and Chippewa Indians of Michigan (Blackbird 1887, 74). Prehistoric Indians quarried chert from this source, the *Pi-wan-go-ning*

quarry, to make arrowheads, knives, scrapers, and other artifacts (C. Cleland 1973).

In the origin mythology of the Potowatomi, *Ka-ponka* (the cold weather–maker) has elbows made of flint arrowheads. *Ka-ponka* kills his mother with his elbows and flees north, pursued by *Wi-saka*, who summons the Thunderbirds who kill *Ka-ponka* with lightning (Skinner 1924, 214–15).

4. Ojibwa and Ottawa tradition identifies this creation site with Mackinac Island.

5. Basil H. Johnston, renowned scholar of Ojibwa literature at the Royal Ontario Museum, has kindly helped me with the Ojibwa language, including the distinction made here. Ojibwa dictionaries published by Baraga (1973) and Eklund (1991) were used in the phonetic renderings of Algonquian words.

6. The migration legend of the Ojibwa is recorded in some detail by W. J. Hoffman in his extensive study of the *Midé-wi-win* or Grand Medicine Society (Hoffman 1891). Selwyn Dewdney (1975) carries the topic further through the study of the birchbark scrolls that were used to record the order and substance of *Midé-wi-win* ritual.

7. Warren 1984, 87–88.

8. Dewdney (1975, 57–80) provides a detailed comparison of the several known migration charts as well as the associated place names given by Redsky and other Midé informants for the various "stopping places" of the westward migration.

9. Much of the technical information on Great Lakes archaeology is published in *Michigan Archaeologist, Wisconsin Archaeologist,* or *Ontario Archaeologist,* all excellent journals supported by the avocational archaeologists of those states and the province of Ontario. Other information is presented in professional journals such as *American Antiquity* or *Midcontinental Journal of Archaeology.* For excellent summaries of Great Lakes archaeology, the reader is referred to Fitting 1970 and R. Mason 1981.

10. The sequence of the development of the Great Lakes forest is reconstructed from pollen cores extracted from bog deposits. See Bearrs and Kapp 1987; Ahearn and Bailey 1980; Kapp 1977. Prehistory is the division of the field of archaeology that studies archaeological sites formed before the time of written history. It may be contrasted with the field of historic archaeology or classical archaeology, which studies sites occupied after the advent of the literate traditions. The term *prehistory* does not imply that Indians were without history since the formation of each archaeological site is itself proof of Indian history. It is true, however, that prehistorians are more interested in the process and patterns

of culture that can be gleaned from the study of sites in general than they are in the unique or "historical" aspects of particular sites. The two are of course interrelated in the sense that in order to understand, for example, how Archaic people built their houses and how these houses may have changed over time, it is first necessary to study evidence that results from the remains of many particular houses that are each unique, that is, a product of history.

11. The only instance of animal bone being found on a Paleo-Indian site in Michigan was a caribou bone from the Holcomb site reported by C. Cleland (1965). It is widely assumed that these animals were the primary food source for Great Lakes Paleo-Indians. It should be noted, however, that many other potential game species inhabited the early postglacial landscape. Wilson (1967) and Holman, Fisher, and Kapp (1986) provide detailed information on this subject. Both Fischer (1984) and Garland and Cogswell (1985) have presented evidence for the butchering of mastodons. However, no direct evidence for the killing of Pleistocene elephants has been forthcoming from the eastern United States although such evidence exists in the western part of the country. Despite arguments to the contrary, it is unlikely that ancient Indians played a significant role in the extinction of the Pleistocene megafauna.

12. There have been many isolated Paleo-Indian fluted point finds reported in the literature, but our understanding of Paleo-Indian lifeway is best gleaned from excavated sites. For more detail on such sites as well as opinions of archaeologists concerning the interpretation of Paleo-Indian material, see Wright and Roosa 1966; Roosa 1977; Fitting, Devisscher, and Wahla 1966; Simmons, Shott, and Wright 1984; Voss 1977; R. Mason 1986a.

13. Larsen (1987) presents a readable summary of the complex geological processes that led to the formation of the modern Great Lakes. Karrow and Calkins (1985) offer an edited volume with several detailed papers on this topic.

14. Buckmaster and Paquette 1988, 101–24.

15. Mason and Irwin 1960, 43–57.

16. Fitting 1963, 87–96.

17. Brown and Vierra (1983) include papers by several authors discussing general Archaic adaptations in the American Midwest. Lovis and Robertson (1989) focus on the Archaic sequence of the Saginaw valley and are successful in suggesting a sensible Archaic chronology for this important region.

18. See Lovis 1989.

19. N. Cleland 1989, 175–89; Smith 1989, 143–74.

20. See Brown and Vierra 1983.

21. See Garland 1984.
22. See Lovis and Robertson 1989; Harrison 1966; Lovis 1989; Papworth 1967; Taggart 1967; Wright and Morlan 1964.
23. The burial ceremonies and trade system of the Late Archaic period have been described in a number of reports that treat sites in Wisconsin, northern Illinois, and Indiana as well as Michigan. See Stoltman 1986; Mead and Kingsley 1985; Papworth 1967; Binford 1963; Cunningham 1948; Fogel 1963; Griffin 1961; Hruska 1967; Ritzenthaler and Quimby 1962; Wittry and Ritzenthaler 1957. Fitting (1970) and R. Mason (1981) provide summaries.
24. See Griffin 1961.
25. See Conway 1979; J. V. Wright 1972.
26. Garland 1984, 691–711.
27. H. T. Wright 1964, 17–22; Parachini 1984, 757–86.
28. The two major reports describing Early Woodland finds are those by Garland (1984) and Ozker (1982). See also Fitting 1972.
29. See Prahl 1991.
30. See Ozker 1982.
31. Kingsley 1981, 132–78; Flanders 1977, 144–51.
32. See C. Cleland 1966; Yarnell 1964.
33. See Fitting 1972.
34. Ford 1981, 6–27.
35. Kingsley 1981, 132–78.
36. Griffin, Flanders, and Titterington 1970; Quimby 1941, 61–161.
37. See Griffin, Flanders, and Titterington 1970; Flanders 1969; Prahl 1966.
38. See J. V. Wright 1967.
39. Janzen 1968; Brose 1970; Fitting et al. 1969. Laurellike sites occur as far south as the mouth of the Au Sable River, Little Traverse Bay, and Green Bay.
40. See C. Cleland 1982.
41. See Brose 1970.
42. See Holman 1984.
43. See McPherron 1967.
44. See C. Cleland 1982, 1985; S. Martin 1989. There has been some debate on the origin and nature of the Great Lakes fishery. Martin uses statistical analysis of the location of sites to argue for the slow development of a generalized subsistence strategy.
45. See Yarnell 1964.
46. See map 5 and the accompanying essay on the "Distribution of Late Prehistoric Cultures" by Charles E. Cleland in H. Tanner 1987 (24–28).

47. See Brashler 1981.
48. See Fitting 1965; Brose 1976.
49. See Greenman 1937; Murphy and Ferris 1990.
50. See J. V. Wright 1966; Finlayson 1989.
51. See Bettarel and Smith 1973.
52. Gibbon 1986, 314–38.
53. See Quimby 1966.
54. See Cleland and Brantsner n.d.; C. Mason 1986.
55. Anderson 1991, 218–36.
56. Sahlins 1981, 14.
57. The term "people without history" is borrowed from Eric Wolf from the title of his book documenting the expansion of European mercantilism and colonialism between the fifteenth and nineteenth centuries (see Wolf 1982).
58. Fogelson (1989) contrasts the events of written history with what he calls the nonevents of Indian history. In his classification of nonevents, he reveals the contrast between the way history itself is incorporated in the cultural context of Indian and Western intellectual traditions. Oral tradition and its historical implication has, of course, been given serious consideration by folklorists and, more recently, by historians; see especially Vansina 1985; Cohen 1989; Trigger 1984.
59. Grace Rajnovich of Sault Ste. Marie, Ontario, shared this view of an Ojibwa leader with whom she worked in designing an archaeological project near Kenora, Ontario.

Chapter 2

A Sense of Time, a Sense of Place

A question most often asked of the ethnologists who study the cultures of native Americans is, "Which tribe lived in this area when white people first arrived?" This is clearly a question of "non-Indian history" because, as we will see, the very concept of "tribe" as it is used now had little if any meaning whatsoever to native peoples before they had extensive contact with non-Indians. If we could have asked an Indian woman living in what is now Michigan in A.D. 1600 to identify herself, she would probably have answered that she was of the *Anishnabeg* or in the singular an *Anishnabe*. This term would indicate her to be an Algonquian speaker who shared that identity with her neighbors who spoke the same or mutually intelligible dialects. Our informant would also tell us that these people shared very similar customs and traditions. Among the beliefs held in common would be that the *Anishnabeg* were "true" people, that is, the descendants of people created in their mythology and, there-fore, "real," superior to those of whose mythological origins were separate or unclear. Other people, non-*Anishnabeg,* were given specific names, and not only had ambiguous human status but were people with whom hostile or potentially hostile relationships existed.

Beyond this identity, our informant would probably make refer-ence to membership in smaller, named groups. One would be a kin group, those who are family by virtue of birth. This family would be defined on the basis of the father's kin identity, so that we might be told that our informant was a member of a particular clan. We also might be told of membership in a particular band, a small local eco-nomic and sociopolitical group. The band might take its name from its leader, a river or other geographic landmark, a village, or perhaps

39

an animal. In any case, the band would have a territorial dimension. Thus, our informant might tell us that her name was *Binesi-kwe* (Bird Woman), that she was an *Anishnabe,* that she was of the *Migisi* (eagle) clan, and belonged to the *We-qua-dong* (Keweenaw Bay) band.

Given this means of thinking about cultural identity, it makes little sense to describe the Indians of the contact period in terms of nineteenth-century political configurations—even these, incidentally, had almost no meaning to Indians. It is true, of course, that the people we call Ojibwa and Potawatomi were descendants of contact-period *Anishnabeg* in the same way they were, in turn, the cultural and geneological descendants of earlier, Late Woodland people in the area. The important point, however, is that tribal labels originally held little meaning; as James Clifton so ably stated it, "The core of each individual personal identity comes not from being Potawatomi but from the close, intimate relationships of everyday life."[1]

In order to understand the course of the subsequent history of the cultural contact between the native peoples of the upper Great Lakes and non-Indians, it is necessary to have a cultural baseline. From this we can ask such questions as what were the traditions, customs, and values that shaped Indian interaction with the newcomers? How did the interplay between these cultures change both traditional Indian and Euro-American strategies and perceptions? What cultural mechanisms did Indians use to deal with fur traders, missionaries, or colonists?

For purposes of cultural description, the protohistoric *Anishnabeg,* that is, those at the cusp of European contact, will be described in two geographic divisions, the northern *Anishnabeg* and the southern *Anishnabeg.* This distinction is based on the major economic orientations that divide the corn farmers of the south from the fishing/hunting peoples of the north.

To establish the cultural baseline, I will use a distinctively anthropological kind of historic reconstruction called the "ethnographic present." This is really a conjectural kind of history, in a sense a hypothesis about how these cultures were organized.

When we discuss Indian society at the time they were first contacted by Europeans, the adjectives often used to describe them are "primitive" or "simple." In contrast to today's large, complex, and highly stratified industrial society, these descriptions have some merit. As we will see, however, these seventeenth-century Indian cultures were far from "simple." In fact, it could reasonably be argued that their very simplicity made them infinitely complex. Consider, for example, that these Indians lived without laws, police, or courts, yet they had to punish people who did not conform to expected norms of behavior. To do this in the absence of legal institutions involves social subtleties that are not at issue in modern law enforcement. Perhaps this is what we recognize when we describe a really tough cop by saying he would "arrest his own mother." Within a seventeenth-century Indian band, everyone was a relative! In this sense, nothing was "simple." Greed, ambition, jealousy, and other human frailties are difficult to deal with, particularly so within the confines of a very small group of related human beings who absolutely depended on each other for their survival. Cultural systems provide people with the beliefs, values, and ideals with which to solve the problems common to all humans, and in this context "primitive" has no meaning.

A survey of Great Lakes Indian cultures shows us that there were substantial differences from society to society. In fact, great contrasts often existed, as, for example, between the Iroquoian speakers east of Lake Huron and the Algonquian people to the west, where we find totally different principles used to trace descent and to organize political life. These differences often confused the early explorers and certainly sometimes confuse modern students of native American ethnography. It is also true that beneath these different social practices we find principles of organization that are common across much of native North America. If we are to explore beyond our simple curiosity about specific customs, we must try to understand the values upon which they are based. If we can do that, we are also in a position to rethink and reevaluate our own values and culture.

The Web of Kinship

At the heart of *all* social relationships among Great Lakes *Anishnabeg* is kinship. The unique kin relationship between any two Indians determined everything else about the way they interacted with each other, from the form of address to how food was shared to obligations of mutual help. If no kin relationship existed, a fictive device, for example, adoption, had to be provided. Each person was born into a family. Among both the northern and southern *Anishnabeg,* this family consisted of a group of people related through the father to a distant, and perhaps, mythical progenitor. Birth, of course, provides one with a sex, generation, and birth order, all important in determining one's role and relationship within the family. These features of self are, in turn, encoded by means of a kinship system that groups certain classes of people and distinguishes them from other groups, each designated by kin terms. In our own system, we group the female siblings of our mothers and fathers and call them aunts. Likewise, the offspring of these people who are members of our own generation, we call cousins, irrespective of their sex. To show that splitting, lumping, and naming is arbitrary rather than natural, as we tend to think, it would be possible for us to separate the female siblings of our mother from those of our father and to call them by different terms. Thus, maternal aunts might be called by different terms than paternal ones. Similarly, cousins might be designated by sex so that female offspring of our mothers' and fathers' sisters and brothers might be called our "hickles" while the males might be called "parpits."[2]

It is true that modern Americans, like the *Anishnabeg,* establish identity of their children by reference to the father's family, but here the similarity between the two kinship systems ends. Strictly speaking, the American kinship system is bilateral; we trace our descent from both our mothers and fathers, and we do not feel more closely related to one or the other. The *Anishnabe* system of descent recognition was lineal; a person belonged to the lineage and clan of the father. It was through this line alone that descent was traced and from which rights and obligations of the children were derived. This did not mean that the *Anishnabeg* lacked identity with their mother's family. In fact, that connection was important, but those people were not part of one's family. The brothers and sisters of a family shared with the father the rituals and duties of clanhood. They knew its songs and signs, and, with the death of their father, they would inherit his property. The mother's interests were in the clan of her birth, her family of blood.

In the case of the northern *Anishnabeg,* the term *noss* is used to refer to males of the older generation of my own descent group. This term may best be translated as 'my father.' Similarly, the word for my mother, *ninga,* is used for both a biological mother and her sisters.

In effect, people in these categories, those referred to by the terms *noss* and *ninga,* are really fathers and mothers. Being a father or mother had very little to do with biology in *Anishnabe* society. These are social categories. Thus, it is likely that any person would have numerous mothers and fathers and, because the children of these mothers and fathers would be classified as real siblings, one would also have lots of brothers and sisters. Such a system minimizes the possibility of children being orphaned and maximizes the number of close and cooperating kin in each generation. The *Anishnabeg* kinship system also distinguishes between these blood relatives and others who do not belong to one's own familial group. Thus, mother's brothers and father's sisters are called by terms that indicate them to be potential parents-in-law. As we might expect, their children, part of the broad group we call cousins, were designated by the *Anishnabeg* as potential mates in marriage.

When a couple married, the newlyweds would reside with the husband's family. Thus, a family group would comprise several generations of related males, their wives, and children, a patrilineal/patrilocal band, composed of several households. Since the daughters of each band are required to marry into other families, a custom known as exogamy, bands, in effect, trade daughters. As the daughters become wives of men in the families of other bands, they transform unrelated people into in-laws. Thus, marriage bonds are very important for economic, social, and political reasons. These bonds tie family to family and band to band through a network of mutual kin rights and obligations.

In this way, the patrilineal bands of the *Anishnabeg* were based upon the need for the close cooperation of males in hunting. Exogamy and patrilocal residence would assure this outcome, because males would never leave the home territory that they shared with fathers and brothers.

To people of a society such as ours where residence is seldom fixed for long and where moves of considerable distance are common in the life of nearly every individual, it is difficult to imagine a sense of place in the way the *Anishnabeg* perceived it and the way many of their modern descendants still do. It is not just that the experience of many generations living in the same territory gave them intimate knowledge of each hill and stream, but that their kinship was tied to the land itself. As they traveled from place to place, they recognized the localities in which specific animals and features of the landscape itself had been created. Other spots reminded them of the legendary deeds and heroes of old who were known to them from song and myth. Other landmarks brought to mind the birth and burial places of family ancestors.[3] The land and the *Anishnabeg* were one complete thing, neither to be understood apart. This relationship was one of kindred expressed by them as the relationship between dependent children and the provider, *Nokomis,* grandmother earth.

Let us return now to the nuclear family: father, mother, children, and perhaps an attached grandparent or unmarried brother or sister. It is this group that is the minimal working unit of *Anishnabeg* society because its members possess the knowledge, time, energy, and skill needed to perform all the tasks required for survival. These tasks are assigned, by custom, according to sex and age. For example, men are responsible for hunting, women for cooking and making clothes, children for collecting wood, and grandparents for education, and on and on. This division of labor within the family is vital to survival, because no person alone could hope to know enough and do enough to stay alive. All people are, therefore, members of families at all times. There is no escape from the family.

The division of labor is interwoven in an extremely complex way; something as simple as a fish net provides an example. The plants needed for fiber are collected by women, who also process and prepare the fiber and manufacturing cordage. Men, however, weave the nets from the cordage, and mostly, but not exclusively, fish with them. In most things, the division of labor was fairly strict and work was not divided on the basis of the physical effort required. Euro-American observers, and particularly those of the Victorian era, missed the subtlety of this enterprise and often condemned Indian men as lazy because women, who carried the burden of domestic chores, performed heavy work as well. One keen observer of the early nineteenth-century Ojibwa, libertarian adventurer Ann Jameson, freely attested to the drudgery performed by Indian women. She goes on to observe, however, that the heavy work of women had to be understood in terms of the responsibility of husbands, fathers, brothers, and sons for feeding the family. It is part of the reality of hunters that women must labor. She contrasted this to the enforced leisure of the female members of the English aristocracy and the exploitation of working-class women in English factories. She concluded with the remark that "however hard the lot of an (Indian) woman, she is in no false position. The two sexes are in their natural and true position relative to their state of society, and the means of subsistence."[4]

The composition of a work group, that is, the number of people of each sex and age needed to perform specific tasks, is highly variable. A large number of men may cooperate in hunting or large, mixed-sex and -age groups may help with clearing fields. It is actually the necessity of forming specific kinds of work groups at specific seasons that creates the first important differences between the northern and southern *Anishnabeg*.

The people of the northern Great Lakes forest occupy a region that, except for a few areas, is unsuited for the cultivation of corn, beans, and squash because of the short growing season. The *Anishnabeg* living in this region think of themselves as hunters. Indeed, this is strangely true, despite the fact that they primarily gained a living from fishing. Johann Kohl, who traveled extensively among the Ojibwa of Lake Superior in the mid-nineteenth century, remarks that they rarely speak of fishing but constantly of hunting. Their medicine bags are made of animal skins and not from fish and this is also true of their totemic signs.[5] There are no magical songs for catching fish and even their word for whitefish, the cornerstone of their subsistence, is *Atikameg,* a variant of the word for caribou, *Atik.* Even as the Ojibwa fish, they hunt.

During the summer, the northern *Anishnabeg* formed small villages on the shores of the Great Lakes. These villages were typically occupied by fifty to seventy-five people. Houses were round or oval, made of bent-over saplings and covered with sheets of birchbark. Such villages must have been very active, with children laughing and running, dogs barking, and adults working at various tasks. Non-Indian visitors to such villages in later times also tell us they smelled horribly from garbage and waste that was strewn among the houses. During the warm season, men made periodic hunting excursions into the forest while women collected a large variety of plants for food, building material, and medicines. Small gardens were planted and tended by women, and both sexes fished with hook and line and gill nets. Men speared and harpooned large fish species. In late fall, some of the small summer villages coalesced at a few very productive fishing sites.[6] From these villages, the men ventured onto the storm-tossed waters of the Great Lakes to set gill nets on the offshore reefs where whitefish and lake trout spawned in fantastic numbers. The huge harvest of fish put a premium on the labor of women who cleaned the catch and preserved it by smoking or freezing for winter use.[7]

Once the fish harvest was complete, the village disintegrated as each independent family took up residence in a customary interior hunting territory. The winter season was spent hunting moose, caribou, deer, and bear as well as trapping and snaring smaller mammals and birds. Fish were also taken through the ice by means of both gill nets and spears. Late winter was the most difficult season for the northern *Anishnabeg* because travel was difficult and game was in poor condition. At this time, stored resources became critical. Corn produced in summer gardens, dried berries, and smoked or frozen whitefish, even in small amounts, could make the difference between survival and starvation.

Alexander Henry, an eighteenth-century trader, provides a detailed account of the travels and activities of the *Wawatam* family during the winter of 1763–64.[8] These activities are probably fairly typical of those of earlier times. After fall fishing in St. Martins Bay, just east of the Straits of Mackinac, the family made its way south along Lake Michigan, going inland to winter between the headwaters of the Manistee and Muskegon rivers near present-day Cadillac. During that winter, the *Wawatam* family consisted of *Wawatam*, his wife, and his eldest son and his wife and a baby born the previous summer. The remaining family members were *Wawatam's* younger son and a daughter who was thirteen years old and considered an adult. There was also Alexander Henry, who was attached to the family as an adopted older son and brother. The family consisted of four adult males, three adult females, and an infant, a work force of seven people.

As the ice began to leave the lakes, the northern *Anishnabeg* families made their way back to the shores of the Great Lakes and camped near the mouths of streams, where they fished for suckers and sturgeon that were entering the waterways to spawn. Families stayed on the lakeshore fishing, hunting, and collecting plant foods through the summer in the company of other families, thus recreating the summer villages.

In this cycle we see cooperation centered in the nuclear and extended family. Spring, summer, and winter activities required no economic need that could not be met by small groups of men and women. The village configuration of the summer was purely social. In the context of these groupings, people performed ceremonies, found mates, visited with relatives, and arranged future activities. With the fall fishing villages, it was different. Here the huge catch put a demand on the collective labor of women. The temporary formation of large villages by the coalescence of bands was probably arranged by the joining of families through in-law relationships, that is, fathers and brothers appealing for help from the families of married daughters.

Given the small number of widely scattered fishers and hunters who comprised the northern *Anishnabeg*, this lifeway seems to have been stable and relatively secure. The balance of a steady supply of fish, a high-quality protein, with wild and garden-raised vegetables produced a high-quality diet.

The southern *Anishnabeg* were farmers. Their major subsistence was gained from raising corn, beans, and squash, crops first cultivated in Central America and Mexico and subsequently diffused north during the prehistoric era. Like their northern neighbors, the southern *Anishnabeg* spent summers in small villages. These villages were located on, or adjacent to, the flood plains of large rivers and streams. These water courses served as the transportation routes through the deciduous forests and marshlands that covered the southern two-thirds of Lower Michigan.

Typically, a village might be composed of ten to twenty households consisting of perhaps seventy-five to one hundred fifty people. In total, the number of southern *Anishnabeg* in what is now southern Michigan was probably about ten to fifteen thousand. Despite a more stable food supply, villages in the south were only slightly larger than those in the north. This condition would seem to indicate that social, rather than economic, constraints limited village size.[9] Given the few means for resolving disputes and limited incentives for close cooperation of large groups of people, band size seems to have been regulated by minimum work group size at the lower end and the fission of groups that grew too large at the other.

The typical southern village was made up of small, round houses made of sapling frames and covered with cattail leaf mats and bark. Houses were snug, only about ten to twelve feet across. The realities of heating these homes in the cold winter months precluded the luxury of ample personal space. *Anishnabeg* were great cuddlers. In the summer, however, most activities took place in the open around the fireplaces, earth pit storage places, wood piles, and drying racks that were to be found around the houses.

The agricultural methods employed by these farmers of the woodlands were ingenious. Here and there, some distance from the village, one would see patches made in the forest by girdling trees in order to kill the overstory of vegetation and allow light to reach crops on the forest floor. The dead trees not only produced firewood, but the limbs and brush from the clearings were burned to release their nutrients to the soil. Burning also killed weed seeds and the eggs of insects. Of course, this clearing and burning was hard work requiring the labor of men, women, and children. Once the "fields" were cleared, women planted crops in scattered hills using hoes made from deer and elk scapula. Corn, beans, and pumpkins were all planted in the same hills. As the gardens grew, the bean plants would climb the corn stalks and the pumpkin and squash would run between the hills. To non-Indian eyes, the fields looked messy and jumbled, but by mixing crops, there was less soil depletion and crop diversity made it more difficult for insect pests to destroy an entire planting of any one species.

As crops matured, women and girls cooperated in the heavy labor of weeding. Meanwhile, men were hunting deer, elk, and bear in the woods surrounding the village. Rock weirs were also constructed in rivers so that sturgeon could be speared as they ascended and descended the streams at spawning time. Ripening crops had to be protected from predators such as passenger pigeons and blackbirds, which appeared in huge flocks, as well as from raccoons and deer. This was the task of boys who might live in the fields during the late summer and fall.

Harvest was a time of great abundance and also tremendous work. Corn and beans had to be brought in, dried, and bundled; that portion to be used for food had to be shelled and stored. Pumpkins were cut into long strips and dried in the sun for future use. Here again, the entire village, men, women, and children, young and old, worked hard and, often, cooperatively to produce food for each family.

As important as these crops were to the southern *Anishnabeg,* it must be remembered that these people were also hunters and gatherers. Food and supplies collected in the forest were important in summer and vital in winter. For this reason, these southern Indians maintained territories that were comparable in extent to their northern counterparts. It should be noted that diets based on cultivated plants (particularly corn) often lack essential nutrients and were often insufficient, especially for infants and children. However, when wild foods and particularly animal protein was added, a very good nutritional balance resulted.

The reliance on animal protein was seen during the winter months, at which time the villages temporarily fragmented as families departed for winter hunting territories. A great variety of game was taken by hunters, but deer was far and away the favored target of the hunt since they provided both food and the hide used to make clothing. As the weather warmed in the spring, families returned to the summer villages and began the hard work of preparing fields for planting.

Here again we see flexibility in group size and composition to accommodate labor needs. It is apparent that agricultural production demands an enduring, cooperative labor force and it is perhaps for this reason that we see more permanent villages among agricultural people. It should be noted, however, that a larger population did not necessarily result from agricultural production, because excess production of food was not the goal of these woodland cultivators. When stored food was scarce, they maintained the economic flexibility to use other resources and the social flexibility to spread themselves thinly on the landscape.

It would seem that the economic and social life of the *Anishnabeg* required a means to formalize and extend the net of kinship that could unite patrilocal households. This is especially true among the southern *Anishnabeg*, who accomplished this end through groups that might best be thought of as "superfamilies," that is, a group of patrilineal kin who thought of themselves as descendants of an ancient ancestor. Though these people were scattered throughout the tribal domain and many would remain unknown to each other personally, they were all members of the same *Ototomen*. This root Algonquian word, which becomes *Dodems* or *Ododents* among the Ojibwa, is usually rendered into English as totem. Literally, the word means 'my blood relations.'[10] In anthropological jargon, these descent groups are referred to as clans and if, as is usually the case, the ancestral form is an animal, then they are called totemic clans. The clan members shared origin mythology, ritual paraphernalia (sometimes including clan medicine bundles, songs, and chants), methods of face decoration, clan symbols, food taboos, and other devices to set themselves apart from members of other clans. Most important, however, clan members shared a strong feeling of family loyalty. In many ways, this is similar to the clans of eighteenth-century Scotland, where independent families of a clan shared common customs and dress and fought together in battle.

The origin of clan groups among the *Anishnabeg* is unclear and subject to debate among ethnologists. It has been suggested that, originally, clans were small regional or even village groups and that these were later dispersed as a result of European contact.[11] Clans, like families, are not fixed social entities but sometimes die out while new clans are born by the fission of old ones.

The kin nomenclature of the patrilineal family is extended to the clan. Thus, clan members of the older generation become fathers and of one's own generation brothers and sisters, that is, blood relatives. Thus, like the families, clans too are exogamous. Clanship among the northern *Anishnabeg* did not extend much beyond the function of regulating marriage, although it is true that some interclan politics were linked to clan mythology. We might recall here the migration allegory that set forth the political relationship between the Crane and the Loon clans. It was the Crane (clan) that led the way and provided the head chief, while the Loon (clan) followed and provided the "voice" or chief speaker.

Ojibwa tradition of the nineteenth century relates that the northern *Anishnabeg* originally had five totems that were the descendants from five mysterious beings in human form who emerged from the deep (Atlantic Ocean). This produced the original clans: *Awas-e* (catfish), *Bus-in-aus-e* (Echo Maker, in reference to the voice of the crane), *Ah-ah-wau-k* (loon), *Noka* (bear), and *Waub-ish-ash-e* (marten). Eventually, these original clans gave rise to about twenty clans, each associated with these original five. For example, the Sturgeon, Pike, Whitefish, and Sucker clans would all recognize themselves as coming from the *Awas-e* totem. A list of nineteenth-century Ojibwa clans include: Crane, Catfish, Loon, Bear, Marten, Reindeer, Wolf, Merman, Pike, Lynx, Eagle, Rattlesnake, Moose, Cormorant,

Goose, Sucker, Sturgeon, Whitefish, Beaver, Gull, and Hawk. Apparently, about 80 percent of the northern *Anishnabeg* belonged to either the Crane, Catfish, Bear, Wolf, Marten, or Loon clans.[12]

Clanship among the southern *Anishnabeg* is much more complex and the clans themselves were more prominent in social and political life owing to the importance placed on the ceremonial relationship among clans. Some of the increased complexity results from the fact that various clans are grouped into larger descent units. Such grouping of clans are called phratries by anthropologists. People who belong to the clans of a given phratry feel these clans to be more closely related to each other than to the clans of other phratries. For this reason social custom requires that people marry members of clans grouped into phratries different from their own. The forty or more clans of the nineteenth-century Prairie Potawatomi were grouped into the following phratries: Water, Bird, Buffalo, Bear, Wolf, and Man. The Buffalo phratry, for example, was composed of people belonging to the Buffalo, Moose, Elk, and Deer clans. Each clan had reciprocal social and political functions so that if one of the clans of the Water phratry was holding a feast, the servers would be provided by the Man phratry and the Thunder clan, while speakers would come from the Bear phratry and the Bald Eagle and Thunder clans. Duties extended from political roles (for example, the principle chief was always drawn from the Fish clan) to ritual ones, since obligation bound members of one clan to bury the dead of another. Clans played an important part in the regulation of warfare, diplomatic initiatives, and in maintaining internal order.

Among the Potawatomi each clan has a series of traditional personal names so that, in most cases, a person's clan affiliation is apparent. *Kakita-pe* (No tail), *Kakinikisha* (Sharp claw), *Mat-wa* (Gets angry), *Sha-beni* (He has pawed through), and *Mukopin* (Bear potato) are but a few of the personal names that make reference to bears and are property of the clans of the Bear phratry.[13]

The clans each hold ceremonial medicine bundles containing clan fetishes that in turn make reference to clan origin mythology. Clans observe an annual round of ceremonies featuring the singing of traditional clan songs and the display of ritual paraphernalia. This promotes the general well-being and fertility of the clan.

Since clan exogamy is practiced and since clans feel a closeness of kin within phratries, a person of the Raven clan could not marry

Origin of the Fish Clan and Bundle Origin Myth

In the beginning of the world a young couple had a man child who died. The parents went away from the village where they lived to mourn in solitude. One day, while the man was away from the lodge hunting, the woman went down to the water's edge to wash some clothes, and while she was so engaged she happened to catch a pretty little sunfish. She was so lonely for her lost child that she played with it, and sang to it. She made it swim, and petted it, until, behold, it turned into a real human baby! She put it to her breasts, and it nursed.

After a time, the husband came back from the hunt laden with much meat. He saw the cradle with the enchanted baby in it, and thought at first that it was a doll, but when he peeped in he discovered that it was really a child. His wife was disturbed and cried out:

"Oh, what are you doing?"

"Why, isn't this our child?" asked the man.

"Yes, but you should have asked me first, before you disturbed it. Now I will tell you all about it."

So they made a feast of the breast of a deer and carried the meat to the shores of the sea and gave it to the fishes and thanked them for sending back their child. They returned to the lodge of the woman's parents, and they were surprised to see the baby, whom they naturally thought was some adopted orphan. The mother, however, told them the facts of the matter, and called upon them to sing the chief's song, because her child had come back alive to her.

The relatives gathered and made a feast called *Tcipa' Kikwao*, or Feast of the Dead. Their speaker announced to the guests what the ceremony was for, and recounted the circumstances of the return of the child for their benefit. Then they gave a great feast in honor of the fish. In their dreams a trout came and told them that the Fish clan would be the greatest division of their people, and none should ever equal it.

Years passed, and the Fish boy grew up. His parents later had nine other sons, but they were never told the strange history of their elder brother. One day he said to his mother, "I would like to go hunting and take my brothers with me." His mother was pleased, and told the others to obey him.

When the party of brothers was a long way off in the woods, the Fish boy said to the others: "My brothers, it may seem strange to you, but I am not to live on this earth always, like the rest of you. What I am about to tell you comes from the Great Spirit. Now kill me, sprinkle my blood everywhere, cut off my head and throw it away. Burn my body in a brush pile. Hunt, you will have success, and then go home and tell my parents and my people. It will sound cruel, but they know how I came into this world, and it will not hurt them. We are all here only for a short time anyway.

"Now, when you have done what I told you, stay away from this place for one year. At the end of that time tell father to invite all the men to come here with him and camp. Tell mother to take tobacco and go to a certain place and pray for me. She will see corn, beans, pumpkins, and melons there, that will be me myself. Let her gather as much as she needs, and then tell her to bring the rest here to feast on me. These vegetables will be on earth with you until the last Indian. But, remember this, women in the course of their sickness must keep away from the fields."

—Alanson Skinner, *The Mascoutens or Prairie Patawatonmi Indians.*

another Raven nor a member of any of the eight bird-named clans of the Bird phratry. Marriage was thus to nonrelated clans and had the effect of tying these together with in-law bonds.

Clans are, of course, interest groups. In disputes among people of two different clans, a person could count on support from all fellow clan members (brothers, sisters, mothers, and fathers). The clan lines are thus points of possible social schisms. This danger is somewhat offset by the phratry structure because, by including many more people, obligation is extended to more distantly related people and thereby diminished. Of course, it is also worth remembering that the more social divisions created through patrilineal families, clans, and phratries, the more social identity can be compounded. Thus, a man of a specific patrilineage of the Fish clan may claim various degrees of identity from the Great Sea clan, and with the other clans of his Water phratry; his mother's clan (Elk) and the four clans of her phratry (Buffalo) as well as the Bear clan into which he marries and the three other clans of the Bear phratry. Of course, the ties of patrilineage are strongest, with a continuum of loyalty and obligation extending from the closest relationship of blood through the less compelling obligations of marriage and friendship. In loyalty or obligation, the clans form the major divisions. It is for this reason that, when the Prairie Potawatomi played the violent game of lacrosse, the threat of serious social disruption (such as might occur if clan was pitted against clan) was avoided by drafting teams that crosscut clan membership. Thus, a moiety or two-part division was used. Teams were composed by people first, third, or fifth born, the *Oskush,* or second, fourth, and sixth born, the *Kishko.* These divisions are without reference to sex or clan.

The clan and phratry divisions among the southern *Anishnabeg,* if we can use this nineteenth-century model as a guide, emerged as a powerful integrative force in society. Exactly when this happened is uncertain, but it certainly made a major difference in how they conducted themselves in later times.

The Chain of Gifts

As capitalists, we learn at an early age that the law of supply and demand is both natural and logical. After all, if something is scarce it is bound to be more valuable, and if it is not scarce, it could not have great value.[14] Supply must be the primary difference between glass and diamonds, because they look the same to most people. With this understanding of economics, we separate what is "economic" from what is "social." If we buy a theater ticket, the transaction is an amount of money for an equivalent value of ticket. The transaction is purely economic. As tickets become scarce, their value rises, scalpers demand higher prices, and people with tickets guard them more jealously. The value of the ticket is not changed by the relationship between ticket buyer and the seller in the booth and the inflated cost charged by the scalper does not change if he happens to be a relative. This is not to say that social relations never matter in a capitalist economy. It is true that economic exchange is either economic or social but it is very seldom both, and most often purely economic. In the economy of the *Anishnabeg,* kinship does matter. In fact, economic exchange cannot be understood apart from it, for there is no such thing as a purely economic transaction. Exchange might be "economic" in the sense that goods and services flow from person to person, but exchange cannot be asocial since, among the *Anishnabeg,* all social interaction is conditioned by kinship. The *Anishnabeg* could not, by definition, be capitalist, or for that matter socialist or communist, because their economics was always strictly personal. *Anishnabeg* "economics" was an economy of gifts where exchange produced both economic benefit and a feeling of good will that cemented the social bond between the people who conducted the exchange.

Gift giving as a type of economic exchange is a two-edged sword. Giving the proper way makes people feel good but giving too much, not enough, or at the wrong time creates the opposite effect. As a result, customs that govern gift giving among *Anishnabeg* were well developed and commensurate with its importance in society. As we might expect, the kin relationship conditioned expectations of exchange.

Basically, the rule of giving was this: the closer the kin relationship between people, the greater the reliance, and therefore, the implication of trust. Exchange would balance out in the long run. This type of exchange is called general reciprocity by anthropologists and is the kind of exchange that occurs within households and among members of a nuclear family. This holds true in nonnative families as well, where, for example, on Christmas there is no insistence on the exchange of equally valuable gifts. As we say, "It's the thought that counts."

At the other extreme of *Anishnabeg* exchange is the type that takes place with very distant kin or strangers. Here, the things exchanged should be of equal value and both parties should be immediately satisfied. Although this sounds like our ticket buyer and seller, it is not, since the exchange is still in the form of a gift and still carries social implications—goodwill and the promise of future relationships. It was for this reason that, when Europeans first contacted the *Anishnabeg*, "barter" (an economic term in our context) was conducted in a social atmosphere with prolonged greetings, pipe smoking, and present exchanges as preliminaries to the main event.

The confusion over social versus economic emphasis in exchange during the early years of Euro-American and Indian contact also accounts for a common term in American folklore about Indians. Because the Indians placed gift giving in an economic as well as a social context, a present made to a distant kinsman or to a stranger, the category into which non-Indians would be placed, required the immediate return of a present of equal value. To a person ignorant of this expectation, as many non-Indians were, the gift was usually accepted with a grateful "thank you," a social response. Since no economic recompense was forthcoming from the ill-mannered stranger, a return of the gift was demanded. The Indian, for his trouble, was branded as an "Indian giver."

Since reciprocal giving was both economic and social, many customs determined the conditions and decorum of giving. The first of these is that there is as much obligation to receive as to give, and as much right. Custom dictated that visitors be fed, and that tools required to complete a task were available to all, irrespective of ownership. No thanks was required and no thanks was expected; giving and receiving were equivalents. To the *Anishnabeg*, it was "blessed to give and receive." Unlike our gifts, which require transfer of ownership or use rights and imply future obligation, *Anishnabeg* required neither. Obligations were implicit in the kin relationship and were, in turn, structured by the nature of the social interaction.

For example, if an *Anishnabe* hunter killed a deer, various relatives, blood and in-law, would have customary claims on certain portions of the deer governed by their relationship to the hunter. A brother-in-law might get one of the haunches, a father the other, an older sister a forequarter, and a wife the liver. The brother-in-law may have a wife and a son who would each receive a portion of his meat. The deer is thereby divided and redivided. As each piece changes hands as a gift, the social relationship between the giver and receiver is reinforced and the mutual obligation rekindled. The social whole was reinforced as the people were fed.

Taking another view of *Anishnabeg* reciprocity, it might be observed that the obligation of gift exchange is like a life insurance policy. That is, in a sense, true, because as food becomes scarce, the *Anishnabeg* are more anxious to give it away. The deer is divided and redivided as each person gives away more meat. The effect is that the deer is shared by a greater number of people, all of whom get less meat. This behavior is directly opposite of what we would predict on the basis of the notion that scarcity creates increased economic value, a proposition that would lead one to expect hoarding. By acting in the opposite manner, the *Anishnabeg* are storing food in the stomachs of relatives. Giving is a social investment yielding an economic return.

Dependent as the *Anishnabeg* are on the caprices of nature, a steady supply of food could not be guaranteed by any one family. If, however, several families cooperatively shared food, the unevenness of production could be brought into better balance with the steady demand of consumption. Even when food is available periodically, people like to eat regularly. To some extent, this can be offset by food storage, and storability is no doubt the reason agricultural production, the harvest of wild rice, and the cold storage of smoked fish, were so important. These foodstuffs can all be produced in excess and stored for future use. But these strategies alone were still not sufficient; as a result, a reciprocal exchange system arose, allowing the survival of the group over survival of the individual.

Cooperative giving started in the family, where it was linked to the division of labor. Husbands gave meat and skins, wives gave cooked food and clothing, children received food and clothing and gave blueberries and firewood. In this system of giving, the boy who snared a rabbit was given the same respect as a hunter who brought home a bear. This exchange, as in contemporary families, produced a sense of interdependency, security, and satisfaction.

In *Anishnabeg* society, the chain of gifts extended outward beyond the nuclear family in an important manner. Exogamy means that the daughters of one group become the wives of other groups. They are, in effect, precious gifts given from one family, band, or clan to another. As we might expect, marriage is thereby both a social and economic institution. In-laws, as relatives, have mutual economic obligations. For this reason, the *Anishnabeg* carefully arranged marriages so that links between families and clans were not duplicated. Marriages were too important to squander, because they provided the conduit for cooperation between social groups. Families routed from their territory by a disastrous forest fire could seek refuge with in-laws of other bands. A family needing extra labor could call on such relatives to help preserve fish or to help avenge a wrong. The importance of these in-law connections cannot be overemphasized.

In fact, they were emphasized by the *Anishnabeg* to the extent that a social means was found to preserve the economic relationships created by the marriage even if one of the partners died. These are the customs of levirate and sororate. In the former case, if a man dies, his brother is encouraged to marry the widow; in the case of sororate, a widower would marry the sister of his deceased wife. Here we see that marriage is, first of all, a social affair and, to a lesser extent, an individual one. Romance may enter marriage but marriage is not a romantic institution; it was the institution of *Anishnabeg* survival.

According to *Anishnabeg* thinking, if one marriage created favorable social relations, two marriages were better. A man would certainly increase his family's security by arranging an additional marriage; however, polygyny also meant that more people had to be supported. For this reason, polygynous marriages seem to have been the exception.

One would think that the economic incentives associated with marriage would have produced stability in marriage partnerships. This is apparently not true. *Anishnabeg* people seem to have been married to many different partners during their lifetimes. This is, in part, due to fairly high mortality, but also to the ease of both marriage and divorce. If a marriage was not working, it was a threat to everyone's survival and the couple simply split up, the wife returning to her family. The children in these patrilineal societies stayed with their kin, that is, the father and his relatives. Given the need for a balance of labor, people did not stay unmarried for long.

A Society of Equals

In the course of everyday life, it is inevitable that situations arise that require or favor the cooperation of people in groups larger and more complex than the nuclear family. Hunting expeditions, movements of villages, and dealing with problems that affect several families all call for coordinated effort and, therefore, leadership. In the context of American culture, we tend to think about leadership in terms of the exercising of authority or power on the part of a leader, and to think about the use of authority in a hierarchical structure of decision making. That is, we assign authority to positions filled by individuals upon whom we bestow the right and responsibility to make decisions for others. It seems to us that this system is the very basis of our civilization; without such a structure, everyone would do as they saw fit and the resulting anarchy would bring chaos.

Among the *Anishnabeg*, leadership was not based upon power except insofar as each person was willing to personally delegate authority to another. Inside the family, males held more authority than females, and adults more authority than children. Outside of the family, the *Anishnabeg* were a society of equals. Even inside the family, authority relationships were not based upon the power of one person to make decisions for another. The principle of individual sovereignty extended even to the rearing of children. Even in situations dangerous to the safety of the child, parents did not command or demand, but taught by patient insistence, appeals to expectations of proper behavior and occasionally to the fear of supernatural beings. The use of force or corporal punishment was unthinkable to the *Anishnabeg* because it would require the willful use of one's power over another, an action, even between parent and child, that was inconsistent with the use of authority in *Anishnabeg* society.

In seeking leaders, the last quality the *Anishnabeg* sought was the desire to lead. The ideal leader was a person who was wise by virtue of experience and demonstratively successful in life through generosity and humility. Parenthetically, it may be added that these characteristics are respected to this day in the Indian community. People who meet Indians for the first time often perceive them to be "shy" because they may not offer a firm handshake or make eye contact during conversation. These characteristics, which are a means of expressing polite openness, are associated with submissiveness in American culture.

Among small groups of people who are well known to each other, everyone is familiar with the strengths and weaknesses of others. It is, therefore, true that when needs of leadership arise, the people know where to turn to find the necessary skill and knowledge to meet any contingency. Given that stability was more characteristic of *Anishnabeg* experience than change, and given that all people develop different skills as a result of their unique abilities, all *Anishnabeg* had occasion to be leaders. It is also, of course, true that some people seem to have more leadership talents than others. This is the case no matter how leadership is defined. There are always those with charisma. In the true sense of the word, *Anishnabeg* leaders were charismatic leaders that people followed willingly for their talents and not because they had greater authority.

The principle of individual sovereignty in *Anishnabeg* political life meant that all group decisions were made as a matter of consensus on the part of the people who participated in them. Groups acted cooperatively and leaders merely offered advice. Here again, this tradition is still much in evidence in modern tribal politics. Decisions are seldom made on the spot because tribal leaders feel the necessity to discuss matters with kin and friends "behind the scene." Often enough, when non-Indians who are unfamiliar with this mode of leadership and decision making present proposals to tribal councils, they are later disappointed to find that silence or the lack of questions they took as a sign of assent did not indicate agreement with their proposal.

Returning to the protohistoric *Anishnabeg,* it is true that leadership has some structure beyond the needs of the moment. For one thing, leadership seems to pass in families; accomplished fathers seem to have accomplished sons who tended to assume leadership roles. This trend seems to be due to education and, to some degree, the acquisition of supernatural powers. Among the southern *Anishnabeg* it is also due to the fact that leadership is more structured by the existence of "offices" within and among clans. In popular usage, the term *Ogama* or *Okama* is used to mean chief; *Okemos* is a diminutive, therefore 'little chief.' Clifton, however, points out that these terms alone mean little, in the sense that leadership among the *Anishnabeg* was more complex. Speaking of historic Potawatomi,

Clifton reminds us that *Okamek* came in a variety of sexes, ages, and roles.[15] *Okama* may be a leader of a clan, village, or extended family; *Kiktowenene* was a speaker; *Skabewis,* a crier; *Okamakwe,* a women's leader; and *Shkenweyowokama,* a leader of young people. Some of these traditional leadership roles were more or less permanently held by prominent leaders, while others were filled for the occasion. Often as not, leadership roles might be referred to by clan membership and positions within the clan as well as personal names. For example, a northern *Anishnabeg* speaker would be drawn by tradition from the *Ah-ah-wauk* (Loon) clan in reference to the loud and distinctive voice of the loon. A speaker would be a person of demonstrated oratorical skill and might, as a result, be named *Nodin,* 'wind,' in reference to the metaphorical relationship between the power of the wind and skillful articulation.

Lacking any reliance on built-in authority, the *Anishnabeg* who rose to positions of widely recognized leadership were people with the ability to convince others. As nineteenth-century American diplomats often discovered, *Anishnabeg* leaders were accomplished speakers and shrewd negotiators. As they also discovered, however, decision making took place in the context of the families that composed individual bands, and agreement among bands required laborious discussion until consensus could be reached.

In this last point lies a fundamental principle in understanding not only *Anishnabeg* politics but also many other aspects of *Anishnabeg* culture, that is, that society is composed of like parts. Like people comprise like families, like families comprise like bands, like lineages form like clans, and like clans form phratries. Each of these "pieces" of *Anishnabeg* society is different in important ways but, in the context of the social order, perfectly equivalent. The ethic of equality that organizes personal relationships also organizes all other levels of society.

Maintaining Order

It would be a vast mistake to picture the life of the *Anishnabeg* at the eve of contact with Europeans as idyllic. Certainly an economic system based upon gift giving or a pattern of leadership based upon egalitarian principles has romantic appeal, yet the *Anishnabeg* were real people living in a real world. Sickness, starvation, and other calamities were always immediate to the *Anishnabeg* and the principles that organized their cultures reflected their means to cope with potential tragedy. An example that could be cited is social discord, a problem in every human society. It is true that the *Anishnabeg* seldom assaulted each other and that murder was very rare. Theft was inconceivable because there was no point to it in a society where things could be taken and used without asking. This does not mean however that the *Anishnabeg* lived their lives in peace and tranquility.

In any society there are expected modes of behavior. These can be codified as laws and rules, as in the case of American society, or as customs and etiquette, as in the case of the *Anishnabeg*. In each case, there are recognized norms and permissible deviations. We know the law prescribes driving at 65 miles per hour but that we can get away with 70. In the same way, an *Anishnabeg* would know that it is improper to speak of personal matters in front of a brother-inlaw, but might do it anyhow.

Education was an important means of teaching young people proper or expected roles. Much of this was done by correcting young people as they learned by imitating adult work in everyday apprenticeships. When we consider that there was no escape from the family group, every person had to learn to resolve life's problems. Our options, of stalking off in anger or avoiding people we do not particularly like, were not solutions available to the *Anishnabeg*.

Humor, and in particular sarcastic humor, were devices that helped maintain social norms. When a person hoarded food or shirked obligations to relatives, family and friends responded with sharp ridicule, biting words, and songs that were difficult to withstand. In a way, the community acted as a grand jury, always in session and always ready to prod the lazy, stingy, and boastful back into more acceptable behavior.

Now and again people transgressed in more serious ways, behaving in a way that threatened the unity of the social fabric. Murder, wife stealing, and sorcery were major "crimes." In the case of murders, which were exceedingly rare, relatives felt obligated to avenge such deaths. Thus, a murder could set a family and their clansmen against another family and another clan in a self-perpetuating round of revenge and counterrevenge involving more and more people. When murder occurred, mutual kin of the two parties tried to settle the matter by an exchange of property. Wife stealing and adultery seemed to be an almost constant source of friction in *Anishnabeg* communities. Here again, the social seriousness of the offense forced kinsmen to take sides and, therefore, threatened both internal and external relations.

The same was true of sorcery. Since all sickness and misfortune was believed to stem from supernatural sources, and since some individuals were known to have the power to alter events by supernatural means, accusations of sorcery were quite common. The remedy for magical spells was counterspells and, thus, people who knew the use of magic were both respected and feared.

People who persisted in causing disruption in *Anishnabeg* communities through behavior that threatened the close cooperation so necessary for survival would find themselves increasingly isolated within society. This, of course, meant increasing difficulty in performing life's necessary tasks and a powerful nudge toward conformity with community norms. If, in the case of the most serious offenses, no accommodation could be reached, the offender would be entirely isolated, a sentence tantamount to death.

The trauma of Euro-American contact, as we shall see in subsequent chapters, often led the *Anishnabeg* (along with other native people of the eastern woodland) to war. As a result, American mythology and history often casts these Indians as a race of warriors. This is a false image in the context of the protohistoric *Anishnabeg*. It is certain that warfare did exist well before the arrival of Europeans; fortified Late Woodland villages bear evidence of this fact. The question remains, however, what was the extent of precontact warfare? In the case of most tribal peoples, war between neighboring groups seldom had territorial objectives and was almost never sustained. More likely, *Anishnabeg* war took place in the form of periodic raids by small war parties. Warfare, whatever its extent or duration, was a serious concern because of the difficulty of resolving disputes between unrelated people. Almost certainly, the *Anishnabeg* would have been hesitant to engage in war with their neighbors and never would have seen total annihilation of enemies as an objective. Glory, adventure, honor, and prestige were the rewards of war, and revenge was its objective. While it is probably true that the threat of war was a constant reality to the *Anishnabeg*, as a practical matter they lived mostly in peace.

An Ojibwa Joke

Humor provides more than amusement for Indian people; it is often a way to teach a lesson or a means to encourage correct behavior. It is perhaps for that reason that Ojibwa humor usually has a sharp and obvious point. Bill Twain of the Bear Island Reserve on Lake Temagami, Ontario, told this story, which got a huge laugh from his audience.

A man and his son were hunting moose and, in fact, succeeded in killing a young bull at some distance from camp. The son was lazy and kept up a constant quibble about the work as the pair skinned and butchered the dead animal. In order to take meat back to camp, the two men each prepared a bundle of meat to carry and they set out. As they walked along, the son soon began to complain that his burden was the heavier of the two. Finally the father had enough of his son's bickering. He placed a heavy stick across a low tree limb and put his bundle of meat on one end. "Now," he said to his son, "you put your meat on the other end and we will see which is heavier." As the son hung his bundle on the stick the father let go and the stick on the son's side flew up, striking the son a wicked blow on the point of his chin. The father picked up his bundle and headed home.

Bodies, Shadows, and the Supernatural

One of the fundamental keys to understanding the *Anishnabeg* and their descendants lies in the ways they structured their relationships as human beings to the world around them. Our own tradition clearly partitions the world into contrasting categories. As we see it, things are either animate or inanimate, natural or supernatural, savage or civilized, human or nonhuman. The *Anishnabeg* did not draw these neat categorical distinctions.

As far as it may be ascertained from much later accounts, the *Anishnabeg* concept of life was tripartite. All things had an outward manifestation, a perceptual essence, and a life force. These are generally referred to as the body, *wiyo,* shadow, *wdjibbon,* and spirit or soul, *wdjitchog.* In this fundamental conception, there was no distinction made between animate and inanimate or human and nonhuman. A rock had a spirit as much as a fish did. As *Pegahmagabow,* an Ojiibwa of Perry Island, explained it to Diamond Jenness in 1928, "Sometimes a tree will fall when there is not a breath of wind. Its soul dies just as the soul of a man dies and goes to the land of the west. But whither the tree's soul goes no one knows."[16] The shadow, in nineteenth-century Ojibwa conception, resided in the brain and was invisible under most circumstances. It provided perception and intuition, the truth that precedes logic. The spirit or soul resided in the heart and was the life force and intelligence of the being. Amazingly, the body, shadow, and spirit were all independent and interchangeable entities. In dreams, the spirit left the body and wandered freely to commune with other spirits. This produced a vulnerable and, therefore, dangerous state because a permanent separation of one's body and spirit would produce insanity or death. This is also a notion of our own not too distant past and is a source of the custom of blessing a person after a violent sneeze for fear the person's soul would rush out of the body. Among the *Anishnabeg,* spirit flight was also an acquired power used by shamans to facilitate the healing of the sick. People of exceptional magical power claimed the ability to enter a trance state where the spirit would leave the body and either commune with other spirits or fly forth and survey distant places. Information thus gained could be either communicated in the trance state or in posttrance sessions after the body and spirit had been safely reunited. In these instances, the trance was regarded as a pseudodeath and a demonstration of remarkable power and knowledge.

Since the body, spirit, and shadow were regarded as independent entities, they were, to varying degrees, interchangeable. For example, in that instant when you think you see a person that you know is really far away, it is that person's shadow that let itself be seen for a brief second. Similarly, the nineteenth-century Ojibwa believed that two people passing on a road would not get in an argument if they passed each other and then turned back to talk since their spirits and the source of the intelligence would have continued down the road.[17] Likewise, the appearance of the spirits of one life form in the bodies of others was, to some degree, a natural process. This is why, according to the Ojibwa, so many sturgeon appear at some times of the year and so many bear at others; they are really "the same animal."[18]

The fact that body, soul, and shadow could be disarticulated and interchanged meant that the world could be a mysterious and terrifying place. The reality we find in the "natural" world with its physical laws and predictable relationships did not exist for the *Anishnabeg*. Indeed, things were often not at all what they seemed.

Power and the Supernatural

In his *Animal World,* Berger tells us that animals have always been central to the process by which men form an image of themselves.[19] The same thought is expressed by French anthropologist Levi-Strauss, who reminds us that animals figure prominently in totemic discourse not because they are good to eat but because they are good to think with.[20] This is certainly true in the case of the *Anishnabeg,* where the conceptual distinction between human and nonhuman and between natural and supernatural realms of experience does not follow the strict Cartesian dichotomy of Western thought.[21]

Recall first that the mythology of totemic descent does more than link humans to animals. In the *Anishnabeg* conception, humans are often transformed from animals. Members of the Fish clan came from a sunfish that was transformed into a human body. This blood relationship among Fish clan members is acknowledged by exogamy and the observance of incest taboos among descendants from this mythical progenitor. Animals themselves are not always the product of original creation, but are transformed in appearance and behavior by interaction with the spirit *Nanabojo* who is himself quasi-human. Thus, the morphology of animals and plants, their color, the form of their tails or the way their tails are carried are all the product of natural and cultural interaction. Animals became metaphors for the relationships that the *Anishnabeg* draw for themselves in balancing human needs against the unforeseeable forces of the natural world.

The needs of survival, however, require human and cultural intervention in the natural world, and these needs disrupt the order imparted by creation. In interacting with animals, and particularly in killing them, the *Anishnabeg* acknowledged the superiority of the creation order and the mystical forces that control human and nonhuman interaction. Rituals to placate the spirits of slain animals were common. A bear killed by hunters might have been decorated, had smoke blown into its mouth, and been offered prayers of forgiveness so that its spirit would not be offended. Similarly, the *Anishnabeg* took the precaution of leaving sacrificial offerings when they collected plants, a practice still common among modern Indians. These actions and much other taboo and ritual were extended to preserve the sanctity and balance of creation. In this sense, the relationship between humans and the nonhuman world was one of reciprocal exchange and cooperation. The natural world provided the means for food, clothing, and shelter in exchange for the human acknowledgement of their potentially disruptive role in nature's order.[22] It is important to understand that people are not the takers but that animals and plants are the givers. It is not the hunter's skill with a bow that brings down the deer, but the deer's willingness to give its body to the hunter. If the spirit of the deer is willing, the hunter's arrow cannot miss. To the *Anishnabeg,* the relationship between the hunter's success and his power to manipulate animal spirits is obvious. As we say, "Nothing succeeds like success." A good hunter demonstrates, time and again, his ability to manipulate the spirits of his quarry.

This last idea introduces the concept of power. In Algonquian thought, "Power is manifest in the land, in the dialectic of the sacred and profane, and in the pattern of space and time. Power is the transformative presence in cycles of day and night and the seasons, in the fecund earth and in the vision and deeds of spirits, ancestors, and living people. Power is manifestly present and it is itself the explanation of all transformations."[23]

Given a view of the natural world in which the boundaries between perception and reality are ambiguous, people would have no
hope without power. Power provides the means to control the un-
imagined and unforeseen, the means to balance the moral inferiority
incumbent upon people by the need to intervene in the natural order
imposed by creation. Power guides human action; it is a gift given to
human beings, as is perception and wisdom. Power may be bestowed
in a dream or vision and it may be earned by study; it may even be
purchased from others. Power may be collected in the form of me-
dicinal formulas or in physical things—charms, amulets, or medicine
bundles (*pinji-gosan*). Songs, personal names, and places are all loci
of varying degrees of power. One of the most important sources of
power is dreams and visions acquired by young people who fast and
undergo privation in order to obtain this source of power. Often it
comes in the guise of spiritual helpers or guardians that protect the
person through life and provide the dreamer with special control
over some realm of human experience such as curing the sick or
forecasting the future. In the world of the *Anishnabeg*, "religion"
was distinctly individual.

The *Anishnabeg* believed in distinct, independent, and unranked
sources of power or spirits called *manidog*. Some were remote and
related to creation, while other *manitou* resided in particular places.
Some appeared in natural guise with distinct personalities; *Nanabojo*
is one of these. Others were thought of in animal form and thus as
supernatural beings such as the thunderbird or horned snakes. Some
manitou were beneficial to human interests and others decidedly
malevolent. There is no sense of good and evil here, however, but a
natural balance of deeds, much like the concept of Yahweh and
Satan in the Old Testament of the Christian Bible. The *Anishnabeg*
did recognize a supreme spirit or *kitchimanitou* ('big spirit'). This
spirit was not all powerful, but the prime mover of creation—the
"master of life." In fact, this spirit was often confused by Christian
missionaries with the Christian God. *Kitchimanitou* is more properly
envisioned as having started the earth but, after creation, withdrawing to leave the affairs of the world to many *manidog*. As twentieth-
century Canadian Ojibwa John Manatuwba explained it, "There is
a big boss manido, the chief of all the manidos. He stays somewhere
in one place, sitting quietly and supervising everything. He is like

the captain on a steamboat, or like the government that remains in Ottawa, yet has servants all over the country."[24]

In order to survive in a world of unknown and dangerous spirits, the *Anishnabeg* used their power to enlist the aid of spiritual beneficiaries and to ward off by prayers, sacrifices, and spells the malevolent *manitou* who would bring sickness, misfortune, or death. Often, the *manitou* had particular known abodes, often noticeable features of the landscape such as huge rocks along shorelines or caves or small lakes. It was at these spots that the *Anishnabeg* left offerings.

As we might expect, some people were more successful in obtaining and using power than others. These became spiritual leaders known to anthropologists as shamans. Insofar as the nineteenth century was typical of earlier times, the *Anishnabeg* recognized several specialists: *Jessakkid*, *Wabeno*, and *Mashkikikewinnini*.[25]

Jessakkid was a seer and prophet whose power was bestowed by the thunderers or thunderbird *animiki*. The *jessakkid* were also curers who specialized in the removal of offending foreign bodies from the sick by means of a sucking tube made of bone. In these manipulations the *jessakkid* were skilled in slight-of-hand magic. Most famous of the *jessakkid* performances was the shaking tent ceremony. Enclosed in a tall, narrow tent open to the sky and only barely large enough to hide them, the *jessakkid* called forth spirits who announced their presence inside the tent by violently shaking the tent poles. These spirits came in animal form and answered questions posed by people outside the tent using different voices and, often, different languages. In the shaking tent ceremony, the turtle *makinak* was the major intermediator.[26]

Wabeno ('men of dawn') refers to a class of religious specialists whose power was obtained in youthful visions. *Wabeno* were skilled in divination and could provide love and hunting magic or cast spells and predict the presence of game by looking into a bowl of water. *Wabeno* held boisterous dances and feasts featuring exhibitions of power, including fire handling and putting hands into boiling maple sap without apparent harm.

The third type of shaman was the herbalist or *mashkikikewinnini* ('medicine men') who were, in fact, often women. These specialists had detailed knowledge of the mysterious properties of a huge variety of plants, herbs, roots, and berries. *Anishnabeg* pharmacology was, in fact, extensive, including not only thousands of kinds of plants and plant parts, but also complex prescriptions prepared by mixtures of different species whose compound potency often made these medicines extremely dangerous. The nineteenth-century missionary at Fond du Lac at the west end of Lake Superior, Edmund Ely, reported that local Ojibwa were astounded at the power of cattle when they first encountered them. Unfamiliar with wide spectrum grazers, the Ojibwa observed that cattle consumed, with apparent immunity, combinations of plants that they regarded as deadly poisonous.[27]

It should be emphasized that the power wielded by *Anishnabeg* shamans was no different than that in the hands of any individual; it was just more concentrated. Custom recognized that power could be used for both good and bad effect. These outcomes were the reverse sides of the same coin. The same magic could lure animals into a trap or could ensnare an unsuspecting person in misfortune. Some shamans practiced harmful magic on their own behalf or for others and, therefore, were treated with both respect and fear. Witchcraft and sorcery represented a two-edged sword that inevitably, it is said, was turned back on its originator.

The Earth and Beyond

The earth as the *Anishnabeg* knew it was flat, and the cosmos was constructed like a layer cake covered by a dome. People, of course, occupied the surface where they had been created along with the plants, animals, and features of the land. The events of people's lives and the lives of ancestors for countless generations were played out in this changeless and timeless world. Indeed, it was not a mundane earth, but one filled with the supernatural as well as the usual. Among the ordinary creatures were those of extraordinary dimension, which included the cannibal giant *windigo*, the little wild people (*bagudzinishinabe*), mischievous water elves (*maymayggayshi*), and many more. There were, however, other realms of the cosmos that were more remote to humans and, therefore, more mysterious and dangerous. Tradition places these other domains at anywhere from four to sixteen in number. At the very least, they included, besides the earth's surface, the air above the earth, the sky vault, and the underworld.

The air above, like the earth, was visible and known to the *Anishnabeg* as the abode of the birds as well as the thunderers or *animiki*. The thunderbirds were believed to cause thunder by the flapping of their wings and the hurling of lightning from their talons. *Animiki* could bestow power and were regarded with both respect and trepidation.

Above the sky was the upper sky or sky vault, home of the stars as well as the moon and sun, both power spirits associated with female and male personas. The sky vault and its junction with the air above was the home of many spirits. These included those associated with the cardinal directions and winds such as *kewaytin* ('north') and the spirits that control the cycle of the seasons. The celestial bodies of the sky were linked with both physical light and symbolic light, enlightenment, and wisdom. It was here, too, that the *Anishnabeg* envisioned the land beyond death, a mirror of the earth where the departed lived in a pleasant village without deprivation, a land reached by spirits that traveled the road of souls.

Below the earth and the surface of the earth's waters was the dark and dangerous underworld. Here was the domain of huge serpents, the *mishikinebik* envisioned with horns and sometimes legs, as well as the underwater panther *michipishiew*. The underwater panther with its huge thrashing tail, dorsal spines, and horns was particularly feared for its habit of causing violent storms on the lakes by slashing its tail. These dreaded creatures occasionally made their appearance by emerging on the surface of the Great Lakes or through "faults" between the surface and the underworld such as caves, crevices, or whirlpools. It is said that they could travel by means of underground rivers to appear in certain inland lakes, a tradition that, no doubt, accounts for such modern names as Devils Lake, Spirit Lake, or Manitou Lake. Humans were not alone in dreading the underworld creatures. In this, they had allies in the thunderbirds, who often flung lightning bolts at these underworld adversaries.

To a great degree, the four or more layers of the cosmos were separate from each other. In fact, contact between these domains was regarded as mystical and usually dangerous. Dreams, shamanistic spirit voyaging, death, legends about the origin of the earth and fire all involve travel from one plane to another. Snakes, toads, and frogs are likewise travelers between the earth and underworld while otters and turtles accomplish the same in water. These creatures are assigned magical significance; the former being potentially dangerous and the latter beneficial to human interests.

The layers of the *Anishnabeg* cosmos were united by a single *axis mundi*, the great medicine tree, which was the white cedar. With its roots in the underworld, the cedar grew from the earth through the air until its very tip broke though the vault of the sky permitting light to reach the earth. The white cedar is the source of much medicine and, in the Ojibwa language, white cedar is called *gijik*, which is also the word for light. Symbolically, light is equated with the enlightenment of wisdom and knowledge and it is perhaps for this reason that this word occurs commonly in personal names.

Conclusion

I hope it is apparent from this summary of the principles that must have organized *Anishnabeg* society that it was far from simple or primitive. It might be emphasized, again, that people who organized their lives around small, kin-based groups where reciprocal exchanges and an egalitarian ethic prevailed needed to develop impressive social skills. To make a living from the land they had to have encyclopedic knowledge of the plants and animals around them. Each person needed the know-how of hundreds of skills to turn wood, bone, skin, and bark into the necessities of survival. The *Anishnabeg* were a knowledgeable, skillful, and resourceful people. It is from this baseline that we must analyze the impact of the Euro-American conquest and try to understand the changes that were to occur in the cultures of native peoples of the northern Great Lakes.

NOTES

1. J. Clifton, 1986, 45.
2. A more detailed description of Great Lakes Indian kinship can be found in Callender 1978 or Eggan 1966. For those interested in contrasting Indian kinship systems with those of modern American society, see Schneider 1980.
3. There is a large and fascinating literature on the place names of the Great Lakes country that derive from various Indian languages. Vogels's work (1986) is most comprehensive, but Bernard Peters (1981 and 1985) also offers a variety of papers on the topic, many of which deal with the south shore of Lake Superior.
4. Jameson 1870, 3: 303–4; Landes 1971.
5. Kohl 1985, 327–31.

6. The rapids of the Saint Marys River and the Straits of Mackinac seem to be places where people of otherwise independent bands joined forces to cooperate in the fall fish harvest. Agnatic or in-law bonds provided the social mechanism that brought people temporarily together in large groups.

7. See Cleland 1991b.

8. Quimby 1962, 217–39.

9. The arguments for the validity of these figures are set out in Cleland n.d. Essentially, they are drawn from the first reliable Indian census of the Ottawa and Chippewa of Michigan and Wisconsin compiled by Henry R. Schoolcraft in 1838. Cleland argues that these figures are roughly indicative of the population level and settlement sizes at the time of European contact. Cleland also deals with the size of band territories.

10. Densmore 1970, 9–10.

11. Hickerson 1970, 39–50; Clifton 1986, 45; Bishop 1989, 43–61.

12. Warren 1984, 44–53; Densmore 1970, 10.

13. Skinner 1924, 16–30.

14. My own understanding of the principles upon which *Anishnabeg* society was organized leans heavily upon the perspectives provided by Marshall Sahlins (1968) and Elman Service (1971), both former professors at the University of Michigan. In addition, Sahlins's book, *Stone Age Economics* (1972), must be acknowledged as helping to shape my own thoughts regarding tribal economics.

15. Clifton 1977, 57–58.

16. Jenness 1935, 21.

17. Jenness 1935, 19.

18. Jenness 1935, 80.

19. Berger 1971, 1042–43.

20. See Levi-Strauss 1964.

21. Ingold, in the introduction to his *What Is an Animal?* (1988), provides an excellent overview of the complex philosophical relationship between people and the creatures of the "natural world." Richard Tapper's essay in that volume, "Animality, Humanity, Morality and Society," is also pertinent to the subject.

22. Tapper 1988, 52.

23. Grim and St. John 1989, 118.

24. Jenness 1935, 30.

25. Hoffman 1891, 156–59. Grim (1983, 65) claims another variety of shaman, *manandaw* ('tribal herbalist'), but there seems to be little evidence to support this idea.

26. Brown and Brightman 1988, 146; Verwyst 1892.

27. Edmund Ely Journals, Minnesota Historical Society, St. Paul.

Chapter 3

Coming of the *Wemitigoji*

In our imaginations we might conjure an image, a scene that must have repeated itself again and again through the Great Lakes country during the first half of the seventeenth century. The *Anishnabeg* had heard of the coming of the strange men through stories spread from village to village. Some people even managed to acquire a few glass beads and pieces of hard metal wire through trade with Indian travelers from the east. One did not know the truth of these tales, for strange beings were always reported and certainly trade did, from time to time, produce objects never seen by the *Anishnabeg*.

In the year the French calculated as A.D. 1634, a young French adventurer, having left the small settlement of Montreal in May, traveled to the north and west with seven Ottawa Indian guides and skirted the place of the giant turtle *Michikackinakong* (Mackinac Island) to enter Lake Michigan. Now, in the moon of *Meenigeesis* (July), they paddle along the north shore. The noise of their paddles alerts an *Anishnabe* family collecting blueberries in the dunes. Ever cautious of the approach of enemies, the family silently sinks into the hollows behind the dunes. The wary men peek over the crest to see a strange, high-ended canoe with flaring sides emerging from the morning mist.[1] The paddlers rest, letting the bark canoe bob in the gentle swells. Vaguely, the *Anishnabeg* make out the roached hair style and tattooed torsos of some of the men. "*Adawa*"! ('Ottawa') whispers the father of the family. Then, a strange nasal speech drifts across the water. Alerted, they see that one of the men in the canoe has no color. He is dead; only a *wdjibbon* ('shadow') whispers the father's brother. As they watch from concealment, clutching their bows in fear, the canoe drifts closer. The strange being is covered with a material that looks like woven carrying bags. His face is covered with dark hair like his head! He is *"Wemitigoji!"* ('French') whispers the father. They then notice that the long object held by the creature that they had at first taken for a bow is actually a dreaded fire stick. Stories have already reached the *Anishnabeg* telling of the awesome power of the thunderers concentrated in these weapons. By pointing them, the *Wemitigoji* could shoot instant death in a crash of lightning and thunder. The men sink back behind the dune, afraid. They are relieved sometime later. When rested, the *Adawa* stangers and the *Wemitigoji* spirit paddle on.

The native peoples of the Upper Lakes did not hide from the French for long. They soon learned that the French were people too, and useful for some purposes. The French, British, and people of many European nationalities would eventually have important relationships with the *Anishnabeg,* but it was the French who made the first, most profound, and most lasting impact. To this day, many native Americans bear French surnames, have French genes, and often greet each other with the Algonquianized French term *boo-zhoo* ('bon jour').

The specific historical and cultural circumstances of European-Indian contact will emerge as the experiences recorded in the written records of European travelers, missionaries, military commanders, and fur traders are reviewed. It is certain, however, that the meeting of their alien cultures produced remarkable changes in both. For example, the English language and the modern Great Lakes landscape is sprinkled with hundreds of Algonquian words: canoe, moccasin, moose, Mackinac, Chesaning, Dowagiac, and Michigan. Corn and beans, both products of native American cultivation and the staples of our midwestern agricultural economy, now feed a substantial share of the world's population. Further, the art and literary contributions of Great Lakes Indians have had an important influence on the modern world.

French and other non-Indian societies had a profound influence on Indian cultures as well. Perhaps the ultimate measure of this change is the contrast that may be observed as a result of contact over three hundred years or more. Though very substantial, it is

worth remembering that this change did not occur at a uniform rate
nor did it occur uniformly in all realms of Indian culture. For example, the history of Indian-European experience indicates that technological change was made rapidly in comparison to changes in religious beliefs and language, which changed very slowly. For many
years, anthropologists supposed that cultural change took place
through the process called acculturation. The underlying assumption
was that Indians would slowly lose their own cultures as they gradually adopted the culture of the "dominant society." According to this
theory, as they adopted European-style clothing, lived in houses,
spoke English, accepted Western views about property, and became
Christian, they became less "Indian" at each step. Finally, they
would be incorporated in the great American melting pot. The fact
that, after three hundred years, Indians still think of themselves as
Ottawa or Ojibwa belies the basis for the disappearing American
Indian theory.

The study of the historical archives, which bear witness to the
process of cultural change, shows that acculturation is an outmoded
theory. It is more accurate to think about social change as a process
in which conscious decisions are made that result in the substitution
of functional equivalents. It must, of course, be admitted that future
consequences can never be fully perceived. The adoption of firearms
to replace bows and arrows is not simply an obvious choice adding
efficiency, but a choice that has perceived advantages and disadvantages. Further, the choice to use guns was made in the context of
French policy as well as *Anishnabeg* culture. In theory at least not
all people chose to use guns because, despite obvious advantages,
possession of a gun required investment of energy in the fur collection process, raised expectations in the community of the gun owner's
role as a provider, and made the owner reliant upon the French for
powder and shot. Likewise, guns were perceived to be status items
(a critical consideration in the balance of power with neighboring
tribes) and a tool that could have significant impact on hunting success. The use of guns could, thus, change patterns of seasonal movement, which could, in turn, disrupt ceremonial activities, and on and
on. The point is that the use of guns, like the use of the French
language, blankets, and iron knives, had complex ramifications. The
theory that seems to best deal with the decision-making process and
its outcomes is called the adaptive strategy theory. This theory sees

change as part of a decision-making process that seeks to preserve various interests while changing others. It assumes that the process of change is complex and foretells no ultimate outcome.[2] Another important idea in adaptive strategy theory is that change is not the result of any single cause. It is tempting to say that firearms, or the fur trade, or the use of alcohol, or population loss due to newly introduced European diseases was *the* important impetus of culture change. The cause of such change is, however, very complex, involving informed choices and deliberate actions as well as historical accidents and unforeseen consequences. It is naive to assume that change can be explained by a single paramount cause.

Of course Indian cultures did change as the result of both European and indigeneous influences. As members of a society where rapid change is expected and technology is often seen as the primary impetus of social and political transformations, we are tempted to view change in seventeenth- or eighteenth-century Indian culture in the same way. Rapid technological change did, indeed, occur in this context, but what were its implications for change in other social customs and institutions? Perhaps quite naturally modern archaeologists who work almost exclusively with objects of material culture tend to overemphasize the importance of technological change, while ethnologists, for example, might see the persistence of mythology as an indication of long-term cultural stability.

One thing we can observe is that non-Western peoples tend to be conservative when it comes to change. Tradition holds more appeal than innovation. All things considered, it is reasonable to predict that a seventeenth-century *Anishnabe* would adopt tools that made life easier but would reject ideas that would challenge deeply held beliefs. In fact, evidence indicates that this is exactly what happened in the course of contact between Indians and Europeans. Technology changes very rapidly but many other aspects of culture do not. In religion, social conventions, economics, and modes of political decision making, the *Anishnabeg* were slow to change. Great Lakes natives had developed coherent, effective, and comfortable means of coping with life's requirements and had no desire or reason to adopt customs or beliefs that they saw as repugnant or nonsensical. As an example, the French had no clans and, as the Indians saw it, this meant that they were continually committing incest because they had no way to keep track of their ancestry over the long term. The pathetic point from the Indian perspective is that the French just did not seem to care. No wonder they acted so strangely.

Of course, it cannot be argued that the *Anishnabeg* rejected all aspects of French culture. They enthusiastically welcomed, even craved, items of European technology. While they were not, at first, dependent on these things, guns, iron knives, axes and strike-a-lites, kettles, and, most especially, tailored cloth clothing made life much easier.[3] These items had a real impact on indigenous technology and lifeway. Pottery making, for example, was lost almost immediately because metal containers were much more serviceable than ceramic pots. It might be noted, parenthetically, that the loss of aboriginal ceramics creates a barrier for archaeologists trying to link historically known ethnic groups with prehistoric cultures, because the latter are largely identified through ceramic decorative styles. Other French influences were less popular. These included ideas about property ownership, capitalistic values related to trade, and Christianity, all of which were based on ideals foreign to *Anishnabeg* cultural principles.

Perhaps the most important of the early European influences on Great Lakes natives were those that were inadvertent and had unforeseen consequences such as the forming of kin bonds between the French and Indian through marriage and procreation, the appearance of bilingual individuals with knowledge of both cultures, and the devastating epidemic diseases that swept native American populations both in advance of and in the wake of the fur trade frontier.

The point is often made, with some truth, that the French got along better with Indians than either their British or American successors. One of the reasons for this is not the innate goodwill of the French but because there were so few of them. The French that did go among the Indian tribes also seemed to be tolerant of Indian cultures. They saw the value and clear necessity of learning Indian languages, adopting appropriate Indian dress and technology, such as the canoe, and taking up residence with Indian women thereby creating the kin links so important to all aspects of *Anishnabeg* life. It could also be said that the French were interested in getting from the Indians things that were compatible with their life-style, such as their services as hunters, trappers, and warriors; their skills as builders of canoes and makers of skin clothing; and the goods they could supply in excess, such as corn, wild rice, meat, and fish. The French were interested in manipulating Indian politics and economics but, for the most part, they were not interested in changing their customs or occupying Indian land. Missionaries were the exception: the French Catholic fathers who established missions wanted Indians to renounce pagan idolatry and to embrace Christ through the public act of baptism. Although compared to later Protestant missionaries they were more flexible and permitted some accommodation of Christian theology to make it more understandable and appealing to Indians, they expected total change and they were, as a result, constantly disappointed.

For the purpose of describing the relationship between the Great Lakes native peoples and the French, it is convenient to divide events into three periods. The first, from the origin of French settlement on the St. Lawrence in 1603 to the beginning of the Iroquois War of 1649, details the information available to the French on the original placement of native peoples as well as their discrete social and political divisions. The second period, from 1649 to 1700, the period of the Iroquois Wars, describes the tremendous suffering and displacement of native people as a result of European contact. Finally, the period from the end of the Iroquois Wars until the expulsion of the French from Canada in 1760, shows the critical role of native peoples in both American history as well as the beginning of their own adjustment to the European presence.

Discovering the French

By the beginning of the seventeenth century, sailing ships of many nations and regions were visiting the coasts of America on a regular basis. Crews of Basques, Biscaynes, Bretons, Portuguese, and English fished, hunted whales, captured Indian slaves, and occasionally traded for furs from the Hudson Straits to Florida. The French explorer Champlain, following in the footsteps of Cartier, who visited the St. Lawrence valley in 1535, pushed up river to establish Quebec in 1608. From this small settlement the French began to explore the Great Lakes region and soon established a cooperative relationship with the Algonquian-speaking peoples who occupied the valley and the country to the north and west.

During the summer of 1609, Champlain committed a strategic error when he accompanied a Montagnais war party on a raid against

their Iroquois enemies who lived south of Lake Ontario. At the south
end of Lake Champlain, the Montagnais, who were joined by some
western Algonquians and Hurons from Georgian Bay, encountered
a party of two hundred Iroquois. The Iroquois were unprepared for
this first sight of a Frenchman and were not familiar with firearms;
they were routed by the first French volley, which struck down a
major chief. The victorious northerners were soon scalping and tor-
turing prisoners and were able to capture many Iroquois women and
children. Though shocked, the French accepted the results as a part
of tribal warfare, but they alienated the Iroquois even further when
they again accompanied their new allies south on a raid the next
summer. In this adventure, Champlain made enemies of the Iroquois, a mistake for which France would pay dearly in the future.

At about the same time France was establishing its presence in the
St. Lawrence valley and sending explorers westward, traders in the
employ of the Dutch West Indian Company were moving up the
Hudson valley establishing trade relationships with the Iroquois.
Fort Nasson, later called Fort Orange, was built near the present site
of Albany in 1614. To this fort came the Mohawk, Oneida,
Onondaga, Cayuga, and Seneca, tribes of small size that formed a
political confederacy known as the league of Ho-de-no-sau-nee
('League of the Iroquois'), the Five Nations.

During the summer of 1615, Champlain explored the headwaters
of the Ottawa River, where he encountered the Huron on their own
ground. He estimated them to number about thirty thousand people
living in eighteen villages.[4] The Huron rapidly became fast allies of
the French and among their most important Indian trading partners.
On the same trip, Champlain also met the Algonquian-speaking
Nipissing and people who the French called the Cheveaux Releves
and who later became known as the Ottawa. Both groups, though
Algonquians, were longstanding trade partners of the Iroquoian-
speaking Huron. During the next summer, Champlain, in company
with a Recollect priest, visited the Bruce Peninsula on the Georgian
Bay of Lake Huron and became better acquainted with the Ottawa
as well as their immediate neighbors, the Petun or Tobacco Huron.
Following this trip, Champlain returned to France extolling the virtues of Canada, the Indian people, and the likelihood of discovering
the passageway to China beyond the Lake of the Hurons.

During the second decade of the seventeenth century, there were

fewer than seventy-five French in Quebec while the English and
Dutch settlements along the Atlantic coast were prospering and
growing rapidly in population.[5] It was evident that the Algonquian
and Huron trade partners of the French, and the Iroquois who were
equally attached to Dutch interests, had their own longstanding disputes that were demonstrated by raids and counterraids. As more
guns were acquired by these old enemies, particularly the Iroquois,
the frequency and ferocity of war seemed to steadily increase. More
will be said of this warfare later (particularly about its causes and
consequences), but one thing is certain: it existed well before the
arrival of Europeans.

Most of what we know about the location of aboriginal communities and groups prior to the disruption caused by European contact
comes from the writing of Recollect and Jesuit priests who resided
as missionaries among the Huron and their neighbors. Despite some
obvious biases in their reporting, flowing from their fervent desire
to convert Indians to Christianity as well as to impress European
audiences with the implications of "savagery," the priests were excellent observers.[6] Most were well educated, literate, and spoke native
languages relatively fluently. This set them apart from most French
traders, explorers, and military men, who moved among the Indians
but left few written records. The observations of the priests, among
whom Father Gabriel Segard should be mentioned prominently, relied on direct observation as well as indirect reports about distant
lands and people. It is from this intelligence that we have the earliest
written reports of the *Anishnabeg* of the basins of Lakes Huron,
Michigan, and Superior, including their own names for themselves
and their neighbors. Any story of their history must however start
with the Huron.

The Huron Confederacy

The word *Huron* apparently came into use among the French because the traditional Huron hairstyle reminded them of the head of
a wild boar (or *hure* in French).[7] As the French priests came to know
them better, they discovered that the Huron were a confederacy of
at least four distinct tribes that were recorded as *Attingneenong-
nahac* ('barking dogs'), *Attignaouantan* ('bear'), *Tahontaenrat* ('deer'),
and *Ahrendaronnon* ('rock'). These territorial groups of about twenty

thousand people lived between Lake Huron and Lake Simco in a relatively small area that included the peninsula between Nottawasaga and Matchedash Bays.[8] It is perhaps from this that the Huron derived their own name for themselves: *Ouendant* or *Wendat,* which means 'dwellers on a peninsula.' These people were speakers of an Iroquoian language and were closely related in both language and culture to the Five Nations Iroquois, who were likewise organized as a confederacy of independent tribes. The social basis for these confederacies was the matrilineal clan that, to varying degrees, crosscut the tribes and villages.[9] Among the Huron there were eight exogamous clans: Turtle, Wolf, Bear, Beaver, Deer, Hawk, Porcupine, and Snake. Some people belonging to these maternal groups could be found in each tribe and village of the Huron.[10]

Huron villages, composed of enormous houses, were heavily fortified with encircling stockades and fences. The houses were 25–30 feet in height and width, and could be 200 feet long. The sides and domed roofs were covered with slabs of cedar or elm bark. Each house sheltered a local segment of a matrilineal clan, that is, a matrilineage or clan segment consisting of a grandmother, her daughters and granddaughters, and their husbands and children. The matrifocused system of tracing descent and organizing family relationships was found in the northeastern part of North America among the Iroquoian speakers; that is, the Huron, Petun, the Five Nations Iroquois, and their neighbors, the Neutral. The reputed function of the matrilocal ethic is to promote a work force of women who cooperate on a permanent basis. Matrilocality seems to be a condition of intensive agricultural production, although it is not found among the Algonquian speaking agriculturalists of the same region.

Each nuclear family of the matrilineage occupied a small apartment in the clan longhouse. This form of residence is called matrilocality and, although not strictly practiced among the Huron, was certainly their dominant tradition, as it was also among the Five Nations Iroquois. The matriclans held the house and agricultural fields and both title and property were inherited through the female line; among males, inheritance was from brother to sister's son.[11]

The matrilocal Huron family was organized around shallow lineages of perhaps four or five generations that were, in turn, linked by mythical descent from a common female ancestor. Matrilocality meant that Huron men, as husbands and fathers, were outsiders in the houses they shared with their wives and children. Their real loyalties and interests were in the longhouses of their own matrilineage, those occupied by their mothers and sisters and their families. Of course, these houses could be the longhouse next door or longhouses in a distant village. The distant crosscutting loyalties to the tribe and the Huron as a whole certainly gave cohesive strength to the confederacy. This was not its most important basis, however. For the *Ahrendaronnon* to fight the *Tahontaenrat* or for one village of *Tahontaenrat* to fight the next would mean that clan brothers would be pitted against each other. Wolf would fight Wolf and Deer would kill Deer. Internally, war was fratricidal. The social and political strength provided by the dispersed clans cannot be stressed enough. In fact, throughout Huron history, clan solidarity maintained Huron integrity through unbelievable adversity.

The French who visited Huronia in the early seventeenth century were not well prepared by their own experience or understanding to deal with matrilineality or matrilocality.[12] To Jesuit eyes, it appeared that these customs functioned to preserve family lines in the face of what they regarded as the promiscuity of Huron women. The priests contended that, since the paternity of the child could not be established, the clan affiliation of the mother was assigned to the child since that relationship was known as a consequence of birth. This idea was typical of the cross-cultural biases that often entered the written record. For their part, the Huron thought the French fairly strange as well. Consider the Huron who, observing a Frenchman blowing his nose in a handkerchief, said, "If you like that filth so much to keep it in your pocket, give me your rag and I will help you fill it."[13]

The Huron were fierce warriors and, like the other agricultural peoples of the eastern forests, were in a state of constant hostility with their neighbors. Beyond the usual terrorist tactics that constituted tribal war, the torture of war captives added an extra specter of fear. In addition, the Iroquois, as well as many Algonquian-speaking groups, ritually consumed part of a slain enemy in the hope that his bravery and skill would be bestowed upon aspiring living warriors. Torture was a ritual sacrifice in which the war captive's spirit was given to the spirits of war, death, and destruction. Captives of the Five Nations Iroquois were sacrificed to *Aireskoi,* the spiritual essence of hunting and war. The longer and more bravely the captive suffered, the more successful the sacrifice. Among both these people and the Huron, captive sacrifice flows from creation mythology, which sharply balances positive creative forces of life and growth associated with female activities against the destructive forces of fire, war, death, and cold, which are associated with males.

Before the participation and influence of Europeans in Huron warfare, war was likely characterized by periodic blood feuds between lineages or villages. Torture was probably accepted with stoicism and taken in the spirit in which it was given. Jesuit captives of the Five Nations Iroquois also expected and accepted such death, though for different, but perhaps related, reasons.

Another extremely important aspect of Iroquoian-Huron warfare was the practice of wholesale adoption of vanquished enemies, particularly women and children. In the last half of the seventeenth century, the Five Nations Iroquois nearly reconstituted themselves by taking in war captives, including Huron.[14]

It would appear that Huron tribal government was vested in chiefs who held their positions and prerogatives of government by virtue of their position within a specific matrilineage. Both village councils and tribal councils were held to mediate disputes between clans or villages,[15] while councils that included several tribes were mainly concerned with "foreign affairs." Councils reached decisions as a result of compromise and consensus rather than on the basis of delegated authority or plurality.[16] Certain Huron chiefs were apparently men of great renown and, therefore, beneficiaries of privilege not accorded to others, such as the control of trade routes that were apparently regarded as the stewardship prerogative of certain lineages.[17] These and other advantages were contrary to the egalitarian principle of Huron social interaction. Possibly such privileges were greatly expanded because of the new and rapidly developing opportunities created by the fur trade as well as the escalation of intrigue and warfare surrounding the maneuvering of various tribes for a better position in that trade.

The Huron observed four basic kinds of feasts or ceremonies: celebrating farewells, giving thanks, dining and singing, and for curing sickness.[18] The ceremonial cycle had complex formal dimensions, including a schedule for the celebration of various spirits as well as the more informal occasions that also required feasting and ceremony.

The *Awataerohi* feast for the curing of sickness took on special meaning after European contact because of the new prevalence of disease. As the Huron saw it, disease, mental or physical, has several causes. First there were those caused by natural agents that could be treated with herbal remedies. Other illnesses were caused by the unfulfilled desires of the soul that were revealed in dreams. Finally there were diseases caused by witchcraft. The last category was treated by special shamans, *Aretsan.*

Witchcraft and fear of witchcraft was an important element of Huron society. At least this is true of the Huron society described by the Jesuits, although admittedly this was a society filled with suspicion. Witches, *Oky Ontatechita* ('those who kill by spells'), could be identified through the dreams of the sick or by the unusual behavior of the witches themselves.[19] Refusal to give feasts, insufficient generosity, or other unusual behavior was taken as a clue to the identity of witches.[20] Witches, as well as the shamans who specialized in treating illness caused by witches, were thought to possess a power, called *oky*, to influence humans. *Oky* was often incorporated in charms that were valued and inherited from generation to generation.[21]

The Huron had a number of curing societies and special ceremonies to treat various kinds of illness. Some involved dances in costume, while others required participants to be completely naked. The Jesuits approved the participation of Christian converts in these ceremonies on a case by case basis.

Neighbors of the Huron

When the French arrived in Huronia, they soon discovered that the Huron had extensive trade contacts with their neighbors, both Algonquians to the north and west and Iroquoian people to the south. In the trade with the Algonquians, agricultural products flowed north in exchange for products of the chase, furs, skins, meat, and fish, and some manufactured items such as fish nets and charms. The nearest neighbors to the Huron in culture as well as location were the people they called the *Tionnontatehronnon* or, as the French called them, the *Petun* ('tobacco') Huron. They are historically called the *Tionnontate* Huron. These people occupied the base of the Bruce Peninsula (see map 1).

Toward the end of the same peninsula, on adjacent Manitoulin Island, were several autonomous groups that the French called the *Cheveux Releves,* because of their roached hair style, or, sometimes, the *Courtes Oreilles* or short ears. Most of the early information about these people was collected by Jean Nicolet, who was sent by Champlain to live among the Algonquian people as a boy in 1618. They referred to themselves collectively as *O-dah-wah* or *Adawa* ('trader'), which the French rendered as *Outaouacs* and which in modern usage is *Ottawa.* In the seventeenth and early eighteenth century, they were subdivided into four distinct groups: *Outaouosinigouek* (Sinago or 'black squirrel people'), *Kichkagoueiak* (Kiskakon or 'cut-tail people,' in reference to the bear), *Negaouichiriniouek* (Sable or 'people of the sandy beach'), and the *Nassauaketon* ('people of the fork').[22]

Nicolet also described other Algonquian-speaking groups who occupied the coast of Lake Huron west and north of Huronia as far as Lake Superior. These small, independent bands fished the lake in the summer and fall and hunted up country in the winter. Beyond these to the north were people who were described as "hunters with no fixed abode." West of the *Nipisiriniens* or the Nipissings, sometimes called the Sorcerers, were several bands near the mouth of the French River, the *Atchiligouan.* To the west were the *Amikouai* ('beaver people') and still further west the *Oumisagia* ('eagle people') or *Mississauga,* and beyond them at the falls of the St. Marys River, the *Pahouitingwach Irini* ('people of the falls'), who were known to the French as the Saulteaur.[23]

On the east end of the north shore of Lake Superior were the *Outchibous* ('voice of the crane people') and the *Marameg* ('catfish people'). The south shore of Lake Superior and the eastern Upper Peninsula of Michigan including the coast of Lake Michigan were the homes of the *Mikinac* ('turtle people') and the *Nouquet* ('bear people').[24] It is clear that these people living near Lakes Superior and Michigan were the ancestors of the modern *Ojibwa* or *Chippewa.* These two synonymous terms are apparently derived from *Ocipwe,* which means to 'pucker up' in reference to the method used to sew the toe of the moccasin.[25] Collectively, these independent Ojibwa bands refer to themselves as *Anishnabeg* or 'true people,'[26] a term also used by other Algonquians.

To the south of the Huron lived people called the *Attiwandaronk* ('people of a slightly different language'), who were populous, occupying more than forty villages scattered over what is today southwestern Ontario. Known historically as the Neutral, they were allied with neither the Huron or Five Nations Iroquois and were usually at peace with both groups. It was from the Neutral that the Jesuits first heard reports of the people who occupied lower Michigan. In the Iroquoian language, they were called the *Atsistaehronons* or the 'fire nation.'[27]

The Neutrals as well as the Ottawa were at war with the "Fire Nation" and apparently sent a huge number of warriors against them in the early 1640s. This party returned across the Detroit River with 800 captives. The Jesuits contended that the "Fire Nation" was more populous than the Neutral, Huron, and Five Nations Iroquois combined, but, of course, they had no real way of knowing.[28]

After many years of discussion and speculation, most scholars now seem to agree that the "Fire Nation" was not a single group but included a large number of small, independent Algonquian-speaking swidden agriculturalists who occupied the southern third of what is now the Lower Peninsula of Michigan. Historically, these people came to be known as Potawatomi and Mascouten and included related groups such as the Miami.

In 1634, Champlain sent his accomplished Algonquian Indian expert Jean Nicolet on a westward voyage to explore, meet the natives, and locate a water route to China and Japan. Making his way up the Ottawa River route, Nicolet reached Lake Huron and followed the coast west and, instead of entering Lake Superior, he turned south. Passing into the Straits of Mackinac, Nicolet became the first non-Indian to visit Mackinac Island. Still heading west, he followed the north shore of Lake Michigan and proceeded with his seven Ottawa Indian guides around the Garden Peninsula into Green Bay. Donning a great Chinese robe embroidered with bright birds and flowers that he brought to greet the emperor, Nicolet waded ashore to the shouts of hordes of Winnebago Indians. No doubt they were as bewildered as Nicolet.

Winnebago were a very numerous people, agriculturalists who spoke a Siouan language. Their name was derived from the Potawatomi word *Winpyeko* ('people of dirty water'). They were also known to the French as the *Puans* or 'stinking people.'[29]

North of the Winnebago, around the mouth of the Menominee

River and the Lake Michigan and Green Bay shore, was an Algonquian-speaking group, the *Oumalouminek* ('wild rice people') or, as
they called themselves, the Menominee, from *manomin* ('wild
rice').[30] The Menominee occupy the same general area in eastern
Wisconsin today as they did when they were first encountered by
Nicolet in 1634.

The Destruction of the Huron Confederacy

Of all the pressures that came to bear on the Hurons and their neighbors during the early seventeenth century, three are generally considered to be instrumental in the collapse of the Huron Confederacy
and the expulsion of the Neutral, Huron, Petun, and Ottawa from
their homelands on the eastern shore of Lake Huron. These are
disease, Christianity, and warfare. It is difficult to assess the separate
effects of these and other factors that contributed to the destruction
of the Huron Confederacy since they are closely interrelated. Certainly the political solidarity of the Huron was diminished by both
population loss and factionalism involving Christian converts. Both
in turn contributed to the diminished capacity of the Huron to meet
the military challenge of the tribes of the Five Nations.

During the mid 1630s, the first outbreaks of European disease
appeared among the Great Lakes Indians. These plagues, which
continued to wreak devastation among native people of North America for at least the next two hundred years, were caused by diseases
endemic in European populations. Unfortunately, North Americans
had no "immunity" to them. That is to say, because they had no
previous exposure, they lacked defending antibodies and were subject to extreme mortality. It is estimated that mortality among Indians due to smallpox, whooping cough, measles, and influenza was
between 60 and 70 percent. This meant that within several decades
of contact with Europeans, at least two out of every three Indians
died. The Huron were reduced from a precontact population in 1615
of 21,000 to between 8,700 and 10,000 twenty-three years later.[31]
Presumably, other groups, particularly those living in the crowded
villages favored by agriculturalists, suffered a similar fate.

Since the germ theory of disease was not yet understood by either
native Americans or Europeans, the devastations of these epidemics
were explained in historical and cultural terms rather than as a mat-

ter of biology.[32] The Huron correctly observed that the onset of the
epidemics was coeval with the appearance of the French. Only making a general association, some of the western Indians assumed the
use of trade goods was causing the diseases and hoped that, by dis-
carding metal kettles and other European goods, a cure would result.
Lacking the means to treat these new diseases, the Huron sought
their cause in the power of witchcraft. Suspicion pointed to the Jesuit
priests and the Huron began to accuse them of being *Oky Ontatechita*
('those who kill by spells'). First of all, the Huron knew that the
priests were the white men's shamans. The fact that the French sent
so many of their shamans to live among the Huron was itself grounds
for suspicion. Considering that the principle means of identifying
witches was their unusual behavior, the priests were again prime
candidates. They did not have wives or families, they did not give
feasts and, in fact, tried to discourage them, they mocked respected
elders and medicine men, and they were both secretive and obviously selfish. Direct confirmation for the Huron, however, was in the
theology and symbolism of seventeenth-century Catholicism. The
priests made no secret of the fact that they wanted to capture the
souls of the Huron for Christ. To people of animistic belief, this
confession was bound to produce fear and terror.[33] Biblical stories
told to impress the Huron with God's power must have seemed nonsensical to them, especially given their matrilineal orientation. The
Eucharist, with the miracle of Christ's rising from the dead, would
have particularly terrified the Huron and their Algonquian neighbors, because they greatly abhorred the spirits of the dead. The use
of relics, especially those involving body parts of saints, was a sure
sign of sorcery, as was the skull and crossbones often affixed to the
crucifix distributed by the black-robed priests. It is little wonder that
the Jesuits were regarded as witches and sorcerers and greatly
feared.

   There were, however, some aspects of Christian dogma and practice that were understandable to the Huron. The Jesuits eventually
became more sophisticated in appealing to these linkages as they
became more fluent in Huron language and more familiar with their
culture. The concepts of heaven and the soul as well as the use of
magical amulets such as the cross and crucifix were understandable
to the Huron in the context of their own culture. Even the burning
torment of eternal hell used to threaten the unrepentant recalled to

the Huron the torture and sacrifice of war captives. Likewise, there were economic and social benefits to be enjoyed by Huron converts to Christianity. They received favored consideration in trade relations with the French. For example, the Christian Huron alone were able to acquire firearms in trade, presumably because the French feared that their pagan brethren would turn them against the priests. Christian Huron often became intermediaries in relationships with the French and especially between the Huron and the powerful Jesuits. By the late 1640s about five hundred Huron had converted to Christianity, approximately 15 percent of the now vastly reduced population.[34] The degree to which these Huron were Christian in the French meaning is, of course, a matter of speculation. Many of the conversions claimed by the priests were of the dying or by the baptism of very young children. ·

Among the Huron as well as other animistic people of the Great Lakes, the addition of a new deity or spirit for veneration was presumably a common occurrence and a decided benefit. It is true that the priests had some notable successes among the Huron, including the conversion of some principal elders and chiefs. These people and other converts who professed Christianity and supported French interests increasingly withdrew from traditional ritual and custom and eventually formed a Christian faction within Huron society. If it had not been for the devastating population loss and the many new problems created by the presence of European interests, the Christian element would have probably been of little consequence. As it turned out, however, the divisive influence of Christianity was probably a factor of some importance in the inability of the Huron to withstand the onslaught of the Five Nations Iroquois.

The catastrophe waiting the Huron was the escalating warfare with the Five Nations Iroquois. According to many historians, this struggle was related to economic competition.[35] Briefly stated, the demand for furs quickly reduced the availability of beaver in the territory of the Five Nations Iroquois by 1640. By this time, the Five Nations were dependent upon European trade goods and particularly guns. The Huron, by virtue of their long-term trading relationships with the Ottawa, Nipissing, and other northern Algonquians, were now in control of the flow of furs. The better armed but perhaps less numerous Five Nations saw their old enemies gaining the upper hand as the trade was diverted to Quebec and Montreal. Other scholars dispute the economic theory of the war between the Huron, their neighbors, and the Five Nations. In this view, longstanding inter-tribal animosities were aggravated by the appearance of Europeans who, in turn, provided the means of one protagonist to destroy the other.[36] Whatever the roots of the conflict or the relationships be-tween the tribes that made up the two confederacies, and whatever role guns played in the situation, the strategy of war changed. After a brief peace between the Five Nations and the French and their Indian allies lasting from 1645 to 1647, the Niagarian frontier burst into violent war. In 1647, a combined Mohawk and Seneca force fell upon Huronia to counter the Huron chief *Ondagiondiont*'s attempt to split their confederacy by making peace with the Onondaga.[37] In March, 1649, the Five Nations sent a war party of one thousand well-armed warriors against the Huron villages. Never before had so many warriors massed for battle, and never before had the tribes fought in winter. Although the Huron gave a good account of them-selves, inflicting nearly equal losses, the Iroquois kept up the pres-sure. The Huron seemed to totally panic and, by May, had aban-doned most of their villages.[38] Refugees fled to Christian Island in Georgian Bay and later to Manitoulin Island in northern Lake Huron where they joined refugee Petun and Ottawa who were somewhat better organized. In the winter of 1650, the Five Nations turned their attention to the Neutral, who were attacked and, in fact, utterly destroyed. Large numbers of Neutral and presumably Huron war captives were adopted by the Seneca, Mohawk, and other Five Na-tions tribes. In only two years, the Iroquois had completely evicted the native people of southwestern Ontario and vastly increased their own numbers.

A great deal of debate has focused on the causes contributing to the defeat of the Huron and their Algonquian allies. The popular idea, that it was all the result of economic competition over access to technological abundance (a trade war), seems to require us to ascribe capitalistic motivations that were inconsistent with Huron and Iro-quois culture in the seventeenth century. If the Huron had such an economic advantage over the Iroquois, why are there so very few trade goods associated with Huron archaeological sites of the period and so many in Five Nations sites? From this evidence, it would seem the Huron were disadvantaged, not the Iroquois. It has also been suggested that superior fire power in the hands of the Iroquois gave them a tremendous military advantage. This conclusion, too, may be questioned because, in actual battle, the Huron often held their own against the Iroquois, who had been better armed for decades. Others have suggested a vital role for the Jesuits, who undermined Huron political solidarity by creating a Christian faction. Although the Christian element was strong and gaining strength, its role should not be overemphasized. Traditionalists composed the vast majority in the total population and a majority in all but a few villages.

Certainly all of these factors contributed to the end of the Huron Confederacy, but it is worth remembering that the Confederacy was not a state but a fragile set of alliances between people tied by the bonds of kinship. The huge population loss, factionalism over Christian conversions and Jesuit influence, and the terror of massive war on their home ground simply fragmented the social reality that was Huron. Those many who survived, did so as individuals and those individuals became Oneida, Mohawk, and Seneca. Their inclusion into the Five Nations villages strengthened the League of the Iroquois and made them a single people.

The Great Diaspora

The half-century following the destruction of the Huron and Neutral confederacies and the flight of the surviving Huron, Petun, Ottawa, and their Algonquian neighbors to the relative safety of the lakes and forests of the northern Great Lakes was the most traumatic in their tribal histories. Their worlds were turned upside down. First, the epidemics that had earlier struck the Huron with such disastrous effect now visited the western fringes of French contact and beyond. Much of this devastation is unrecorded, but, from what we know from the spread of such plagues in other places, whole villages must have perished one after another. More notable in the historical record is the massive population displacement resulting from the continued aggressive onslaught of war parties sent out by the tribes of the Five Nations Iroquois to capture fur and prisoners and to disrupt trade along the Ottawa River route. One western group after another fled westward in terror of the Iroquois, who were now even more heavily armed with Dutch and English guns. As they sought refuge beyond Lake Michigan and in northern forests, families often found it difficult to live in strange, new environments. Want and starvation were a common companion in their flight. As refugees, the *Anishnabeg* of lower Michigan found themselves in the company of families or individuals who belonged to other bands; strangers sought aid not as kin but as people whose dialect or language was understandable. With a huge population loss, it was not always possible to find those who knew the words or order of important ceremonies or even the hands to process skins into clothing. People began to come together out of the necessity of sustaining life. As we know, disaster and extreme need often produces innovation, and the late seventeenth century certainly produced new cultural institutions and new identities. *Anishnabeg* bands independent and self-sufficient before the appearance of Europeans were fragmented and dispersed, but the surviving individuals, families, and sometimes larger groups were metamorphised into the more inclusive social units that we now know as the Ottawa, Ojibwa, and Potawatomi tribes, that is, groups united by new social institutions and some measure of political integrity. Still, each of these tribes has its own story.

Following the winter attacks of 1649, the Huron briefly tried to regroup, but fearing the effectiveness of the new, large war party tactics of the Five Nations, they fled. Some Huron headed east to Quebec under the supervision of the Jesuits while others sought refuge among the Neutral or the Petun (*Tionnontate*) Huron. This latter group, in company with a large number of fleeing Ottawa, moved west to Manitoulin Island, then on to Mackinac Island in the Straits of Mackinac.

Meanwhile, encouraged by their defeat of the Neutral in 1650, the Iroquois raiders turned their attention to the Algonquians in Michigan's Lower Peninsula as well as to those along the canoe routes to the north. These raids were so destructive and so overwhelming that southern Michigan was almost totally abandoned. The *Anishnabeg* of the "fire nations," as they were known to the Ottawa and Neutral, also abandoned their ancestral lands. Since these were not canoe people, they walked south and west around Lake Michigan and congregated around Green Bay. The refugee Petun and Ottawa likewise moved west again and established villages on Rock Island at the mouth of Green Bay.[39] Rumors of the approach of a large Iroquois war party again sent the Petun and Ottawa fleeing west in 1653. Making their way down the Wisconsin River to Lake Pepin on the Mississippi, the refugees met the Siouan people indigenous to central and western Wisconsin.

Since they possessed French trade goods in abundance, they were treated by the Sioux as if they were deities. The newcomers began to take advantage of this position and soon had made themselves enemies to the Sioux. By 1658 the Petun were encamped on the Black River and the Ottawa were living around Lac Courtes Oreilles in northern Wisconsin; neither place was conducive to the corn cultivation that was so important to these groups. Both the Petun and Ottawa, fleeing new enemies, found themselves at Chequamegon Bay of Lake Superior in 1661.

The new and rapidly growing refugee communities around Green Bay were located in a region with extremely fertile soil that was also rich in fish and game. Between the visit by Nicolet to Green Bay in 1634 and the arrival of the refugees after 1650, a series of tragedies had beset the populous Winnebago who traditionally occupied this region. In the 1640s, the Winnebago had already been severely devastated by disease, but on top of this they suffered a tragedy of horrible dimension. At war with the *Mesquakie* ('red earth people'), who the French called the Renards (Fox), a Winnebago war party of five hundred men set out for an attack. The entire fighting force drowned in a Lake Michigan storm, a loss that doomed the Winnebago.[40]

By the mid-1650s the land left vacant by the Winnebago was filled with Menominee, Fox, Potawatomi, Petun, Mascouten, Noquet, Ottawa, Salteaur, Nipissing, and Sauk (see map 2). The major town of the region was occupied by Potawatomi and was called *Mitchigami* ('big lake'). It was against this principle target that the Iroquois now sent the largest war party they had yet fielded, apparently in the hope of opening access to new fur sources west of Lake Michigan. Ironically, by the time the Iroquois raiders reached the vicinity of *Mitchigami* they were weak with hunger and, in good Indian tradition, asked for food from the very people they were about to attack. The Potawatomi offered corn that they had taken the precaution of lacing with poison. The invaders detected the plot, however, and retreated in two groups. One headed south around Lake Michigan where they were drawn into battle with the Illinois, who ultimately destroyed them. The other party of one hundred warriors headed north against the Saulteaur at the rapids of the St. Marys River. Here, the well-armed Iroquois were met by an equal force of Saulteaur armed with bows and stone-tipped arrows. Like their companions, these raiders never returned to their villages south of Lake Ontario.[41]

The falls of the St. Marys River, like the shore of Green Bay, became an important Algonquian refuge, particularly for the people who lived on the north shore of Lake Huron. Long the residence of a band of approximately 150 people who called themselves the *Pahouitingwach Irini* ('people of the falls') the region was used by a large number of nearby bands, of which the most prominent was the *Outchibou* ('crane people'). Collectively, these bands were known to the French as Saulteaur. In fact, in 1688 Lahontan refers to the people of the Sault as *Outchipoues* alias Saulteaur.[42] Father Dablon described the major attraction of the region in 1669.

It is at the foot of these rapids, and even amid these boiling waters, that extensive fishing is carried on from spring until winter, of a kind of fish found usually only in Lake Superior and Lake Huron. It is called in the native language *atticameg,* in ours whitefish because in truth it is very white and it is most excellent, so that it furnishes food, almost itself, to the greater part of all these people.

Dexterity and strength are needed for this kind of fishing; for one must stand upright in a bark canoe and there, among the whirlpools, with muscles tense, thrust deep in to the water a rod, at the end of which is fastened a net made in the form of a pocket into which the fish is made to enter. . . .

This convenience of having fish in such quantities that one has only to go and draw them out of the water attracts the surrounding Nations to the sport during the summer.[43]

Though the Saulteaur already had the reputation as tough warriors by their staunch defense of their homeland against Iroquois raiders in 1653, this acclaim was sealed in 1662 with the destruction of a Mohawk and Oneida war party intent on disrupting the flow of furs from Lake Superior. On a point of land jutting into Lake Superior near the modern Bay Mills Indian Reservation at Brimley, Michigan, a group of Saulteaur, Ottawa, and Amikwa out hunting happened upon the Iroquois. Under the leadership of a Saulteaur war chief, they crept up on the enemy camp. At dawn the next day, they

rushed in with gun, bow, and war club, killing all of the dreaded
Nadoway ('big serpents'). This great victory gave its name to the
place, which today is known as Iroquois Point. The victory also gave
comfort to the Saulteaur and their relatives living in villages along
the Lake Superior shore.[44]

The refugee Petun and Ottawa, probably representing the Sinago,
Nassauakuetons, and the partially Christianized Kiskakon bands at
Chequamegon Bay, were involved in increased hostilities with the
Sioux. The Algonquian groups clustered around Green Bay were
having similar problems as they pressed the eastern boundary of the
Sioux. Further, the huge concentration of people on the west shore
of Lake Michigan was causing both hunger and social discord. Fortunately, there was a reprieve from Iroquois raiding. Weakened by
disease, epidemics, and war with their powerful southern enemies,
the Susquehannocks, the Five Nations sought a temporary peace
with the French in 1667. Almost immediately, the northern peoples
started back east searching for homes where they could pursue their
former lifeways. In 1670, the Petun and many of the Ottawa moved
to the Straits of Mackinac, where they established two large villages
on the shore of St. Martins Bay at the modern town of St. Ignace.
Some of the Ottawa moved back to Manitoulin Island and others
moved to Green Bay. The decrease in Iroquois pressure also led the
Miami and some Potawatomi to begin to filter south around the end
of Lake Michigan toward their ancestral homelands in southern
Michigan.

During the time when the Algonquians were concentrated in refuges at Green Bay, at the Falls of the St. Marys, at Chequamegon
Bay, and later at Michilimackinac, the Jesuits had the opportunity
to establish missions among them. These had very limited success.
Father Allouez, describing the Ottawa, tells us "the savages of these
regions recognize no sovereign master of heaven and earth, but believe there are many spirits—some of whom are beneficent, as the
sun, the moon, the lake, rivers, and woods; others malevolent, as the
adder, the dragon, cold, and storms. And, in general, whatever seems
to them either helpful or hurtful, they call a *manitou* and pay it the
worship and veneration which we render only to the true God."
Allouez goes on to explain the manner of what he calls public
sacrifices through the use of tobacco as an offering. "During storms
and tempests they sacrifice a dog, throwing it into the lake. That is

to appease thee, they say to the latter; keep quiet. At perilous places in the rivers, they propitiate the eddies and rapids by offering them presents; and so persuaded are they that they honor their pretended divinities by this external worship that those among them who are converted and baptised observe the same ceremonies toward the true God, until they are disabused."[45]

A practical example of this latter point occurred when Allouez explained to a *Mesquake* (Fox) Indian whose parents were at the point of death that they could be cured by bleeding. The desperate man sprinkled his black gown with tobacco, saying, "Thou art a spirit, come now, restore these sick people to health. I offer thee this tobacco in sacrifice."[46]

The Potawatomi at Green Bay were described in 1666 as being "extremely idolatrous, clinging to their ridiculous legends, and are addicted to polygamy."[47]

The most notable success was among the Petun Huron. At the mission of St. Espirit at Chequamegon Bay, the Jesuits reported that more than five hundred baptized Hurons and some Christianized Ottawa (Kiskagon) were part of a large concentration of Indians that also included Ottawa, Saulteaur, and Illinois.[48]

Lahontan, a soldier in the service of the King of France, had a jaded view of the successes reported by the Jesuits. In 1688, he said of Michilimackinac that the fathers who minister to the Huron "lavish away all their Divinity and Patience to no purpose, in converting such ignorant Infideles: for all the length they can bring 'em to, is that sometimes they'll desire Baptism for their dying children and some few superannuated persons consent to receive the Sacrament of Baptism, when they find themselves at the point of death."[49]

Temporary peace with the Iroquois also permitted resumption of a more regular fur trade. Now, Ottawa and the Potawatomi visited Montreal, thus ushering in a new trade era as well as new competition among the Algonquians for favor with the French suppliers. Part of the competition was the result of the entry of the English into the trade when they acquired New Netherlands by treaty in 1664, followed by the chartering of the Hudson Bay Company in 1670. From this latter date onward, the French were challenged from both the south and north by the British, who offered better quality and cheaper goods. This not only created problems for Montreal and Quebec merchants, but a great temptation for the Indian trading partners of New France. As part of their response to this new threat, the French sent Saint Lusson to Sault Ste. Marie, where, in the presence of fifteen assembled tribes, he claimed the Lake Superior country and its resources for France. Of more importance to the local people was the killing of a Sioux emissary on the same spot three years later, in 1673. This event was perhaps the first blow in two hundred years of periodic warfare between the Ojibwa bands and the Sioux to the south and west of Lake Superior. Collectively, the people soon to be known as the Lake Superior Ojibwa were beginning a slow and steady encroachment into the territory of the Sioux known to them as the *Nadowessi* ('little serpents').

The Ottawa and Huron of Michilimackinac

In 1671, after traveling a great circuit from their homelands east of Georgian Bay, the *Tionnontate* Huron and their Ottawa neighbors arrived at the Straits of Mackinac via Green Bay, Lake Pepin, Black River, Lac Courtes Oreilles, Chequamegon Bay, and Sault Ste. Marie. For the next thirty years, they remained settled at Michilimackinac, as St. Ignace was then known. Here they lived in close proximity to the French who established a Jesuit mission and Fort du Baud, a trading center, nearby. Both the missionary Marquette and Cadillac, who was briefly the commandant and chief trader at Fort du Baud, have left descriptions of the Ottawa and Huron settlements.[50]

The Ottawa, mainly Kiskagons under the influence of the priests but with the other tribes of Ottawa represented as well, occupied a village separate from the Huron. It is clear that these two groups, though closely tied by historical circumstance and allegiance to the French, were much different in culture and political goals. They were frequently at odds and occasionally on the verge of armed aggression. Perhaps it was not just the Iroquois threat that caused the Michilimackinac people to heavily fortify their villages with stockades.

The Huron village was composed of traditional, bark-covered longhouses. Despite the considerable influence of the priests, archaeological evidence indicates that the Huron and Ottawa managed to maintain much of their traditional culture. The longer growing season at the Straits permitted a return to the mixed agricultural and hunting-fishing economy of earlier times. Both groups put in large corn crops in order to grow enough for their own use as well as having enough to sell to the French. These people were also market hunters, and it was not long before the surrounding forests were depleted of large game. In fact, the substantial population of Michilimackinac, which probably numbered between 2,500 and 3,000 people, could not have subsisted without the whitefish and lake trout obtained from the remarkable Straits fishery. As Cadillac reports: "But I ought to mention the pleasure of seeing them bring up, in one net, as many as a hundred whitefish. This is the most delicate fish in the lake."[51] Whitefish was normally boiled in a pot with ground corn meal to make a very nutritious soup called *sagamity*, which looked like milk.[52] Fish and meat were eaten baked, fried, boiled, roasted, and smoked, and corn meal ground in a wooden mortar and pestle was made into bread cooked in the ashes of an open fire.

Women grew corn and engaged in domestic duties while the men were busy hunting, trading, and making war. These latter activities were the path to prestige and leadership for Huron men, although the strong matrilineal tradition of the Huron may have somewhat quashed the degree to which status could actually be achieved apart from that afforded by positions under the control of particular matrilineages.

The major Huron leader of the Christian element at Michilimackinac was *Kondorant*, "The Rat" ('muskrat'), also called *Adario*, who was a great friend of Governor Frontenac and influential in the politics of New France as well as among the Indian tribes. The French regarded him as a skillful and cunning diplomat whose interests only partially corresponded to their own. Thanks to *Kondorant*, the small Huron community at Michilimackinac had far more influence than their numbers would have otherwise provided. As an aside, *Kondorant* is also the central character in Lahontan's romantic satire on French culture called *A Dialogue between the Author and Adario, a Noted Man Among the Savages*.[53]

Lahontan also used *Kondorant*'s family to illustrate what was, to the French, the strange custom the Huron used in naming.

The Savages go always by the Mother's name. To make this plain by example: the leader of the Nation of Hurons who is called *Sastaretsi* being married to a Daughter of another Huron Family,

Grandma Kishigo's Corn Soup Recipe

At most gatherings of Michigan Indians, the menu features venison, corn soup, and fry bread. Corn soup, a traditional dish of the Ottawa and Potawatomi, is always the favorite. No wonder, it is nutritious and delicious too. In 1972, Amelia Kishigo (*Animiquam Gijigowi*) gave her famous corn soup recipe to my wife as a Christmas present, and I have now convinced her to share it here.

In preparation for making the soup, sweet corn must be toasted. This can be done on a grill or in an oven at low heat. The corn is roasted on the cob, turning it frequently until it is golden brown (some charring won't hurt). Once roasted, let the corn dry and then remove the kernels from the cob. If the kernels are dried properly, they can be stored almost indefinitely in this condition.

Ingredients: 2 cups of roasted corn
                deer or beef soup bone with meat
                1, 16 oz. can of red beans
                3–4 potatoes

Rinse the corn and soak overnight in a 6 to 8 quart kettle, three-quarters full. In the morning, add soup bone and meat to the soak water with the corn, and bring it to a boil. Now reduce the heat and simmer for about 6 hours. One or two hours before serving, add drained, presimmered red beans and pared, cut up potatoes. Season to taste and enjoy!

by whom he has several Children, that General's name is extinct at his Death, for that his Children assume the Name of the Mother. Now, it may be ask'd how the Name of *Sastaretsi* has been up for the space of Seven or Eight Hundred Years among that People, and is likely to continue to future ages? But the Question is easily answered, if we consider, that the Sister of this *Sastaretsi* being married to another savage, whom we shall call *Adario,* the children Springing from that marriage, will be called *Sastaretsi* after the Mother and not *Adario* after this father. When I asked them the reason of the Custom, they replyed, that the Children having received their Soul from their Father, and their Body from their Mother, 'twas but reasonable that the Maternal Name should be perpetuated.[54]

Traditional economic ideals were also in force at Michilimackinac, despite the influence of the French. As Cadillac reports,

... so, among the Indians the good hunters profit the least from their hunting. They often make feasts for their friends or relatives or distribute the animals they have killed among the cabins or the families of the village. One proof of the liberality or the vanity which they acquire from this occupation is that those who are present when they arrive at their village are permitted to appropriate all the meat in the canoe of the hunter who has killed it, and he merely laughs. This is sufficient reason for believing that their only idea is to feed the people, and as the whole tribe get the benefit, it is interested in praising such a noble calling, especially as it often happens that a single hunter provides food for several families which but for his aid, would at certain times and places perish from hunger and want.[55]

Likewise, we see in the complaints of priests concerning the idolatry of the Huron and Ottawa that traditional ceremonies were being performed in preference to Christian rituals. The priests particularly objected to dances that involved nakedness or the imitation of animals. The Bear Dance, a curing ceremony performed by women, seemed to be particularly objectionable to the Jesuits, undoubtedly because of its similarity to pagan carnivals still performed by French peasants.[56]

The New Tribes

By the late 1680s, the Miami and Potawatomi were beginning to drift out of the Green Bay area and to establish new villages along the western and southern shore of Lake Michigan as far as the St. Joseph River valley of southwestern Michigan. This was a homecoming after two generations of exile.[57] The Potawatomi, however, did not abandon their new ground on the west shore of Lake Michigan; like the Ojibwa moving west along the Lake Superior coast, they were also expanding their geographic sphere of influence.

This could not have been accomplished except for the fact that the people expanding out of Green Bay, Chequamegon Bay, and the St. Marys River refuge were socially transformed by the refugee experience. As a result, they emerged with new modes of social integration and enhanced political solidarity. These changes founded in the seventeenth century experience were more important during the eighteenth century.

Pioneer ethnohistorian Harold Hickerson was the first to point out this process in reference to the identity of the Lake Superior Ojibwa.[58] He noticed that the animal-named local groups first described by the French explorers in the seventeenth century, such as *Amikwa* ('beaver'), *Oumisagia* ('eagle'), *Noquet* ('bear'), *Marameg* ('catfish'), and so forth, emerged in the eighteenth century as clan names. He hypothesized that village or band identities became geneological totems as members of these local groups, reduced by disease and concentrated for common defense and support, formed large villages. Thus, the sanctuaries at Green Bay, St. Marys, and Chequamegon Bay were composed of villages of people who had common identities as speakers of the same or similar dialects but who came from different local groups. Some of the new villages might consist of Ottawa from any of the four original Ottawa bands, while another might be composed of people who had formerly identified as *Marameg, Amikwa,* and *Noquet.* As people expanded out of the refuges, new villages were composed of people of many local origins. Identity was no longer *Amikwa* or *Noquet* but Ojibwa of the Beaver or Bear clans. This new identity did not emerge overnight and we find local terms in French usage until the turn of the eighteenth century. Cadillac, writing toward the end of the seventeenth century, says that "the Noquet tribes is now overthrown; there are so few of them left that they are not entitled to any distinct name, since they are incorporated in a number of other tribes."[59] It is also true that new clans were added as populations expanded. Hickerson's hypothesis about the origin of Ojibwa clans may not hold totally for other tribes. The Potawatomi, for example, were always identified by the general term and may have had dispersed clans since before their expulsion from Lower Michigan in the mid-seventeenth century. On the other hand, the Ottawa were clearly identified by the general term *Ottawa*, but the French also understood that they were composed of at least four distinct "tribes" or local groups. The extent to which they may have been geographically and linguistically distinct is found in Cadillac's comment, circa 1695–97, that "these four tribes are allies and are closely united, living on good terms with one another, and now speaking the same common language."[60] Clanship among the Ottawa appears to have always been quite weak, perhaps as a result of the strong tribal identities. The terms *Kiskagon Ottawa* or *Sinago Ottawa* are used well into the eighteenth century.

Clanship, however, became an important mechanism of social and political solidarity. As Potawatomi people expanded by forming new villages, the families of these villages were linked by clan membership to people and families of other Potawatomi villages. It was to these larger families that their loyalty belonged, but with these feelings also came an identity as Potawatomi. The same was true for the Ojibwa and Ottawa.

Indian Fur Trade Commerce

By the beginning of the last quarter of the seventeenth century, the Ottawa had given up the cold, forbidding coasts of Lake Superior for the Straits of Mackinac, where they had established villages at the location of the modern city of St. Ignace; here they resurrected an agricultural economy. This new location soon became the Ottawa "capital" and their numbers grew to about 1,300.[61] The Ottawa reinstituted another old tradition as well, their propensity to trade. Because Michilimackinac was the major staging point for the western fur trade, the Ottawa were soon doing a thriving business, not only in collecting and transporting fur but in supplying the growing French community and traders with canoes, fish, game, and, particularly, corn. Speaking of both Huron and Ottawa, Lahontan remarked

A Dialogue between the
Author and Adario, a Noted Man among the Savages

Lahontan. These are fine distinctions indeed, you please yourself with idle Flams. Haft not thee the sense to perceive, after twenty years conversation with the French, that what the Hurons call reason is reason among the French. 'Tis certain that all men do not observe the laws of reason, for if they did there would be no occasion for punishments, and those judges thou haft seen at Paris and Quebec would be oblig'd to look out for another way of living. But in regard that the good of the society conflicts is doing justice and following these laws, there's a necessity of punishing the wicked and rewarding the good; for without that precaution murders, robberies, and defamations would spread everywhere, and in a word, we should be the most miserable people upon the face of the earth.

Adario. Nay, you are miserable enough already, and indeed I can't see how you can be more such. What sort of men must the Europeans be? What species of creatures do they retain to? The Europeans, who must be forc'd to do good, and have no other prompter for the avoiding of evil than the fear of punishment. If I ask'd thee, what a man is, thou wouldn't answer me, he's a Frenchman, and yet I'll prove that your man is rather a beaver. For man is not entitled to that character upon the score of his walking upright upon two legs, or of reading and writing, and shewing a thousand other instances of his industry. I call that creature a man, that hath a natural inclination to do good, and never entertains the thoughts of doing evil. You see we have no judges; and what's the reason of that? Why? We neither quarrel nor sue one another. And that's the reason that we have no lawsuits? Why? Because we are resolved neither to receive nor to know silver. But why do we refuse admission to silver among us? The reason is this: We are resolv'd to have no laws, for since the world was a world our ancestors liv'd happily without 'em. In fine, as I intimated before, the word laws does not signifie just and reasonable things as you use it, for the rich make a jest of 'em, and 'tis only the poor wretches that pay any regard to 'em. But, pray, let's look into these laws, or reasonable things, as you call 'em. For these fifty years, the governors of Canada have still alledg'd that we are subject to the laws of their great captain. We content ourselves in denying all manner of dependence, excepting that upon the great spirit, as being born free and joint brethren, who are all equally masters: Whereas you are all slaves to one man. We do not put in any such answer to you, as if the French depended upon us; and the reason of our silence upon that head is, that we have no mind to quarrel. But, pray tell me, what authority or right is the pretended superiority of your great captain grounded upon? Did we ever sell ourselves to that great captain? Were we ever in France to look after you? 'Tis you that came hither to find out us. Who gave you all the countries that you now inhabit, by what right do you possess 'em? They always belong'd to the Algonkins before. In earnest, my dear brother, I'm sorry for thee from the bottom of my soul. Take my advice and turn Huron; for I see plainly a vast difference between thy condition and mine. I am master of my own body, I have the absolute disposal of my self, I do what I please, I am the first and the last of my nation, I fear no man, and I depend only upon the great spirit: whereas thy body, as well as thy soul, are doom'd to a dependance upon thy great captain; thy vice-roy disposes of thee; thou haft not the liberty of doing what thou haft a mind to; thou'rt afraid of robbers, false witnesses, and thou dependest upon an infinity of persons whose places have rais'd 'em above thee. Is it true, or not? Are these things either improbable or invisible? Ah! my dear brother, thou seest plainly that I am in the right of it; and yet thou choosest rather to be a French slave than a free Huron. What a fine spark does a Frenchman make with his fine laws, who taking himself to be mighty wise is assuredly a great fool; for as much as he continues in slavery and a state of dependence, while the very brutes enjoy that adorable liberty, and like us fear nothing but foreign enemies.

Lahontan. Indeed, my friend, thy way of reasoning is as savage as thy self. I did not think that a man of sense, who hath been in France and New England, would speak after that fashion. What benefit hast thou reap'd by having seen our cities, forts, and palaces? When thou talk'st of severe laws, of slavery, and a thousand other idle whims, questionless pleasure in discanting upon the felicity of the Hurons, a set of men who mind nothing but eating, drinking, sleeping, hunting, and fishing; who have not the enjoyment of any one conveniency of life, who travel four hundred leagues on foot to knock four Iroquese on the head, in a word, who have no more than the shape of men: whereas we have our conveniences, our unbending diversions, and a thousand other pleasures, which render the minutes of our life supportable. To avoid the lash of those laws which are severe only upon wicked and criminal persons, one needs only to live honestly, and offer injuries to no man.

Adario. Ay, my dear brother, your being an honest man would not avail you; if two false witnesses swear against you, you'll presently see whether your laws are severe or not. Have not the Coureurs de Bois quoted me twenty instances of persons that have been cruelly put to death by the lash of your laws, whose innocence has appear'd after their death? What truth there is in their relations, I do not pretend to know; but 'tis plain that such a thing may happen. I have heard 'em say farther (and indeed I had heard the same thing in France before) that poor innocent men are tortur'd in a most horrible manner, in order to force 'em by the violence of their torment to a confession of all that is charg'd upon 'em and of ten times more. What execrable tyranny must this be! Tho' the French pretend to be men, yet the women are not exempted from this horrid cruelty, no more than the men; both the one and the other choose rather to die once than to die fifty times. And indeed they are in the right of it: for if it should happen that by the influence of extraordinary courage, they were capable of undergoing such torments without confessing a crime that they never committed; what health, what manner of life can they enjoy thereafter? No, no, my dear brother, the black devils that the Jesuits talk so much of, are not in the regions where souls burn in flames, but in Quebec and in France, where they keep company with the laws, the false witnesses, the conveniencies of life, the cities, the fortresses, and the pleasures you spoke of but now.

—Emma Blair, editor, *The Indian
Tribes of the Upper Mississippi Valley
and the Region of the Great Lakes.*

that "sometimes these savages sell their corn very dear, especially when the beaver hunting happens not to take well."[62]

The Potawatomi at Green Bay and at the southern end of Lake Michigan had a similar geographic advantage. They controlled access to the water routes west to the Sioux and south to the Illinois. As beaver became scarce in Michigan, these areas became increasingly important in the trade. This fact was not lost on the Five Nations, who once more began to raid west, turning most of their unwanted attention on the tribes of the Illinois country.

The French also began to take a more aggressive role in conducting the western trade. Nicolas Perrot, an able Indian agent, was dispatched to Green Bay in 1668. The Green Bay Algonquians, particularly the Potawatomi, were now key players in controlling the flow of furs from the south and Sioux country to the west. Although more military-trading posts were established, of greater long-term importance was the appearance of French Canadian traders, the *coureurs de bois*. These men, though often poorly capitalized, were entrepreneurs who hoped to make their fortune in the trade, and they were not about to let the official trade monopoly get in the way. The *coureurs de bois* lived among the Indians, often had Indian wives and children, and adopted Indian dress and customs. As Perrot put it, "The Canadians make themselves like unto the savages."[63] Partially as a result of the lack of control of the trade and the entrepreneurial spirit of French traders on the distant frontier, the rift between civil trading interests and the Jesuits grew into a chasm. The latter claimed that the *coureurs de bois* and French soldiers were ruining the Indians with brandy and debauching native women by turning them into trade goods, prostitutes. Although there was justice in this claim and although the Jesuits were to win some battles in protecting their parishioners, they would lose the war to capitalism and imperialistic interests.

As it was conducted by the French and their English competitors on the Great Lakes frontier, the fur trade had two objects. One was to acquire fur to be sold at a profit for the manufacture of felt. The other was to market the manufactured goods of English and French industry at a profit.

When the Indians were first exposed to objects made of metal, glass, and woven fabric, they assumed these to be the wondrous possessions of deities. La Potherie relates an early encounter of Perrot with the Potawatomi in which they believed Perrot to be *manitou*. The chief took Perrot's knives and hatchets and "incensed them with tobacco smoke from his mouth."[64]

The Algonquians were people accustomed to exchange and the earliest trade was conducted by their own rules, those they had used since prehistoric times. Since it is sometimes assumed that once Indians were exposed to trade goods they rapidly took on a Western economic perspective, it is important to briefly examine the nature and assumptions of the fur trade as the Indian trading partners would have perceived it.

The early trade was conducted as if the French were simply members of another tribe. The assumptions of reciprocity were in force. Goods moved between groups through the medium of the personal relations between trading partners. Since the Indians and the earliest French traders were not related in blood or marriage, the exchange would be immediate and balanced. The French, for some mysterious reason, valued beaver skins and the Indians, for obvious reasons, coveted trade items. On the Indian side, the passing of goods required social boundaries. Indian traders represented kin groups who were exchanging with sociological equivalents. An Indian trader represented his group and "profited" by achieving prestige in circulating goods back into that group. That is, status was attained by giving— the Indian trade was social as well as economic. For whatever economic, political, or military value trade goods had, it was the social and political aspects of the trade that made it work. Its value was a collective benefit because trade enhanced the prestige of the group. Trade opportunities were, therefore, of benefit to everyone.

Guns provide the most powerful example because they had immediate economic and military application. Indians got along fine without guns. The bow and arrow provided food and, at least in some hands, were sufficient to defeat well-armed intruders. Guns came from the French through Indian "trading captains" who probably represented kin groups. Since the Indian trading enterprise was a group venture and not an individual one, individuals got guns through internal social pathways.

The French soon learned the social importance of reciprocal exchange and also that exchange was a political venture. Radisson at Chequamegon laid out "three presents" that were actually groups of goods, each to be given separately to the men, women, and children. The men's present was a kettle, two hatchets, six knives, and a sword blade. Each item had its symbolic value, so that the kettle was to remind the Ojibwa to renew their friendship with all nations (French included) by feasting the dead. The hatchets were to strengthen young men in protecting themselves from their enemies, and the knives to show the might of the French. The sword shows the French to be masters of both peace and war, able to help friends and destroy enemies. Even gifts directed toward the children had messages that were made explicit in the speeches and feasting that accompanied the exchange.[65] Good trade made good social relations and good social relations made political alliances. In the tribal world, peace equaled trade. Again we see, at least initially, that trade was not an economic enterprise between individuals.

Indians also learned to understand the extremely petty, jealous, and greedy ways of French traders, whose usual objective was to make a profit. They learned about supply and demand, price equivalents, and competition and that exchange could be conducted with the French on the merest pretext of civility.

It is also important to note that furs were only one item of trade and, to many groups, not the most important. Indian people around Green Bay and Michilimackinac became provisioners for fur brigades and this was true of people around most French establishments. Galinee, speaking of the Ojibwa at the falls of the St. Marys in 1670, says, "The fish is so cheap that they give ten or twelve of them for four fingers of tobacco . . . and that meat was so cheap that for a pound of glass beads I had four minots of fat entrails of moose."[66] It is clear from records made throughout the fur trade frontier that Indians were quick and efficient as market entrepreneurs. Corn, meat, fish, bark, twine, skin clothing, baskets, canoes, berries, and many other products were soon offered for sale to the French.

Does this mean they were capitalists? No, it does not. For the next century or more, the furs and trade goods were exchanged amicably and willingly in a system of trade that was neither capitalist or reciprocal but a third type, the wonderfully practical invention of willing partners. Within these two very different societies, however, traditional forms of exchange were maintained. Thus, the same wild rice that might be sold to a Frenchman at a price he would consider outrageous would as easily be given away to a brother-in-law with no thought to its market value.

Some of the intertribal politics and warfare of the late seventeenth and eighteenth centuries can be directly related to the idea that Indian exchange was more social and political than economic. As we have discovered in the case of the Huron, Potawatomi, Ottawa, and Fox, these groups are often portrayed as middlemen in trade.[67] It is assumed that they were motivated to enhance their economic position by interdicting or manipulating the supply of furs in order to effect demand. This would put potential competitors at an economic disadvantage by controlling the flow of goods. In short, they behaved like rational capitalists. This conclusion stretches credulity, because it requires us to believe that trade goods were critical to survival and that, to acquire these goods, traditional values of economic exchange were rapidly discarded.[68] It is certainly true that, from almost the earliest contact, one Indian group after another tried to block French traders from contact with their neighbors, and great energy and imagination was obviously devoted to this goal. Understood as a group dynamic and within the context of tribal exchange, this does not require us to assume profit as a motivation. Remembering that exchange to Indians was not just an economic venture but a political and social relationship ratified by a transfer of property, trade was like a marriage between two families sealed with a dowry. Once the French began to exchange with a tribe's neighbors, the social and political value to the group, in Indian eyes the main basis for continued trade and friendship, had slipped away.

Because of the French licensing system, traders, French and Indian, were encouraged to take fur to the St. Lawrence settlements. This pattern fit nicely with the Indian trade system, particularly the Ottawa one, which normally sent out large trade expeditions. Entire villages or lineages were represented by a few "trading captains" who returned from the French settlements with trade goods to distribute. While it may be true that some of those traders may have accumulated goods as individuals, their motivations have to be understood in the context of indigenous culture not capitalist ethics. The prestige of these traders was once again based upon the giving of trade gifts—not economic profit or wealth.

There was another important dimension to the trade, the Indians' clear demarcation between friends and enemies. To them, trade and war were mutually exclusive; trade meant giving, giving meant friendship, and friendship meant trade. Conversely, the lack of trade meant greed, greed meant hostility, and hostility led to warfare or potential warfare.

If the Indian partners of the fur trade were caught up in its social and political dimension, so, eventually, were the French. By 1685 it was obvious that the fur market was becoming oversupplied with pelts. It took another ten years, however, before the government was forced to curtail the flow, and, by then, the storage houses in Quebec and Montreal had a ten year reserve. This situation hardly seems the product of rational economic practice. In fact, the French could not curtail the trade because they were as much prisoners of it as the Indians were. As Canadian historian William Eccles put it, "If the French were to have ceased to provide them with trade goods and the services of blacksmiths and gunsmiths, the French feared that the Indians would have gone over to the English, who, ironically, had never proved able to provide these services for more than brief periods."[69]

By the beginning of the last decade of the seventeenth century, the French had "discovered" and explored the Great Lakes. They understood the geography of its interconnecting waterways, they had at least limited contact with all of the indigenous tribes, and appreciated local differences in language and culture. Military and trading establishments and missions had been strategically placed at Green Bay, Michilimackinac, on the St. Joseph River, and at several other locations that controlled interconnecting waterways south and west of Lake Michigan and north and west of Lake Superior.

In 1696, this entire French trading system was abandoned as the result of a royal decree revoking trade licenses. The decree was partially the result of a worldwide glut of beaver pelts and partially the result of lobbying in the French court by the Jesuits, who resented the presence and influence of the military-trade alliance on western Indians.

The sudden demise of the trade in 1696 not only created economic hardship for Indian families supplying the trade, but also caused hardships associated with the loss of tools and implements. It was not that Indians were dependent on these items so much that they had found an important niche in the status and warfare systems of the

Algonquians. More than anything else, however, the respite in the trade demonstrated to the western tribes the limited political power of their French trading patrons. Iroquois attacks on the St. Lawrence settlements and the killing of the French citizenry at La Chene in 1689 convinced many western Indians, particularly the Ottawa, who had the most invested in the French alliance, that their future might be more secure with the Iroquois and their English traders. Governor Frontenac acted quickly, however, to hold the French-Algonquian alliance by sending French troops to the upper lakes with the message that "the Five Nations were like five muskrat lodges in a marsh which the French propose to drain and burn."[70] The French were, of course, not without local support. At a council at Michilimackinac, a *Sinago* Ottawa chief advised his people to "vomit forth thy hateful feelings and all thy plots. Return to thy Father, who stretches out his arms and who is, moreover, not unable to protect thee."[71]

It is clear that the French presence, though of considerable influence, was in Indian eyes exactly equivalent to another tribe. As the seventeenth century closed, the Ottawa, Potawatomi, Huron, French, Saulteaur, Miami, Fox, and Sioux were all engaged in plot and counterplot, alliance and betrayal, war and peace. Even the staunchest French allies, the Potawatomi, Ottawa, and Huron, were not French puppets. At a time when the French and the Iroquois were negotiating the Treaty of Montreal in 1701, bringing an end to the Iroquois wars, the Ottawa had already independently arrived at an agreement that opened northern hunting grounds to the Iroquois in exchange for "an open path to Albany."[72]

Peace with the Iroquois in 1701 opened new potential for fur trade prosperity, but it also made the *Anishnabeg* keenly aware that the old French promise of military protection of allies was hollow. The French could not protect themselves.

Growing French Influence

As the seventeenth century wore on, the native peoples of the upper Great Lakes had a more difficult time dealing with the French. The French, it seemed, always wanted something; missionaries wanted them to forgo old beliefs, traders wanted them to abandon hunting in favor of trapping, and civil authorities wanted to reorient their external relations to conform to French interests.

Two separate events in 1684 show the degree of French influence. Determined to carry war to the home country of the Iroquois, who were making serious raids into the upper Mississippi valley, the Governor of New France ordered Duluth and Perrot to organize the northern tribes for an attack. After great difficulty, they managed to raise four hundred warriors from several tribes, mainly the Ottawa. This was the first of many war parties that would leave the safety of the northern lakes to do battle for France.[73]

The party was led by Perrot, who had to continually fuel the reluctant warriors' enthusiasm for the venture. To the Indians, who conducted war on a religious as well as a political basis, the project was bad medicine from the start. Between Saginaw and Detroit, a French soldier accidentally discharged his musket and killed himself. Such a bad omen would normally be cause to scrub the mission, but Perrot talked them into going on. At Detroit, a herd of elk were driven into the river among the war canoes and a young Ottawa, attempting to fire at them, mistakenly shot his brother who was paddling in front. The brother soon died of his wound and his brother died from grief. Again, Perrot convinced the party to continue toward Iroquois country. As they approached the enemy, the Ottawa sent out scouts on foot and determined a place of rendezvous with the main party. While waiting for the others to appear, the scouts amused themselves by imitating the calling of elk. Their mimicry was so successful that a Frenchman with the main force shot and wounded one of the scouts. After this incident, Perrot had a real challenge convincing the Indians to proceed; as he reports, some of the Ottawa were, by that time, ready to attack the French since as they had properly concluded "it was the French who were killing us not the Iroquois."[74] As it turned out, the Iroquois had been forewarned of their approach through the inept bargaining of the French Governor La Barre. The French were then forced to sign a humiliating peace agreement with the Iroquois that gave temporary respite to the St. Lawrence settlements in exchange for abandoning the French allies in the west to Iroquois aggression.[75]

The second incident involved an early indication of the desire of French authorities to impose civil authority over the Indians. During the fall of 1684, a French trading party was attacked on the Keweenaw Peninsula of Lake Superior, and the Ottawa chief *Achiganaga* as well as two Menominee were implicated in the murder of two Frenchmen and their ten Indian companions. Violence from various causes happened occasionally on the Great Lakes frontier and in this case was attributable to the drunken behavior of Indians who were supplied intoxicants by the traders. According to Indian custom, amends were later made by "covering the dead," a metaphor indicating the making of a substantial gift to allay the grief of kin, to "dry their tears." In this case, however, the accused were tracked down by the French, taken to Michilimackinac, tried by a committee of Frenchmen, and convicted, despite the efforts of a large assembly of relatives and supporters. One of the Menominee and the eldest son of *Achiganaga* were given death sentences. Duluth reports the execution as follows.

> After this I left the council, and informed the Reverend Fathers, so that they might baptise those two wretched men which they did. An hour afterwards, I put myself at the head of 42 Frenchmen, and, in sight of more than 400 men, and 200 steps from their fort, I had their heads broken in.[76]

French justice had come to the Great Lakes.

Indian Relations at Detroit

Day in and day out, the French probably had little effect on the home life of Indians. Certainly, however, they were an important force in external relationships. The Indian turmoil around Detroit in the first dozen years of the eighteenth century serves to illustrate the extent of French influence in this realm.

In 1701, Cadillac returned from France with the French court's blessing for the establishment of Fort Ponchartrain and a new trading concession on the Detroit River. In theory, this concession was to hold France's Algonquian trading partners loyal by blocking their access to English traders who were pushing into the Ohio valley. The French were keenly aware that several Great Lakes tribes, especially the Ottawa, were making trade overtures to the Iroquois, who had promised the Ottawa access to British traders at Albany. Since there were few Indians in the eastern part of Lower Michigan or adjacent Ontario, Cadillac invited his old acquaintances from Michilimackinac, the Ottawa and Huron, to join him at Detroit. Consequently, the Huron, some of the Ottawa, and villages representing Potawatomi and Ojibwa soon settled in the Detroit River valley near the new French fort. It was claimed that this multiethnic assembly sometimes reached six thousand people.

To a large degree, the Detroit phenomenon was a part of the reoccupation of land earlier abandoned as the result of the Iroquois menace. The Miami and Potawatomi left the west side of Lake Michigan and moved south to the St. Joseph and Wabash valleys. The Kickapoo pushed south toward the Illinois, and the Mascouten settled along the west shore of Lake Michigan. The Fox now inherited control of the Fox River portage south and west of Green Bay. Meanwhile, the Ottawa established villages along the northwest coast of Lower Michigan and in the Saginaw valley, which was also occupied by some Ojibwa. Missisauga Ojibwa were likewise spreading their villages south into southwestern Ontario. For their part, the French were trying to control these movements to limit contact with the British (see map 3).

In the early eighteenth century, two arenas of conflict arose, the Ohio valley and Green Bay. In the latter case, the Fox and their allies, the Sauk, Kickapoo, Mascouten, and Winnebago, were disrupting the lucrative French trade with the Sioux. In order to try to smooth relationships and, perhaps, distract their attention, the French invited the Green Bay groups to establish villages at Detroit.

In the spring of 1712, two large Fox bands under the leadership of *Lamyma,* a peace chief, and *Pemaussa,* the major Fox war chief, along with a Mascouten village under the prominent chiefs *Kisis* and *Ouabimanitou* ('White Spirit') established villages near the French. One Fox settlement was within fifty feet of the pallisades of Fort Ponchartrain. Cadillac had by then been transferred to Louisiana, leaving the fort under the command of Dubuisson, an inexperienced officer with no garrison. As most of the Indian allies of the French had not yet returned from winter hunting, the Fox and Mascouten seized the opportunity and terrorized the French and resident Indians by "insults" and by plundering livestock.[77]

At some point, news reached the Fox and Mascouten that a Mascouten village on the St. Joseph River had been attacked the previous winter by *Saguina,* an Ottawa war chief, and his Potawatomi counterpart, *Makisabe.* Over 150 people were killed in the attack. Outraged, the Fox and Mascouten took hostages and threatened to kill the few Ottawa in residence and to attack the French who were allies of the Ottawa and Potawatomi. Dubuisson quickly sent a message to hasten the return of his Algonquian allies. Shortly, *Makisabe* arrived with six hundred men. Also arriving was *Saguina* with local Ottawa and Huron as well as Illinois, Missouri, and Osage warriors under the leadership of the Illinois chief *Makovaandely*. The Fox and Mascouten were immediately driven inside their "fort." With the French supplying the shot and powder to the besieging "army," the Fox were trapped and became increasingly desperate for food and water. Nonetheless, they hung red banners over the pallisade of their village and flew red flags, shouting that they would turn the ground as red with the blood of their enemies. The Fox also exhorted their Indian attackers to join them and the English against the French. The siege dragged on, with the Fox finally having to crouch in trenches to avoid musket fire from platforms built to look down into their village. The French set up two mortars that had murderous effect and resulted in the Fox and Mascouten seeking council under a white flag. The Fox war chief, *Pemaussa,* appeared and asked a truce to permit time to consider options. He sealed this request by offering to return three Ottawa women hostages taken before the appearance of the French allies. One of these women was the wife of the Ottawa war chief *Saguina*. In accepting the hostages, Dubuisson told the Fox that "if you had devoured this flesh of mine which you have brought me, you would not be alive now. . . . " To this, Illinois chief *Makovaandely,* speaking for the Indians, chided the Fox, "You are dogs, who have always bitten him (the French); you have never been grateful for the benefits you have received from the French." Their offer rejected, the Fox and Mascouten returned to their fort and fighting began again.[78]

Four days went by with fighting so heavy that the Fox sometimes fired two to three hundred arrows at once. Some were fire arrows and others contained lighted fuses affixed to powder charges. These had a good effect on the thatched roof of Fort Ponchartrain. As French supplies of food ran out, the Indian allies threatened to leave, causing great panic among the French. Dubuisson began working to rally young war chiefs to stand firm. To attain his end he stripped himself of all he had to give these men presents. As he later reported to Governor Vaudreuil, "You know, Sir, that one must not be stingy with the savages."[79] In general council, Dubuisson tried to shame his allies by telling them that all the other tribes would say, "Those are the brave warriors who fled in so cowardly a manner and deserted the French. Be not troubled: take courage. We will try and find a little good (goods) yet; the Huron and Ottawa, your brethren, offer you some for me...."[80] Supported by the young war chiefs, the Algonquian allies stood fast and again forced the Fox to parley.

This time all of the Fox and Mascouten chiefs appeared in full regalia and, with great ceremony that included singing, presented the French and their allies with presents, including slaves. Their object was to beg for the lives of their women and children. Dubuisson left this decision to the chiefs, who refused all mercy and sent the Fox and Mascouten back to their forts.

On the nineteenth day of the siege, the Fox and Mascouten were able to sneak out of their forts in the midst of a violent midnight thunderstorm. Fleeing north and east, they were soon overtaken at the south end of Lake St. Clair. After four more days of fighting, the Fox surrendered. One hundred fifty men were taken prisoner along with some of the women and children; hundreds of others were killed. Many of these prisoners were tortured and killed a few at a time outside Fort Ponchartrain.

During the siege, the French lost thirty men, the Indian allies sixty, and the Fox-Mascouten suffered a thousand casualties. A few, no doubt, escaped to report the news at Green Bay, where their relatives stepped up harassment of French traders with renewed vigor.

The French, in turn, eventually mounted several expeditions against the Fox, including one in 1716 when an army of two hundred French and six hundred Indians succeeded in capturing chief *Pemaussa* and temporarily opening the trade with the Sioux.[81]

By 1720, the Fox were divided into two factions and the one led by *Kiala* was violently anti-French. *Kiala* traveled widely in hope of building a tribal alliance to fight growing French influence. As part of his plan, the Fox not only attacked the Illinois tribes and French settlements on the Mississippi but continued to interdict the trade west of Lake Michigan.

Governor Beauharnois faced this threat by convincing the Potawatomi, Ojibwa, Huron, and Ottawa to send a stream of small war parties against the Fox and their allies. In 1729, their victories over the Fox reduced their fighting efficiency and, in 1733, *Kiala* was forced to surrender. In this final episode of the "Fox Wars," the true intent of the French toward the Fox is revealed. Their object was nothing short of ethnocide. Chief *Kiala* was exiled to the West Indies to die at hard labor, while captured Fox women and children were divided among Christian Indians as slaves.[82] Those few Fox who remained free joined the Sauk, while others crossed the Mississippi to join the Iowa. In the end, however, these brutal French actions were so severe that they actually undermined their support among other Algonquians.

Diplomacy and War

The early eighteenth century in American history books is usually devoted to the French and Indian Wars. This label is entirely misleading because it was the French and British who were at war or, more precisely, were engaged in a series of four wars. In the New World, much of the warring was carried out by Indian proxies who, in effect, became French and British mercenaries. The ramifications of the distant French and British conflict had some very direct and terrible impacts on the Great Lakes tribes. These often did not involve Europeans, but were played out in repeated, hostile encounters between their Indian allies. Through the first four decades of the eighteenth century, French, British, and various Indian interests fanned hostility as they tried to outmaneuver their rivals. Following the outbreak of the final struggle in 1754, which would lead to the ultimate surrender of France's Canadian interest less than a decade later, Great Lakes Indians were increasingly supplied and led by the French military. They were also involved more directly and continually in fighting for French objectives. The degree to which the political goals of the various tribes were served in alliance with France seems to vary greatly. Some tribes, such as the Ottawa, emerged as powerful political forces by the mid-eighteenth century while others, such as the Illinois, were scattered and weakened. Whatever the social and political significance of the French and Indian alliance, the human toll paid for partnership with the French father was terrible.

Although the Treaty of Montreal in 1701 assured the neutrality of the Five Nations in French-British relations on paper, the French, fearing that peace between their allies and the Five Nations would lead to the loss of their critical support against the British, did their best to maintain the hostility between the Algonquians and their old *Nodaway* enemies. This was, indeed, part of a new, aggressive imperial policy on the part of Louis XIV, who sought to block British expansion west of the Alleghenies. Such a policy was partially necessary because the Algonquians were rapidly expanding into the Ohio country earlier abandoned as the result of the incursions of the Five Nations. The Potawatomi, Mascouten, and Miami all returned east to occupy southern Michigan and northern Indiana while the Shawanee, Delaware, and various refugee Algonquian and scattered Iroquois bands filled the rich forests and prairie lands of the central Ohio valley. Much of this expansion was completed during the first two decades of the seventeenth century. In these new territories, the French Indian allies were in close and permanent contact with British traders. Moreover, they were often impressed with better prices, the superior quality of manufactured goods offered by the British, and by a more consistent supply. The French had good reason to worry about their fragile alliance with the Great Lakes Algonquians.

Several additional points need to be raised as background for understanding the complex nature of eighteenth-century Indian history. First, Western history tends to paint the French as large and powerful in their relationships with Indians. In reality, the French were only influential insofar as they were able to manipulate Indian action to French objectives. Occasionally they were successful but, in fact, the relationship between the French and specific tribes was not unlike that between the tribes themselves. Alliance with the French by tribes or tribal segments was for specific purposes and temporary. Agreements of peace and friendship were based on the ceremonial and ritual traditions of the tribes, slightly modified to accommodate European conventions such as written records of transactions. In Indian practice, individual chiefs took a prominent role in arrangements and negotiation of agreements. This necessitated the appointment of functional counterparts in the French camp. Thus, military people and prominent citizens such as Tonty and Cadillac, who knew Indian affairs and who had their own interests within tribes, became, in effect, French chiefs. As we might expect, these men, drawn into an extant system, were instruments of both self-interest and French policy.

In the latter regard they tried to make agreements with Indian tribes that would further the policies of the French colonial government. These agreements, however, were made in the name of the various governors who were referred to by the Iroquoian term *Onontio* ('father'). This term was also used in reference to the even more remote and powerful king of France. Consequently, as we might expect, the Indian-French relationship was at least symbolically filial, the Indians collectively and the chiefs personally being "children" of the king and governors. The relationship had no semblance of servitude or authority, as indeed the father-child relationships did not within the Indian family. Neither did this role imply jural authority of the French father, again a concept foreign to the relationships among extended kin. The new kin relationship of French "father" to Indian "child" did, however, bind the two in the tradition of economic reciprocity in which the Father was obliged to give freely and generously in proportion to his ability and status. The children could expect the protection of the father's strong arm in the vigorous defense of their interests. To the Potawatomi, Ottawa, and Ojibwa, their relationship to the French had the same clear expectations of mutual obligation as that found within their own families and clans.

The French, of course, had a different understanding. Children were to bend to the will of the parent, to obediently do their bidding, and to remain steadfast at all costs. To the French, the father-child relationship was more remote, much more symbolic and political. Perhaps due to differences in the understanding of the meaning of their relationship, French attempts to blatantly manipulate tribal interests for their own advantage were perceived by Indians as a fundamental betrayal of family trust. Chiefs soon learned that their French counterparts could be greedy, untruthful, and unforgiving, all characteristics that Indians did not admire in a father.

Another significant discovery on the part of the Algonquian tribes was that the English enemy of the French Father was growing in strength and offering goods and promises at least equal to those of the French. When it became apparent that it was possible to bargain by threatening the loyalty of political alliance, the Algonquians began to form and pursue their own political goals. In many cases, this meant continued alliance with the French, in others, alliance with the British and their Iroquoian partners, and for some, an independent path. The latter two options set a collision course between some tribes and French interests, of which the fate of the Fox serves as an example.

It is also necessary to understand the change in warfare that occurred during the early eighteenth century. During the seventeenth century, we see the elaboration and embellishment of what was essentially a prehistoric warfare system. Cycles of revenge and replacement of slain kin were the driving factors that fueled raid and counterraid against fortified villages. As guns entered the picture, their impact can be seen in the history of the Huron-Iroquoian warfare to the east of Lake Huron. While bows and arrows, the ax, and the club were still probably the main weapons of war, firearms provided long-range firepower and changed military tactics. Now, larger and larger war parties went forth to besiege forts strongly pallisaded in the French style of single lines of huge posts, rather than a complex maze of brush pickets. Capture of prisoners for wholesale adoption became even more important to offset losses through more sustained warfare and epidemic diseases.

In the second third of the eighteenth century, warfare was substantially changed again when both the French and British began to supply arms and ammunition to their Indian allies in order to transform war parties into irregular military units. Now, groups of heavily armed warriors directed by French officers descended upon British installations and settlements and fought against professional army units. The one advantage that remained to the tribal warriors was their skill at fighting in small, mobile units and the use of ambush in heavy forest cover. These tactics were used with devastating effect against British troops who fought in organized ranks in fully visible positions.

Ottawa, Potawatomi, and Ojibwa warriors still clung to the prime expedient of tribal war, which was to do as much damage as possible to the enemy while taking as few losses as possible. Attackers did not give warning, recognize noncombatants, or spare the wounded, nor did they see the slightest disgrace in running away in the face of defeat or in the use of trickery to gain advantage. Even given its social overtones, tribal war was a serious enterprise. As English frontier settlers knew, and British regular army units soon came to realize, France's Indian allies, "the bloody claws of New France," were worthy of mortal fear.

Indian Mercenaries

The French now turned their attention to their British rivals on both banks of the Ohio River. Under French auspices in 1737, upper Great Lakes warriors formed war parties that moved south into the area that is now western Tennessee and Mississippi to fight the Chickasaw trading partners of the British. The main battleground, however, became central Ohio and eastern Indiana.

After the outbreaks of the war between Britain and France in 1744, English traders brought their trade goods to the Ohio valley in large quantities.[83] The French were faced with defection on the part of some of their oldest and strongest allies including the Huron and Ottawa at Detroit. The Huron, in fact, split into two factions: one remained loyal to the French while the other, under the leadership of *Orontony* or Nicolas, moved south to Sandusky Bay to be in closer contact with British merchants. The Sandusky group called themselves *Wendats* or *Wyandots*. In using this term to describe themselves, the "Huron" of Sandusky were rejecting the old French alliance and constructing a new identity for themselves.[84]

The success of the English was evident on the Great Miami river, where the village of *Pickawellany* had as many as fifty British traders in 1750. This Miami town was under the leadership of the chief known to the French as La Demoiselle and to the English as Old Briton.[85] The French at Detroit tried to recruit a passing Nipissing war party to attack *Pickawellany* and, although they were willing, local Ottawa would not permit them to proceed because, as they explained to the Nipissings, they were intermarried with the Miami. Next the French fell back upon their northern Ojibwa and Ottawa allies from Michilimackinac who were counseled at Fort Michilimackinac (and later at Green Bay) by a half Ottawa–half French war chief, *Akewaugeketauso* ('he who is fierce for the land'), who learned his trade as a small boy by following his maternal uncle *Nisowaquet* against the Fox. *Akewaugeketauso,* whose French name was Charles de Langlade, was one of a growing number of people of dual Indian and French descent, custom, and language called *Métis,* who could function effectively in both cultural contexts.[86] Thus, the young de Langlade, *both* an officer in the French militia and an Ottawa *ogamaw* or chief, raised 240 Ottawa warriors to descend on *Pickawellany.* The town was looted and burned and Old Briton was killed, cooked, and eaten by de Langlade and his fighting men. As in other cases where enemies were overcome and consumed, the warriors hoped to ingest and incorporate the spirit of a brave adversary as well as to terrorize the survivors.

During the 1750s, France struggled to preserve Canada with its pitifully small French population against the pressure of millions of English-speaking colonists now filling the Atlantic seaboard and beginning to spill over the Alleghenies. Time and again upper Great Lakes Indian warriors were recruited and sent east in small parties to fight in the French cause. Sometimes they participated as irregular troops in sustained military action, but, as often as not, they raided and looted British towns and settlements. The French were well aware of the terror that tribal war created on the frontier and often sought to reinforce it by denying that they had any control over the actions of their "savages." During the summer of 1760, war parties of twelve hundred Potawatomi, Ottawa, and Ojibwa left the upper lakes to participate in the battle for Quebec. Though they undoubtedly fasted before battle and evoked spiritual help and protection through prayers and special charms, they could not forestall the French defeat. As they returned home in the autumn, the fall chill over the lakes was also in their hearts. They well knew that the hated British redcoats would soon appear in their forest sanctuaries.

NOTES

1. Adney and Chapelle 1964, 113.
2. Branstner (1991, 40–57) sets out a long and complex model of Huron decision making that is rooted in Huron culture as well as external pressure.
3. D. Anderson (1991) offers a fascinating study of the goods purchased and packaged for the western fur trade by a group of Montreal merchants. His study provides a list of the wide variety of European- and Canadian-made goods offered to Indians in exchange for furs. Time and again, Anderson demonstrates that cloth and ready-made clothing were the most important trade items during the eighteenth century.
4. Modern estimates vary somewhat from the 30,000 reported by Champlain and the French Jesuits to 18,000 favored by Trigger (1976, 32). An extensive analysis by Heidenreich (1971, 103) presents a convincing argument for about 21,000.

5. Sauer 1980, 107.
6. Walsh 1982, 13–26.
7. Thwaites 1896, 16: 231–32.
8. Heidenreich 1971, 28.
9. For a more detailed description of the Huron and their history, see Trigger 1969 and 1976; Heidenreich 1971; Tooker 1964. Plates 33–36 in the beautifully illustrated *Historical Atlas of Canada* (edited by Harris and Matthews) add rich detail to our understanding of French activities from the exploration of Cartier in 1535 to the conquest of the Huron in 1649.
10. Heidenreich 1971, 28.
11. Thwaites 1896, 10: 233.
12. Thwaites 1896, 44: 306; Champlain 1902, 130–31.
13. Thwaites 1896, 44: 297.
14. Trigger 1969, 47–49.
15. Trigger 1969, 75.
16. Thwaites 1896, 10: 255.
17. Thwaites 1896, 10: 225–26.
18. Thwaites 1896, 10: 178–79.
19. Thwaites 1896, 33: 221, 119.
20. Trigger 1969, 47–49.
21. Thwaites 1896, 33: 211.
22. Kellogg 1925, 69; Feest and Feest 1978, 772; Kinietz 1940, 226–27.
23. Thwaites 1896, 54: 133–35; Rodgers 1978, 768–70; Ritzenthaler 1978, 743.
24. Hickerson 1970, 35–50.
25. Rodgers 1978, 768.
26. The Late Woodland archaeology of northern Michigan and the northern Lake Huron coast indicates that, from about A.D. 800 to historic contact, there was a widespread ceramic style tradition common to the region. This Juntunen tradition includes territory bounded by the eastern Lake Superior coast from the Michpicoten River on the north to Keweenaw Bay on the south and east along the north shore of Lake Huron as far as the Spanish River. On Lake Michigan, the Juntunen tradition extends from the Garden Peninsula east to the Straits of Mackinac and the adjacent tip of northern Lower Michigan. This region is what Thor Conway (1979) has called the "heartland of the Ojibwa."
27. Thwaites 1896, 21: 193–99.
28. Kellogg 1917, 421; Champlain 1902, 100–101.
29. Lurie 1978, 706.
30. Spindler 1978, 723.
31. Heidenreich 1971, 98.

32. Calvin Martin, in his book *Keepers of the Game* (1978), has argued that Algonquian associated the new diseases with disharmony between humans and the natural world. This disjuncture set off a war between men and animals that led to the near extermination of the beaver. Many scholars have objected to this theory on the basis of the fact that animism does not necessarily imply a conservationist ethic nor did fur trade participation need to have a philosophical rationale.
33. Trigger 1976, 534–38.
34. Trigger 1976, 700.
35. See Hunt 1940.
36. Heidenreich 1990, 5.
37. Hunt 1940, 88.
38. Hunt 1940, 93.
39. The Rock Island site was discovered and excavated by Ronald Mason (1986b), who illustrates artifacts related to the Ottawa-Petun as well as subsequent Potawatomi occupation.
40. Kellogg 1925, 88.
41. Kellogg 1925, 98.
42. Thwaites 1905, 152.
43. Thwaites 1896, 54: 130–31.
44. Blair 1911, 179. As a testimony to the accuracy of oral history, a nearly identical account of this battle was given 235 years later (1893) by Charles Kobawgam of Marquette, Michigan, to Homer H. Kidder; since Kobawgam could not read English there is very little chance he could have acquired details of this event except as it was passed down through the generations as part of tribal history. See Kobawgam n.d.
45. Thwaites 1896, 50: 285–87.
46. Thwaites 1896, 51: 44.
47. Thwaites 1896, 51: 27.
48. Thwaites 1896, 54: 167.
49. Thwaites 1905, 146.
50. Susan Branstner (1991) provides a detailed description of Huron life at the village associated with the Jesuit mission. Still extant in a city park in downtown St. Ignace, the site is annually visited by thousands of tourists. The Museum of Ojibwa Culture and History located on the site displays artifacts excavated at the Huron village, although the museum is primarily devoted to the protohistoric Ojibwa, the indigenous people of the Straits of Mackinac region.
51. Quaife 1962, 13.
52. I am grateful to Beverly Smith for pointing out to me that *sagamity,* which combines small amounts of fish with a corn base, gave the Great Lakes Indians a soup that was of extremely high nutritional quality.

This is the result of the supplemental protein phenomenon that can be achieved by combining a small amount of complete protein with an incomplete protein, in this case fish with corn. The complete amino acids found in fish enhance those that are deficient in corn and also provide missing vitamins of the B complex. The soup mixture also tends to better preserve water-soluble vitamins of the B and C groups that are destroyed by prolonged cooking. Thus, *sagamity,* like other meat-vegetable mixtures, provides a better food than the meat and vegetables eaten separately.

53. Blair 1911, 517–18.
54. Blair 1911, 461–62.
55. Quaife 1962, 21.
56. Walsh 1982, 13–26.
57. Clifton 1977, 66–68.
58. Hickerson 1970, 47.
59. Quaife 1962, 64.
60. Quaife 1962, 10.
61. Feest and Feest 1978, 774.
62. Thwaites 1905, 148.
63. Blair 1911, 230.
64. Blair 1911, 309.
65. Adams 1961, 128–29.
66. Kellogg 1917, 207.
67. See Hunt 1940.
68. In reassessing the role of trade goods in social and political change among the seventeenth-century Huron, Trigger (1984) concludes that their desire to secure and maintain access to European goods was the primary agent of cultural change.
69. Eccles 1988, 327–28.
70. Blair 1911, 246.
71. Blair 1911, 51.
72. Miquelon 1987, 21–22.
73. Kellogg 1925, 229.
74. Blair 1911, 232–43.
75. Kellogg 1925, 229.
76. Ourada 1979, 21.
77. Dubuisson to Vaudreuil, June 15, 1712, *Michigan Pioneer and Historical Collections* 33: 538.
78. Dubuisson to Vaudreuil, 545.
79. Dubuisson to Vaudreuil, 546.
80. Dubuisson to Vaudreuil, 547.
81. Kellogg 1925, 288.

82. Kellogg 1925, 331.
83. Jacobs 1950, 90.
84. Clifton (1983) presents the history of the formation of the Wyandot group of Sandusky from the larger Huron community at Detroit. He argues that the division occurred along clan and phratry lines reflecting the old Huron-Petun understanding of the size and ranking of these groups. Contrary opinions are expressed by Branstner (1991) and Campeau (1987). Whatever the grounds for the social division, it seems clear that the emergent Wyandot were traditional in religious belief and politically independent.
85. Kellogg 1925, 421. Multiple identifications, each specific to the separate cultures in which the person functioned, were not unusual on the eighteenth- and nineteenth-century frontier. Many people, particularly those of prominence or those with unusual language abilities, had three or, in some cases, four sets of names, languages, and modes of behavior appropriate to specific sociopolitical contexts (see Clifton 1989).
86. Grignon 1904, 236.

Chapter 4

Foreign Invasion: The *Jagonash* and the *Chemokmon*

In the late fall of 1760, small groups of *Anishnabeg* warriors paddled home to their upper Great Lakes forest sanctuaries from the summer battlefields of the east. This was a pattern now repeated for several generations, as son followed father east to fight in the service of the French father. War leaders and their men set forth armed with presents to insure their participation and returned with captured plunder. Men in the canoes were dressed in a striking mixture of traditional and European garb. Leather breech cloths and moccasins, bright cloth leggings, cotton shirts, and thick woolen trade blankets formed their attire beneath traditional turban headdresses festooned with feathers. Garters of glass beads, arm bands, earrings, and gorgets of bright trade silver flashed in the sun and contrasted sharply with the vestiges of ghostly vermillion, white, and black war paint. Costumes, like the weapons and utensils they carried, were mostly obtained from Europeans in trade or war. As they pushed their canoes rapidly up the streams and across the lakes for home, these warriors did not know that the latest battle in which they had participated, the defeat of the French army of General Montcalm at Quebec, would seal the fate of French Canada. The king of France, they would say during the next few years, "has gone to sleep but will shortly awaken to return to his Indian children."

At about the same time the fighting men of the northern Lakes were returning home, a group of thirty Ottawa warriors with war chief Pontiac met Major Robert Rodgers advancing west along the south shore of Lake Erie to receive the surrender of Detroit. The Ottawa, prudently carrying the British flag, were assured by George

Crogan, the Indian agent with Rodgers, that they would "enjoy free trade and possession of the country as long as they adhered to his Majesty's interest."[1]

Such arrogance on the part of the British was highly offensive to the western Indians, who did not consider themselves to be vanquished enemies of the British. This point is nowhere better made than by an incident at the post of Ft. Michilimackinac in the late fall of 1761.

With the rapid withdrawal of the French garrisons from the scattered northern trading posts, British traders were soon drawn to the riches of the fur trade. One of the first Englishmen to arrive at Fort Michilimackinac was Alexander Henry, who landed on the south shore of the Straits of Mackinac in the early fall. Although he disguised himself as a Canadian trader, his identity became known and he soon received a visit from *Minavavana,* the war chief of the local Mackinac band, and sixty Ojibwa warriors.

Minavavana welcomed Henry with preliminary comments to an interpreter about the bravery of the British to come among their enemies. Then, as custom dictated for important diplomatic occasions, *Minavavana* and the warriors smoked their pipes. Taking a few strings of wampum in his hand, *Minavavana* addressed Henry as follows.

Englishman, it is to you that I speak, and I demand your attention.

Englishman, you know that the French king is our father. He promised to be such; and we, in return, promised to be his children. This promise we have kept.

Englishman, it is you who have made war with this our father. You are his enemy; and how, then, could you have the boldness to venture among us, his children? You know that his enemies are ours.

Englishman, we are informed, that our father, the king of France, is old and infirm; and that being fatigued, with making war upon your nation, he is fallen asleep. During his sleep you have taken advantage of him, and possessed yourselves of Canada. But his nap is almost at an end. I think I hear him stirring, and inquiring for his children, the Indians; and when he does awake what must become of you? He will destroy you utterly!

Englishman, although you have conquered the French, you have not yet conquered us! We are not your slaves. These lakes, these woods and mountains, were left to us by our ancestors. They are our inheritance; and we will part with them to none. Your nation supposes that we, like the white people, cannot live without bread and pork and beef! But, you ought to know, that He, the Great Spirit and Master of Life, has provided food for us, in these spacious lakes, and on these wooded mountains.

Englishman, our father, the king of France, employed our young men to make war upon your nation. In this warfare, many of them have been killed: and it is our custom to retaliate, until such times as the spirits of the slain are satisfied. But the spirits of the slain are to be satisfied in either of two ways; the first is by spilling of the blood of the nation by which they fell; the other, by covering the bodies of the dead, and thus allowing the resentment of their relations. This is done by making presents.

Englishman, your king has never sent us any presents, nor entered into any treaty with us, wherefore he and we are still at war; and until he does these things, we must consider that we have no other father, nor friend, among the white men, than the king of France, but, for you, we have taken into consideration, that you have ventured your life among us, in the expectation that we should not molest you. You do not come armed, with an intention to make war; you come in peace, to trade with us, and supply us with necessaries, of which we are in much want. We shall regard you, therefore, as a brother; and you may sleep tranquilly, without fear of the Chipeways. As a token of our friendship, we present you with this pipe, to smoke.[2]

At the conclusion of this speech, the Ojibwa passed around a pipe that was smoked by all, after which they shook hands. *Minavavana* then asked Henry if they might taste English milk (rum), since they had not tasted any in a long while and wanted to ascertain if it was different from the French.

As *Minavavana*'s speech clearly states, the western Indians, though mostly firm allies of the French, were neither dependent upon Europeans nor did they believe themselves defeated in the recent wars. In tribal tradition, peace could have soon been concluded with the payment of reparations in the form of gifts. Being ignorant of this fact, the British regarrisoned the western posts but neglected to supply these detachments with Indian presents. This greatly angered local tribesmen, who viewed the same arrangement with the French as a form of rent on the land where the forts were erected.

In fact, the Indians of the upper lakes were very anxious to resume the fur trade. As *Minavavana*'s comments indicate, the disruption of the trade during the war between France and England did work hardships on many Indian families who had adopted many items of European manufacture among their tools, weapons, and costumes. Unfortunately, British trade policy, the attitude of colonial administrators toward Indians, and the bad character of many traders gave the British fur trade a shaky start and a nasty turn.

The period of initial British penetration into the upper Great Lakes country, that is, between the close of hostilities in 1760 and the Treaty of Paris, which concluded peace in 1763, was one of turmoil. This trouble, in fact, led to armed hostility between the British and Indians, and later between Indians and American colonial settlers. Great Lakes Indians became increasingly upset by two major problems, the encroachment of white settlers on Indian lands in the Ohio valley and the restrictions placed on trade. The second problem was paramount for the northern groups (see map 4).

At the conclusion of the French and Indian Wars, Lord Jeffery Amherst was appointed military governor. Amherst had a very low opinion of Indians, once referring to them as "pernicious vermin" and an "execrable race." In fact, he had written to Colonel Henry Bouquet at Fort Pitt suggesting that blankets contaminated with smallpox be distributed to hostile Indians.[3] His basic distrust of Indians led Amherst to restrict the flow of arms and ammunition for fear that they would be used against the British. From the Indian point of view, such a policy was vindictive and, in practical terms, meant that it would be much more difficult for hunters to feed their families.

Other new trade policies also created antagonism. Present giving, an important prelude to trade and, therefore, friendly relationships, was at first dismissed by Amherst as "bribery." Sir William Johnston, the able superintendent of the Northern Indian Department and the English Board of Trade, tried to regularize the trade by establishing a system of standard price equivalents and by restricting the use of liquor. Neither worked thanks to the ignorance and arrogance of

British officials and the villainy of the traders. The latter were described by Lieutenant Governor Henry Hamilton at Detroit as "the most worthless vagabonds imaginable, they are fugitives (in general) from lower Canada or the colonies, who fly from their debtors or the law and being proficients in all sorts of vice and debauchery, corrupt the morals of the savages. . . ."[4] Without the family connections of the French traders or knowledge of Indian customs, the English were often brutal in their dealings and especially in the use of intoxicants in the trade. Although the use of "strong water" was not new, it reached unprecedented proportions during the last quarter of the eighteenth century. The traders justified its use by citing sharp competition between traders and Indian demand. In rum they had found the perfect trade good: cheap, addictive, and immediately consumed.

It must be recognized that intoxicants, particularly East Indian rum, were demanded by Indians. Beyond its "recreational" appeal, its use in native contexts was complex and at least two factors enhanced its desirability. First, liquor was a purely European commodity. Prior to their arrival, the Indians of eastern North America did not use either intoxicants or hallucinogens. They did, however, very highly value "out of body" experiences in trances, dreams, or visions. In fact, they went to great lengths to induce visions through privation and exposure. Liquor represented a powerful new shortcut to these same experiences, and it is perhaps for this reason that it was consumed in huge amounts by men and women, young and old.

The second factor is a symbolic one. Liquor came to represent the mutually dependent relationship between the European "fathers" and the Indian "children."[5] In the Algonquian idiom, intoxicating beverages were referred to as "milk" and they therefore expressed their wish for liquor in terms of suckling. Complaining of Major DePeyster's stinginess in issuing rum at Detroit, an Indian told him, "Father you have only given milk at one breast. . . ."[6] Thus, in a sense, liquor nurtured the social relationship between the father and his children. It also had a terrible effect.

The literature of the North American fur trade is replete with accounts of violence induced by liquor. Lake Superior trader John Long describes a typical "frolic" as follows.

The rum, being taken from my house, was carried to their wigwam, and they began to drink. The frolic lasted four days and nights; and not withstanding all our precautions (securing their guns, knives, and tomahawks) two boys were killed and six men wounded by three Indian women; one of the chiefs was also murdered, which reduced me to the necessity of giving several articles to bury with him, to complete the usual ceremony to their interment. These frolics are very prejudicial to all parties, and put the trader to a considerable expense, which nevertheless he cannot with safety refuse. On the fifth day they were all sober, and expressed great sorrow for their conduct, lamenting bitterly the loss of their friends.[7]

Since Indians probably saw drunkenness as more or less equivalent to a dream state, it was also involuntary and entailed disassociation of conscious action. With no means of cultural control over intoxicated behavior, violence and mayhem were accepted parts of the use of liquor. For the trader, the inherent dangers were part of doing business and not a moral concern. Benjimen Roberts wrote to Guy Johnson in 1767 that traders had left Michilimackinac in the dead of night for Green Bay with a large quantity of rum in order to pick up all their skins; he observed it was also likely to get all the traders scalped.[8] Enterprising trader John Long found he could avoid the violence of liquor use. To quiet a woman demanding rum, Long laced a glass of *scuttaywabo* (rum) with "forty drops of cantharides (Spanish fly) and the same quantity of laudanum (opium). After a repeat dose, the woman remained in a deep sleep for twelve hours. Long reported, "I have always found laudanum extremely useful; in general it may be considered an essential article in commerce with the Indians, as it proves the only method of overcoming their intoxicated senses and making the life of a trader more tolerable, by putting a stop to their impertinence."[9]

Cheated by traders, ravaged by the violence brought about by the use of intoxicants, unfairly treated in the restriction of firearms in trade, and humiliated by the contempt of English soldiers and administrators, Great Lakes Indians seethed in growing anger. Finally, in the spring of 1763, the resentment resulted in open war, a war led by the southern Ottawa war chief, Pontiac.

The Beaver War

During the summer of 1762, war belts distributed by Pontiac and Seneca war chief *Kysutha* circulated widely among the western Indians, urging a general attack to drive the British from the forts they had recently inherited from the French. The message gained general acceptance, especially among northern people who had limited contact with British goods and traders. At the south end of Lakes Huron and Michigan and in the intervening country, factions of the Huron, Ottawa, and Potawatomi and nearly all the Miami were inclined toward British interests. This was also true of many of the Iroquois, whose ranks had been increased in 1722 by the admission of the *Tuscarora* into the League and who thereafter were called the Six Nations. Nonetheless, most of these groups, increasingly concerned with the encroachment of colonial settlers, took up the cause of ridding the west of the British.

Between May 8 and June 22, 1763, every British fort west of the Alleghenies was attacked. Eastern Indians took Forts Presque Isle, Le Boeuf, and Venango on the upper Allegheny River and besieged Fort Pitt. In the west, local Indians captured Forts Michilimackinac, St. Joseph (Niles, Michigan), Miami (Ft. Wayne, Indiana), Sandusky, and Ouiatenon (Lafayette, Indiana) while Fort Edward Augustus (Green Bay, Wisconsin) was abandoned. Fort Detroit, the principal military establishment in the Great Lakes, was besieged by Pontiac and a combined force of southern Ottawa, Huron, Potawatomi, and Ojibwa from Saginaw and the Thames River in Canada. Knowing that they could not overpower these heavily armed positions manned by professional troops, the Indians used surprise and subterfuge to gain entry and to overwhelm the garrisons.[10]

The story of the siege of Detroit is well known thanks to several journals that preserve many details of the engagement. They also offer insights into Pontiac as a man and war leader and particularly into the difficult task he faced in organizing the interests of the fiercely independent Indian allies. That he was successful at all perhaps speaks more to the general dissatisfaction with the British and Virginian settlers in Kentucky and Ohio than of Pontiac's skill. Pontiac's genius should not, however, be underrated. In an arena where authority was practically nonexistent, and where pro- and anti-British arguments competed with pro- and anti-French arguments for a best fit with several different Indian objectives, any cooperation was remarkable. Pontiac and *Kysutha* managed, within a period of several months, to temporarily paralyze British interests over thousands of square miles. They also substantially altered the course of American history.

Pontiac's charisma was partially built on a widespread revitalization movement that was based upon the teachings of a Delaware Indian, *Noelin,* usually referred to simply as the "Delaware Prophet." In laying out his rationale for an attack on the English, Pontiac evoked a parable based upon *Noelin's* teaching. In the story, a supplicant, the Wolf, visits the Master of Life and, after several trials, receives instruction to promote general well-being among the Indians. The Wolf is told to reduce the use of liquor, to refrain from polygyny and adultery, to stop fighting among themselves, to put away sorcery, and, finally, to cast out the whites and all their goods. The Wolf is told by the Master of Life that "this land where you dwell I have made for you and not for others."[11]

Unquestionably, the message of *Noelin* contains elements of Christian influence, but it also appeals for the rekindling of traditional values, beliefs, and lifeways. In using this message, Pontiac attacked those behaviors that were most damaging to tribal social fabric as well as invoking behavior that would promote Indian unity against an external aggressor. Pontiac's hatred for the British was tempered by his understanding of the importance of trade and his insistence on friendship and political alliance with France. It was probably, in fact, not so much his affinity for the French that motivated Pontiac, but a necessity to choose between lesser evils. Certainly, just as Pontiac used the teachings of *Noelin,* he also used the promised reappearance of the French father, his "awakening," as a political and military inducement in recruiting allies and in holding them to his cause.[12] In this, Pontiac displayed a skill and determination that deserves our respect.

The Victory at Fort Michilimackinac

Roughly two hundred years after the initial capture of Fort Michilimackinac, a group of Indians, who no doubt counted in their number descendants of the Indian warriors who captured the place in 1763, again attacked. Now they protested the image of their ancestors

Bowon-diac (Pontiac)

Asked to name famous American Indian chiefs, most Americans would list Pontiac along with the likes of Crazy Horse and Sitting Bull. In fact, it is doubtful that any other native American is so prominent in our popular culture. Besides giving his name to the automobile that we encounter on nearly a daily basis, cities and towns in several states, street names, and subdivisions are often named for this prominent Ottawa. Given all this notoriety, it is surprising that so little is known about Pontiac as a person. Most of what we do know comes from the careful analysis by historian Howard Peckham, author of the book *Pontiac and the Indian Uprising.*

It would seem that Pontiac was born in the mid-1720s in an Ottawa village along the Maumee River where the city of Toledo, Ohio, now stands. While his father was Ottawa, there is reason to believe that his mother was a Miami; intermarriage between the southern Ottawa and the Miami was quite common at that time. Virtually nothing is known of Pontiac's early life, but presumably he grew to early manhood learning skills as a hunter, trapper, and warrior. Pontiac probably had several wives at various times but we know one, *Kantuckeegun,* by name. He also had two sons, *Skegenabe* and *Hebahkohum,* as well as other children of unknown identity. One of these, a small daughter, died of a disease in 1767. When he was not engaged in political activity, Pontiac supported his family in the normal fashion, that is, by hunting and trapping.

Pontiac first comes to notice in 1757, when he was a young war chief fighting against the English and Virginians around Ft. Duquesne on the upper Ohio. At this time, it is clear that his role in Ottawa politics was a very limited one. Certainly his rise to prominence is linked to warfare and closely associated with the transition from French to British control of the fur trade.

As a public figure, Pontiac was a person of energy, intelligence, and great oratorical skill. Shortly after the British arrived in Detroit in 1760, we begin to hear Pontiac's voice protesting British practices and policies. According to a contemporary French writer at Detroit, Pontiac was proud, vindictive, and easily offended. In fact, Pontiac himself condemned the arrogance of British military commanders in their treatment of him, as well as other Indians. Leading up to the outbreak of the Beaver War in May, 1763, Pontiac's anti-British stand became increasingly hostile. At some point, Pontiac decided that the best solution for the tribes would be to attack the British forts and to drive the English soldiers from their country. It was this position that attracted other southern Ottawa and eventually many Ojibwa, Potawatomi, and some of the Huron and northern Ottawa to his leadership. In advancing his cause, Pontiac extolled the virtues of alliance with the French as well as the revivalistic teachings of the Delaware prophet. It was, however, a pro-Indian appeal that was the backbone of his campaign and that earned him wide respect. As George Crogan, the British Indian agent, once remarked, Pontiac commanded more respect among other nations than most chiefs do among their own tribe.

Like most heroic figures, Pontiac also had a dark side. For example, he stabbed to death a prominent Illinois chief in the streets of Detroit in what was likely a drunken quarrel; he was also implicated in the drowning death of a seven-year-old captive French girl in 1764. He must also have been bitterly disappointed in the failure of his campaign against the British.

In 1766, Pontiac was forced to pledge his fidelity to Britain at a peace conference at Niagara that officially ended the Beaver War. He then returned to the Maumee valley but also spent considerable time in the Illinois country. There, in the village of Cahokia in 1769, he was killed by Illinois, perhaps in revenge for the chief he killed in Detroit. His body was taken to St. Louis for burial, although the specific grave site is unknown. On hearing of his death, Pontiac's old northern ally, the Ojibwa chief *Minavavana,* set out for Cahokia to extract the necessary revenge for his friend.

Pontiac, for all his considerable strengths and human failings, today enjoys a larger-than-life reputation woven of both fact and fancy. Some historians have judged him as a pawn of the forces of his time; others contend that he was a master politician of extraordinary skill. For whatever his personal assets, his political intentions, or however we may judge his success, Pontiac rose to the challenge of defending the interest of his people in a difficult hour. While the name Pontiac means something different to us all, Pontiac the man was, is, and deserves to be a hero of the Ottawa people.

portrayed in a reenactment of the event staged each Memorial Day
by citizens of Mackinaw City at the reconstructed fort. The title of
the pageant was "Massacre at Michilimackinac." One Ottawa remarked that, while he appreciated alliteration as well as anyone, he
found it strange that when white people won battles, great military
victories were touted, but when Indians won, they became massa-
cres. After initial resistance, the townsfolk retreated and the "Battle
of Fort Michilimackinac" was born. It is still to be seen each spring
before the gates of the reconstructed fort.

The original event began on June 4, 1763, with the celebration of
the English king George the Third's birthday. Among the day's activities was a game of *baggatiwag* (lacrosse) to be played between a
local team of Ojibwa and some visiting Sauk. As traders and soldiers
lounged against the outside of the stockade, scores of Indian players
dashed to and fro slashing at the ball amid shouts and the whack of
racket against racket and human flesh. Suddenly, the ball rose high
in the morning sun and sailed over the top of the stockade. In a flash,
players were in pursuit. As they surged through the open gates,
women who had concealed weapons beneath their blankets passed
them to the players. In seconds, an armed war party, under the
leadership of the famous war chief *Matchekewis,* was inside the fort
and took the British garrison totally by surprise.

Fighting was hand to hand; it was a fight of gunbutts, clubs,
knives, and hatchets. Shouts in Ojibwa and English mingled with the
plaints and screams of dying men. As the struggle subsided, seventy
British had been killed and the remaining soldiers and British traders
were taken prisoner. It should be noted that nearly three hundred
French Canadians lived within the fort—not one was harmed.
Clearly, the Ojibwa were not caught up in an antiwhite or anti-
European objective, but an anti-British one.

So many of the details of the battle of Michilimackinac are known
because of a journal kept by trader Alexander Henry, who two years
before had been sternly lectured by *Minavavana.* After successfully
hiding during the heat of the fighting, Henry was captured and later
released into the care of his adopted Ojibwa father, *Wawatam* ('Little
Goose').[13]

On June 6, Henry and four of the prisoners were stripped naked
and loaded in a canoe to be taken to Beaver Island. As the canoe
passed Waugoshance Point west of modern Mackinaw City, they

were hailed by some Ottawa who, incensed that they had been cheated out of participation in the taking of the fort, captured the prisoners. Immediately, they were loaded into Ottawa canoes and returned to Michilimackinac, where they were again held. Meanwhile, the Ojibwa and Ottawa counciled to split up the goods taken with the fort. In the ensuing exchange, the prisoners ended up with the Ojibwa under *Minavavana* or, as he was known to the British, the "Grand Salteaur." Fortunately for Alexander Henry, he was again rescued by *Wawatam* and spirited away to his lodge.

The next morning Henry awakened and peeked out of the wigwam and was horrified to see seven dead soldiers being dragged to a central area of the village where they were dismembered and thrown into kettles of boiling water. *Wawatam* soon departed with his bowl and spoon and returned with some soup from which a human hand protruded. Henry remarked that the kindly *Wawatam* did not appear to relish the war feast, but explained that the ceremony inspired the warriors with courage in attack and allowed him to meet death with fearlessness.[14]

Of the British traders captured in the battle, only one was killed. The twenty surviving officers and men, as well as those captured at Fort St. Joseph and those who had abandoned Fort Edward Augustus, eventually came into the hands of the Ottawa from L'Arbre Croche (Cross Village) and were taken to Montreal, where they were ransomed.

Similar stories emerged from the capture of the other British forts. The Indian victory had all but wiped away the British presence west of the Allegheny mountains. In truth, the tribes had no use for the fortifications and soon left them to their local French and mixed-blood communities. In the fall of 1763, Pontiac's siege of Detroit was finally broken as his "army" dissolved and the warriors returned to hunting to feed their families. Pontiac and his supporters *Minavavana* and *Matchekewis* of the northern Ojibwa, *Wasson* of the Saginaw Ojibwa, *Ninivois* and *Waskee* of the Potawatomi, and *Sekahos* of the Thames River Ojibwa won all the battles but lost the war.

As we might expect of these deeply religious people, Great Lakes Indians let the spirits guide their important decisions. After the conclusion of the Beaver War, Indian agent Sir William Johnston arranged for a huge Indian peace council to be held at Niagara in the summer of 1764. The Ojibwa of Mackinac, like every tribe in the

Tchissakiwin or Indian Jugglery

We will give here a short account or description of a certain species of
Indian jugglery, as still practiced by pagan Chippewa Indians. They
call this ceremony or incantation: *Tchissakiwin,* the lodge, in which it
is performed, *Tchissakan,* and the medicine-man, who performs the
incantation, *Tchissakiwinini.* The object of these incantations is to help
the sick, to know what medicines, roots, or herbs are to be used to cure
him; also to ascertain the whereabouts of absent husband, friends, and
others, or how they are getting along and when they are going to
return, or to revenge themselves or punish some enemy.

The lodge, *Tchissakan* is generally constructed of eight poles, 8–10
ft. in length, and stuck about two or three ft. into the ground. They are
generally very narrow, so that a man inside can easily reach across
from side to side. The lodge-poles are interlaced with willow branches
or something similar, forming a kind of octagon or circle. The sides are
covered with birchbark or blankets. The top is open and there four
shishigwan are hanging. These *shishigwan* are gourd bottles or small
tin cans, containing shot, which rattle whenever the lodge sways back
and forward. They also use them when performing superstitious rites
for curing the sick. Many a time have we heard the jing, jing, jing of
the shishigwan, when passing by a pagan Indian's wigwam.

The *Tchissakiwinini,* or medicine-man, is supposed to communicate
with the manitous or spirits, whom he consults in behalf of his Indian
friends as to past or future events, ailments of the sick, means of
recovery, etc.

First he goes around the *Tchissakan,* or juggler-lodge, muttering
some unintelligible words. At other times he thus addresses his peculiar
manitou, be it the buffalo-manitou, or the bear-manitou, or bird-mani-
tou: *"Rin, ke ği-jawenim iw tchi tchisak kuan; kin ki ği-mij mash-
kawisiwin tchi tchissakiian; ki nandomin jaigwa tchi bi-ijaian oma.
Anishinabeğ oma eiadjib nind anonigoğ wi-nondokwa tchi ğağigitoian."*

Translation of this invocation: "Thou hast helped me to do the
incantation-rites; thou hast given me the power to perform them. I
summon thee now to come here. The Indians here present employ
me to hear thee speak."

These words he says before entering the lodge, into which he de-
scends from the top. Sometimes, however, the medicine-man crawls
on all fours through an aperture into the lodge. Having entered he
sings, addressing his favorite manitou:

"*Bi-pindigen eiashing nin wigiwaming.*" "Come, enter my wig-wam." This song he repeats several times.

On the bottom of the lodge spruce-boughs are spread, on which the juggler lies, or kneels, bent forward, with his face towards the ground. The Indians sit around the lodge and a small fire is kept burning, into which tobacco is thrown from time to time by way of sacrifice to the manitous.

The coming of the manitous is announced by a loud, wheezing sound or sigh, as of a man tired after coming from a great distance, also by a loud stamp on the ground, like that of one jumping down from a great height, and by a violent blow from within against the side of the lodge. There are said to be two manitous present on such occasions. The head-manitou is called: *Mishike* the turtle, and he talks a language unintelligible to the Indians. The other manitou is the servant or messenger of *Mishike,* and he is called: *Ishkabewis.* As his name indicates, he is the messenger or servant of *Mishike;* he interprets the mysterious words of his master and does his errands.

When the manitous have manifested their presence, one of the outsiders stands up and addresses the manitous as follows:

"*Nin gi-anonanan nidjikiweinan tchi nandomineg; geget nind animisimin; anin ged-ijitchigeiang, jigwa wi-ishkwa-bimadisid waaw.*" We have employed our friend (the medicine-man) to summon you; truly we are suffering; what shall we do as that person there is on the point of dying? The sick man or woman is generally present or nearby in a wigwam. "*Gego na aiamagad ge-ondji-mino-aiapan?*" "Is there anything by which he may recover?" The chief manitou answers in a language, which the Indians do not understand, but which his servant, *Ishkabewis,* interprets. He says: "*Aiamagad ge-ijit chigeiegoban.*" "There is something you ought to do." The Indian on the outside of the lodge asks: "*Wegonen iw? Windamawishin iw,*" "What is it? Tell me!" The answer generally is: "*Ta-medewi, mi tchi mino aiad.*" "Let him perform the great medicine dance [i.e., let it be performed for him, for his recovery] then he will recover." Sometimes the manitous tell him the roots or medicines, which the sick man is to use in order to recover. Occasionally the outsiders inquire about their absent friends: "*Anin eji-aiad nin widigemagan? Anin iwapi ge-dagwishing!*" "How is my husband? When will he return?"

Perhaps an Indian is angry at someone and wants to injure him or revenge himself on him. We will then say:

"Waaw assema nind assa; ki wi-anonin tchi nanad bejiġ anishinabe, mi wedi aiad, o tchitchaġwan, - nin ġi-nish kiiġ aw anishinabe, mano oma ta-aiawan o tchitchaġwan tchi kotaġumind." "I put this tobacco (for a sacrifice) on the fire. I want to employ you to get a certain Indian; he is in such a place; he has offended me; let his soul be here to be tormented." He does not mention his enemy's name for prudential reasons. Then *Ishkabewis,* the messenger-manitou, does as he is told, and gets the soul of the offender. The latter is then asked by the offended party, the one who had employed the manitous: *"Wegonen ġa-ondji-ijitchiġeian?"* "Why did you do that?" The poor soul in the grip of *Ishkabewis* answers contritely: *"Rawin ondjita nin ġi-ijitchiġessi, mano jawenimishin, mano ninga-sagaam."* "I did not do it intentionally—did not mean to wrong you, offend you—have mercy on me; let me go out."

Madjiġabaw—"He who begins to stand"—an intelligent Indian of Bad River Reservation, Wis. told the writer once that his father was a great medicine man in his time and that one evening he was performing his jugglery. He said to his son, who was then about 6–7 years old: "My son, look!" The little fellow peered inside and saw many small fires or lights, like small stars, and he says they spoke a few moments, though not when he was looking at them.

The Bad River Indians tell of an Indian medicine man, who was tied very strongly with ropes in every possible manner. His hands were tied behind his back; he was bent together and tied up like a ball and thus bound was thrust into the lodge. As soon as the juggler was heard singing his incantation-song and the *shishigwan* began to rattle that were attached to the top of the lodge, he was at once freed from his ropes and he threw them out through the opening at the top of the lodge; none of the knots having been untied.

When the manitous enter the *Tchissakan*-juggler-lodge—it trembles and is violently moved backward and forward, and this rocking motion is kept up as long as the manitous are present.

—Fr. Chrysostom Verwyst, O. S. F.
Bad River, Wisconsin, 1892

northwest, were invited to attend. Naturally, the tribes were suspicious of the motives of the British. The Sault Ojibwa called upon a great shaman (*jessakkid*) to evaluate the invitation. Constructing a "shaking tent," the *jessakkid* evoked the presence of the Turtle Spirit, who was then questioned by the village chief. Would a trip to Niagara be safe or were the British preparing for war? Were there British troops in Niagara? Upon hearing the questions, the tent shook violently as the spirit departed to reconnoiter. After a half-hour of silence, the Turtle Spirit returned and, in an ancient tongue intelligible only to the *jessakkid,* reported that there were few soldiers at Niagara, but that the lower St. Lawrence was filled with boats containing troops. Should they go to Niagara? If they did so, the spirit answered, William Johnston would "fill their canoes with presents." And so they went, and the wisdom of the Great Turtle proved correct. This scene was likely repeated again and again in villages throughout the northwest; so it was that the Beaver War finally ended on the exchange of gifts and on the good advice of the spirits.

The Crown Proclamation of 1763

Even before the outbreak of the Beaver War, Great Lakes Indians were aware of the encroachment of colonial settlers on Indian lands in the Ohio valley. Perhaps an irritant to the upper Lakes tribes and a threat to the Five Nations who claimed much of this land as hunting grounds, the intrusion was an outrage to the Shawnee, Delaware, and Mingo, who made their homes north of the Ohio River (see map 4). The British military was also concerned because they knew that the tribes would not take such aggression peacefully. As a result, the Commissioners of Trade and Plantations authorized a new policy that prohibited white settlement beyond the crest of the Alleghenies.[15] Given the recent demonstration by the western Indians of their power to disrupt the British administration of the northwestern territories newly acquired through the Treaty of Paris (1763), the king issued the Crown Proclamation of 1763. The proclamation reaffirmed the "no settlement policy" and essentially made the Ohio valley–Great Lakes region a huge Indian hunting and trading preserve. Despite the fact that this territory was still recognized as Indian property by the right of aboriginal occupancy, influential colonists had heavily invested in western land speculation enterprises and began agitating for the repeal of the Crown Proclamation to no avail.[16]

As the tribes became hostile and began to raid American settlements, the colonists appealed to the military for protection that steadily grew more costly to the crown. As the British saw it, colonists would either have to support the army with taxes or they would be at the mercy of the Indians. George Grenville, the minister who implemented the infamous Stamp Act, thought it ironic that Britain should pay to defend those who denied that she had a right to tax them.[17]

Notwithstanding the danger and official restrictions on settlement, squatters continued to settle and expropriate Indian land and speculators continued to purchase land from Indians; the settlers, in turn, began to demand civil government. Fearing another general Indian war, parliament ultimately passed the Quebec Act in 1774. This act expanded the Province of Quebec from its western boundary on the Allegheny Crest to encompass all of the territory included in the old French province of Quebec, that is, the Northwest Territories. The act also provided for a system of civil governance and courts. In the same year, however, Lord Dunmore and an army of Virginians marched north to assert their right to settle "their side" (the south) of the Ohio. An ensuing battle with the Shawnee and Delaware set off a long and bitter struggle for the Ohio country. This warfare gradually drew in the Indian people of the upper Lakes and reshaped their political future.

Most likely, the outbreak of the American Revolution received little notice by the tribes of the upper Great Lakes. If it did, they probably would have equated it with their own occasional intertribal conflicts. At any rate, it had little direct impact on their history. It could be argued that the reverse is not true. In fact, Pontiac and the Potawatomi, Ottawa, and Ojibwa war leaders had a profound influence on the course of American history. The Crown Proclamation of 1763, which they were so instrumental in instigating, became one of the "intolerable acts" that set the American colonies on a collision course with Great Britain and the English king against his colonial children.

The shelter used by a *jessakkid* ('revealer of hidden truths'), Lac Courte Oreille, Wisconsin, circa 1900. (Photograph courtesy of the Smithsonian Institution.)

The *Jagonash* (British)

As heirs to the French interests, the first few British soldiers and traders who made their way to the northwest found themselves not only recent enemies of the local inhabitants, both *Anishnabeg* and French, but very much strangers confined to Detroit, Michilimackinac, and a few other remote trading forts. Most of these locales had small French settlements and it was to these communities that Indians continued to have their closest ties with the non-Indian world. Over one hundred years of contact with native people had produced frequent ties of blood and a great deal of bilingual fluency. Ojibwa/Ottawa and French not a combination of the two was the lingua franca of the fur trade. The fact that the Great Lakes region never produced a true pidgin language for the conduct of its extensive trade is an indication of the ability of a great many people to communicate in both the Algonquian dialects and French. Lacking kin ties to Indian communities and speaking neither French nor any of the Algonquian tongues, the British were, in many ways, starting a new wave of exploration. They were, of course, aided by maps and other information provided by French sources, yet initial English-language documents reveal ignorance of geography as well as Indian languages and customs. In these first sources, the Miami are "Tweeghtwees," the Ottawa the "Tawa," and the Potawatomi the "Poes."[18] Nonetheless, detailed descriptions of Indian life became more frequent, thanks in part to the memoirs of British traders and those who spent time as Indian captives. From these we know that, by the turn of the nineteenth century, the Great Lakes tribes had more or less occupied the territories that today are regarded as "traditional." Some groups had ancient roots in these territories and some were relative newcomers. In any case, the gross tribal categories used in English description, for example, "the Potawatomi," had little reality for the Potawatomi who continued to closely identify with families, clans, bands, and emerging political factions within these social groups.

By the beginning of the last quarter of the eighteenth century, the eastern or Missisauga Ojibwa had moved east and south around Lake Huron and come to occupy the territory vacated more than a century earlier by the Huron, Neutral, and Tobacco (see map 5). Small bands of these Ojibwa hunters occupied the hinterlands of the Ontario Peninsula, while those who resided on the shores of Lakes Ontario and

Erie became proficient gardeners. Other Missisauga bands settled the Lake St. Clair basin and moved up the Black River, eventually settling in the rich Saginaw valley.[19]

The Saulteaur Ojibwa, who occupied the northeastern tip of the Lower Peninsula south to Thunder Bay as well as the Upper Peninsula of Michigan and the shores of Lake Superior, continued to push westward against the Dakota (Sioux). South of Lake Superior, new communities were established at Lac du Flambeau and at Lac Courte Oreille, from which they fought for control of the St. Croix valley. Likewise, Ojibwa from Fond du Lac and other Lake Superior bands fought westward to Sandy and Leech lakes in Minnesota and eventually formed the Pillager Ojibwa, who carried the brunt of the war against the Dakota.[20] North of Lake Superior, the Ojibwa established themselves from the lake west to the prairie margins and beyond, increasing their access to prime beaver territory.[21]

From their initial foothold north of the Straits of Mackinac, the Ottawa shifted their base in order to better supply fur brigades leaving Fort Michilimackinac, which was the hub of the eighteenth-century fur trade. Early in the eighteenth century they founded several villages along the coastline of northwestern lower Michigan where fertile soil and a moderate climate was favorable for corn agriculture. With their success as farmers, traders, and fishermen, their numbers grew until the coast from the Straits of Mackinac to Little Traverse Bay was covered with closely spaced Ottawa villages. The most famous of the Ottawa towns was *Waganagisi* ('Crooked Tree'), which today we know by the French form, L'Abre Croche. The northern Ottawa pushed even farther south along the coast, establishing major villages on Grand Traverse Bay and on the Manistee and Muskegon rivers and finally settled the Grand River valley. Ottawa historian Andrew Blackbird relates that Ottawa tradition tells that this expansion was at the expense of the Mascouten.[22]

At about the same time that the Ottawa first settled northwestern Lower Michigan, other Ottawa groups along with the Huron established communities in the Saginaw and Detroit River valleys. Fission in this community resulted in a third major Ottawa settlement at Sandusky Bay and in the Maumee valley (see map 5).

The area around Green Bay continued to be held by the Menominee, who were one of the few among all the Great Lakes tribes who managed to continuously hold their pre-European territory. Further south and west were the Winnebago and, on the Wisconsin River, the Sauk and Fox.[23]

The Potawatomi, having moved east, expanded their domain into the southern part of Lower Michigan, establishing villages in the rich prairie openings and bottomlands of the Kalamazoo and St. Joseph rivers east to the Huron River and the western shore of Lake Erie. They also occupied the shore of Lake Michigan west to Green Bay as well as northeastern Illinois and northern Indiana. Over time, these settlements tended to identify more closely with either the St. Joseph bands or those known as the Potawatomi of the Huron in eastern Michigan.

It should be acknowledged that these "tribal territories" represented only concentrations of Indians of particular ethnic affiliation. A more detailed map of village location such as those presented in the *Atlas of Great Lakes Indian History* shows that villages of many different affiliations often existed close together.[24] In fact, a more fine-grained analysis would reveal that any given village would likely have representatives of several tribal groups because marriage between people of neighboring villages was common. Thus, "tribal territories" were not political domains in the modern sense.

To be sure, however, territories had economic reality because their inhabitants were dependent upon the resources found in such territories for subsistence. Their residents were also strongly linked to the landscape emotionally, cherishing landmarks of special historical and religious significance. It is no surprise, therefore, that territories were defended despite the fact that Indian people felt no sense of land ownership per se.

Life in the Indian villages of the Great Lakes has been described by a number of English visitors, of which our friend Alexander Henry is a good example. Following his release into the hands of *Wawatam*, Henry spent the winter of 1763–64 as an adopted son and an active partner in the day-to-day life of the *Wawatam* family.[25]

In preparation for the forthcoming winter, the *Wawatam* family journeyed from Mackinac to St. Martins Island to secure a supply of sturgeon. This accomplished, they headed south by canoe, stopping to visit the village of *Waganagisi* (Cross Village) where they obtained dried corn from the Ottawas. Proceeding south, they came to the Big Sable River, the gateway to their family hunting territory in the interior. At the river's mouth, *Wawatam* sacrificed a dog and appealed to the spirits for favorable hunting. From their first camp fifteen miles above the mouth (near present day Freesoil in Mason County), they hunted deer, bear, racoon, beaver, and martin as well as fish and waterfowl.

On the first of November, the family held a renewal feast, similar to the ones still held by Indians today, called a "ghost supper." *Wawatam* made an hour-long speech calling upon the spirits of his dead ancestors and friends to be present and to partake with the family in a feast of boiled corn. At the conclusion of the ceremony a new fire was kindled, pipes were smoked, and singing and dancing lasted the entire night.

Moving slowly east, the family hunted its way into the wilds of central Lower Michigan, probably to the vicinity of Houghton Lake. One day in January Henry found a huge, hibernating bear, which he killed. Once the bear was dead, his adopted Indian mother took the animal's head in her hands and, stroking and kissing it, begged pardon for taking its life. Addressing the bear as "grandmother," she requested that its spirit not blame the Indians since, in reality, it had been killed by an Englishman. The bear's head was later decorated with silver arm bands and wampum belts and was placed on a special scaffold in *Wawatum*'s lodge with a quantity of tobacco near its nose. Thus, the bear spirit joined in a feast given in its honor. As *Wawatum* explained to the bear, "The necessity under which men labored, thus to destroy their friends." He concluded by saying that "this misfortune was unavoidable since it was the only way for men to subsist." That said, the family feasted on the flesh of the bear.

Hunting continued during the late winter until at last it was time to pack the huge load of winter furs to market at Michilimackinac. On the way, the family paused with other related families that had wintered near them to make maple sugar somewhere along the Lake Michigan shore. While encamped here in the month of April, the camp was terrorized by a mountain lion that had attacked and carried off children at times.

The band was also very apprehensive about an anticipated attack by the British in retaliation for the taking of Fort Michilimackinac. In council they consulted Henry, whom they believed to be capable of foreknowledge of events and able to dream of all things going on at a distance. When Henry pleaded ignorance of the whereabouts and intentions of the British, the Ojibwa did not doubt his supposed power of clairvoyance, but were suspicious that he was concealing his knowledge.

The *Chemokmon* (Americans)

To this very day, the Indian descendants of Algonquian speakers refer to non-Indian Americans as *Chemokmon*. The term relates to the word *kitchimokomon* ('big knife') and apparently arose out of the first terrifying encounters between Great Lakes warriors and mounted, saber-wielding Virginia and Kentucky militia in the years shortly before the American Revolution. From that time until late in the eighteenth century, the western tribes were locked into a series of violent encounters with Americans that helped shape the nineteenth-century American stereotypes of Indians as savage, warlike barbarians. This stereotype, in turn, strongly influenced the formation and execution of American federal Indian policy. The same encounters angered and confused Indians, who became forever suspicious of the motives and veracity of a people who were willing to so arrogantly and self-righteously possess the earth and to dispossess its rightful occupants without sympathy or understanding.

As an aspect of civil government required by the Quebec Act, Henry Hamilton was appointed as lieutenant governor and Indian agent at Detroit. From that strategic post he was able to orchestrate Indian raiding on the Ohio frontier. As part of his campaign, Hamilton modified the ancient Algonquian custom of taking war trophies by instituting a bounty system. Originally, such trophies were taken by victorious warriors to strengthen themselves because the trophy was thought to contain the fighting spirit of the slain enemy. Now, Hamilton began to pay cash for the trophies, particularly in the form of scalps, although he also paid a ransom for war captives. This practice, which naturally outraged American frontiersmen, who labeled Hamilton "the hair buyer," probably actually saved lives because higher bounties were paid for prisoners. One benefactor of Hamilton's policy was Daniel Boone, who, with twenty-six of his men, was ransomed at Detroit in 1778.[26]

As hatred for the *Chemokmon* invaders increased, so did the ties between the British and the tribes strengthen. This was not, however, true in all quarters. The Potawatomi of the Milwaukee area and, to perhaps a lesser degree, those of the St. Joseph valley of southwestern Michigan maintained strong ties with the French communities at Green Bay, around Fort St. Joseph, and in the Illinois country. The Americans had captured the Illinois country, and George Rodgers Clark appealed to the northern tribes as common allies of the French and Spanish with whom the Potawatomi traded at St. Louis. In 1781, a Spanish force from St. Louis along with Potawatomi under *Sigenak* (Blackbird) and *Nakiyowin* (Wind Spirit) marched into southwestern Michigan and, by convincing the local Potawatomi to remain neutral, attacked and captured the British garrison at Fort St. Joseph. The next day, the Spanish retreated back to the Mississippi.[27]

Revenge, booty, or hatred were not always the motives for Indian raiding. In the winter of 1788–89, a woman of the Saginaw Ojibwa, *Negigwoskitchmequa* (Otter Woman), lost a young son to disease. Although she also had several daughters, a young son *Benaissa* (the Bird), and an older son *Kishkauko* (the Crow), she suffered cruelly from her loss. In the spring, she convinced her husband, *Manitogezik* (Enlightened Spirit), that they must replace the dead child. *Manitogezik* along with *Kishkauko* and two other warriors proceeded south through eastern Ohio until they arrived at the confluence of the Big Miami and the Ohio rivers. Crossing the Ohio at night, they found an isolated settler's cabin occupied by an immigrant Virginian preacher, John Tanner, and his family. The Ojibwa watched from concealment until they saw their chance to snatch an eleven-year-old boy playing behind the cabin. The captive was soon spirited back across the Ohio and north to Saginaw, eluding would-be rescuers. On seeing the frightened boy, *Negigwoskitchmequa* began to cry and, at the same time, began hugging and kissing him. The next day, an adoption or replacement ceremony was held at the grave of the dead son. *Manitogezik*'s family had brought presents of sugar, corn, beads, cloth, and tobacco that were given away to the unrelated families (other clans) of the village. The captive, John Tanner, Jr., was now a son and was later rechristened as *Shawshawwabenase* (Falcon). Like many captives who survived the trauma of kidnapping and mistreatment at the hands of his captors, Tanner was eventually socialized into tribal society. This was, however, an incomplete process and although Tanner was able to function in both Indian and American frontier society he never seemed successful in either place. He remained among the Indians for many years, and, like his adopted brother *Kishkauko,* became a figure of prominence and controversy on the American frontier.[28]

Another story of the terrible years of the Ohio wars involved a group of Delaware and Shawanee refugees who had been converted to Christianity by Moravian missionaries in several towns in the Tuscarawas and Muskingum River valleys of southeastern Ohio. Although neutral in the struggle around them, they were deported to Sandusky by the British. After great suffering, including the slaughter of ninety men who had returned to the Tuscarawas to try to obtain provisions, the British permitted the Moravian Indians to settle near Detroit. Obtaining leave from the Ojibwa of Lake St. Clair, about a hundred Indian brethren under the leadership of Reverend David Zeisberger established a colony on the Clinton River, near the present city of Mt. Clemens. Until their welcome ran out in 1786, this small colony, called New Gnadenhütten, supplied meat and other collected and manufactured products such as canoes to the population of Detroit in exchange for flour and corn. In 1785, they cut an overland road twenty-three miles to Detroit and this first interior road in Michigan was soon called the Moravian road.[29]

After the Revolution, the Moravian community again became refugees and finally settled at Fairfield, Ontario, near Chatham, where their town was again ravaged during the battle of the Thames during the War of 1812.

The War for the Ohio Country

Following the second treaty of Paris, which concluded the American Revolution in 1783, the new American government fell heir to British interests in the northwest. Remote and weak, the Americans could not dislodge the British from Detroit and Mackinac, where they remained and continued to influence Indian decision making. Rich now in land but its treasury drained by years of war, the Washington administration set out to convert western land to money. In a series of treaties at Fort Stanwix (1784), Fort McIntosh (1785), and Fort Finney (1786), Americans claimed purchase of large blocks of Indian land. Much of the selling was done by Indians who did not occupy the land, or who did not legitimately represent those who did. When the rightful occupants were present, they were usually woefully outnumbered.

With settlement pressure on the lands north of the Ohio River increasing rapidly, the Congress of the United States was forced to provide an orderly means of settlement and a process for establishing civil government. The result was the Northwest Ordinance of 1787. Given strong Indian contention for the same land, Congress apparently felt compelled to give lip service to their interests by inserting the following paragraph into the ordinance.

The utmost good faith shall always be observed towards the Indians; their lands and property shall never be taken from them without their consent; and in their property rights and liberty they never shall be invaded or disturbed unless in just and lawful wars authorized by congress; but laws founded in justice and humanity shall, from time to time, be made, for preserving peace and friendship with them.

The effect of the land cessions and border hostility in southeastern Ohio was a gradual retreat of the Shawnee, Delaware, Mingo, and Miami to the north and west, where they established a second line of defense along the Maumee and Wabash rivers. These settlements consisted of clusters of villages on the portage between the two rivers near modern Fort Wayne, Indiana, and on the upper Sandusky River.[30] The Miami and Shawnee established their villages on the tributaries of the Wabash; the most important of these was the trading center of *Kekionga*. The Sandusky villages were mainly occupied by Wyandot and Ottawa. These groups, as well as Detroit area Potawatomi and Ottawa and occasional Ojibwa war parties, now stepped up their raiding on the Ohio and Kentucky settlements. Likewise, American militia units operating from Pittsburgh, Cincinnati, and Vincennes struck north, burning villages and corn crops in the Wabash and Maumee valleys. The Washington administration sanctioned these raids as a means of "chastising" the Indians and soon mounted organized military expeditions against the Maumee-Wabash line.[31]

As warfare became more intense, Indians were increasingly supplied by the British from Detroit. The British were cautious in this regard, however, for fear that their support would be considered an act of war.[32] As Henry Hamilton told the assembled tribes at Detroit, "The King has ordered me to give you an ax (war hatchet), he has not as yet told me to bring it, whenever he does my children shall know it immediately."[33] They were also advised by loyalist field agents married to Indian women, including Alexander McKee, Matthew Elliot, and the Girty brothers. These Indian allies were reviled along the American frontier as "traitors and renegades."[34]

During the years between 1786 and 1794, at least seven major military expeditions were sent against the Indians of the so-called Ohio Confederacy; most ended in disaster. In 1790, General Josiah Harmar attacked *Kekionga* and the Miami towns with 320 U.S. regulars and 1,100 Kentucky militia. He was met by the Miami war chief *Meshekmnoquah* (Little Turtle), the Shawnee war chief Blue Jacket, and *Buckongahelas,* a Delaware war leader with 1,040 warriors including Michigan Ottawa, Ojibwa, and Potawatomi, who carried the left side of the line in the Indian attack. The Americans suffered 270 men killed in a battle that sent the army retreating south in panic. The next summer and autumn, General Arthur St. Clair marched north with 1,400 regulars and was handed one of the worst defeats in U.S. military history. The assembled tribesmen under Little Turtle's leadership killed 630 American soldiers and wounded 280 more.[35]

These campaigns were waged in the tradition of tribal warfare. Both sides killed without mercy, tortured prisoners, and mutilated the dead. Both took prisoners for ransom and both burned the homes and crops and slaughtered the domestic stock of the other. With the exception of the fact that the Indian combatants were fighting to defend their homes and families from invaders on their own territory, the two sides were on an approximately equal footing. The lack of training and discipline among the American conscripts and militia cancelled out the advantage usually held by a disciplined army over warriors fighting on their own authority. Thanks to the British, the Indians were also fairly well supplied and were also able to raise a sufficient force to meet the enemy. In one regard, the Indians had clear superiority, that is, in leadership and tactical skill. Little Turtle and Blue Jacket were simply able to organize, collect intelligence, and deploy their fighters more efficiently than their American counterparts.

Reeling from the disastrous defeats dealt to Harmer and St. Clair by the combined Indian tribes and the humiliating presence of British forces and agents operating on "its soil," the American government resolved to renew the Ohio Indian war with vigor. After much consideration, Anthony Wayne was appointed major general commanding the Army of the United States and ordered to punish the Ohio Indians. He immediately began preparations for a campaign against the Wabash-Maumee line.

In the meantime, a more conciliatory position was developing among the tribes, given that much of the southern Ohio was already abandoned. The moderate faction led by Joseph Brant and the Iroquois urged negotiation with the Americans for a boundary line north of the Ohio River.[36] This position was supported, to some degree, by Little Turtle, who had come to suspect promised military help from the British even though, by 1794, they had constructed Fort Miami on the lower Maumee. This heavily armed British outpost, built to support Indian operations and to defend the southern approach to Detroit, was an outrage to the Americans, who viewed its construction as a premeditated act of aggression.

As Wayne's legions moved north from the headwaters of the Wabash, then down the Auglaize to its junction with the Maumee during the summer of 1794, a force of about 1,600 warriors was forming to meet him. At least half of these were Ottawa and Ojibwa from northern Michigan. Food supply became a very difficult problem for such a large concentration of men. As they advanced toward Wayne's columns, the warriors needed to procure an estimated 200 deer and several hundred turkeys for food each day.[37]

The initial Indian attack by a combined force of Potawatomi, Ottawa, and Ojibwa was directed against Fort Recovery, built by Wayne at the site of St. Clair's defeat. Badly shot up in a direct assault on the pallisaded fort, the northern warriors became angry over the lack of support on the part of the local Shawnee and Delaware. The Huron River Potawatomis as well as most of the Ottawa and Ojibwa returned to their villages in disgust, reducing Indian forces by a third.[38] Many of the St. Joseph River Potawatomi remained, and by the time Wayne advanced up the Maumee a month later some of the northern Indians had returned.

Battle was now joined a short distance upstream from Fort Miami at a place known as Fallen Timbers because of old windfalls and heavy undergrowth. Such a locality provided an advantageous site for the ambush tactics favored by Indians and it also neutralized the danger of a cavalry charge by saber-wielding soldiers. After several days of fasting in anticipation of battle, many Indian warriors had returned to Fort Miami to be resupplied. The center of the remaining Indian line consisted of southern Ottawa led by the war chiefs Little Otter and *Equshawa*. At the approach of Wayne's legion, the warriors fired a musket barrage and charged forward only to be stalled and thrown back by an American advance. In the ensuing confusion of battle, the Indians became disorganized and were routed by a bayonet charge.[39]

In many regards, the fight at Fallen Timbers was no more than another in a long series of skirmishes; the Indians lost forty men while the Americans had thirty killed and one hundred wounded.[40] Yet Wayne's action subsequent to the battle and the lack of response on the part of Major William Campbell, commander of the British forces at Fort Miami, totally demoralized the Indian warriors. As the retreating tribesmen made their way to Fort Miami, they found, to their utter disbelief, that their British allies had closed the pallisade gates in their faces. Adding insult to injury, General Wayne boldly proceeded to burn Indian and trader dwellings and the mature corn crop under the cannons of the British fort.

Although both commanders knew that conflict between them would lead to war between the United States and England, the apparent cowardice and treachery of the British compared to Wayne's bravado destroyed Indian confidence in British support for a continuing struggle. It was clear to Indian leaders that the British had used them to promote their own ends. As General Wayne put it, "These events must produce a conviction in the minds of the savages that the British have neither the power nor inclination to afford them the protection they had been taught to expect."[41]

The Treaty of Greenville

In September, 1794, Anthony Wayne issued a summons for the tribes to meet him to discuss a peace with the United States.[42] The resulting congress took place in July and August of 1795 at Greenville, Ohio. The Treaty of Greenville was the first important treaty in a long series of agreements between the United States and the tribes of the upper Lakes. In several ways it set precedents for those that followed.

The Treaty of Greenville was both a treaty of peace between the tribes and the United States as well as a treaty of land cession.[43] The tribes, some with little or no real claim to the land in question, agreed to cede the southern two-thirds of Ohio as well as a large number of strategic locations throughout the Old Northwest that had earlier been the sites of French and British settlements. Included were Detroit, Sandusky, Chicago, Mackinac Island, Michilimackinac, and Bois Blanc Island, the latter a voluntary gift of the Ojibwa. In exchange, the United States relinquished claim to all other land in the northwest and agreed to pay the tribes $20,000 in goods every year—forever. Indians retained the right to use their lands free of "molestation" by the United States or its citizens with the understanding that, if they should wish to sell any of it in the future, the United States would be the sole purchaser. The treaty gave Indians the right to drive off settlers who encroached on their land "in such a manner as they shall think fit." Indians were also at liberty to hunt upon ceded lands as long as they "demean themselves peacefully."

The treaty also provided for the regulation of Indian trade by requiring licensing of resident traders by the president. Finally, the treaty called for the full exchange of prisoners and, wisely, outlawed private revenge as a result of the recent wars. Clearly, the Americans were learning how to "cover the dead."

Among the chiefs who were instrumental in negotiating the Treaty of Greenville were New Corn, *Michimang, Asimethe,* Sun or *Gizes,* and *Okia* of the Potawatomi; Blue Jacket and Red Pole for the Shawnee; *Tarke* or Crane of the Wyandot; *Bukongehelas, Peketelemund,* and *Tetabokshke* of the Delaware; *Agooshaway* for the Ottawa; and the Ojibwa chiefs *Mashipinashiwish* (Bad Bird) and *Masass.*

Meshekimnoquah (Little Turtle), the leader of the "Ohio Confederacy," represented the Miami, and, although he believed the agreement to be totally unfair, he deported himself with as much dignity in peace as he had skill in war. Apparently Little Turtle came to the Greenville treaty convention armed with a copy of the Northwest Ordinance, for he remarked to General Wayne:

> Here are papers which have been given to me by General Washington, the great chief of the United States. He told me they should protect us in the possession of our lands, and that no white person should interrupt us in the enjoyment of our hunting grounds, or be permitted to purchase any of our towns or land

from us; that he would place traders among us, who would deal fairly. I wish you to examine these papers.[44]

In this first important treaty with the *Chemokmon,* the Indian participants addressed Wayne not as "father" but as "elder brother." Clearly, they still regarded the British king as "father," despite the fiasco at Fort Miami. Wayne, in the ceremonial form necessary for occasions of importance, presented himself as the war chief of the "fifteen fires," that is, the fifteen states of the American Republic. It seems to have been in this same context that the first mention is made to the council of the "three fires," that is, the loose political confederation of lake Indians that included the Potawatomi, Ottawa, and Ojibwa.

Ottawa chief *Augooshaway,* addressing the assembled Indians, offered the red stone calumet pipe of peace to the Shawnee, saying, "All you nations present, you know this to be the calumet of the three fires. It is six years (about 1789) since it was sent from the north to Michilimackinac, to the three fires who live at the gate [the Miami village, now Fort Wayne, Indiana] to be presented to the Wyandot, Delaware, and Shawnee, with an injunction always to hide it when anything bad was in motion, but to display it when any good was contemplated. You all know the importance of this sacred token to peace among us Indians."[45]

Little else is known of this calumet or the origin of the council of the three fires other than Chief *Masass*'s hint at Greenville that it did not originate on "this little lake near us, [Erie] but from the great Lake Superior home of great Ojibwa chiefs and warriors." Like most of us, *Massass* could not resist a plug for his home country.

One provision of the Greenville treaty caused great commotion on the Great Lakes borderland, the requirement that Indian traders be licensed by the United States. This was regarded by the British and Canadian fur traders as an attempt to move them out of the extremely profitable trade in favor of American newcomers. The Jay Treaty had, of course, already secured their right to trade on U.S. soil and to cross the border. Although this problem was resolved in favor of the British traders, who continued to monopolize the trade, the Indians, who also had free access across the border, used this advantage to pose a problem for the United States. By continuing friendly relations with the British, who had to abandon their posts on American soil by June, 1796, the Great Lakes tribes were able to gain political leverage with the Americans and considerable economic benefit from both England and the United States.

American Occupation Begins

In the summer of 1796, American troops took possession of the forts at Detroit and Mackinac and thus began the American occupation of the upper Great Lakes. It was, however, a very tenuous occupation at best. Although they abandoned "American soil" by condition of the Jay Treaty, the British did not move far. New posts were established at Malden, across the river from Detroit, and at Fort St. Joseph, on St. Joseph's Island, commanding the St. Marys River and thereby the entrance to Lake Superior. From these equally strategic locations, they maintained regular contact with their Indian allies and British citizens who remained as traders on the American side of the border. For their part, most of the Potawatomi, Ojibwa, Ottawa, Menominee, and other lakes tribes, though suspicious of British interests and angered at the Fort Miami betrayal, saw British alliance as preferable to close cooperation with the *Chemokmon*.

The British at Forts Malden and St. Joseph began to step up gift giving to Indians who visited these forts on an annual basis. Originally, gift exchanges between Indians and the commandants of the forts had been a custom in which the tribes demonstrated good will and friendship by giving post commanders presents of corn, meat, grease, and other supplies while the commandant, in turn, presented powder, shot, blankets, decorative items, and rum as a sort of rent.[46] Now, however, to the great delight of the Indians, the gift giving took a new turn, involving an expensive competition between the British and Americans for their loyalty. At Fort Malden (Amherstburg) and at Fort St. Joseph, the British handed out gifts worth £7,855, an enormous expense in 1799.[47] Among the gifts given were silver arm bands, bracelets, ear bobs, brooches and gorgets, glass beads, blankets, buttons, cloth, lace and bunting, guns, powder, flints and shot, kettles, knives and axes, fishing hooks and lines, needles, scissors and thread, ribbon, saddles and bridles, traps, tomahawks, vermillion, hats, files, grindstones, medals, and trunks, presumably in which to carry away the loot.

The political intent of this competitive gift giving was apparent in the fact that more and better gifts were given to Indians that the British and Americans perceived to be authority figures. Thus, "chiefs" and "chiefs' ladies" received more than "common warriors" and "Indian women." In fact, an age-graded series was created to dispense gifts from the oldest people to the youngest children.[48] Beyond these attempts to manipulate legitimate chiefs, both British and American commanders used commissions in attempts to create "chiefs." For example, Captain William Doyle, at Fort Mackinac in 1796, issued the following certificate to *Keehwitamigistcan,* an Ojibwa at Sault Ste. Marie.

> In consequence of your attachment to the English of which you have given repeated proofs by voluntarily coming forward in Defense of the traders residing at the Sault Ste. Mary when their lives and property were in Emminent danger from open and daring attacks of some Evil disposed Indians, I hereby constitute and appoint you a chief of the Chippewa Indians residing at the Said Sault Ste. Mary.[49]

As Colonel Alexander McKee explained to his superior, "By this means Chiefs may be made and unmade at pleasure and therefore indefinitely increased or diminished at the direction of every succeeding commanding officer. . . . "[50] Such commissions must have been a great joke among the Indians, who, of course, maintained their traditional mode of political leadership. The fact that such blatant attempts were made to manipulate Indians and the way these attempts were made shows a gross misunderstanding on the part of both British and American military men and civil authorities of the principles upon which Indian society was organized. The receipt of more goods by genuine chiefs would have simply provided an additional way for them to demonstrate their generosity by giving it all away. "Made chiefs" would gain no additional respect as a result of their favored treatment. It is, nonetheless, worthy of mention that the gift-giving cycle and the fur trade did affect opportunities for individuals, particularly bilingual persons, to enhance their prestige as intermediaries between the Indian and non-Indian worlds. Frequently, such roles were filled by the children of white fathers and Indian mothers.

NOTES

1. Two early, though still useful, texts on the British occupation of the Old Northwest are Russell 1939 and Kellogg 1935. A discussion of the encounter between Rodgers, Crogan, and Pontiac is in Russell 1939, 11.
2. See Henry 1969.
3. It is not known whether the scheme to infect Indians with smallpox was actually put into effect. It is known that upper Great Lakes Indians fighting in the Ohio valley did carry the disease to their villages. Blackbird (1887, 9–10) relates a similar story, contending that smallpox was passed to the Ottawa by means of infected material in a small box sold to them in Montreal. Parkman (1883, 39–41) discusses the documentary evidence for Amherst's suggestion and Bouquet's reply.
4. Hamilton to Dartmouth, August 29, 1776, in Haldimand Papers, *Michigan Pioneer and Historical Collections*, 10:268.
5. See B. White 1982.
6. De Peyster to Haldimand, November 3, 1781, in Haldimand Papers, *Michigan Pioneer and Historical Collections*, 10:537.
7. Thwaites 1904, 93.
8. Roberts to Johnson, August 20, 1767, in Haldimand Papers, *Michigan Pioneer and Historical Society*, 10:225.
9. Thwaites 1904, 149–50.
10. The widespread warfare between various Indian groups and the British during the summer of 1763 has been the subject of much scholarly discourse as well as popular writing. Francis Parkman (1883) called the warfare the "conspiracy of Pontiac" and credited the Ottawa war chief with masterminding coordinated Indian resistance to the British. Howard Peckham's study of the same events (1947) led him to the conclusion that Pontiac had far less control over the "Indian uprising." Recently, Gregory Dowd has provided a new and insightful discussion of "Pontiac's War" (1990). War, uprising, or conspiracy? In my discussion, Pontiac's own description is used, "The Beaver War" (Peckham 1947, 111). Allen W. Eckert's historical novel, *The Conquerors* (1970), is based upon these same events.
11. Burton 1912, 28–31.
12. See Dowd 1990.
13. Henry 1969, 77–104.
14. Henry 1969, 103.
15. Sosin 1975, 62.
16. Sosin 1975, 65.
17. Sosin 1975, 64.
18. *The Handbook of North American Indians*, Vol. 15, *The Northeast*,

edited by Bruce Trigger (1978), provides a complete synonymy for each of the groups under discussion. The reader is referred to Clifton (1977, 741), Rodgers (1978, 768), and Feest and Feest (1978, 785), which all illustrate the bewildering variation in the names assigned to these groups by French, English, Americans, and other groups of Indians. Considerable confusion also results from the phonetic rendering of Indian words into these languages and, in turn, their modern English versions.

19. See Ferris 1989; Denke 1990.
20. See Warren 1984.
21. However, as Greenberg and Morrison (1982) have shown, much of the alleged movement of Ojibwa into the northern boreal forest was not really a movement of people but resulted from the more general application of the term "Ojibwa" to groups that were previously known by local names.
22. Blackbird 1887, 90–91.
23. Parker 1976, 75–76.
24. H. Tanner 1987, maps 20, 25.
25. A readable version of Henry's journal has been published by the Mackinac Island State Park Commission under the title *Attack at Michilimackinac,* edited by David Armour (1971).
26. H. Hamilton to G. Carleton, April 25, 1778, in Haldimand Papers, *Michigan Pioneer and Historical Collections,* 9:435.
27. Clifton 1977, 164–66; Council Held with the Potawatomis of St. Joseph, Detroit, March 11, 1781, *Michigan Pioneer and Historical Collections,* 10:453.
28. See J. Tanner 1956.
29. H. Ford 1888, 107–15; Bliss 1885, 262–63.
30. H. Tanner 1987, maps 14, 18.
31. Sword 1985, 131.
32. Sword 1985, 122–23. Ultimately, the supply and provisioning of Indians became not only expensive, but the use of rum also created a controversy in British policy. General Haldimand reported that the expenditure for rum at Detroit "was beyond his comprehension since it brought poverty and disease to the Indian families." In 1779, it is estimated that 17,502 gallons of rum were consumed by Indians at Detroit and, in 1780, 1,800 gallons were used by those at Michilimackinac (Russell 1939, 81). When Haldimand tried to reduce the flow of British rum, Lt. Governor Patrick Sinclair wrote from Michilimackinac on February 5, 1782, "The Indians cannot be deprived of nearly their usual quantity of rum, however destructive it is, without creating much discontent" (*Michigan Pioneer and Historical Collections,* 10:549).

33. Council held at Detroit, June 17, 1778, Lieutenant Governor Henry Hamilton, in the Haldimand Papers, *Michigan Pioneer and Historical Collections*, 9:446.
34. Sword 1985, 126.
35. Sword 1985, 195.
36. Sword 1985, 241.
37. Sword 1985, 271.
38. Edmunds 1978, 30.
39. Nelson 1985, 266.
40. General Wayne's Orderly Book, August 20, 1794, *Michigan Pioneer and Historical Collections*, 34:545–46.
41. General Wayne's Orderly Book, 34:547.
42. General Wayne to Indian Sachems, September 12, 1794, Copies of Papers on File in the Dominion Archives of Ottawa, Canada, Pertaining to the Relations of the British Government with Indian Tribes in North America and to Military Posts and Marine Interest of the Great Lakes, 1762–1799, *Michigan Pioneer and Historical Collections*, 12:143.
43. Treaty of Greenville, 4th Cong., 1st sess., December 9, 1795 (see Cochran 1972, 4:150).
44. Cochran 1972, 4:169.
45. Cochran 1972, 4:162.
46. Endorsed Outlines of a Reformation of Expenses in the Indian Department, in Haldimand Papers, *Michigan Pioneer and Historical Collections*, 10:555.
47. Requisition for Stores, Copies of Papers on File in the Dominion Archives at Ottawa, Canada, Pertaining to the Relations of the British Government to Indians, *Michigan Pioneer and Historical Collections*, 12:285–89.
48. State of Equipment Commonly Given to Indians, Copies of Papers on File in the Dominion Archives at Ottawa, Canada, Pertaining to the Relations of the British Government to Indians, *Michigan Pioneer and Historical Collections*, 12:264.
49. Copy of a Commission by Major Doyle to *Keehwitamigistcan*, Copies of Papers on File in the Dominion Archives at Ottawa, Canada, Pertaining to Relations of the British Government to Indians, *Michigan Pioneer and Historical Collections*, 12:217.
50. A. McKee to J. Chew, June 19, 1796, Copies of Papers on File in the Dominion Archives at Ottawa, Canada, Pertaining to Relations of the British Government to Indians, *Michigan Pioneer and Historical Collections*, 12:237.

Chapter 5

The End of Power

The Prophet and His Brother

John Tanner, the white boy captured on the Kentucky frontier by the Saginaw Ojibwa in 1789, had grown to early manhood and was himself a hunter with an Indian family by the first decade of the nineteenth century. Some years after his adoption at Saginaw, he was traded to an Ottawa woman, *Netnokwa*, by his Indian father for a keg of whiskey. Tanner was then forced to leave his brokenhearted Ojibwa mother to make his new home among the Ottawa at Mackinac. Soon thereafter this new family decided to travel west to the valley of the Red River in Minnesota, where they would become involved in the fur trade. One day, as Tanner and his family were camped near the junction of the modern Canadian border with Minnesota and North Dakota, a stranger approached their camp. Sensing his unusual demeanor, Tanner at first feared him to be a Sioux enemy but soon discovered that he was an Ojibwa holy man preaching the message of the Shawnee Prophet. The stranger appealed to Tanner and the Ojibwa and Assinneboine residents of the region to "take the hand of the Prophet" in a number of unusual practices. They were to discard their medicine bundles and cease the use of liquor and making war on other Indians. They were never to strike another person or to permit their fires to die. Perhaps the most controversial admonition was to kill their valued hunting dogs. Tanner, after going to a white trader for advice reasoning that "if the Divine will had an important revelation to make to men, white men would be the first to receive it,"[1] decided to accept the new religion but was skeptical enough that he did not kill his dogs. The prophet's teachings were

widely accepted among the Red River people, and Tanner remarked
that the impact of his teaching was felt by even the most remote
Ojibwa, although as far as he could discern the doctrines were not
meant to unite them for any human purpose.[2]

This fact was not apparent nine hundred miles away in the
Wabash, Maumee, and Detroit River valleys and in the forests bor-
dering Lakes Huron, Michigan, and Superior. Here it was not easy
to separate religious revitalization from political cause nor, for that
matter, the interests of two Shawnee brothers who were the focus of
these diverse but interrelated objectives. In fact, the Tanner encounter owes its origin to the Shawnee shaman *Tenskwatawa* (The One
That Opens the Door), who, after a series of revelations in 1805,
founded a new religion. He hoped to revitalize Indian culture by a
combination of teachings that required rejection of some traditions
and the strengthening of others. The prophet admonished his followers to refuse whiskey and some aspects of European material culture,
such as flint and steel for fire making, guns for hunting (but not war),
and woven clothing. Certain traditional dances and the use of medicine bundles were banned, while the faithful were required to refrain
from intertribal war. Explicit in the teaching of *Tenskwatawa* was
that Americans alone among non-Indians were evil, having been
formed as scum on the ocean and blown westward by a strong wind.[3]

The new religion reached fever pitch among the Indians west of
Lake Michigan and on Michigan's peninsulas. *Le Maigouis* (The
Trout), an Ottawa warrior from L'Arbre Croche (Cross Village), became a leading advocate of the new religion and was eminently
successful in spreading its message among the northern Ottawa and
Ojibwa. In the summer of 1808 it was reported that Ojibwa villages
along the south shore of Lake Superior were almost totally deserted
as the new enthusiasts traveled south to visit the prophet.[4] Among
the Potawatomi, the very powerful shaman *Main Poche* (Withered
Hand) embraced the prophet's teachings, albeit reluctantly, and, at
the same time, also became the rallying point for anti-American feelings among his people.

Much of the hostility felt against Americans was directly traceable
to the threat of American expansion and occupation of the land. This
latter fact was also the heart of a political movement that was nearly
as popular and widespread as the prophet's revivalistic teachings.
Led by *Tenskwatawa*'s immensely talented brother *Tecumseh,* a co-

alition of tribes and tribal factions sought to stop American expansion by political and, if necessary, armed resistance. Although the northern line set by the Treaty of Greenville in 1794 was to be a permanent boundary between the United States and Indian country, the cession filled so rapidly with settlers that, by 1802, the United States government was pressing Indians for even more land to expand its agricultural frontier. By 1810 Ohio had nearly a quarter-million inhabitants and settlers who were pushing into Indiana and Illinois.[5] The event that focused Indian hostility was the Treaty of Fort Wayne, negotiated by Governor William Henry Harrison and chiefs representing the Delaware, Miami, and Potawatomi.

With this treaty, the United States acquired nearly three million acres of land in Indiana and Illinois for an annuity in the form of money and trade goods amounting to a few cents per acre. The cession was negotiated by chiefs including *Winamek* (Catfish) and Five Medals of the Potawatomi, Little Turtle and Pecan for the Miami, and *Tarhe* (The Crane) of the Wyandot. These men, as well as others (such as Black Hoof of the Shawnee and the Wyandot Walk in the Water) who tended to be impressed with American power, urged peace and accommodation with American interests. They also rejected the teachings of *Tenskwatawa*. As occupation of their hunting lands by American settlers created severe food shortages, these village chiefs increasingly relied on their ability to procure supplies and services from the American government to support their people.

The opposing factions in these same tribes had similar problems but rejected accommodation as the solution. Wyandot led by Roundhead, Potawatomi under *Main Poche*, the hostile *Winamek*, and the Shawnee who followed *Tecumseh* and *Tenskwatawa* as well as most of the Indians of the west shore of Lake Michigan, especially the Winnebago and the Ottawa and Ojibwa of Michigan, were decidedly anti-American. It was among the people on the northern and western margins of the American invasion that the exhortations of the Shawnee brothers had the most appeal. Still in control of their lands, they were witness to the consequences of the onslaught of the American farmer on their southern kinsmen. They were, for the first time, able to clearly observe the meaning of the American idea of land ownership and to see that it meant exclusive possession rather than shared use. No wonder that those who rejected accommodation had such strong feelings—following the Treaty of Fort Wayne, *Tecumseh* and his followers threatened to kill all the chiefs who signed the document.

The threat of American expansion into the upper Great Lakes country and the division it produced in the political alignments within each tribe also led to several new twists in traditional polity. The movements led by *Tecumseh* and *Tenskwatawa,* though not new in concept, succeeded in rallying support to factions that crosscut the lineage, clans, and band alliances that formed the traditional foundation of tribal politics. Political consensus was no longer possible within these social institutions. The new alliances that crosscut these old social units produced political alliances that had no basis in kin or ethnicity. Now, Potawatomi or Shawnee of like religious and political persuasion became aligned with people of other tribes against fellow Potawatomi and Shawnee. Along with the appearance of new, extratribal factions came a new kind of leader. Clearly, chiefs such as *Tecumseh* and *Main Poche* acquired authority not so much from traditional means as by their ability to create political division, encourage consensus among dissidents, and meld these factions for political action.

New residential groups also formed as part of this process. One such, Prophetstown, located at the junction of Tippecanoe Creek and the Wabash River in northwestern Indiana, became the focus of anti-American activity. Indians from many tribes journeyed there to hear the teachings of the prophet and to council with *Tecumseh.*

In these meetings, *Tecumseh* advocated a well-planned and coordinated attack to drive the American invaders from Indian land. In the summer and fall of 1811, *Tecumseh* journeyed south to try to bring the Creeks, Choctaws, and Chickasaws into alliance against the Long Knives. Failing in this, he returned to the Tippecanoe to find Prophetstown destroyed. Taking advantage of his absence, Harrison had moved troops against the village, and *Tenskwatawa,* perhaps seeking to enhance his own prestige, had attacked the approaching American army in defiance of *Tecumseh*'s advice. After destroying the village, Harrison's army burned five thousand bushels of corn and beans and, finding thirty-six dead warriors, stripped the bodies and scalped and mutilated the corpses. In terms of casualties, the Battle of Tippecanoe was a draw, but the destruction of Indian food stores and the fact that *Tenskwatawa* had not demonstrated the magical power he claimed to have over the enemy led to a major loss of credibility. The prophet could neither support nor protect the true believers. From that point on, anti-American opinion had a political rather than religious focus.

Likewise, William Henry Harrison was to glorify and exaggerate the importance of the Tippecanoe battle for his political benefit. Three decades later, he became "Old Tippecanoe" and rode to the White House on the slogan "Tippecanoe and Tyler Too."[6]

The Prophetstown attack effectively dispersed hostile warriors across the Great Lakes frontier and they began to systematically attack American settlers. The most serious of these attacks was the attempt of the Winnebago to capture Fort Madison in Iowa.[7] Lacking a means of sustaining an offensive against the Americans, *Tecumseh* and his cohorts were increasingly enamored by calls from the British for a closer alliance. This was particularly so when the British sweetened the appeal with supplies. As both England and the United States anticipated the outbreak of hostilities between them, both also appreciated that victory in the west would depend upon success in controlling the Indians. For his part, Harrison tried unsuccessfully to organize a junket to Washington so the chiefs could meet the president; at about the same time, the British sent these same chiefs a huge red wampum belt that measured three by six feet. This war belt was called the "King's Great Broadax" and it was said that it had medicine to cut down all before it.[8]

The Warriors' Final Hour

War broke out between the United States and Great Britain during the early summer of 1812. The peace of the western frontier had already been periodically marred by violence between Great Lakes Indians and the Long Knives. Though in theory neutral, the British tried to encourage these conflicts from their posts at Fort Malden opposite Detroit and Fort St. Joseph on the lower St. Marys River. By the time war was declared, the tribes, already fighting with the Americans, found their own best interests aligned with those of the British. Likewise, it was immediately apparent to U.S. and British military leaders and to tribal chiefs that Indian participation or the lack of it would likely determine the outcome of the struggle.

Brigadier General William Hull, commander of the U.S. Northwest Army, knew that it was highly unlikely that Indians could be

FT. ST. JOSEPH

FT. MACKINAC

↑N

MORAVIANTOWN

DETROIT
SPRINGWELLS → SANDWICH
BROWNSTOWN FT. MALDEN
FRENCHTOWN AMHERSTBURG

FT. DEARBORN

PUT IN BAY

FT. MEIGS

FT.WAYNE

PROPHETSTOWN

0   40   80
MILES

Sites of battles in the Great Lakes during the War of 1812. (Drawing by B. Nemeth.)

drawn to his cause. Consequently, in the early spring of 1812, he issued a message to Indian leaders to remain home and at peace should war break out. The message also contained the threat that he was advancing with a sword in one hand and an olive branch in the other.[9] It is doubtful that the chiefs knew the symbolic meaning of the olive branch, but they certainly understood the sword. After arriving in Detroit, Hull issued a proclamation to the inhabitants of Canada declaring that "no white man found fighting by the side of an Indian would be taken prisoner. Instant destruction will be his lot."[10] As a further precaution he also assembled representatives of the Ottawa, Ojibwa, Potawatomi, Wyandot, Delaware, Kickapoo, Sauk, and Six Nations Iroquois to request their neutrality. He optimistically reported to Washington that they would remain neutral.[11] This was not to be.

To be sure, a few chiefs did keep their people neutral and some even fought on the American side, but the vast majority soon yielded to exhortations of the British Indian Department and wholeheartedly joined the British. It is also clear that they did so not to advance British interests, but in an attempt to rid themselves of American interference in their affairs.

Initially, the Americans had some success. Hull invaded Canada and captured Fort Malden. As it became obvious that large numbers of Indians would fight on the British side, Hull was forced to abandon Malden and retreat back across the river to Detroit. By mid-August, General Hull surrendered Detroit to General Isaac Brock.

Indians played an important role in this major defeat. Their role was partially tactical and partially psychological. Unlike the British, who were supplied by water from Ft. Niagara on the east end of Lake Erie, Hull depended on a long and very vulnerable supply line to the Ohio River. In early August, warriors under *Tecumseh* supported by Canadian militia and a few British regulars had twice disrupted the American supply line along the Lake Erie shore south of Detroit. Further, Hull was aware that Fort Mackinac had fallen to a mixed army of regulars, Canadian militia, and Indians on July 17. Indians made up two-thirds of the attacking force and represented mostly local Ottawa and Ojibwa with a contingent of Menominee, Winnebago, and Sioux recruited from Green Bay.[12] Hull thus believed that these and many more northern warriors would soon be sent against him at a time when he could well be cut off from supplies and reinforcements. These military considerations, though important, did not outweigh the less tangible psychological ones. Hull, like other whites on the western frontier, was extremely fearful of tribal warfare.

The terror of tribal war is difficult for us to comprehend. Beyond the fact that much of the actual combat involved fighting hand to hand with knives, war hatchets, and clubs, and that no mercy was shown to the wounded and noncombatants, there was also the frenzy that came over warriors in the heat of battle. Even hardened frontiersmen with firsthand experience were often aghast at what they considered to be pure blood lust. Canadian militiaman Thomas Vercheres, who often fought beside Indian warriors in the War of 1812, described preparation for war by the Shawnee, Potawatomi, Ottawa,

Ojibwa, and Winnebago assembled at Fort Malden for an assault on Detroit.

> We on our part were inspected by the General [Brock] before crossing on to the opposite shore. While this was going on, the savages arrived in their bark canoes to the number of three hundred. According to custom they had spent the preceding night at Amherstburg dancing the war dance. It is an extraordinary spectacle to see all these aborigines assembled together at one time, some covered with vermillion, others with blue clay, and still others tattooed in black and white from head to foot. Their single article of clothing was a breechcloth, always worn when going to war. A European witnessing this strange spectacle for the first time would have thought, I truly believe, that he was standing at the entrance to hell, with the gates thrown open to let the damned out for an hour's recreation on earth! It was frightful, horrifying beyond expression. Accustomed as I was to seeing them on such occasions I could not but feel overcome, as though under the influence of some kind of terror which I was powerless to control.[13]

The "horrifying spectacle" observed by Thomas Vercheres was certainly a concluding part of the long ritual performed in preparation of war. Among the northern *Anishnabeg,* the ceremonies leading to war were called *baunindobindidowin* (war path).[14] Preparation for battle required a long and complex series of ceremonies, including consultation with elders and shamans, the consecration of protective medicines, a formal invitation to war, ritual cleansing and purification, and the war dance. The *baunindobindidowin* was not just a preparation for fighting but also an opportunity to restrain warriors and prevent war; at the very least, war had to be justified and supported by the entire community. The formal songs and dance recounted the rationale for the forthcoming battle and bolstered the spirits of the warriors through an outpouring of emotions that, in turn, sent them forth charged with strength for defending their common interests.

General Brock, like other British military men, relied upon a campaign of terror against the Americans. In his demand for the surrender of Detroit, Brock told Hull, "It is far from my inclination to join in a war of extermination, but you must be aware that the numerous body of Indians, who have attached themselves to my troops, will be beyond my control the moment the contest commences."[15] In his court-martial for surrendering Detroit, Hull later revealed part of the basis of his decision as well as his own attitude about his Indian opponents. It was in part, he said, to spare the women and children under his protection, since the "savage will have blood for blood, though he draws it from the veins of the defenseless. Victory only heightens his inhuman thirst."[16]

Two events soon demonstrated that Brock's prediction and Hull's fears were correct. The day before Detroit's surrender, Captain Nathan Heald, commander of Fort Dearborn at Chicago, carried out Hull's order to evacuate his post for Fort Wayne or Detroit. On the morning of August 15, 96 soldiers and civilians marched through the stockade gates and were soon confronted by over 600 Potawatomi warriors following Blackbird and Mad Sturgeon.[17] After a brief and fierce fight, Captain Heald surrendered his column on the guarantee of safety. This was a mistake in judgment. Once in control, the warriors began to kill or claim the survivors. Of the 45 prisoners, at least 28 were killed and many were tortured and dismembered. Many of the captives also subsequently died of exposure. Those who did survive did so with the aid of friendly Potawatomi. Subsequently, newspaper accounts from survivors spread terror across the frontier.[18]

In January, a similar incident occurred at Frenchtown on the River Raisin in Michigan. British forces now under the command of General Henry Procter along with 600 Indian warriors under Wyandot war chief Roundhead advanced against an American army of equal size near Frenchtown. The Americans were hopelessly defeated, in part because Indian warriors were willing to fight on open ground. The American commander, General James Winchester, was captured and taken before Roundhead and was told that, if he failed to surrender, the Indians would kill his entire force. On Procter's promise that they would be treated as prisoners of war, Winchester surrendered his army. Taking the Americans who could march, Procter immediately retreated back to Detroit, but he left 80 wounded American prisoners under the guard of 50 Potawatomi. Thirty prisoners were soon killed and the remaining claimed as captives and marched off to distant villages. When word reached the American frontier, the population was outraged by both the fate of the prisoners and the failure of the British to control their Indian allies. "Remember the Raisin" became the battle cry of the American army in the remaining campaigns of the war.

In the spring, *Tecumseh* found himself in partnership with General Procter, a person he respected neither as an individual nor as a warrior. Nonetheless he managed to muster large numbers of Indians for two attacks on Fort Meigs, which the Americans had built near the remains of old Fort Miami on the lower Maumee. In both battles, Indian participants outnumbered British troops and Canadian militia. The warriors proved again they would fight on open ground. They could not, however, overcome the barricaded enemy and were disappointed at the failure of British artillery to accomplish this task. Perry's victory over the British fleet on Lake Erie in September, 1813, substantially revised the strategic picture in the west. Now it was Procter who lacked a sound line of supply. Consequently, he took the defensive, falling back to Malden and proposing to retreat farther east.

Tecumseh and the other chiefs, fighting for their own homeland, strongly opposed retreat. In fact, *Tecumseh* was so angry he publicly berated Procter for cowardice and lack of candor, telling him, "Every word you say evaporates like the smoke from our pipes. Father, you are like a crayfish that does not know how to walk straight ahead."[19] Notwithstanding this stinging rebuke, Procter and his Indian allies retreated east up the Thames River.

Finally, the pursuing Americans forced them to make a stand. This occurred near Moraviantown, which was occupied by the same band of Christian Delaware who had waited out the Revolution on the Clinton River north of Detroit. Finally wearing out their welcome among the local Ojibwa, they had established this village on the upper Thames. Here they were witness to the last great battle between northwestern Indians and the Long Knives of General Harrison. Among the thirty Indians who fell in the battle of Moraviantown was the great Shawnee war chief *Tecumseh*. With him died the last hope for armed resistance to American expansion. Before further pursuit of Procter's army, Harrison burned Moraviantown to the ground.[20]

As a postscript to the battle, Procter was retreating so fast that his personal supply wagons were overrun and captured by American cavalry. Later, in order to humiliate the bitterly anti-American Potawatomi chief *Main Poche*, Harrison produced Procter's captured sword and scarlet uniform blouse. "This belonged to your great father and friend," said Harrison, "Don't you think he was a great man to run away and leave his honor behind, no soldier ought to part with this without his life. I present you with this coat to remember your friend by." *Main Poche,* it was reported, "looked like a bear but took the coat."[21]

Following their defeat at the battle of Moraviantown, many of the Indian warriors dispersed to their homes in Michigan, Wisconsin, and northern Indiana and Illinois. They remained hostile to Americans and, until peace was concluded between the United States and England in December, 1814, continued to raid farmsteads and settlements.

The Treaty of Springwells along with over a dozen other agreements officially ended the war between the United States and the upper Great Lakes tribes in 1815. The Indians were never again able to mount a serious military challenge to American encroachment. Despite this fact, the conception of Indians as dangerous, uncontrollable savages so carefully cultivated by the British during the struggle for the Ohio valley and the War of 1812 was emblazoned on the imagination of Americans. The terror of tribal war merged with the Indian identity; suspicion and fear submerged the judgment of policymakers, the curiosity of scholars, and the humanity of the citizenry. On one level, this conception of Indian savagery neatly played to the emerging concept of American manifest destiny; if Indians could not be totally transformed, they could be totally destroyed. Savagery was, after all, incompatible with the march of civilization.

On a more individual level, American frontier settlers continued to react to Indians with fear and hostility. Indians, unencumbered with preconceptions about the barbarism of the civilized, puzzled about why their appearance sent women and children shrieking and men running for their guns.

Furs for Useful Things

Unquestionably, the major point of contact between the native peoples of the Great Lakes and the world beyond was trade. During the seventeenth, eighteenth, and early nineteenth centuries, Euro-American and Canadian traders in quest of furs entered the continent's heartland and, in this sparsely settled region, dealt with Indian producers to obtain the pelts of beaver, otter, mink, marten, fisher, wolf, and bear as well as several other species. Much of the policy and action of the newcomers involved protection and encouragement of these commercial interests.

The trade, as it played out on the local level, was complex. During the seventeenth and most of the eighteenth century it was conducted according to Indian custom. That is to say it was framed as exchange within a social context that had heavy political overtones.[22] Gradually, Indians became more sophisticated about the motivations of their non-Indian trading partners and learned to separate the external economic expectations from customary ones. As a result, Indian traders tried to get the best prices for the furs they produced and knew that they could bargain between competing traders for better prices. At the same time, they were not in business as fur producers but were fur producers to obtain what they needed from the trade. Thus, if the traders lowered prices for goods to get Indians to produce more furs, they would find that Indians would produce less furs because they could get the same amount of goods with less work. Traders responded by labeling them "lazy" and "indolent."

The fur trade was also, of course, a complex business in which New World fur entered an international market. Huge fortunes were to be made by individuals and corporations that succeeded in obtaining the most fur at the least cost in manufactured items. The temptation was to offer Indians cheaply made goods. However, Indians soon became very discriminating in their tastes and demand for quality. Thus, they were at the same time reluctant producers and eager but sophisticated customers.

Goods acquired in trade became an increasingly important part of native life. Modes of dress and the tools used in almost all activities were, by the mid-eighteenth century, likely as not of Euro-American or Canadian manufacture. These same items were incorporated into status systems both as items of exchange and as markers of success. In fact, the goods themselves often became essential to the production of exchangeable items. For example, the use of metal kettles greatly simplified the production of maple sugar, which was exported by the hundreds of tons from the Great Lakes forests. Sugar based on Euro-American technology and Indian know-how became, in turn, a means to acquire such goods as blankets, cotton

netting, twine, and magnifying glasses for starting fires. These devices, in turn, changed the time and effort demanded of people in
making a living from the lakes and forests. Freed by the need to
spend countless hours making skin clothing, women could turn their
attention to producing more sugar and dressing more furs. As the
eighteenth century wore on, Indian participation in the trade became
more and more fundamental to their economy. Fortunately it was
also commensurate with their traditional skills and lifeway. With
very few exceptions, Indians were able to acquire furs with very little
disruption to seasonal rounds, settlement mode, or their sociopolitical
systems.

The U.S. government immediately recognized the importance of
the fur trade to both Indians and the business interests of its own
citizens. In 1790, Congress passed the Trade and Intercourse Act,
which set up jurisdictions for the trade and required bonds and licenses for traders on Indian lands within the bounds of American
jurisdiction (*U.S. Statutes at Large,* 1:137–38). In the latter provision we see the first of many attempts to define and regulate "Indian
country." In the late eighteenth and early nineteenth centuries the
Northwest Territory, that is, portions of the United States not yet
organized as states, was Indian country, and citizens could not enter
without the permission of public officials. In the early decades of the
nineteenth century, Congress passed several acts through which it
tried to protect Indian access to trade goods without exposing them
to the exploitation of unscrupulous traders and, particularly, to the
ungoverned use of alcohol. In fact, the government itself decided to
go into the Indian trade when, in 1802, the so-called Factory System
of government trading houses was established (*U.S. Statutes at
Large,* 2:139–46). In the decades that followed, many laws and regulations were passed by Congress to try to regulate the fur trade.

These good intentions were never effectively realized. In 1822,
after two decades of disastrous operation, the federal trading system
was abandoned. The United States could not regulate the trade,
because it had neither the will nor the power to control it. Prior to
the War of 1812, the upper Great Lakes fur trade was in the hands
of British traders, actually Scots, of the Northwest and Mackinac
companies, which had large, well-organized, and well-financed operations. After the war American policy was designed to wrest control
of the trade from these interests. Officially, the government tried to

limit the number of trading licenses granted to "foreigners" and to suppress the use of liquor. This effort ran afoul of the large and powerful American Fur Company under the leadership of John Jacob Astor. After buying two-thirds interest in the Mackinac Company in 1808, the American Fur Company emerged as a powerful presence in upper Great Lakes economics and politics, including Indian policy. The company was operated from headquarters on Mackinac Island, where it was directed by Ramsey Crooks and Robert Stuart. After the war, the American Fur Company had a virtual monopoly over the Great Lakes fur trade even though its traders were largely Canadian or British citizens. Despite government policy, the powerful political influence of Astor and his allies, Territorial Governor Lewis Cass and Secretary of War John Calhoun, was such that the company was able to operate with near impunity. When William Puthuff, the Indian agent at Mackinac, tried to limit the companies' licenses, he was fired and replaced by a much more cooperative agent, George Boyd, brother-in-law of John Quincy Adams.[23]

A major problem faced by the Office of Indian Affairs and by some Indian leaders was the use of alcohol in the fur trade. One of the best documented cases of the way liquor was used comes from the journal of Michel Curot, a French Canadian trader for the XYZ Company, who spent the winter of 1803–4 as a clerk in charge of the trade on the St. Croix River in northwestern Wisconsin.[24] Curot writes:

> Monday, September 19, 1803—I camped on an island. Four savages came to me again to ask credit. When I had given this I bought a fawn skin of wild rice for three pints of mixed rum. Hail fell today as large as Bullet with very heavy thunder and lightning. The Brother in Law of Smith [an employee married to an Indian woman] came to camp at the end of the island and asked me to his lodge where I went with Smith. He ask me for some ointment to put on his wound having been stabbed with a knife by *Payedigigue,* when he wished to avenge the death of his brother who had been slain three or four days ago by le Razeur's Band, close to the camp of La Prairie. He also ask for a little Rum in order to go off to his father at the river au Serpent [Snake River], to Weep for the son and brother. I gave him some Ointment and Rum, and he delivered to me a Brasse of scarlet cloth, telling me not to be Uneasy with regard to the rest of his Credit,

that the Blow that he had received was not mortal (it was a little below the Left shoulder) that he had nothing from Mr. Reaume, [that is, he had no credit with a competing trader] and that as soon as he was better he would hunt in order to pay me. He had solemnly promised Smith to go to the river au Serpent to get wild rice, saying that the savages there had Cached [stored] a Great Deal.

Tuesday Sept 20—Mr. Reaume having passed this morning I left the island and went into camp near the house of la prairie. I saw Le Grand Razeur [an Indian] who gave me three fawn skins of rice. Savoyard [a French Canadian employee married to a local Indian woman] had 4 chapines of Mixed Rum that he gave his mother in law. I traded for the Rum Four fawn skins of wild rice. I bought 2 lynx and one deerskin For a little sugar and a few Beads. I traded for one Otter and a Large Beaver.[25]

From this and the journals of other traders we can begin to understand the day-to-day economics of the trade. Obviously, liquor played an important role. First, it was frequently given as a gift in order to attach the loyalty of an Indian by establishing a reciprocal obligation. The present obliged the Indian to return a gift at some time in the future. The trader's payment, of course, would come in the form of furs or supplies. Liquor was also used to purchase Indian foods in the fall. Dried meat and fish, berries, and, particularly, wild rice obtained in exchange were used by the trader and, more important, traded back to Indians during the winter in exchange for pelts. Thus, liquor was literally used to starve Indians into producing fur. The journal of Curot, as well as those of many other traders, clearly shows that much of the trade in alcohol took place in the fall, which is consistent with these uses. They also show that its use was usually in the context of social gatherings and associated with trading rituals. It seems that the drunken behavior of Indians was not much different from that of the French Canadian employees of the trading companies. It is evident also that Indians were not always drunk, being far too dispersed and busy for drinking most of the year.[26] Yet the violence and death associated with the drunken binges was appalling.

Publicly, Astor and Robert Stuart, a temperance man, did not approve of the use of liquor in the fur trade. Nonetheless, with the support of Territorial Governor Lewis Cass, who was the de facto

Indian superintendent and a staunch moralist, the American Fur
Company alone imported between five and eight thousand gallons
of liquor to Mackinac Island each year for the trade. Without it, they
said, the British would get the upper hand.[27]

After the War of 1812 and into the second decade of the nineteenth century, the Great Lakes fur trade reached its peak in terms
of both the amount of fur exported and its profitability. To meet
growing competition from the Northwest and Hudson Bay companies
to the north and from independent traders in the south, the huge
American Fur Company devised several strategies to strip the area
of its fur-bearing species. All of these strategies were based on the
knowledge that Indians had to be "encouraged to produce."

The first idea was to hire traders on salary to go out each season
to live near concentrations of Indians. Soon, the country was crowded
with traders, often several competing for the furs of each band. Men
were sent *en derouine*, that is, to travel with and visit individual
families at their winter hunting grounds. Many of these men were
either French-Indian *Métis* or French Canadians who spoke Indian
languages. Often, they were married to Indian women "in the manner of the country." The connection between Indian bands and
specific traders and the role of their *Métis* or mixed blood children
became powerful forces in Indian politics as the fur trade waned. At
Green Bay, traders John Lawe, Jacques Porlier, and Augustus,
Pierre, and Louis Gregnon established strong paternal ties with the
Menominee and Winnebago. In the Grand Valley, Louis and Antoine Campau, Richard Godfroy, Rix Robinson, and the La Fram-
boises established posts for trade with the Ottawa, while in the Saginaw drainage, Henry Conner, Whitmore Knaggs, Joseph Trombley,
and the Williams brothers became Ojibwa traders and the fathers of
Métis children. In the Lake Superior country, John Johnston, the
Cadottes, John Haliday, the Rouassain brothers, and William
Aitken, like their southern counterparts, married local women and
established strong trading relationships with their Ojibwa in-laws.[28]
These relationships are today evident in the large number of Indian
families with these same surnames.

There is no better evidence of the influence of the *Métis* traders
than at Mackinac, where mixed-blood Ottawa families formed a very
large community. It was not only large but powerful, and a community where sex and race were not impediments to success. Madame

Framboise was a famous hostess and a prosperous trader whose daughter, Josette, married Captain Benjamin Pierce, brother of President Franklin Pierce. Another Ottawa woman, Agatha Bailey, was married to Edward Biddle, whose brother Nicholas was president of the United States Bank.[29] Most were not so prominent, but collectively they developed and controlled much of the early commerce and industry of the Great Lakes.

Another technique used by the trading companies was the time-honored debt system. Goods were advanced on credit to individual Indians each fall with the expectation that these credits would be paid off with an equal value in pelts in the spring. Of course, it was prudent to keep a careful watch on the creditors for fear they would take their furs elsewhere. As the number of furbearers declined and competition increased to the point that each band had a resident trader, the trade more resembled employment piecework than independent exchange.[30]

The success of these strategies was evident in a crash in furbearer populations. By the mid-1820s, beaver, otter, and marten had been virtually exterminated from the Great Lakes forests. The traders responded by developing a market for less valuable alternatives, namely muskrat fur and deer hides. Soon these commodities made up the vast bulk of the trade. Now, in order to pay their trade credits and to replenish their supplies of clothing, guns, knives, and kettles, the Indians were forced to kill off their main source of meat. As a result, Indians began to starve as the deer population declined in the late 1820s and early 1830s.[31]

By the late 1820s, the growing popularity of silk top hats began to limit the demand for felt in the hat industry and the fur market plummeted. Faced with decreased profits, many small traders left the business to compete with Indians in supplying immigrant settlers. John Astor, himself, sold his interest in the American Fur Company's Great Lakes enterprise in 1834.

Although the fur trade never totally ended for Indians, it certainly faded dramatically by the mid-1830s. In the last decade of this period, traders continued to run up huge debts for goods forwarded to Indians. This would seem to have been unwise, particularly in view of the decline in both the supply of fur and its value. Despite these facts, the trading companies continued to pay large dividends to shareholders. These practices make sense when we realize that the

companies and individual traders were anticipating a government
buyout in the form of Indian treaties, which regularly provided
money to pay the debts of Indians. For example, the Menominee
Treaty of 1836 permitted $100,000 for trader claims, the Winne-
bago Treaty of 1837, $150,000, and the Ojibwa-Ottawa Treaty of
1836 in Michigan allotted $300,000 for these purposes. At a time
when the country was in the midst of a serious financial crisis, this
was not only a great deal of money but often the only source of hard
currency on the rural frontier.

The major trading families and the American Fur Company eventually received the lion's share of this money. The point to be realized is that the same group of businessmen and prominent traders
who controlled the fur trade also had a huge financial interest in
treaties of land cession, since they profited both directly and indirectly by the money the treaties provided. As we will see, these men
used all of their considerable resources to promote treaty making and
to override Indian resistance.

On the Northern Border

Competitive gift giving across the U.S.-Canadian border continued
after the War of 1812 and became a very troublesome problem for
American politicians who were trying to define and secure the border. Indians had been granted freedom to freely cross the border in
the Treaty of Ghent, which ended the War of 1812. Despite this fact,
American agents tried every means to discourage continued relations
between the tribes and their former ally. The annual trek made by
many of the Ottawa and Ojibwa to Fort Collier on Drummond Island
and later to Manitoulin Island was particularly galling to Lewis Cass,
the territorial governor of Michigan.

During the summer of 1820, Governor Cass assembled an ex-
ploratory expedition to visit the south shore of Lake Superior and to
explore the source of the Mississippi River. Besides looking for min-
eral resources and observing wildlife, Cass wanted to show the flag
and to counteract British influence among local Indians.[32] For the
trip he assembled a group of young men who later played influential
roles in Indian policy and the politics of the Northwest Territory.
Prominent among them was his protégé Henry R. Schoolcraft, who
would become famous as an Indian agent and scholar of Ojibwa

culture. The party, consisting of nine official members, twelve French Canadian boatmen, ten Ottawa and southern Ojibwa guides, and seven soldiers, set forth from Detroit and reached Mackinac on May 24. After resting and adding a military detachment of twenty-two men (under the command of Lt. John Pierce) for its push into hostile Indian country, the expedition set off for Sault Ste. Marie. Arriving at the rapids on June 15, they found a large Ojibwa village of forty to fifty dome-shaped wigwams as well as a cluster of log buildings occupied by five or six families of mixed descent. One of the log homes was the residence of John Johnston, a prominent fur trader, and his wife *Ozhawguscodaywaquay* (Green Meadow Woman) and their nearly grown children. The Johnston household extended its hospitality to the official party, which witnessed an initiation ritual of the *Midé-wi-win* or Grand Medicine society. The event was recorded by the party's engineer, David Bates Douglass.

The party to the number of perhaps thirty were in a wigwam uncovered at the top and on the poles of which some bits of strand & other things intended as I was informed by way of offerings were hung—Round the interior was a circle of Indian men & women highly ornamented and painted & in the center two persons were holding a long kind of drum upon which one of them beat, while the other shook in the same measured time a kind of gourd shell rattle; around them within the circle seven or eight persons were moving with a solemn measured step which they sometimes quickened to a run—In general the time of the drum was marked by all present, those standing on the outer circle as well as those moving around & all occasionally accompanied with the voice in a low moaning tone sometimes swelling out with much emphasis. The old man who shook the gourd in particular uttered a species of Chaunt almost the whole time. I observed that all had in their hands the dressed skins of some small animal as a marten an otter a weasel etc. & occasionally the shrieking of an animal was heard but whether from a real animal or merely an imitation I could not tell. At such times those who walked around & those who held the drum would appear to be wrought up to a frenzy. Their motions were quickened, their chaunting more emphasized & all their exertions redoubled while their eyeballs seemed almost bursting from their sockets. This excitement by the bye was not

always accompanied by the squeaking noise I have mentioned—
But the most remarkable feature in the extraordinary dance was
the apparent deprivation of life which those in the circle suffered
whenever any of those who walked around breathed upon the
mouth or skin which he held in his hand and directed it to them. I
sometimes thought I heard a little snapping noise when this was
done & a little white bean (actually a cowrie shell) appeared to be
shot out of the mouth of the animal at the person to be struck
down, but this was not always the case—The person so shot at, at
all events, fell to the ground for a minute or two appearing to
recover slowly & with great difficulty & to retain some of the
supernatural influence about him even after he rose.[33]

The *Midé-wi-win* society was devoted to perpetuating knowledge
and skill related to herbal curing. The ritual described by Douglass
was the initiation of new members into one of the four degrees of the
society. It was culminated by the shooting of power into the body of
the initiate by means of a small shell (*megis*). The *Midé-wi-win* society gained in popularity after the exodus of the Algonquian people
from their seventeenth-century refuges at Green Bay, Sault Ste.
Marie, and Chequamegon Bay. With the continuing assault of new
diseases and the disruption due to warfare in the eighteenth century,
the *Midé-wi-win* became an important reservoir of traditionalism.
As such, the society was often attacked by missionaries and Indian
agents as a pagan institution and, therefore, became an important
nineteenth-century counterpoint to the growing influence of Christianity.[34]

There was an incident on the morning of June 16, however, that
illustrated the manner in which the United States dealt with the
Ojibwa. Governor Cass summoned the local Ojibwa to council and
announced his intention of obtaining a land cession at the rapids in
order to build a fort. The local chief *Singabawossin* (Spirit Stone), a
powerful shaman and leader of the Crane clan, and his fellow clans-
man and distinguished war chief *Shingwak* (Little Pine) opposed this
suggestion, citing the fact that the proposed location of the fort was
also the traditional cemetery of the band.[35] Cass responded that his
offer was only a courtesy, since the United States had already acquired rights to all former European land grants through the Treaty
of Greenville in 1795. Since the French had a fort at the Sault, Cass

A *midewigan* ('ceremonial lodge') of the *Midé-wi-win* society. Lac Courte Oreille, Wisconsin, circa 1900. (Photograph courtesy of the Smithsonian Institution.)

claimed the United States could occupy the spot whether the Ojibwa "renewed the lease or not."[36] The chiefs were incensed, particularly *Sassaba,* a young war chief who had come to the conference wearing the bright scarlet uniform blouse and silver gorget that indicated his rank as a brigadier general in the British army. *Sassaba* angrily kicked aside a pile of tobacco that the Americans had offered as presents and, before stalking out, violently thrust his war lance in the ground before the stunned negotiators.

As the assembly broke up, the Union Jack was raised over the Indian village. Infuriated by the sight of the British flag flying over U.S. soil, Cass, with interpreter William Riley, rushed into the village, tore down the flag, and warned the assembled warriors that such behavior would cause the United States "to set a strong foot upon their necks and crush them to the earth."[37]

Both camps, separated by only a few hundred yards, prepared for a fight with thirty professional soldiers and another dozen or so well-armed men facing fifty to sixty Ojibwa warriors. After some hours of high tension, Schoolcraft related that some of the chiefs offered peace and that later the same day they acceded to Cass's request by signing a treaty. The treaty ceded four square miles on the south side of the river to the United States in exchange for presents.

Cass's heroic exploits were widely extolled in the American press and the subsequent writings of the official party. What none of these arrogant and naive chroniclers realized was that their lives and those of many of the opposing Ojibwa were likely saved not by the intrepid Cass, but by the Ojibwa woman *Ozhawguscodaywaquay.*[38]

As *Sassaba* and some of the warriors were preparing to attack the Cass party, *Ozhawguscodaywaquay* sent her son, George Johnston, to hurriedly summon the older chiefs to the Johnston home. As they no doubt knew, she had been blessed by a vision that gave her special power to deal with calamity, and they came willingly and heeded her advice not to attack the Americans. *Shingabawossin* consequently faced down *Sassaba* and thus averted bloodshed. The Americans were, of course, oblivious to these maneuvers on the Indian side.

Henry Schoolcraft later married *Ozhawguscodaywaquay*'s daughter Jane and eventually acknowledged his mother-in-law's pivotal role in resolving the near fateful confrontation.

The episode of Lewis Cass at Sault Ste. Marie reveals not only the

bias of the Western perspective in written history, but the fact that
it is strongly dominated by male understanding and interests. Because of these latter views, it is difficult to reconstruct the day-to-day
life in Great Lakes Indian villages during the early part of the nineteenth century. The activities of village life were as strongly attached
to the activities of women as war and politics were to the realm of
men.

Village Life

Anishnabeg family life in the first part of the nineteenth century
consisted of two distinct annual phases, the cold, winter months that
were spent in the company of close kin and the summer, the time of
village life. The summer village (*odena*) was a happy place; relieved
of the long winter isolation, the people enjoyed the company of relatives and friends. People visited, gossiped, courted, and laid plans for
the future. Villages were noisy, cluttered, and full of running children, barking dogs, and people working, over all of which hung the
constant pall of smoke from the cooking fires. Each family had its
dwelling, a low, dome-shaped structure formed of bent poles covered
with bark or reed mats. The dwellings (*waginogan*) were usually
between twelve and fifteen feet in diameter, small but easy to heat.[39]
Inside space was clearly partitioned between a male side and a female side. Adults of each sex occupied the space on opposite sides
of the entrance, while children occupied either side of the central
fire, sons on the side of the father, daughters on the mother's. Grandparents occupied the rear of the structure. Bedding consisted of
tanned deer and bear hides as well as blankets that were thrown
over cedar boughs that, in turn, covered reed mats. Eating and other
activities took place around a fire that, in good weather, was kindled
outside the house.

Many of the descriptions of Algonquian households rest upon gen-
eralities, but the eye of Ann Jameson, who visited an Ottawa village
on Mackinac Island in 1837, was more discerning.

> Though all these lodges seem nearly alike to a casual observer,
> I was soon aware of differences and gradations in the particular
> arrangements, which are amusingly characteristic of the various
> inhabitants. There is one lodge, a little to the east of us, which I

call the Chateau. It is rather larger and loftier than the others: the mats which cover it are whiter and of a neater texture than usual. The blanket which hangs before the opening is new and clean. The inmates, ten in number, are well and handsomely dressed; even the women and children have abundance of ornaments; and as for the gay cradle of the baby, I quite covet it—it is so gorgeously elegant. I supposed at first that this must be the lodge of a chief; but I have since understood that the chief is seldom either so well lodged or so well dressed as the others, it being part of his policy to avoid anything like ostentation, or rather to be ostentatiously poor and plain in his apparel and possessions. This wigwam belongs to an Ottawa, remarkable for his skill in hunting, and for his habitual abstinence from the "fire water." He is a baptized Roman Catholic, belonging to the mission at Arbre Croche, and is reputed a rich man.

Not far from this, and almost immediately in front of our house, stands another wigwam, a most wretched concern. The owners have not mats enough to screen them from the weather; and the bare poles are exposed through the "looped and windowed raggedness" on every side. The woman, with her long, neglected hair, is always seen cowering despondingly over the embers of her fire, as if lost in sad reveries. Two naked children are scrambling among the pebbles on the shore. The man wrapt in a dirty ragged blanket, without a single ornament, looks the image of savage inebriety and ferocity. Observe that these are the two extremes, and that between them are many gradations of comfort, order, and respectability.[40]

Much of the business of town life was the business of women. As mothers, wives, and sisters, they placed high value on industriousness and hard work. Each day they labored long hours to collect wood and water, tend gardens, and collect food. They joined together in these tasks, enjoying the company of other women and the help of other hands. Children were their constant companions. Babies hung swaddled on cradleboards within easy reach while naked toddlers and young children played games underfoot. Older girls joined in the tasks, thus learning to cooperate and, through practical application, all the skills that would be so important when they reached adulthood.

Ozhawguscodaywaquay
(Green Meadow Woman)

Sometime around 1780, *Ozhawguscodaywaquay* was born to the Reindeer clan of the Ojibwa who resided at *Shaugawaumikong* (Chequamegon Bay, Wisconsin). Her father, *Waubojeeg* (White Fisher), and
her grandfather, *Mongazid* (Loon's Foot), were both very influential
chiefs among the people of western Lake Superior. As a young woman,
Ozhawguscodaywaquay, like most Ojibwa youths, fasted for power and
was the recipient of an extraordinary vision. In this dream she was
visited by a white man who offered her food, and, although a stranger,
he was accompanied by a dog that seemed to know her. As part of the
same vision she dreamed of being on a high hill surrounded by water
and from which she beheld many canoes full of Indians coming to
honor her. She was then snatched into the sky, only to look down and
see the earth on fire. Afraid, she cried out in fear that the Indians
would be burned. "No," a voice answered, "they will be saved."
Ozhawguscodaywaquay recognized the voice of the white stranger and
knew that he was a spirit and that he would become her lifelong
guardian.

Even though she knew of her special power in dealing with danger
to her people and the role of her white spirit in these matters, she
reacted with aversion when her future husband, the Irish fur trader
John Johnston, approached her father to ask for her hand in marriage.
After a suitable waiting period, the couple was married and *Ozhawguscodaywaquay* left her family for her new home at Sault Ste. Marie.

After a difficult period of adjustment, she and John Johnston
formed a warm home and successful fur trading business, the latter
depending in part on *Ozhawguscodaywaquay's* extensive kin networks
in which her husband was now an in-law. Of these kin, her oldest
brother, *Iahbewadic* (Firstborn), also known as *Waishkee,* and his son
Waubojeeg became very important trading partners and men of
influence in northern Michigan.

After moving to the Sault and becoming the mistress of the
Johnston household, *Ozhawguscodaywaquay* was also known as Susan
Johnston, but she remained very much an Ojibwa woman her whole
life. She could understand a little English and French but spoke only
Ojibwa. She continued to practice the traditional subsistence activities
such as fishing and gathering and, with the help of her relatives, made

thousands of pounds of maple sugar each year for market. Thomas McKenney, who visited her home in 1826, described her as "tall and large but uncommonly active and cheerful. She dresses mainly in the costume of her nation, a blue petticoat of cloth, a short gown of calico with leggings worked with beads and moccasins."

Ozhawguscodaywaquay and John Johnston had four daughters and four sons. These children in the idiom of the day were *Métis* or half-bloods. All had both English and Ojibwa names. The eldest son, Louis, served aboard the British frigate "Queen Charlotte" and, during the battle of Put-in-Bay, received wounds that were so severe that he never recovered his health. Both William and George Johnston were prominent figures in the fur trade and in Indian affairs, serving as agents and interpreters. Daughter Jane (*Obahbahmwawazhegoqua,* Star Music Woman) married Henry Schoolcraft, prominent Indian agent and Ojibwa scholar, while daughter Anna Marie (*Omishkabugoqua,* Redleaf Woman) married Henry's brother, James Schoolcraft, and Charlotte (*Ogebunnoqua,* Wild Rose Woman) married the very prominent Canadian Episcopal clergyman, Reverend William MacMurry.

Ozhawguscodaywaquay was an intelligent, determined, and extremely capable woman in the context of not only her native culture but also in the emerging *Métis* and American communities of the early nineteenth-century frontier. Her influence and confidence is readily discernable in her role in averting a violent encounter between the Sault Ojibwa and the Cass expedition in 1820. In this incident, it is likely that she saw the fulfillment of her vision and literally saved her relatives from destruction. As a mother, she raised her children as competent and educated members of two different societies while maintaining her own strong identity as an Ojibwa woman. As a wife, she supported her husband and, for fifteen years after his death, was successful as a trader and businesswoman. When *Ozhawguscodaywaquay* died in Sault Ste. Marie in 1843, this remarkable woman left an enduring legacy that is a force in the history of the upper Great Lakes region.

The relationship between women and their daughters and between sisters was usually very close. Although much more formal, brothers and sisters also often formed close bonds of mutual help. Of course young women lost the day-to-day contact with these family members when they married and moved to be with their husbands in other bands. No wonder joyful summer reunions were such an important part of village life.

At the onset of the first menstruation, girls, like their mothers, retired to the isolation of a special hut where they lived, tended by other women, until their periods ended. While isolated, they were subject to a number of taboos, including a prohibition against scratching with the fingernails. A special stick was used for this purpose. The belief that underlaid both isolation and menstrual taboos was that menstrual fluids were a powerful contaminant that had to be neutralized by these practices. Usually some form of public recognition accompanied a young woman's entry into puberty and after this the woman was considered ready for marriage.

Although marriages were arranged by the couple's families with some further purpose in mind, marriage was also often preceded by courtship. Men attempted to court eligible girls by playing a flute or singing from the darkness near the girl's wigwam. Young women were strictly monitored and very modest in their conduct toward marriageable men. Jealousy was not unknown in courting behavior, and girls sometimes got into spirited fits of hair pulling or cutting of braids, but never slapping or scratching.[41]

Marriage was sealed with an exchange of gifts between the couple's families. Often the couple resided for some time with the bride's band and then, after the birth of a first child, would make their permanent residence with the husband's group. Women were sometimes faced with the prospect of sharing the household with a second wife, since polygyny was an ideal of many men. The difficulty of supporting additional wives and children, however, usually outweighed the advantages. Unless the new wife was a sister of the first and, therefore, they were used to working together, polygyny had a tendency to create tensions in the family.

The care of children was a task that did not often conflict with the work of adults. This is because older siblings and grandparents spent a good deal of time babysitting and because of a wonderful device— the cradleboard. Soon after birth, babies were swaddled in soft skins and laced to a cradleboard, which was a combination pack frame and cradle. A hoop on the cradleboard above the baby's head protected the child not only physically, but also by serving as a place to attach charms that magically shielded the baby from harm. One standard charm was a decorated case containing the dried umbilical cord, which was believed to secure wisdom for the child. Woven spider web fetishes were also attached to "catch something evil, as the spider catches flies."[42] The cradleboard could be hung out of harm's way while the mother worked, or it could be carried on her back. In either case, the mother and baby were constant companions.

After some period of time, a person of acknowledged power was asked to name the child. This occasion was accompanied with feasting. Among the Potawatomi, children were given names that were traditional within specific clans, while Ottawa and Ojibwa names usually referred to dreams, so that the child could grow to inherit the power of its name. Jonas King of Perry Island explained this practice.

One baby I was asked to name I called "Eagle swoops down from the sky" after an incident in my adolescent vision. I cannot tell you the vision because that would destroy its potency and the potency of the name.... An old man living on Perry Island, North Wind, has been asked to name two or three babies. To one child he gave his own name, North Wind. Most of us think this is foolish, for he himself has never been remarkable in any way and his name can have little power.[43]

In addition to birth names, people had other names, some secret, often relating to visions associated with youthful fasts. Commonly, however, people were given new names to commemorate special events in their lives. For example, in the fighting around Fort Dearborn, a Potawatomi warrior, *Kawbenaw* (The Carrier), captured and saved the wife of the commandant, Captain Nathan Heald. This action won him a new name, "Captain Heald," with which he signed several subsequent treaties.[44] Likewise, when Ann Jameson became the first white woman to "shoot the rapids" of the St. Marys River in a birchbark canoe, the local Indians changed her Ojibwa name from *Odawyoungee* (Moon Which Changes Places) to *Wahsage-wampqwe* (Woman of the Bright Foam).[45]

At many times during the eighteenth and nineteenth centuries, the joy of village life was diminished by worry over husbands, fathers, and brothers who were engaged in distant warfare. Not only did women have to contend with long periods of uncertainty over the fate of their loved ones but also with the difficult task of supporting families. The absence of men must also have forced greater reliance on foods produced by women including gathered vegetable products and, where agriculture was practiced, the production of gardens. Hunting during those times was done by boys, older men, and some women who were skillful with the bow as well as snares. In the nineteenth century, as furbearing species became increasingly scarce, Indian women took up the slack by increasing the production of marketable commodities. These principally included maple sugar and wild rice, but also included corn and other garden products. Manufactured items and raw materials were also important trade items. Woven bags, mats, baskets, pitch and bark for building, and items of clothing, especially decorated moccasins, became increasingly important in the family economy. Most of these were the result of the labor of women in the summer villages.

As the fur trade declined and warfare ceased, the role of men in upper Great Lakes Indian society was eclipsed by that of women. Increasingly, women were the major producers of goods so vital for trade, and so the village, built around a stable group of cooperating women, became much more important in social life.

Band Territories and Villages

Treaty negotiations between the United States and Great Lakes Indians in the first five decades of the nineteenth century give us our first comprehensive view of tribal political and social subdivisions. This information may be reconstructed by studying the documents signed by the Indian leaders who represented various bands, the largest decision-making groups. Though the United States may have written treaties with such groups as the "Potawatomi" or the "Ottawa and Chippewa tribe," these distinctions had little or no reality for Indians. For them, it was the local band that made decisions by the consensus of its members, decisions that were conveyed by the chiefs or headmen who were the recognized patriarchs of these local groups.

Since each band consisted of a number of related families who collectively used a set of resources, bands had a territorial dimension.

Often bands are named after a prominent landmark such as a river drainage, a major lake, or a large bay. Map 6 shows the approximate location of the territories and major villages of the upper Great Lakes as they must have existed about 1830. Although each territory is shown as a political unit, in truth these were often subdivided into smaller territories. These smaller units seemed to have had more meaning among the northern groups, where the smallest divisions were likely the hunting and trapping territories of particular families. At the other end of the spectrum, the most southern groups were, by the 1830s, factionalized to the point where the tribal domain was divided among conservative or progressive factions or between traditional factions and Christians of various denominations. Nonetheless, for a group such as the Saginaw Ojibwa to sign a treaty, it was necessary to get the concurrence of its constituent bands, those associated with the Tittabawassee, Shiawassee, Flint, Red Cedar, Cass, and Saginaw rivers and Point Au Gres.

Each of the band or even subband territories was associated with the locations of traditional villages. Originally, these were most commonly given place names such as *Weekwitonsing* (Bay Place), now Harbor Springs, *Peonagowing* (Place of Flint), now the city of Flint, or *Chesaning* (Big Rock), now Chesaning. Village chiefs became more prominent as a result of the increased pressure on the part of the United States to get the bands to agree to various proposals, and as the bands factionalized politically, the villages were more frequently named for the leaders of these factional groups. Thus we have *Cobmoosa*'s village or Blackbird's village. Some names, such as *Peshawbestown* on Grand Traverse Bay, are still in use.

Although the territories of various bands were shown on map 6 by tribal affiliation, many areas contained villages associated with two or more ethnic groups. The headwaters of the Grand River in Michigan was a transition area between the Saginaw Ojibwa and the Grand River Ottawa. Likewise the Leelanau Peninsula in northwestern lower Michigan contained both Ojibwa and Ottawa groups.[46] It is also important to remember that people of these ethnic groups commonly intermarried, particularly in areas of transition between tribes. By 1830 it would probably have been impossible to find any village that was purely Potawatomi or Ottawa.

The first systematic censuses of Indians of the northern Great Lakes were also made by the late 1830s, and while it is thought that these figures are about the same as they would have been at the time of first contact with Europeans, this point remains a matter of vigorous scholarly debate.[47] The earliest censuses indicate that there were about 20,000 Indians in Michigan and northern Wisconsin. Perhaps 12,000 to 15,000 were located in the southern third of the Lower Peninsula and the remaining 5,000 to 8,000 in the north. These are likely conservative figures and, adding in Michigan's Potawatomi, it is likely that the total count was closer to 30,000.

As can be seen from map 6, band territories vary in size and shape depending upon the quantity and quality of resources they contain as well as other, less tangible political considerations. The population size per band, however, is remarkably consistent over the region. Discounting the frequently reported concentration of 2,000 to 3,000 people at Mackinac Island and Chequamegon Bay that were temporary encampments associated with treaty payments, summer village populations seldom exceeded 350 people. Although some band villages contained as few as 50 people, probably 150 people was about average. Given that size for the typical band and an average family size of about 5 people, each band would have been composed of about thirty related families.

It is perhaps surprising that much larger bands are not found among the southern horticulturalists who produced more storable food. Since overall population among the horticulturalists is higher and band territories are often much smaller, that is, 2,000 to 3,000 square miles in the south as opposed to 3,000 to 4,000 square miles in the north, it must be concluded that bands of approximately the same size are simply more densely spaced. We might, therefore, observe that band size per se is not the result of the availability or lack of food but the result of political and sociological factors. It would seem that groups united by egalitarian principles are likely to form at optimal size for good practical purposes. If they are too small, they must grow by recruitment of population; when they become too large, conflicts result in fission.

When we think about the cultural landscape of the Great Lakes country before the time of American settlement or even as the first settlers did, it was a vast and mysterious wilderness. This was certainly not the case for the Indians who lived in Michigan in 1690, 1750, 1830, or at any time in the past. Because they moved widely in the course of hunting and warfare and for summer visiting, they would have had a detailed knowledge of the geography of the whole region. Besides riverway portages and sacred landmarks, they would have known the locations of the principle villages. There is every reason to think that an Indian living in Michigan in 1830 would have been able to name routes, landmarks, and stopping places for travel as well as a modern resident could describe highways, reststops, and motels.

Since there were really so few Indians in the upper Great Lakes country, it is also possible that they were either personally or by gossip acquainted with a large circle of people living in distant places. Of course the practice of exogamy contributed to this pattern as did the extent of travel in the course of seasonal rounds. It is therefore likely that an Indian person in 1830 could name a long list of relatives, friends, and people of political renown who lived in very distant places.

NOTES

1. J. Tanner 1956, 145.
2. J. Tanner 1956, 147.
3. Edmunds 1983, 38.
4. Edmunds 1983, 53.
5. Horsman 1963, 62–63.
6. Edmunds 1983, 115.
7. Edmunds 1983, 115.
8. Edmunds 1983, 127.
9. J. Anderson n.d., 13. Also see Allen 1988, 2–24, and Calloway 1987 for an appraisal of British policy during the period leading to the War of 1812.
10. Hull's Proclamation to the Inhabitants of Canada, July 13, 1812, *Michigan Pioneer and Historical Collections,* 40:409–10.
11. W. Hull to W. Eustis, July 21, 1812, *Michigan Pioneer and Historical Collections,* 40:419–21.
12. Lt. Porter Hanks to Gen. W. Hull, August 4, 1812, Anonymous 1812, 267.
13. Vercheres 1940, 107–8.
14. B. Johnston 1982, 59.
15. J. Brock to W. Hull, August 15, 1812, *Michigan Pioneer and Historical Collections,* 40:451.

16. Testimony of General William Hull, March 16, 1814, *Michigan Pioneer and Historical Collections,* 40:640.
17. Clifton 1977, 207.
18. Kirkland 1893, 113.
19. Vercheres 1940, 142.
20. Gilpin 1958, 227.
21. J. Anderson n.d., 45.
22. Bruce M. White (1987) provides a fascinating discussion of the motivations and perceptions of Ojibwa involved in fur trade exchange with Euro-Americans during the early nineteenth century in Wisconsin and Minnesota.
23. Humins 1983, 27.
24. The Journals of Francois Malhoit and Michel Curot edited for publication by Ruben G. Thwaites (1910, 163–233, 199, 396–471) provide excellent insight into the fur trade at the turn of the nineteenth century. Curot's journal is for the year 1803–4, when he was a clerk for the XYZ Company on the St. Croix River. Malhoit records his life as a North West Company trader at Lac du Flambeau, Wisconsin, during the winter of 1804–5. John Sayer also left a journal of his daily life as a trader on the Snake River in east central Minnesota during the same winter Malhoit was at Lac du Flambeau. These journals make it apparent that the trading practices employed were consistent and widespread, at least among the Lake Superior Ojibwa (see Birk 1989).
25. Thwaites 1911, 407–8.
26. Waddell 1985, 246–68.
27. Voelker 1990, 15.
28. Johnson 1971, 127.
29. McClurken 1988, 129–30.
30. Gilman 1974, 18.
31. See C. Cleland n.d.
32. M. Williams 1953, 8.
33. M. Williams 1953, 369–70.
34. See Hoffman 1891.
35. As a historical note, it might be mentioned here that fifty years later the soldiers from Fort Brady removed the knoll containing *Boweting* band burials to use the soil as fill around buildings. Burial sites were desecrated and local newspapers carried pictures of soldiers posing with skulls and other relics. This event is well established in the oral history of the people of the Sault Ste. Marie band of Chippewa and today evokes strong and bitter recollections.
36. M. Williams 1953, 97.
37. M. Williams 1953, 99.

38. *Ozhawguscodaywaquay* (Susan Johnston) was a truly remarkable woman. We know of her life from several published sources, including Superintendent of Indian Affairs Thomas McKenney (1959, 182–84), who visited her home in 1826. Besides a written description, McKenney also had a portrait drawn of *Ozhawguscodaywaquay*. During the summer of 1837, Ann Jameson (1970, 183), a noted traveler and chronicler of the Canadian frontier, visited *Ozhawguscodaywaquay* and talked with her extensively, including learning of her vision quest. Among the George Johnston papers at the Bayliss Library in Sault Ste. Marie is an unpublished manuscript by Charlotte E. Killaly, a descendent of the Johnston family, that is a biography of John Johnston but includes details about other members of the family. As for *Ozhawguscodaywaquay*'s part in the events of June 16, 1820, they are described by her son George Johnston in Henry Schoolcraft's journal of the Cass Expedition (M. Williams 1953). C. Cleland (1991a) provides a further study of her identity and influence on the Lake Superior frontier.

39. A *waginogan*, the classic dome-shaped bark or reed mat covered domicile, was the usual dwelling for both the summer and winter seasons. A bark-covered conical tipi (*nasaogan*) was built for temporary shelter while traveling. The term *wigiwam,* which has come into modern usage as wigwam, is a generic term to indicate any type of dwelling (Densmore 1970, 12).

40. Jameson 1970, 51–53.

41. Densmore 1970, 72.

42. Densmore 1970, 51–52.

43. Jenness 1935, 93.

44. Clifton 1977, 207.

45. Jameson 1970, 199–200.

46. Montfort 1990, 57–59; McClurken 1988, 293.

47. See C. Cleland 1991b.

Chapter 6

Not the Feelings of Their Hearts

At the beginning of the nineteenth century, Great Lakes Indians occupied millions of acres of land, almost all of the territory that now makes up the upper Great Lakes states and the province of Ontario. Fifty odd years later they were a people dispossessed, owning in total about as much land as may be found in a few counties. In almost every case, they did not give up their land willingly. Although not required to cede it by force of arms, they were nonetheless totally powerless to resist the pressure brought upon them by the United States and England. The story of the tactics used to separate Indians from their ancestral land holdings and their subsequent concentration on tiny reservations is perhaps the most morally despicable story in North American history. It is also one of the culturally most complex, involving a mix of paternalistic good will, racism, arrogance, and ignorance that is difficult to understand. Perhaps more important for today's world, these same events leave modern Americans with a legacy of guilt that powerfully influences the relationship between Indian and non-Indian citizens.

At the conclusion of the War of 1812, the young and struggling United States was left with a huge war debt as well as a variety of other economic woes. It did have within its immense borders, which by now included the Louisiana Purchase, a tremendous potential asset in land. By inducing Indians to relinquish their aboriginal title, the U.S. government saw the opportunity, long since perceived by private investors, to convert land to money. At the same time, the United States could expand its population, secure its distant borders, and stimulate its economy through agricultural production and manufacturing. The first impediment to this vision was, of course, the legitimate interest of aboriginal peoples in the same land holdings. The fact that aboriginal peoples held legitimate title to the land and its resources by virtue of their original occupancy was a well-established construct of Western law. Aboriginal title could be extinguished by a variety of means including both by conquest in rightful wars and by purchase. The Crown Proclamation of 1763 claimed that aboriginal title could only be extinguished by the Crown, a prerogative that on American soil was passed to the United States by the Treaty of Paris that concluded the American revolution. In claiming this exclusive privilege, the governments of both Britain and the United States recognized a filial commitment to an exclusive relationship with the sovereign tribes within their boundaries.

Two national policies were eventually formulated as a means to promote American dominion. The first was the removal policy during the first half of the century; this was later followed by the so-called civilization policy. Both were based on a common underlying theory about the relationship between Indian and non-Indian peoples and cultures. Simply stated, the aboriginal people of the eastern United States were regarded as pagan savages, a state of being that was regarded as incompatible with Christianity and civilized life. It was clear to most nineteenth-century Americans that either Indians would have to radically change or they would have to be eliminated; the two ways of life simply could not coexist. In a message on Indian removal, President Andrew Jackson made this opinion clear: "All preceding experiments for the improvement of the Indians have failed. It seems now to be an established fact that they cannot live in contact with a civilized community and prosper."[1]

This idea of incompatibility rested on the belief that Indians were biologically and culturally inferior. In the science of the day, antiquarians were busy cataloging Indian mounds and earthworks in the newly acquired land of the Ohio valley with the hope that excavated bones and artifacts would shed light on the origins of the "red race." Intellectuals such as Thomas Jefferson were beginning to formulate competing theories of Indian origins and trying to investigate these by means of archaeology.[2] Among the most popular beliefs was that Indians were the descendants of various wayward European expeditions of exploration. Rumors of tribes of "blue-eyed" or "Welsh-speaking" Indians fueled this speculation. Of equal popularity was the idea that Indians were descendants of one of the ten lost tribes of Israel. Here, however, it was necessary to account for the fact that these "Israelite descendants" were also apparent savages. This conflict was rectified by the "fall from grace theory," which proposed that the original Israelite immigrants had long ago succumbed to an emergent faction of savage warriors—the ancestors of modern Indians. Thus, it was conjectured that the mounds and earthworks were the monuments of the earlier, enlightened people who had been exterminated by their savage successors. Reports of finds of hieroglyphic tablets, usually of gold, and other sacred artifacts in Indian mounds seemed to confirm this idea; today it provides the basic theological underpinnings of the Church of Jesus Christ of Latter Day Saints.

Another line of support for these theories of Indian inferiority was to emerge from the new "science" of phrenology—the study of the bumps and lumps on the human skull. Reports out of Harvard and other eastern universities supported the idea that excavated Indian skulls showed fewer propensities for civilized skills than those of whites. To many, this condition was more or less permanent, the result of the divine creation of static races.

Samuel Morton, the father of phrenology, conducted a quantitative comparison of the size and shape of human skulls from around the world. In the case of native Americans, he concluded

the benevolent mind may regret the inaptitude of the Indian for "civilization," but sentimentality must yield to fact. The structure of his mind appears to be different from that of the white man, nor can the two harmonize in the social relations except on the most limited scale. "Indians" are not only adverse to the restraints of education, but for the most part, are incapable of a continued process of reasoning on abstract subjects.[3]

In the thinking of the day, races, usually described in terms of blood, were each provided with innate qualities of intelligence, industriousness, physical abilities, and so on. Travelers among Indians often provided descriptive details compatible with these preconceptions. Chiefs or Indians of accomplishment were given such backhanded compliments as "he has a dignified bearing and quick intelligence unusual for his race."

Beyond the implied racial defects, Indians were burdened with other stereotypes that eroded their status as real human beings. Men were "warriors of keen eyesight, cunning, speed, and great endurance," in short, superlatives usually reserved for wild animals. Women, it seemed, were either "squaws" or, if physically attractive, "dusky maidens." Both early nineteenth-century science and theology thus supported what most Americans already believed as a result of the Indian Wars of the trans-Allegheny west: Indians were *by nature* cruel and warlike savages with limited potential.[4]

The first suggested solution to the perceived incompatibility between American civilization and Indian savagery was the removal policy, which was hotly debated in the 1820s and was enacted into law by Congress in May, 1830 (*U.S. Statutes at Large*, 4:411–12). The removal policy had an insidious aspect in that it was at once supported by both liberals, who hoped to save and protect Indians, and by those who hated them as an impediment to Americans' "manifest destiny." Since coexistence was deemed unworkable, either because Indians could not change in the conservative view or because they would be unmercifully exploited and despoiled in the liberal view, it would serve all interests to remove them. To put them beyond the reach of civilization, the government proposed to buy their land and to transport them to the "unsettled" land west of the Mississippi River. Here, the eastern Indians would be free to roam and to continue to hunt by traditional means. This out of sight, out of mind policy was pushed hard by the likes of old Indian fighter President Andrew Jackson and Christian missionaries who hoped to establish utopian Christian Indian colonies in the west. Conveniently, these advocates of the cruelest of America's Indian policies ignored the fact that the people to be removed were village farmers and that they would be unwelcome in the west, which, of course, was already settled by indigenous tribes.

The strongest opposition to removal was organized by Jeremiah Evarts, secretary of the American Board of Commissioners for Foreign Missions, who led a national fight against Congressional approval. Unfortunately, most of his support in this unsuccessful cause came not from those supporting Indian rights but from Whigs and anti-Jackson forces who hoped to embarrass the administration.[5]

The second stage of the formation of nineteenth-century policy was based upon the same notions of the savage state of Indians but suggested a different and more humane solution, their conversion to a civilized state. The rationale behind this "civilization policy" rested more heavily on cultural than racial concepts. Although not specifically published until later in the century, the idea of cultural evolution contributed importantly to American ideology about Indians and to the government's Indian policy. Formulated in part by pioneer ethnologist Lewis Henry Morgan, this theory saw mankind as evolving through a series of fixed stages, from savagery, to barbarism, and finally to civilization. Each stage was characterized by items of material culture, the use of bow and arrow or metallurgy, for example, or certain other signs of progress, literacy, laws, and modes of kin recognition. The emergent field of anthropology was beginning to reveal the diversity of cultural life on the planet and, to many, it was obvious from this information that Europeans and their descendants were at a much "higher" evolutionary stage than others—including, of course, native Americans. There was a saving grace, however—savages and barbarians could be willfully lifted to the civilized stage. To nineteenth-century Americans, the magic formula for transformation involved teaching Indians to read, write, believe in Christ, and use modern agricultural methods to farm land that they owned as individuals. As good Jeffersonian farmers and as civilized people, Indians would stand shoulder to shoulder with their fellow Americans and be absorbed into American society.

As the horrors and injustice of removal began to penetrate the consciousness of the American public, the civilization policy gained support. Clearly, many Americans, particularly the clergy and those most familiar with Indian affairs, saw a duty as well as a moral responsibility to civilize the savages. It was thus with good will and utter righteousness that the American government, often by employing Christian missionary societies, set out to save Indians by destroying their economy, language, social systems, and religions.

It is perhaps somewhat misleading to focus attention entirely on the cultural devastation of Great Lakes natives because other "primitive" people in every corner of the globe were in for an equal share of salvation. Perhaps it is not fair to say that Indians alone were being herded to the melting pot when the same destiny was seen for the thousands of European immigrants beginning to flood America's shores. It is probably even somewhat cynical to suggest that the underlying motive for these good intentions was to simply separate Indians from their land. What is true is that the self-righteous paternalism that permeated American Indian policy during the nineteenth century allowed our government and its agents to justify unconscionable acts of genocide and ethnocide in the name of progress and civilization. The United States, of course, also acquired the land.

In hindsight, the nineteenth-century relationship between the United States and the Indian tribes within its boundaries can only be described in terms of imperial agression. By means of treaty and within the mythology of sovereign equals, the U.S. government acquired nearly all Indian land. In the process, it usurped control of the resources of the land from productive soil to timber and minerals. Indians were forced onto tiny island "reserves," where they were surrounded by hostile neighbors. Here they could not pursue traditional means of livelihood and they were subject to intense indoctrination. American society imposed its cultural institutions, including language, American law, patterns of land tenure, modes of marriage, inheritance, and child rearing. Despite the high hopes and professed ideals explicit in this civilization experiment, the productivity of Indians was ultimately diverted to the agricultural and industrial areas where they were ultimately exploited as unskilled laborers. One could ask again, in hindsight, were there alternatives? Clearly there were, but was nineteenth-century America able to perceive them?

The Father's Helpers

The administrative mechanisms for handling the rapidly expanding and increasingly complex relationships between the United States and Indian tribes grew erratically during the early years of the Republic. At the beginning of the nineteenth century, the secretary of war assigned a few clerks to administer various federal laws concerning regulation of trade, control of liquor entering Indian country, and operation of government trading houses. Much of this work was done in conjunction with local military commanders, who were barely cooperative. In 1818, Congress authorized the appointment of Indian agents for these purposes, including one at Mackinac (*U.S. Statutes at Large*, 3:461) and, in 1822, Secretary of War John Calhoun created the Bureau of Indian Affairs within the War Department. Thomas McKenney, an exceedingly able man, was appointed as head of the bureau, which was often referred to as the "Indian Office."[6]

The Michigan Superintendency was established in 1805, the year

that Michigan was organized as a territory. Governor William Hull
was ex officio Superintendent of Indian Affairs and was succeeded
by Governor Lewis Cass, who held the post until 1831. By 1818, the
Michigan Superintendency included all of present-day Michigan,
Wisconsin, and Minnesota east of the Mississippi. After the organization of the Bureau of Indian Affairs, agencies (local offices) were
opened at Mackinac, Sault Ste. Marie, Green Bay, Chicago, Fort
Wayne, and Piqua. Subagents and interpreters were employed at
these as well as at various subagencies. The Sault Ste. Marie
Agency, which was under the supervision of Henry Schoolcraft, included a subagency at La Pointe.

By the act of June 9, 1832, Congress authorized a Commissioner
of Indian Affairs to deal with Indian relations (*U.S. Statutes at Large,*
4:564). Thomas McKenney was the first commissioner. The act also
permitted the hiring of additional agents, subagents, interpreters,
and mechanics; the consequence was the first well-organized and
staffed Indian Department. It was, however, a small bureaucracy.

As a result of the new arrangement, the Mackinac and Sault Ste.
Marie agencies were consolidated and the agent, Henry Schoolcraft,
moved to Mackinac in 1833. From 1837 until 1850, subagents were
assigned at Sault Ste. Marie.[7]

When Wisconsin became a territory in 1836 the Michigan Superintendency was reduced to the boundaries of the state. Since Michigan was, itself, on the verge of statehood, Henry Schoolcraft was
designated to act as superintendent. Theoretically, the superintendent was to spend summers at Mackinac and winters at Detroit but,
in fact, the business of the Michigan Superintendency was increasingly centered at Detroit; in 1837, the Detroit subagency was moved
to Saginaw and assigned the duties of dealing with Indians in the
southern part of the state. Henry Conner was appointed to this new
post. The Saginaw subagency was discontinued in 1846, followed
by the Sault Ste. Marie subagency in 1852. The duties of both were
transferred to the Mackinac agency after the Michigan Superintendency was abolished in 1851.[8] Meanwhile, on March 3, 1849, Congress transferred Indian Affairs from the War Department to the
Department of the Interior, where it remains today (*U.S. Statutes at
Large,* 9:395).

Michigan Indian affairs were now placed under the Northern Superintendency, which also included Wisconsin. In fact, however, the

Mackinac agency acted alone and, after 1853, reported directly to the Commissioner of Indian Affairs. After 1852, the Mackinac agency, sometimes called the Michigan agency, had charge over the affairs of all Michigan Indians plus the Lake Superior Chippewa who resided in Wisconsin and Minnesota. The Mackinac agency was abolished in 1889. It was recreated the next year to serve the Lake Superior Chippewa at L'Anse-Ontonogon but was consolidated with the Lac du Flambeau agency in 1927.[9]

Treaties and Treaty Making

From the time of the origin of the American government until 1871 when it stopped making Indian treaties, the formal relationship between Indian tribes and the United States was a relationship between political sovereigns. That is, it was regulated by agreements between governments that stood on an equal legal footing, each recognizing the legitimacy of the other. Such agreements between governments regulated trade, the rights of citizens, and many other matters including, in the case of Indian tribes, relinquishment of specified aboriginal rights, particularly to land. For its part, the United States conducted treaty making with Indians by the same format it did with Spain, England, or any foreign government: treaty commissioners instructed as to specific objectives negotiated the agreement, the signed document was later discussed and usually ratified by the U.S. Senate, and finally declared law by the president.

Indian treaty making often involved a somewhat different process owing to the fact that it was nearly always the United States that was organizing and promoting the treaties. First, the desire to acquire certain territories often led the United States to simply create Indian political entities for the purpose of specific treaties. In fact, such entities as "the Potawatomi Tribe" or "the Chippewa Tribe" never functioned as coherent political bodies, yet the United States insisted on treaty making with these "Tribes." In the case of the Treaty of Washington in 1836, the United States signed a treaty of cession with something it called the "Ottawa and Chippewa Nation" by lumping together bands representing Ottawa on the Grand River, Ottawa on Grand Traverse and Little Traverse bays, and Ojibwa from the eastern Upper Peninsula and the Straits of Mackinac, each having distinctly different interests. This process only worked because the Indians were able to negotiate on the basis of the small bands that actually represented their interests and because the bands managed to reach agreement. It did not matter what the United States wanted to call the collectivity and it does not matter to this day, because it is still the consolidated bands that retain rights under these treaties. Another problem for the United States was that large numbers of Indians had to be assembled for the treaty negotiations, because they had no means to delegate authority. A constant round of discussion among decision makers was required to reach agreement; there could be no minority position, even though there were often very strong minority opinions. Dissenters often simply refused to participate or to sign. Whenever possible, the United States preferred to assemble Indian leaders in Washington or some metropolitan area to negotiate treaties. Here, Indians could be impressed with the power and prestige of the Great Father, entertained, and intimidated.[10] The sheer cost of transporting, housing, clothing, and feeding large numbers of Indian delegates often precluded this tactic and American treaty negotiators found themselves on the home turf of the tribes.

Treaties were uniformly written in the English language and, of course, the verbal negotiations that preceded them required the use of interpreters who were hired by the U.S. government. Language was an immense barrier to progress since Indians had to settle for explanations of proposals that were translated by individuals who were sometimes only marginally proficient in the Algonquian languages. Likewise, Indians skilled in the use of allegory and symbolism had a difficult time making the subtle points upon which their oratory often turned. These difficulties were the result of Indian emphasis on the spoken word, while Americans emphasized the final written document. Because of their training in listening to oration and remembering oral representations, Indians often came away from treaty sessions relying upon what American negotiators stated as bargaining positions. Often what they thought was included in a treaty was simply never written down and, more often, they had very little understanding of what the treaty actually stated.

An incident in July, 1857, at Fort Frances on Rainy River illustrates the point. An American Ojibwa happened to be visiting relatives when the Palliser expedition passed through their territory. The local chief, fearing the visitors would demand a land cession on the part of the queen, told the visitors that they were not interested in parting with any land. He was reassured that the expedition was merely passing through and that "if anybody should wrest their lands from them, our Great Queen would send her soldiers to drive those people back." At that point the American visitor, more experienced in treaty making, rose to advise the chief, "Make him put that on paper."[11]

From the Indian point of view, treaty making was a very important and somewhat mystical process that was taken very seriously. Delegations often arrived at the treaty grounds with great ceremony and dressed in their finest attire. As on other occasions of social and political significance, blessings, which included the smoking of medicine pipes and gift exchanges, preceded business. Treaties, they knew, bound them to take certain irreversible actions that were promises made to the American president as a covenant between father and children. As nonliterate people, the treaty document, which they could not read, took on much significance and magical properties. In the convention of the treaty process, each Indian leader would signify assent by means of an X placed beside his written name, a ceremony called "touching the pen." Instead of writing the X themselves, leaders would literally touch the quill, which in turn would be picked up by the treaty secretary who made the X mark. If Indian leaders personally signed agreements at all, which was unusual during the American period, they drew the animal that was the sign of their clan. Once treaties were finalized, Indians believed that the agreement was permanent. The government, of course, foresaw that conditions might soon require new treaties.

Because Indians took treaty making more seriously than the United States and because they assigned more importance to the ritual does not mean they were naive. In fact they did arrive at strong bargaining positions and were skillful negotiators.

The Carrot and the Stick

Since the United States initiated most treaties in order to acquire land and since Indians were usually very reluctant participants in such enterprises, the United States developed a carrot-and-stick approach to treaty making. With sufficient preparation, these techniques were so effective that no Indian groups were able to resist them.

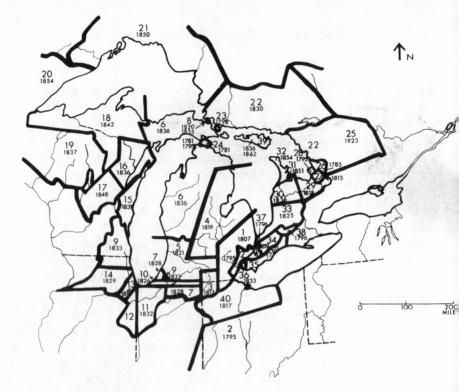

1. Treaty of Detroit (1807)
2. Treaty of Greenville (1795)
3. Rapids of the Miami (1817)
4. Treaty of Saginaw (1819)
5. Treaty of Chicago (1821)
6. Treaty of Washington (1836)
7. Treaty of Carey Mission (1828)
8. Treaty of Sault Ste. Marie (1820) and Treaty of Detroit (1855)
9. Treaty of Chicago (1833)
10. Treaty of Mississinewa (1826)
11. Treaty of Camp Tippecanoe (October 26, 1832)
12. Treaty of Camp Tippecanoe (October 20, 1832)
13. Treaty of St. Louis (1816)
14. Treaty of Prairie du Chien (1829)
15. Stambaugh's Treaty (1831)
16. Treaty of Cedar Point (1836)
17. Menominee Treaty of 1848
18. Treaty of La Pointe (1842)
19. Treaty of St. Peters (1837)
20. Treaty of La Pointe (1854)

21. Robinson-Superior Treaty of 1850
22. Robinson-Huron Treaty of 1850
23. Treaty No. 11 (1798)
24. Treaty of Greenville (1795) and Treaty No. 1 (1781)
25. Williams Treaty (1923) and Robinson Huron Treaty of 1850
26. John Collins Purchase (1785)
27. Treaty No. 16 (1815)
28. Treaty No. 5 (1795)
29. Treaty No. 60 (1818)
30. Treaty No. 45-1/2 (1836)
31. Treaty No. 82 (1857)
32. Treaty No. 72 (1854)
33. Treaty No. 27-1/2 (1825)
34. Treaty No. 21 (1819)
35. Treaty No. 2 (1790)
36. Treaty No. 35 (1833)
37. Treaty No. 7 (1796)
38. Treaty No. 6 (1796)
39. Bond Head Treaty (1836) and Treaty No. 94 (1862)
40. Wyandot Treaty of 1817

Major treaties of land cession. (Drawing by B. Nemeth.)

After the War of 1812, the American settlement frontier was pushing north and west and, for the first time, Great Lakes Indians were feeling the pressure. Squatters were moving onto and clearing farmland on unceded lands in hopes of establishing "preemption" rights when the United States actually purchased the land. Preemption permitted settlers to have first rights to purchase lands they occupied. The completion of the Erie Canal in 1825 and improved water transportation greatly increased settlement in Lower Michigan. In 1820, there were only 8,765 non-Indians in the Michigan Territory, while in 1830 there were 31,640. In the next four years the population almost tripled to 87,278, and by 1836 there were 174,543 non-Indians in Michigan.[12] The *Anishnabeg* were very well aware of the presence of these newcomers and their thirst for farmland. To many Potawatomi, Ottawa, and Saginaw Ojibwa who lived in the fertile woodlands of southern Michigan, the future course seemed inevitable, because it was impossible to resist the U.S. military; treaties represented the only means of securing permanent homes amid the wave of newcomers. This they hoped to achieve by making small reservations that would be withheld from sale. To many, such a tactic was the only hope of preserving their lifeway and traditions. A few leaders even believed that treaties were the only means to acquire the skills, education, and agricultural expertise necessary to compete in the new order. The United States held out these inducements in the form of land and land use concessions, annuities in the form of money and goods in payment for land. The package also included educational opportunities: supplying teachers and schools and the services of mechanics, blacksmiths, and farmers who would teach the American style of agriculture and animal husbandry. Prior to the middle of the century, most of these services were provided by contract with various Protestant missionary establishments. While many Indians recognized the inevitability of change and advocated preparation for it by means of treaty benefits, many others argued that changes of such magnitude would mean the total collapse of all they treasured. These people strongly opposed treaties with the United States.

The United States had at its disposal other powerful inducements that it did not hesitate to use to force Indians to agree to treaties. Implicitly, of course, there was the implied threat of military force: military escorts were often present at treaty sessions. The use of presents to influential people and the use of liquor as inducements or to sway opinion were also effective techniques. In addition, early treaties often contained land grants to specific individuals and often these were to the "Indian children" of non-Indian traders. The influence of traders was perhaps the crucial factor in gaining the acquiescence of Indians to many, many treaties. Since these men had large, extended Indian families and were themselves the link to American society and, therefore, the source of guns, blankets, kettles, and all the other technology upon which Indians now depended, the traders were very powerful. Indians often sought their advice on external affairs and they were likewise consulted by the U.S. government, which hired them as subagents and interpreters.

Treaties profited the traders in several ways. Their children often received large pieces of valuable land, but there were also direct and indirect monetary inducements. Since Indians received annuities in the form of goods and coinage, the traders often sold the goods to the government and quickly received the gold and silver specie from the Indians for more goods and liquor or in payments of debts. This business, particularly the flow of cash into the economy of the northwest during the financially depressed late 1830s when the Bank of the United States was on the verge of collapse, was very significant. Indians were not just big players on the frontier, they were the only game in town. Most of the funds dispersed to Indians in the form of treaty annuities went more or less directly into the hands of the traders, who collected like vultures when the annual payments were made.

Treaties also often specified huge sums to pay the debts of Indians. Knowing this, the traders pressured their Indian in-laws unmercifully for the repayment of debts that, with the depletion of fur-bearing species, Indians had no means to repay, except through making treaties. Again and again the names of traders who were involved in making treaties appeared on debt lists compiled to claim repayment for their "losses." Without a doubt, this small group of traders was greatly instrumental in breaking down Indian resistance to land cession.

Both historical circumstance and government policy affected the way land cession treaties were written. The Great Lakes region illustrates three major types of land cession treaties: those that required removal west, those that provided reservations on the ceded land,

Indian Deed

Potawatomi land grant to Pierre Labady, Raisin River, 1786. (Courtesy of the State of Michigan Archives.)

and those that did not resolve the homeland issue. As examples, we can turn to the Treaties of Saginaw (1819), Chicago (1833), and Washington (1836).

The Treaty of Saginaw

Unfortunately, there are no official minutes of the treaty between the United States and the Chippewa of Saginaw that was negotiated in 1819. It was an important treaty for both parties. For its part, the United States gained 6 million acres, roughly one-third of Lower Michigan, and this concession cost the Chippewa the land that was the core of their identity. Fortunately, there are several accounts of the events that took place during the negotiation of the treaty that were recorded after discussion with people who participated. What we do know rests, therefore, mainly on the oral history of non-Indians.[13] The land ceded was a triangle with its base along the shore of Lake Huron from the Thunder Bay river in the north to the middle of Michigan's thumb on the south. The apex of the triangle was near Kalamazoo.

As ex officio Indian Superintendent, Territorial Governor Lewis Cass received instructions from the War Department to try to gain this territory through a treaty. He was to obtain it as cheaply as possible and, if he could, convince the Chippewa to move west of Lake Michigan. The press of white settlement from the south as well as the desire to collect reparations for Indian "depradations" against white settlers in the Detroit region were cited as the factors that motivated the treaty. In preparation, Cass hired Detroit trader Louis Campau to construct an open council house at the camping place on the Saginaw River called *Bashoaing* ('the place close by'), which is now the site of the city of Saginaw. To his embarrassment, Cass discovered just before his departure that the Saginaw Chippewa had never been paid annuities promised them in prior treaties. He solved this problem by arranging a loan with the Bank of Detroit, which was not difficult since many of the directors were merchants who supplied Indian trade goods to the government.

That problem solved, he proceeded overland to Saginaw with an entourage of agents, subagents, and interpreters. Supplies for the treaty were taken to Saginaw on the U.S. Cutter *Porcupine*, which also carried a company of the U.S. Third Infantry under the command of Cass's brother Charles. Cass came well prepared to deal with the Chippewa. On board the *Porcupine* were Indian presents valued at about $1,500. Also included was a quantity of alcohol. Despite long-standing official U.S. policy against the introduction of intoxicating beverages into Indian country, one of the major proponents of the policy and the person responsible for curbing its use in Michigan was now prepared to supply it to the Saginaw Chippewa in order to induce them to sell their land. Skeptics of Cass's actual intentions in this regard may be convinced by the fact that he prepared for the ten-day parley by purchasing 39 gallons of brandy, 91 gallons of wine, 41 1/2 gallons of fourth proof spirits, 10 gallons of whiskey, and 6 gallons of gin from the Whipple and Smyth Company for a total expenditure of $587.12. This amount was approximately a quarter of the expenses for Indian presents.[14] Clearly, Cass was planning some party.

Assembled to meet Cass were an estimated several thousand men, women, and children mostly of Ojibwa identity but with some Ottawa from the western margins of the valley as well as a mixture of Ottawa and Potawatomi spouses. These represented several distinct bands, including at least those associated with the following river drainages: Au Gres, Rifle, Kawkawlin, Tittabawasee, Pine, Maple, Shiawassee, Flint, and the Cass. The largest number were from the Saginaw proper. Ultimately, 140 Indian leaders signed the treaty, but those of widest acclaim were *Ogamawkeketo* (Chief Speaker), who was from the Tittawabassee, *Kishkauko* (the Crow), who parenthetically was the same *Kishkauko* who helped his father, *Manitogezik,* capture John Tanner in Kentucky before the War of 1812, *Menoquet* from the Cass River, *Neome* from the Flint river, *Wasso* from the Shiawassee, and the Ottawa *Nowkeshuc* (Noonday) from the Grand.

To complete the cast of characters there was a large number of assembled traders, soldiers, subagents, and interpreters, most of whom had some official capacity and all of whom had interests in the outcome of the talks. Besides Lewis Cass, the party included Assistant Commissioner R. A. Forsyth and Secretary John Lieb; J. Marsac, J. Visges, J. Riley, and Henry Conner (interpreters); and Whitmore Knaggs and J. Godfroy (subagents). Excluding Cass, Forsyth, Lieb, and the soldiers, almost all of these men were married to Chippewa women and had Chippewa identities. For example, Henry Conner was called *Wahbeskendip* (White Hair), Louis Campau was called *Netababapinisid,* and Whitmore Knaggs was called *Okeday-bendon.* Most of these men also made their living as Indian traders and from time to time as employees in the administration of Indian affairs. Of special interest is Jacob Smith, *Wahbesin* (Young Swan), a Saginaw trader who was married to both a local woman and to a white woman in Detroit. He had families by both women, and, at the time of the treaty, he had one Indian daughter at Saginaw, *Mokitche-noqua.*[15] As a long-time resident at the portage of the Flint River and as the principle trader of the region, Jacob Smith was to play a pivotal role in the Saginaw Treaty.

The council opened in the second week of September and lasted ten days, during which time there were three formal sessions, the opening, the signing, and one meeting in between. After the usual preliminaries, Cass explained what the United States had in mind through his interpreters Henry Conner and Whitmore Knaggs. First, he extended the paternal regards of the Great Father and his wish for peace between the Ojibwa and the United States. He reminded them that the wave of American civilization was rendering their hunting way of life obsolete and that they would need to turn to agriculture for a living. To help, the United States would buy their land and they could settle down to farm on small reservations. The Ojibwa were both astounded and surprised by Cass's speech. First, they were already farmers, and, second, they probably had not anticipated that the United States would want to buy their land. Because they had been at war with the United States only five years earlier as British allies in the War of 1812 and on none too friendly terms since, they must have assumed the United States would propose an offer of peace. This attitude is apparent in the formal reply to Cass by the chief speaker, *Ogamawkeketo.*

You do not know our wishes. Our people wonder what has brought you so far from your homes. Your young men have invited us to come and light the council fire. We are here to smoke the pipe of peace, but not to sell our land. Our American father wants them. Our English father treats us better; he has never asked for them. Your people trespass upon our hunting grounds. You flock to our shores. Our waters grow warm; our land melts like a cake of ice; our possessions grow smaller and smaller; the warm wave of the white man rolls in upon us and melts us away. Our women reproach us. Our children want homes: shall we sell from under them the spot where they spread their blankets? We have not called you here. We smoke with you the pipe of peace.[16]

The Council broke up with a negative, if not hostile, undercurrent. Cass now unleashed the considerable forces at his disposal. Well-placed presents of liquor took care of some of the opposition. For example, *Kishkauko,* who bitterly opposed land cession, was kept drunk until the time came to sign the treaty. The Indian traders who stood to profit from both the sale of goods to be purchased with the money the Chippewa would get for selling their land and by grants of land reserves to their own children went to work to promote the treaty.

The traders and interpreters offered bribes to individuals for their support; guns, many horses, liquor, and trade goods were promised and eventually delivered. Unquestionably, the key power broker was Jacob Smith, who had a very close personal relationship with *Neome,* the principle Saginaw chief and Smith's main trading partner at the portage of the Flint river where the city of Flint now stands. The vague accounts of the behind-the-scenes negotiations between the chiefs and the traders indicate that little progress was being made until *Neome* was able to extract an agreement that land reserves would be withheld not only for the various bands but also for his friend *Wahbesin* (Jacob Smith). Since they knew the U.S. government did not permit reserves to be made directly to whites, a list of eleven Indian names, supposedly Smith's Indian children, was given to Whitmore Knaggs, who apparently approved the deal on behalf of the government. In article 3 of the treaty, each of these children was to receive 640 acres, a square mile, at the crossing of the Flint River. In addition to *Neome's* deal for Smith, 640 acre reserves were made for the three Riley brothers, sons of *Menawcumegoqua,* for *Kishkauko,* and for the children of *Bokowtonden* (probably Whitmore Knaggs). These private reserves totaled 10,240 acres. The treaty also attempted to make land grants for Dr. William Brown, Henry and James Conner, Peter and George Knaggs, and Jacques Godfroy as well as a cash payment of $1,298.20 to Conrad Ten Eyck as "supplemental articles." These were not approved by the U.S. Senate.

Fifteen other reserves totaling 102,000 acres were made for bands to be held in common. The sizes of these reserves varied from 1,000 to 40,000 acres. Of the total land reserves, one-tenth went to the Indian children of traders. While each of the Saginaw Chippewa received about 25 acres, these individuals received 640 acres.[17] More problematic, however, were the pivotal reserves made for the Smith children. In fact, Smith had only one Indian child; the other ten Indian names were fictitious. Although some of the chiefs later claimed otherwise, presumably to keep these unclaimed lands in Indian hands, litigation concerning ownership dragged on for years.[18]

Resistance broken down, Cass had the treaty prepared for the chiefs to sign. This event was punctuated by a violent fight between Louis Campau and Jacob Smith. Campau, who claimed large trading debts from the Saginaw Chippewa, secretly approached Cass and got him to agree to pay him directly out of the annuity money the Chippewas had coming for their land. Smith and the other traders (who, of course, hoped to get as much of this money as they could for themselves) got wind of the deal at the last minute and sobered up chief *Kishkauko* to object. Faced with this turn of events, Cass had to retract his deal with Campau. Infuriated, Campau attacked Smith and would have killed him if they had not been separated. Campau got his revenge on Cass that same night.

Overjoyed at his success, Cass ordered the U.S. Quartermaster to open five barrels of whiskey and to dispense it to the Indians in celebration. Campau, seeing his chance, added to the festivities by opening ten barrels of whiskey from his trading post and assigning men with ladles to serve all comers. By ten o'clock, the Indians were tremendously drunk and beginning to get hostile. Cass sent a military guard to close down Campau's open bar and soon war whoops were sounded. Cass was terrified and appeared in his night shirt screaming to Campau, "Louis, Louis! Stop the liquors! We will all be killed!" To which Campau replied, "General, you commenced it; you let Smith plunder and rob me, but I will stand between you and harm." Sometime later Campau observed, "I lost my money; I lost my fight; I lost my whiskey; but I got good satisfaction."[19]

The Treaty of Saginaw concluded, the Saginaw Chippewa were now confined to small reservations, and although they also reserved the right to hunt and fish on the land they ceded, this became progressively more difficult. White traders managed to acquire most of the $6,400 appropriated to negotiate the treaty as well as most of the cash paid for land. Account vouchers for the treaty show the key role of the traders, particularly Jacob Smith. Henry Conner made $80 for 20 days' service as an interpreter; Louis Campau, who supplied trade goods and other services, received over $1,000. The *Métis* who acted as subagents and interpreters likewise were generously compensated. Jacob Smith, who had no official position at the treaty, was paid $500 for his "services." This was a great deal of money for a few days' work when the annual salary of a U.S. Indian subagent was an equal amount.

Not all of the Saginaw Chippewa agreed with the treaty and some refused to sign it. One of these men, Chief *Ausawwamic* (Yellow Beaver) from Sebewaing, always came to the annual payments and collected his annuity. He then walked directly to the Saginaw River, where he contemptuously hurled the silver coins into the water.[20] In fact, so much dissatisfaction was apparent that the United States decided to establish a military fort at Saginaw in 1822. A year later it was abandoned after the Americans got a good, firsthand look at their new acquisition. The commandant, Major Daniel Baker, declared the climate so unhealthy that the Saginaw country was fit for nothing but "Indians, muskrats, and bull frogs."[21] Probably *Ausawwamic* and many other of the Chippewa would have agreed.

Eighteen years after the Treaty of Saginaw, Henry Schoolcraft, Superintendent of Indian Affairs, summoned the Saginaw chiefs to Detroit, where the United States offered to purchase their reservations. Now pressured by a crush of white settlers cutting forests and draining swamplands for farms and pressed by traders for the repayment of yet more debts, the chiefs agreed to a treaty on January 14, 1837. This treaty sold most, but not all, of their land reserves in exchange for money that would be raised by the sale of this same land. Out of the proceeds would also come the cost of survey and sale and expenses for the treaty itself. The Chippewa did, however, set apart from the proceeds another fund of $40,000 to pay trader debts and another $10,000 to compensate American citizens for "depredation after the surrender of Detroit in 1812." The Saginaw Chippewa also insisted on the use of some money for schools, smallpox vaccine and medical services, and tobacco. A schedule of payments to individual chiefs and to chiefs representing bands is also included. Among the former is *Wabishkindip,* the Chippewa name for Henry Conner who, in his Indian disguise, collected $3,243.75 when the average payment to real chiefs was about $400. The Treaty of 1837 had one other important provision. The Saginaw Chippewa promised to remove from the region and to reside with "their kindred tribe west of Lake Superior."

Owing in large part to the fact that the Chippewa of Lake Superior were not anxious to receive this huge immigration, the Saginaw people never moved. In fact, they were, instead, joined at Saginaw by the Black River and Swan Creek Chippewa, who, by the Treaty of May 9, 1836, had ceded their reserves in the St. Clair valley made under the Treaty of Detroit in 1807. Now they as well as the Saginaw Chippewa were squeezed on the few small reserves that remained in the Saginaw valley.

Finally, on August 2, 1855, the Saginaw, Black River, and Swan Creek Chippewa concluded a treaty that exchanged their claims in the agriculturally fertile Saginaw region for eight townships of heavily forested land in Isabella County. The United States agreed to provide them with certain services and to allot land to individual Indians. Today, the Isabella Indian community and reservation near Mt. Pleasant is the modern tribal successor to the Chippewa who signed the Treaty of 1855.

The Treaty of Chicago

The Treaty of Detroit in 1807 resulted in the outmigration of many Indians who formerly occupied the southeastern quarter of Lower Michigan. These included many Potawatomi who lived along the rivers that drained into the western end of Lake Erie. The Huron River gave its name to the group that now drifted west, finding less disruption in the unceded territory of the Upper Grand, Thornapple, and Kalamazoo river valleys. Likewise, the Upper Shiawassee, Red Cedar, and Looking Glass drainages sheltered Chippewa fleeing the newly ceded region.

The Huron Potawatomi were but one small band of a great, diverse, and far flung Potawatomi people including the Prairie bands of Illinois and Wisconsin, the Lake bands around Lake Michigan, and the St. Joseph bands in southwestern Michigan and northern Indiana. This latter group was intermarried with the French-Canadian community at Niles and South Bend; some spoke French as well as Potawatomi, and many were inclined toward Catholicism.

Saginaw Chippewa Chief *Nauck-che-gaw-me* (Middle of the Lake), signer of the treaties of 1837, 1855, and 1864. (Photograph courtesy of Leonard Isacc, *Nauck-che-gaw-me*'s great-grandson, and the Historical Museum of Bay County.)

Collectively, the Potawatomi were subject to a barrage of treaty making during the 1820s by which means the United States hoped to acquire all Potawatomi holdings and to remove the Potawatomi west of the Mississippi River. As this process moved forward, the Potawatomi increasingly found themselves on small reserves, islands in the midst of immigrant farmers from the rock-bound country of New England and northern New York who appreciated the rich prairie openings that had been farmed by the Potawatomi.

The Treaty of Chicago in 1821 was perhaps typical of the treaties of cession, though larger than most since it ceded most of the southwest quarter of Lower Michigan. It, too, was negotiated by Lewis Cass, who used the same techniques he found so effective at the Treaty of Saginaw two years earlier. In fact, many of the same individuals were involved. Like the Saginaw Chippewa, the Potawatomi were also extremely reluctant to consider the suggested cession. The respected chief *Topenibe* and the very accomplished chief speaker *Metea* objected strongly, but they were not able to prevail against bribery, the use of liquor, and the duplicity of the traders and *Métis*. The result was, of course, that the Potawatomi, along with the Grand River Ottawa, signed away all of southwestern Michigan south of the Grand except for the area west of the St. Joseph River. Within this territory, they reserved five areas of between three and six square miles and a long list of grants to people of Indian descent, many being members of the extended Burnet, Bertrand, and Riley families.

Just as in the Saginaw case, the government soon approached the Potawatomi to "consolidate" and to remove themselves from the vicinity of the new road being completed between Detroit and Chicago. This the Potawatomi agreed to in the Treaty of September 18, 1827, which exchanged their earlier reserves for 99 sections of land—all of them off the beaten path. In the next year, Cass got the Potawatomi to cede the small triangle of land west of the St. Joseph River. The quid pro quo was again the resolution of trader debts, services, and land grants to individuals.

An important outcome of these treaties was the formation of many small and isolated Potawatomi communities in Michigan. Among the most important were the Potawatomi of the Huron, who took up residence in Calhoun county, the community at the *Nadowesippe* reserve in central St. Joseph county, and the *Pokagon* band, which coalesced at Niles in Berrien county. It should be stressed that by the end of the first quarter of the nineteenth century most Potawatomi in Michigan, perhaps as many as four thousand, continued to pursue their traditional seasonal rounds within ceded territory. Most had adopted American material culture and dress. They also kept pony herds for transportation, but they continued to live in wigwams, to plant summer gardens, and to hunt in family groups during the winter. Most were in occasional, if not frequent, contact with American settlers and at least some Potawatomi spoke Pidgin English.

After the cession of 1821 it became much harder for the Potawatomi to obtain furs to supply their material necessities. They now developed a new economic niche as suppliers for immigrant farmers and townspeople. Meat, hides, collected foodstuffs, corn, honey, and maple sugar were produced for sale or trade as were handicrafts such as bags, split-ash baskets, and bark containers. Settlers were glad to have these products and their relationship with local bands was usually very good. In fact, after the Potawatomi were removed, Michigan citizens often complained at how much their services were missed.[22]

A factor that helped shape Potawatomi views toward the United States and Americans was the presence of missionaries. Just before the Treaty of Chicago in 1821, the St. Joseph bands were being visited by a Baptist missionary, Issac McCoy, who was able to convince some of the chiefs to request a mission school in the forthcoming treaty negotiations. In fact, the treaty did set aside two sections of land as well as $1,000 annual salary for that purpose. Not surprisingly, McCoy got the job.[23] McCoy's mission, called the Carey Mission, was, as other establishments devoted to Christianity and civilizing Indians, supported by the Civilization Fund established by Congress in 1819 as a means of providing education for Indian young people (U.S. Statutes at Large, 3:516–17). These responsibilities were contracted to various Protestant missionary societies.

Even though the St. Joseph Potawatomi would have preferred a Catholic priest, the Carey Mission enjoyed some initial success. Topenibe moved his village nearby, a few Potawatomi tried new methods of cultivation, and some were even baptized. It soon became apparent, however, that McCoy was a strong advocate of the removal policy.[24] It was his hope that the Potawatomi and some of the Grand River Ottawa could be moved west, where he would establish a religious colony among them in an atmosphere uncontaminated by whites, particularly the whiskey peddlers who abounded in Potawatomi country. In a letter of recommendation, Lewis Cass described McCoy as "a man devoted to the moral and physical improvement of the Indians, and to their final location, where they can be secure against evils, which have reduced and threatened to destroy them."[25] After 1827, the Carey Mission rapidly declined as the antiremoval and pro-Catholic chiefs Leopold *Pokagon, Mikasabe,* and *Abtegizhek* (Half Day) resisted association with McCoy. Reverend McCoy then became an agent for the government promoting removal.

Pressure for removal of the Potawatomi was fanned by the Black Hawk War in 1832. Even though the Potawatomi refused to support the Sauk and Fox, and, in fact, although some Potawatomi even acted as scouts for the U.S. Army, American citizens were distrustful and suspicious of Indians in general and agitated for their removal west.[26]

The far-flung Potawatomi bands were summoned to Chicago in the fall of 1833 to negotiate what is probably one of the most complex treaties ever written between the United States and an Indian tribe. In it, the United States agreed to purchase all remaining Potawatomi lands and to pay their outstanding debts and, in exchange, the Potawatomi agreed to remove west. Both the Huron and Pokagon bands staunchly opposed removal. It is reported that special committees were formed during negotiations to watch over and stiffen the resolve of the chiefs, who were under the penalty of death if they signed away the land. When the time came, the Huron band chiefs did agree to remove and it is said that several were, indeed, later assassinated. The Pokagon band, at the stubborn insistence of Leopold *Pokagon* and in spite of the duplicity of old chief *Topenibe*'s son, whom the Americans touted as the new head chief of the Potawatomi, won permission to stay in Michigan. As Catholics, they were to remove north to reside with fellow Catholic Ottawa in northwestern Lower Michigan although the other Potawatomi would have to remove within three years.[27]

In the next few years, scouting parties sent west to visit Kansas, which was to be their new home, reported that the new lands lacked sugar trees and that the arid ground would only produce pumpkins the size of potatoes. It is little wonder that they dreaded the move.

It was not until 1835 that the U.S. Senate finally ratified the treaty of 1833. Although given a short reprieve, the Potawatomi were very apprehensive about their prospects. Removal began to take place further south, in Indiana, where "conductors" hired by the government were paid on contract so many dollars per capita to collect and transport Potawatomi west. Such contracts became an important source of hard money and employment for Michigan frontier settlers during the financial panic of 1836.

The big removal push finally came to Michigan in the fall of 1840, when General Hugh Brady organized a removal roundup with four companies of soldiers and settlers commissioned to support the conductors. Unaware of the exclusion of the Catholic bands, Brady had to be served with a court order obtained by *Pokagon* to permit them to remain. Many of the others were not so fortunate. One example is the band of *Muckmoot,* whose removal from their village near Olivet in Eaton County was the subject of a reminiscence by pioneer John Nichols.[28] Though secondhand and anecdotal, it does provide some of the feelings of the removal episode.

"Captain" Nichols, a farmer near *Muckmoot*'s village, was temporarily commissioned as a tracker to locate *Muckmoot*'s band, who had fled their village for more remote, forested regions in the north. Nichols was personally well acquainted with these Potawatomi neighbors with whom he had dealt for some years. Nonetheless, he tracked them as they fled north on their ponies. Apparently they crossed the Grand River at Grand Ledge and struck the Looking Glass, which they then followed upstream. Nichols found the grave of a woman the band had paused to bury near modern DeWitt and knew he was on the right trail. Striking the Grand River trail west of Laingsburg, they headed east on the open road hoping to escape to Canada. Instead, they decided to turn north into heavy timber country. Nichols finally overtook them encamped, hungry, and cold in the bottomlands of the Shiawassee River near Corunna. An army detachment personally commanded by General Brady soon surrounded them. In the end, the band was captured and marched to Owosso, where they were confined. Later they were taken to Marshall, which was a collection point for the trip west. Each person was permitted fifty pounds of baggage. Edward Foote reported that, during the last night's stay, "the moans and lamentations of the Potawatomi women were heart rending."[29]

The number of Potawatomi who were actually removed is unknown. Many simply hid out until the removal fervor subsided.
Many fled to Canada and the Canadian reserves along the east shore
of Lakes Huron and St. Clair and the Detroit River. These took in
many refugee Potawatomi, including *Muckmoot*'s neighboring band
in Eaton County under the leadership of *Tuckamin*. Walpole Island
on the Canadian side of Lake St. Clair, now an Indian reserve, became an especially important haven for the Potawatomi and one
from which they frequently returned in later years to visit their old
Michigan homelands.[30]

In order to secure his band's future, Leopold *Pokagon* gradually
purchased land at Silver Creek in Cass County until he had accumulated 875 acres.[31] During the last year of his life, the Catholic church
claimed that he had deeded most of this land reserve to the church
for $200. After *Pokagon*'s death in 1841, the band contested the
church's claim in court, which left the matter unresolved until 1848,
when the church was found guilty of fraud. Soon thereafter, however, the inept leadership of Leopold's son Peter led to a fission in
the Silver Creek community. Many of its inhabitants found new
homes in the small, scattered communities they established at Paw
Paw and Brush Lake in Van Buren County and at Nadowesippe
Prairie in St. Joseph County, where *Mgwago* was chief.

The decades after the middle of the nineteenth century were extremely hard on the Michigan Potawatomi communities not only
because of the depletion of natural resources and the restriction of
their seasonal movements owing to white settlement, but also because of the difficulty of collecting back annuities due them from
treaties. It was, in fact, not until 1866, following thirty years of
lobbying, that they were able to obtain these payments.[32]

Later in the century, back migration from both the west and from
Canada increased the Potawatomi population. Dowagiac in Cass
County, Niles in Berrien County, and Athens in Calhoun County
became centers of Potawatomi activity. The latter community, consisting of 120 acres purchased by chief *Pamtopee* with annuity funds,
was deeded to Governor Barry of Michigan and his successors to
that office in 1845. It remains today as a "State Reservation."

Resident and returning Potawatomi in eastern Wisconsin found
themselves without lands and took up life as wanderers on the margins of American settlements, where they became known as the

"strolling Indians." After years of petitions and complaints to the U.S. government by the state and local citizens, who contended that these Potawatomi were a source of disease, a drain on the charity of the counties, and a haven for poachers, the federal government decided to provide them with land. In 1913, the strolling Potawatomi were given homesteads in Menominee County, Michigan, and Forest County, Wisconsin. The Michigan group today constitutes the Hannahville Indian community west of Escanaba.

The Ottawa-Chippewa Treaty of Washington in 1836

In 1835, the people of Michigan's frontier were hard pressed. Smallpox epidemics, a series of hard winters, crop failures, a decline in the fur market, and the scarcity of game made life very difficult. Traders responded to these conditions and to the lack of hard currency in circulation by pushing their Indian creditors for the repayment of debts. In addition to these common problems, Indians were also threatened by conflicts with the growing number of settlers now flooding southern Michigan and by the resulting pressure from their agent, Henry Schoolcraft, for their removal west. Adding to these problems, the Ottawa were divided into several political factions, including small but influential groups organized by the Baptists, Issac McCoy and his successor, Leonard Slater, and by the Catholic priest Frederic Baraga, who founded a competing mission at the rapids of the Grand River. Catholic missionaries also had substantial influence among the northern Ottawa, although in both the north and south, people following traditional religious practices far outnumbered Christian converts. Despite these extreme difficulties and the differences that divided them, the Ottawa and their northern Ojibwa neighbors were united on one point: they totally rejected the idea of removal.

The northern Ottawa, who were heavily indebted to and under great influence of the *Métis* traders, developed a new strategy to meet the debt crisis. They decided to raise money by selling some land that was of marginal use. Toward this end they sent a delegation to Washington to offer the United States Manitou Island and Drummond Island as well as some other land in the Upper Peninsula that they shared with the Ojibwa. They also hoped to secure blacksmith shops, schools, and instruction in plow agriculture so they would be more competitive in the emerging frontier society.

Michigan Superintendent Henry Schoolcraft and Lewis Cass, who had by then moved to Washington as Secretary of War and was, therefore, head of the Indian Department, saw the visit of the Ottawa delegation as an opportunity to exploit the situation and to acquire as much Michigan land as possible. In order to control the negotiations, they decided to conduct them in Washington, D.C., where the Michigan tribesmen could not only be "wined and dined" but separated from contrary influences. Since some of the land in question belonged to the Ojibwa, Schoolcraft called for delegations from the whole eastern part of Michigan's Upper Peninsula as well as the country occupied by the Ottawa, the east coast of Lake Michigan and the valley of the Grand River.

This was a significant treaty for Henry Schoolcraft personally. Since his own relatives were involved on both sides, he had little to lose. The Sault Ste. Marie band was represented by his wife's uncle *Waishkee* and his son *Waubojeeg*, while his brothers-in-law George and William Johnston eventually collected substantial trade debts on behalf of the estate of Schoolcraft's deceased father-in-law, John Johnston. This pattern of vested interest and conflicting responsibility was not unique. In fact, the delegations of chiefs were each conducted to Washington by traders such as Rix Robinson, John Holiday, Henry Levake, Louis Moran, and John Drew, all of whom profited by the treaty by virtue of their status as traders or through their Indian wives and children.

The treaty negotiations, which were held in the District of Columbia's Masonic Hall, began in March and proceeded for some weeks. Records indicate the nature of the questions negotiated but none of the specific details of bargaining. Much of the negotiation seems to have been done by non-Indians, as is evident by the complaint of Augustin Hamlin or *Kanapima* (He Who Is Talked About), an educated *Métis* who had the trust of the Ottawa.[33]

The words the Commissioners had just heard from the chiefs were not their words, not the feelings of their hearts but the words of white men who wanted reservations, and have dictated to them what to say. These men care not for the Indian but they wish to benefit themselves.

He also reported that "their councils, were constantly beset by individuals and disturbed in their private councils, often called and sometimes one—then two and as many as six have been called at one time, their minds were disturbed."[34]

Schoolcraft, who had control over the Ojibwa delegation by virtue of his Indian in-laws, chided the Ottawa that if they did not follow the Ojibwa in approving the treaty, they would "feel ashamed at seeing their Chippewa brothers in possession of many goods, and much money and themselves entirely destitute and very poor."[35]

Finally the chiefs, including *Apokisigan* (Smoking Mixture), *Kiminichaqum*, *Kinoshamaig*, *Naganigobowa*, *Mackatabenese* (Black Bird), and *Chingassamo* (Big Sail), their counterparts *Muckatosha* (Black Skin), *Megisinini* (Shell Power Man), *Waukwindigo* (White Cannibal), *Cobmoosa* (Walker), *Nawbunegeezhig* (Noonday), *Iahbawadik* (First Born), *Wawbojeeg* (White Fisher), *Ainse,* and *Chabowaywa* ceded thirteen million acres of land to the United States. This included the area north of the Grand River west of the Saginaw cession of 1819 north to the Straits of Mackinac. The cession also included all of the Upper Peninsula east of a line between Bay de Noc and Marquette. In most regards, it seemed to the chiefs as well as the non-Indian participants that the treaty solved their problems.[36]

In exchange for this huge land cession, the Ottawa and Ojibwa reserved fourteen substantial reservations scattered through the ceded territory as a place for permanent homes. The government agreed to pay $30,000 annually for twenty years, a $5,000 annuity for education for twenty years, $3,000 for missions, $10,000 for agricultural equipment, $3,000 for medicine and health care, and $2,000 for tobacco, as well as providing $150,000 in provisions. An additional $30,000 was to be distributed among the chiefs and heads of families and $300,000 would go to pay debts to traders. The government also agreed to provide two more blacksmith shops and more farmers, mechanics, and interpreters. An additional $150,000 was set aside to pay *Métis* in lieu of reservations. The treaty also specifically named individuals who would split $48,000 in lieu of reservations. Not surprisingly, these were almost exclusively the *Métis* children of the traders who attended the treaty.

The treaty negotiations were concluded and the treaty signed on March 28, 1836. In normal course it was sent to the U.S. Senate for ratification. As they left Washington, the chiefs believed that the treaty provided the one thing that they desired most—to be able to remain on their own land. Although they had surrendered a significant part of their tribal lands, by securing a guarantee that they could hunt and fish over the entire ceded territory until it was required for settlement they would be able to subsist by moving off their small land reserves to use these resources. In this way, the new order would not, they believed, be radically different from the old, and they would be able to maintain themselves while learning the arts of civilization and agriculture.

The president proclaimed the Treaty of Washington on May 27, 1836, and it was soon thereafter posted in Michigan. The chiefs were utterly shocked when they saw it. The U.S. Senate had unilaterally amended the negotiated document to limit the use of the reservations for a period of only five years. A proviso was also added that this period could be extended by the United States and that, if the Ottawa and Ojibwa wished to remove west, they would be given land.

In July, Schoolcraft summoned the original delegations to Mackinac Island to ratify these changes. No payment of goods, services, or money was to be made unless the Indians gave assent to the new version. Finally and reluctantly they did so, but only after Schoolcraft's assurances that the United States would not need their land for many years to come.[37] According to Schoolcraft, the signing brought "universal joy and satisfaction" to the four thousand Ojibwa and Ottawa and their creditors assembled on Mackinac Island.[38]

The years immediately following the treaty were not filled with "joy and satisfaction" but with fear, controversy, and apprehension. Unsure of their ultimate fate, many Indians were unwilling to invest labor and scarce cash in clearing land and building log homes as the missionaries and agents suggested, because they knew they could well be forced to abandon such improvements if they had to leave Michigan when the five-year provision lapsed in 1841. This dilemma was particularly difficult for the Grand River Ottawa, who were in close contact with American agricultural settlements. As early as January, 1837, the Michigan legislature petitioned Congress to move Michigan Indians west.[39]

Many Ottawa hedged their bets by using the annuity money from the treaty to purchase land from the United States, either individually or in groups. As the removal deadline neared, Schoolcraft showed his true colors by opting for removal over the prospect of civilizing Michigan Indians on their home territory. To support this position, he cited their propensities to savagery and their innate inferiority as a race to be insurmountable barriers to civilization.

In response to heightened pressure for removal perhaps as many as 500 Ottawa and Ojibwa crossed the Canadian border to seek refuge among their relatives, especially those who resided on Manitoulin Island (where the Canadian government was hopeful of consolidating Indian settlement). Many of these people ultimately returned to Michigan.

In 1837, Michigan entered the Union as a state, prompting some Indian leaders to write to Governor Stevens T. Mason asking if land ownership implied Michigan citizenship. When he replied that it did, an avenue seemed to open to secure permanent residence.[40] It also set Henry Schoolcraft on an increasingly confrontational course with his Indian charges.

The national election of 1840 resulted in the expulsion of the Jacksonian Democrats and a new Whig government. Robert Stuart, former Chief Superintendent of the American Fur Company, was appointed to replace Schoolcraft. It was also now apparent that western removal of Indians was making less and less sense; American settlement was proceeding at a faster pace in the western lands to which the Indians would be removed than it was on the northern lands on which they already resided. Robert Stuart, as well as many Michigan politicians and citizens, began to side with the Indians against efforts to move them west. Nonetheless, the decade of the 1840s was a time of trauma. As 1841 passed and the government made no move to resolve the land issue, the majority of Indians who lived either on the reserves or as squatters on public land had learned to expect the worst. Their chiefs frantically petitioned the United States to help them secure permanent homes within the state. To justify this very desirable outcome, the Ottawa and Ojibwa cited their progress in civilization. Similarly, the reports of their agents and missionaries are filled with glowing statistics touting the use of American dress, acres of land cleared, bushels of potatoes grown, days of school attended, and number of pagans converted. The Ottawa and Ojibwa had changed just enough to convince the government they were walking the white man's road. In fact, they continued to maintain their traditional systems of exchange, kinship, language, religion, and customs while giving the illusion of "progress." Beneath this veneer of civilization, they remained fundamentally true to their own cultural traditions.

NOTES

1. President Andrew Jackson's annual message to Congress, December 7, 1835 (quoted in Prucha 1990, 71).

2. Jefferson investigated a mound on his Virginia estate in 1784 with the hope of revealing information about the origins of the "red race." Though fairly skillfully done, the excavation produced no definitive answers. By the early nineteenth century, Rufus Putnam and Caleb Atwater had produced good descriptions of the mounds and earthworks of Ohio; these were published by the American Antiquarian Society, which was founded in 1812. Squire and Davis's study of the ancient monuments of the Ohio and Mississippi valley published in 1848 was vol. 1, no. 1 of the *Smithsonian Contributions to Knowledge* (Jennings 1968, 37–38).

3. Quoted in Gould's book, *The Mismeasure of Man* (1981, 57), from the original, which is found in Morton's classic work, *Crania Americana* (1839, 81).

4. Indians have long objected to the use of some Indian logos and mottos for high school, college, and professional athletic teams. In Michigan, there are over 100 high schools and colleges that use such Indian motifs. In many but not all cases, the logos feature angry Indian faces and warriors brandishing tomahawks and other weapons. Cheers suggesting opponents be "scalped" and stylized war dances embellish the image of Indians as aggressive and savage. Further, slogans and logos often promote racial stereotypes by reference to skin color (Red Skins) or "typical" Indian images—namely the one on the old buffalo nickel. One can imagine the outcry if the same terminology was used in reference to African Americans or people of the Jewish faith.

   In 1990, the Michigan Civil Rights Commission condemned the use of demeaning imagery in reference to native Americans and pointed out the potential damage of this stereotyping on the self-esteem of school children of Indian descent. Many school systems are giving consideration to either dropping violent Indian imagery or adopting nonoffensive logos.

5. Prucha 1986, 75.

6. Prucha 1990, 37.

7. Hill 1981, 24–25.
8. Hill 1967, 93. The Superintendents and Acting Superintendents of the Michigan Superintendency are as follows.
Governors and Ex-Officio Superintendents
   William Hull, 1805–13
   Lewis Cass, 1813–31
   George Porter (Acting), 1831–34
   Steven T. Mason (Acting), 1834–35
   John S. Horner (Acting), 1835–36
Mackinac Agents and Acting Superintendents
   William Puthuff, 1815–18
   George Boyd, 1818–32
   Henry R. Schoolcraft, 1832–41
   Robert Stuart, 1841–45
   William Richmond, 1845–49
   Charles Babcock, 1849–51
   William Sprague, 1851–53
   Henry Gilbert, 1853–57
   Andrew M. Fitch, 1857–61
   DeWitt Leach, 1861–65
   Richard Smith, 1865–69
   William Brockway, 1869
   Major James Long, 1869–71
   Richard Smith, 1871
   George Betts, 1871–76
   George Lee, 1876–80
9. Hill 1981, 165–66.
10. Viola's 1981 book, *Diplomats in Buckskins,* presents a fascinating account of the visits to Washington by many Indian delegations doing business with the government. The rich photographic record of these delegations is a resource of immense historic importance.
11. Spry 1968, 77.
12. Dunbar 1965, 249–50.
13. Nearly every account of the Saginaw Treaty of 1819 is drawn from Charles P. Avery's description (1866), which was based on interviews with participants. Ephrain S. Williams (1886b) presents another account and leans heavily on Avery's description. Fred Dustin's (1919) discussion contains some additional detail.
14. Accounts of the Superintendents of Indian Affairs in Michigan and Missouri (L.C. no. 1, p. 284); see Lowrie and Franklin 1834, 2:284.
15. Williams 1886b, 226; Leeson 1881, 158–64.
16. Williams 1886b, 264.

17. Dustin 1919, 29.
18. Williams 1886a, 140.
19. Mills 1918, 58.
20. Mills 1918, 82.
21. Mills 1918, 60.
22. Foote 1891, 379–81.
23. Edmunds 1978, 223.
24. See Berkhofer 1972; Schultz 1972.
25. Cass to J. S. Dagg, May 26, 1832, National Archives Microforms, series M-21, reel 8:408.
26. Clifton 1977, 234.
27. Clifton 1984, 71.
28. Caldwell 1894, 297.
29. Foote 1891, 382.
30. The details of the Potawatomi exodus to lower Canada across the St. Clair–Detroit River boundary are told by James Clifton (1975). Most Potawatomi much preferred the prospects of life in lower Canada to either Manitoulin Island in the north or Kansas in the west, neither one of which offered prospects for viable horticulture. Of the several thousand Potawatomi who emigrated to Canada, many became "wandering Indians" while others took up land on reserves and integrated with local Ojibwa communities. The United States opposed this eastward migration on the grounds that the Potawatomi had a treaty obligation to settle in the west.
31. Clifton 1984, 69; Claspy 1966, 15–17.
32. Clifton 1984, 89.
33. McClurken 1988, 82–111.
34. Records of a treaty concluded with the Ottawa and Chippewa Nations at Washington, D.C., March 28, 1836, Manuscript in the papers of Henry Rowe Schoolcraft, Library of Congress.
35. Treaty records in Schoolcraft Papers.
36. James McClurken's study, *We Wish to be Civilized: Ottawa-American Political Contest on the Michigan Frontier* (1988), presents a wonderfully detailed account of the heroic struggle of the Ottawa people to maintain their cultural integrity during this most troublesome time in their history. Helen H. Tanner (1974) has written on the details of the resistance of the Michigan Ojibwa and their approach to negotiations of the Treaties of 1836 and 1855. My account is based, to a large degree, on the work of these two accomplished ethnohistorians.
37. Henry Schoolcraft to C. Harris, February 27, 1837, National Archives Microforms, series M-21, reel 37:168.

38. H. Tanner 1974, 64.
39. McClurken 1988, 201.
40. McClurken 1988, 225.

Chapter 7

On White Man's Road

1850—1910

By the mid-1840s, it was evident that the policy of physically separating Indians from whites would not work. Not only was the west filling with settlers, but heavy waves of immigration from Ireland and particularly Scandanavia also resulted in increased settlement of the northern, forested regions. Only the Indian territory of Oklahoma and unceded Ojibwa lands west of Lake Superior were available as places to warehouse "removed" Indians. Although Commissioner of Indian Affairs Medill proposed the establishment of Indian colonies in these regions in 1848, the threat of removal was all but gone.[1]

The new Indian policy that emerged during the middle of the nineteenth century was led by progressives such as Charles Mix, Luke Lea, and George Manypenny. These men rejected not only removal but also the racism and paternalism of Lewis Cass and Henry Schoolcraft, which laid the failures in Indian policy to what they saw as inherent flaws in Indians themselves. As commissioner of Indian Affairs, Luke Lea contended that the failure of removal to civilize Indians was, in fact, the fault of government policy; Indians, he believed, were entirely capable of civilized pursuits and ultimately of assimilation into American society.

To accomplish this end, Lea, and later Manypenny, believed that Indians had to be concentrated on small reservations within their own territories, where they could be protected from undesirable influences and effectively exposed to education, Christianity, the domestic arts, and agriculture. These ends were to be achieved under a new administrative arrangement created in March, 1849, when Congress formed the Department of Interior. The Indian Department was transferred to the new department from the Department of War. George Manypenny, who succeeded Lea as commissioner in 1853, was not only committed to the ideal of civilizing the Indians but also believed that private property, so central to American life, was the concept that could make it work.

During his tenure as commissioner, Manypenny negotiated fifty-two treaties. These he characterized as treaties of peace and friendship, treaties of acquisition with a view of colonizing Indians on reservations, and treaties of acquisition providing permanent settlement of individuals at once and in the future on separate tracts of land for the general abolition of the tribal character.[2] By the latter he meant roving, pagan, and uncivilized pursuits that he saw as being encouraged by providing Indians with too much land, land held in common, and cash annuities that benefited non-Indians more than the intended recipients. The Manypenny policy was thus based on two convergent ideas of how Indians were to be civilized. The first was that the government would temporarily provide support and security to foster the process, and, second, that the allotment of land to individuals would hold out the incentive and means to achieve civilized life. When necessary, protection was provided by defining reservation boundaries and by restricting land transfers to non-Indians.

Manypenny's treaties contained many common provisions. Land was usually set apart in large blocks from which Indians could make selections for family farms. Heads of families were permitted to select 80 acres, and single adults over 21 years of age, 40 acres. Those who were literate in English could dispose of this land as they wished, but those judged by their agents as "not so competent" were required to get permission to sell. In most cases, reservations were created to control the civilization process; while Indians could leave at will, non-Indians could not enter the reservation or use its resources without permission. In effect, reservations became the new "Indian country." Indian agents also assumed broad new powers in administering Indian affairs on reserved lands. Manypenny preferred that Indian payments be made in goods and services, rather than cash that made Indians "indolent and lazy" and thwarted the ethic of honest work for an honest wage. Besides agriculture, education became an important aspect of the civilization policy and day schools were run on contract or, increasingly, by the government itself. Many of these were successful and it was not long before a bilingual generation conversant with both traditional and non-Indian customs and skills appeared on the reservation.

The civilization-reservation policy conformed in many ways to the desire of Indians to remain permanently within their traditional territories and to acquire access to education for their children. These desires were extremely acute, particularly given the legacy of the greed and opportunism of the Cass-Schoolcraft and Stuart tenures, when much of the Great Lakes country was snatched away without providing Indians a viable means to survive or secure their own land.

Consider, for example, that the Treaty of Washington (1836) left the Michigan Ottawa and Chippewa on temporary "reservations" that could be terminated by the government at any time. Likewise in northern Wisconsin and western Upper Michigan, the government had been so anxious to acquire timber in the Treaty of St. Peters (1837) and minerals with the Treaty of La Pointe (1842) that they simply left the Lake Superior Ojibwa wandering the ceded territory. At any time they could be removed by the "Order of the President." The same was true for the Saginaw Chippewa. Most of the reservations made under the Treaty of 1819 were later purchased by Schoolcraft in the Treaty of Detroit (January 14, 1837). It is little wonder that the Indians of the Great Lakes were demoralized and fearful, or that they barraged anyone who would listen with petitions requesting permanent homes.

The treaties negotiated by Commissioner George Manypenny at La Pointe on September 30, 1854, in Detroit on July 31, 1855, and on August 2, 1855, solved these problems but by a method so poorly conceived that it created great hardships that continue to this day. All these were allotment treaties that allowed Indians to select land from townships set aside for this purpose, and all provided a variety of services. In some cases, Indian interests were protected by reservation boundaries created by permanently withdrawing blocks of land for exclusive Indian use; in other cases, Indians were given a time limit to make selections, after which the remaining land was put up for sale to the general public. The result was that the farms of Indians would be interspersed among those of their white neighbors.[3] The Treaty of La Pointe (1854) is an example of the former type, which left the Ojibwa of northern Wisconsin, eastern Minnesota, and western upper Michigan with bounded reservations. The Ottawa-Chippewa Treaty of July 31, 1855 is an example of the latter type, in that it left the Indians of western lower Michigan and the eastern Upper Peninsula scattered. In the treaty of August 2, 1855, the Saginaw Chippewa agreed to give up the remaining reserves in the Saginaw valley and the United States agreed to provide various services at the location of the allotments that were to be made from six adjoining townships in Isabella county.

The six townships of land were selected in a region that had very sparse, if any, settlement in 1855, yet the government knew it must accommodate preexisting interests. For example, it was certain that some sections were reserved for the support of schools under the Northwest Ordinance, and it was almost certain that some areas would be designated as swamplands, and under the Swampland Act, these would go to the State of Michigan. It was possible that the Canal Act, which provided government land to the St. Marys Ship Canal Company, could have resulted in selection of some of the land in the six townships. The United States also had to accommodate American settlers who might have settled in the townships prior to their survey, since the Preemption Act gave such settlers the opportunity of first purchase of the land they occupied at an equitable rate. For all of these reasons, the treaty of August 2, 1855, explicitly stated that the six townships would consist of the unsold lands. That is, it was to exclude from allotment those parcels that may have already been selected, whose use was predetermined or preempted by settlement. The Isabella location was chosen specifically to minimize such conflicts. It was remote and in an area of marginal agricultural worth.

In the case of both 1855 treaties, trouble soon emerged. Bureaucratic inefficiency delayed and snarled the allotment process. Patents were not issued until the early 1870s, long after the expiration of the five-year grace period. Even before it expired, citizens and politicians were clamoring for the right to purchase land from the reservations.

During the late 1850s and the years of the Civil War the Saginaw Chippewa remained in limbo. They still had no secure land and they were coming under extreme pressure from non-Indians to the point that they understood that they were practically powerless to protect their interests without further help from the U.S. government. In early 1864, the Saginaw chiefs petitioned President Lincoln for a new treaty to resolve the myriad problems now before them. Among the problems was the fact that no provision had been made in the 1855 treaty for land to be provided to Indians as they came of age and that whites were threatening the community. The chiefs knew that if whites were allowed to enter the reservation and purchase land, they would again be "scattered."

The government hurried to accommodate the chiefs' request for a new treaty, which was signed in October, 1864, but its agenda was not totally honorable. As active Republican politicians, the Indian agents and their employees were keenly aware of the fact that support for the Republican administration of Lincoln and Governor Austin Blair was eroding, with the governor's margin of victory falling from 20,000 votes in 1858 to 6,000 in 1862. Two of the six members of congress elected in that year were Democrats. Local elections in many districts promised to be tight in 1864. Agent Leach wrote to the Commissioner of Indian Affairs in early October, a little over two weeks before the 1864 Treaty was concluded:

> We hope to make the proposed changes in the treaty of some political use to us. Our Indians are voters and their votes may be of great importance to us at the approaching election. They [the Saginaw Chippewa] reside in the closest Congressional District in the State and hence, anything fair and honorable that we can do to put them in good humor and to favorably dispose them towards the Government we wish to do.[4]

The Saginaw Chippewa, unlike the Ottawa and Chippewa of western Lower Michigan and the eastern Upper Peninsula, were accommodated with a new treaty. As an aside, the Ottawa and Chippewa never got the reservation treaty they so desperately desired. Instead, a remedial piece of legislation called the Indian Homestead Act was passed in 1872 that permitted the Ottawa and Chippewa access to 160-acre homesteads but left them scattered and unprotected as whites were permitted to buy unselected land within the bounds of the land set aside for their allotments in 1855. The result was that they soon sold or were swindled out of their land.

Such was not the case in the instance of the Saginaw Chippewa. The new treaty of 1864 created a reservation from the land within the six original townships for the exclusive use, ownership, and occupancy of the Saginaw peoples. It may be presumed that this provision solved two different problems. First, it provided a pool of land necessary to accommodate Indians both as they came into majority and also those otherwise entitled to selections in exchange for land on Saginaw Bay. Second, the reservation provided a means to safeguard and control the process of civilizing the Saginaw Chippewa. Other articles of the treaty provided for educational and agricultural services and economic support for the community.

There is one other provision of the 1864 treaty that hard and bitter experience had shown to be necessary to maintain individual allotments (even within the bounds of the reservation), a restriction on alienation. The treaty provided a means for the agent to distinguish between literate or "competent" persons and those who did not read or write the English language, the "not so competent." By this method it was presumed that the agent could protect land tenure, since a "not so competent" individual needed the government's permission to dispose of his land. What the government did not foresee is that an agent might use the classification to certify nonliterate Indians as "competent" and to recommend land transactions for "not so competent" people. That is exactly what happened in the case of the Saginaw Chippewa.

As progressive and enlightened as the civilization policy seemed to be in contrast to removal, in practice it did not work at all well. Despite good intentions, the last half of the nineteenth century was almost as difficult for Great Lakes Indians as the first. Although they did achieve their major objective in dealing with the United States, that is, the right to remain in the Great Lakes region, they found the new order difficult and frustrating.

The reported progress of Great Lakes Indians toward civilization is well documented in the annual reports of Indian agents, agency employees, and missionaries. In fact, however, these reports were often self-serving and do not form a basis for an accurate evaluation of the condition of Indians during the late nineteenth century. What agents did, as opposed to what they said, tells the real story.

At the root of the problem was the Indian bureaucracy itself. Once Indians were concentrated on reservations where services could be "effectively" provided, the Indian service expanded. In the years after the Civil War, the business of making annuity payments to individual Indians, supplying goods and services, and managing land and resources such as timber required more people. It also opened many opportunities for corruption. Likewise, agents were now in a position to control the affairs of reservation communities, since Indians became of necessity more dependent upon government subsidies. This dependence resulted from their inability to procure food supplies without access to off-reservation resources and also because the land allotments gave agents more power to make decisions that affected individuals and communities.

During the Grant administration, patronage in government jobs resulted in a deterioration in the qualifications of agents. Many had little or no prior experience with Indian affairs and few stayed on the job for more than a few years. Worse, many were corrupt, more intent on making money at the expense of Indians or delivering the Indian vote in local elections than in managing the affairs of reservations to benefit their inhabitants.

The Reservation Scene

What was life like on Great Lakes Indian reservations and in the many small coummunities of Indians living off reservations during the decades following the Civil War? Although conditions differed somewhat in those places that were closer to the margins of American settlement, the Keweenaw Bay reservation in Baraga County provides a typical example.

Here, six townships of land had been set aside as a reservation under the Treaty of La Pointe (1854). The treaty, one of the first allotment treaties to be written, provided that 80- and 40-acre farms could be selected by adult members of the bands that comprised the community. Although selections were made and submitted to Washington, no patents had been issued by the mid-1860s. This fact alarmed Chiefs David King, *Asinence, Pushquagin,* and *Matyawwosh,* who were veterans in the long and desperate struggle against removal. In fact, however, the desire for patents was more of a political stopgap than a significant economic or social reality. Unlike the case among Indians in the southern part of the state, the allotments at Keweenaw Bay would never be productive farms. The heavily timbered allotments were not places on which the Keweenaw people planned to reside. They were, of necessity, fishing people and so continued to live on the shores of Keweenaw Bay even after the delivery of their patents in the last decades of the century. Even so, some individuals, with the encouragement of the resident government farmer, managed to clear and plant a few acres of potatoes, other root crops, oats, and hay.

Since the 1840s, the Keweenaw Bay community had been divided into three distinct factions, each in turn composed of independent bands.[5] These consisted of a Methodist community on the east side of the bay near the new American town of L'Anse, a Catholic community near Baraga on the west side, and free-ranging traditionalists. Each of the Christian communities had about three hundred people who lived on land purchased before the treaty by their respective missionaries. In 1863, Father Baraga deeded the Catholic lands to his parishioners.[6] Converts in each community had a church, a school run by missionaries, and neat log cabins arranged in rows in which to live. The people wore American-style clothing except for moccasins, which they preferred over stiff leather shoes and boots. A few Methodist Indians spoke English because they were instructed in that language in both church and school. In the case of the Catholics, the catechism and lessons were given in Ojibwa. The Catholic community was also closely affiliated with the French Canadian and *Métis* people, and many spoke French as well as Ojibwa.

Children were given Christian names at baptism and some families were beginning to use Anglicized versions of their Indian names. Thus *Magozid* became Edward Loonsfoot and *Jawaninodin* became John Southwind. Both French and English surnames also appeared, reflecting marriages between white men and Indian women. As a result, tribal rolls contained the names of Nancy Smith, Mary St. Armandt, and John Vizneau. In many cases, Indian names were retained as surnames, as in the case of Joseph *Aishquaygezhiek* or John Battise *Kawmetighyosh*.

Beyond these two small and rather permanent Christian communities, which are the subject of at least 90 percent of the contemporary written descriptions of the Keweenaw Bay community, was a much larger, traditional community. This consisted of perhaps 600 to 800 people made up of four to six bands who resided seasonally at Keweenaw Bay, along the Ontonagon River, or at Lac Vieux Desert near Watersmeet in Gogebic County. The modern, federally recognized Lac Vieux Desert Band is a successor of this latter group.

These people, who continued to follow the seasonal round, dressed in a mixture of traditional and American clothing, lived in wigwams, and practiced *midé-wi-win* and other traditional rituals. They strongly resisted the efforts of Christian missionaries, land allotment, and the English language. They converged on Keweenaw Bay each summer and fall to fish and visit their Christian relatives and, when possible, to receive government annuities and subsidies. To the agents and missionaries, the traditionalists represented an obvious illustration of the failure of the civilization programs. It is no wonder they appear so seldom in written accounts of the reservation—except as a rationale for more appropriations.

To these traditional people, the allotment of land was nonsensical because the land itself was not property but the source of resources that served the common good. It was obvious, moreover, that the government's attempts to settle them could not work because farming could not produce enough food. After all, these people had planted gardens on the shores of Lake Superior for centuries and they knew how undependable agriculture was in this region of cold and severe climate. Traditionalists were caught in a dreadful dilemma: the bay could only support so many sedentary people. To send their children to school, to learn farming, or to live in cabins required a sedentary existence and sedentariness would mean starvation. They had to move to live and, of course, they did.

The government establishment at Keweenaw Bay was on the Methodist side and dispensed services strongly favoring the Protestants. This encouraged competition and resentment between their missionaries and the two groups, an enmity that incidentally still divides the modern community. A government farmer helped Indians clear some land but did most of the farming himself, selling crops for his own advantage. To feed the government oxen, the Indians had to haul hay in their canoes from Portage Lake, fifteen miles away. The chiefs protested the actions of the farmer and asked for a voice in the hiring and firing of government employees on the reservation.

Aside from trying to get the government to send their land patents, the people also tried to collect on unpaid annuities from former treaties. They were also becoming very worried because Americans were beginning to covet the timber growing on reservation land.

As the opportunity arose, Keweenaw Bay men took jobs as wage laborers cutting timber for mine shoring and cordwood for lake steamers. Both men and women were employed in commercial fishing; the former as deck hands or crew members and the women in cleaning and packing fish. Women also contributed to household income by collecting and selling berries and making maple sugar and handicraft items. Sugar was by far the most important export from Keweenaw Bay. Tens of thousands of pounds were shipped annually to eastern American cities in bark boxes called *mokaks*. In 1865 alone the Keweenaw Bay bands sold 453,252 pounds of maple sugar.[7]

For the most part, relationships between the Keweenaw Bay people and their white neighbors at L'Anse seem to have been harmonious, at least in the early years of settlement. There was little racial discord and considerable cooperation.

Like the Keweenaw Bay people, the other Great Lakes Indian communities were trying to maintain the integrity of their culture. Up until the last quarter of the nineteenth century they were successful. Notwithstanding the intense assault on their culture and traditions, the loss of land, and their exposure to broader cultural perspectives, they were able to maintain their language, social and economic systems, political integrity, and religious values. They were not aggressive or hostile in dealing with the U.S. government, but they were single-minded and persistent in representing their views. Many Indians, even the ones who clung most stubbornly to traditional beliefs, saw change as inevitable and believed that the education of their children would serve the entire community. There was, in fact, a growing sentiment among some Indians that they should become citizens of Michigan. This possibility was opened by the second Michigan Constitution, which was approved in 1850. Article 7, sec. 1 provided that "civilized Indians" could become citizens by renouncing their membership in tribes.

Though few Indians opted for Michigan citizenship and even those who did were not U.S. citizens, some Michigan Indians enlisted in the Union army and fought in the Civil War. The most famous Indian unit was Company K of the First Michigan Sharpshooters, composed of Ottawa from Little Traverse Bay led by G. A. Graveract, a *Métis*. The company fought bravely at The Wilderness, Cold Harbor, and Petersburg, but was celebrated for its role in the fighting at Spottsylvania on May 9, 1863.[8] Assigned to protect Union cannon, these Ottawa soldiers withstood charge after charge, taking withering fire from Confederate forces. Both Lieutenant Graveraet and his father, the Bear River band chief *Mankewenan,* were killed along with a large number of men; several were taken prisoners.[9] In vicious hand-to-hand fighting, these Ottawa warriors effectively used their ancient war cries to foment panic in the Confederate ranks.

Learning English—The Language of Civilization

When the chiefs and headmen of the Ottawa and Ojibwa met with George Manypenny and Henry Gilbert to negotiate the Treaty of Detroit in 1855, they inquired about the disposition of the money set aside in the treaty of 1836 to educate Indian young people. Agent Gilbert replied that it had been paid directly by the U.S. Treasury to the missionary societies that ran schools at Sault Ste. Marie, Little and Grand Traverse bays, and the Ottawa colony and Griswold School on the Grand River. Chief *Assagon* later told the treaty commissioners

> My Father in the treaty of 36, you [the United States] appropriated a certain amount for a school fund. I suppose you have since used it—given it to our schoolmasters. But here are your children who might expect to be benefited by it. Here are boys who have not learned enough from those schoolmasters to say in English "give me a drink of water." It is our desire that when you come around to pay our annuities you will bring the school money with you so that we can pay it ourselves. We want to hire our own schoolmasters and then if they do not suit us, we can send them away.[10]

The treaty of 1855 contained $80,000 to be distributed over a ten-year period for a school system to be run by the government in consultation with the Ottawa and Ojibwa. The church-run boarding school system was largely scrapped and a day school system developed. This school system was not just new for Michigan Indians, but was one of the first experiments in large-scale public education anywhere in the world. In many areas the government system was patterned after Michigan's public schools that, thanks to innovations in management, funding, and teacher training, were among the finest public schools in the United States. By 1863, government schools were operating in most Indian communities. In fact, the Mackinac agency became a national model for this approach to Indian education; thirty of the forty-eight Indian schools in the United States were in Michigan. These schools were so good that many non-Indian parents chose to send their children to the Indian schools in preference to public schools.[11] By 1880, the vast majority of Michigan Indians were bilingual.

Regrettably, however, the day school system was deemed a failure by the government and the substantial public lobby that had developed to promote "Indian civilization." A leader among these "friends of the Indian" and Secretary of Interior in the Hayes administration, Carl Schurz, voiced the main complaint: "With the exception of a few hours spent in school, the children remained exposed to the influence of their more or less savage home surroundings, and the indulgence of their parents greatly interfered with the regularity of their attendance and with the necessary discipline."[12] Another problem noted by the liberal reformers had to do with language. Many of the day schools were taught in Ottawa, Ojibwa, or Potawatomi, the dialects of the home. J. D. C. Atkins, commissioner of Indian Affairs from 1885 to 1888, set out to solve this "problem." As he saw it, "To teach Indian school children their native tongue is practically to exclude English, and to prevent them from acquiring it. This language which is good enough for a white man and a black man, ought to be good enough for the red man."[13] The obvious solution seemed to be to remove Indian children from the home, where their education could not be carefully controlled.

In 1887, the government returned to the boarding school system and, thus, ushered in a program of ethnocide that had a profound impact on Indian culture. In twenty-five years, the boarding schools accomplished what armed force, starvation, disease, loss of land, and Christianity could not—a major and irreversible disruption of Indian culture. It also effectively prepared Indian young people, not for assimilation into middle-class America, but as laborers in American fields and factories.[14]

Three boarding schools were operated in Michigan: the Catholic church opened schools at Baraga in 1887 and Holy Childhood at Harbor Springs in 1889, and the government opened the Mt. Pleasant Boarding School.[15]

The Bureau of Indian Affairs School at Mt. Pleasant, which operated until 1933, offered eight years of education and enrolled 300 to 375 children. Professor Alice Littlefield has interviewed Indians who attended the school and was able to draw a comprehensive picture of student life.[16] Like other government boarding schools, it was run in a paramilitary fashion. Students were required to wear uniforms and march to and from school activities. Students not only attended classes to learn English and arithmetic, but also worked in the school farm, bakery, or laundry to learn the "habits of civilization," that is, punctuality, persistence, and attention to detail. Girls, for example, learned "to bake bread and then to place it on plates in a neat attractive manner."[17]

Discipline was harsh for infractions of rules, and, because many students came from impoverished homes, they were lucky to get home during the three-year period of required attendance. During the summers, students were "outed" to non-Indian families, where they practiced domestic and farm skills for fifty cents to one dollar per week plus room and board. It is little wonder runaways were common; the children were completely isolated from their homes and communities. That was, of course, the purpose of the boarding school.

Much emphasis was placed on sports, and Mt. Pleasant athletic teams excelled, usually beating non-Indian opponents. These teams became a source of pride and identity for not only the students but Indians throughout the state.

It is clear from the curriculum as well as the work histories of former students that Mt. Pleasant prepared students to enter American society on the ground floor, as agrarian laborers and domestics. At the turn of the century, the lumber, mining, and fishing industries were booming in the northern Great Lakes and the demand for agricultural labor was very high. This demand peaked, however, during World War I, and thereafter declined dramatically in the north with the bust of extractive industries and in the south with the decline of the small, family farm. Boarding school young people had now been well prepared for a declining and very competitive labor market; further, their newly acquired skills had few applications in the industries of Michigan's emerging urban manufacturing centers.

Perhaps ironically, many of today's tribal elders who were students at the Mt. Pleasant boarding school have good memories of the experience. Many were happy for the relief the school provided from

Graduation picture of Robert Davenport in the uniform of the
Carlisle Indian School, Carlisle, Pennsylvania, 1911.
(Photograph courtesy of the Little Traverse Bay Bands of Odawa
Indians.)

the crushing poverty of the reservations, and all remembered the sense of autonomy and self-esteem it built in the midst of oppression.[18] In many ways, as it was destroying the vitality of their respective cultures, the Mt. Pleasant experience also strengthened their identity as Indians.

In 1900, only 246 Indian pupils attended public schools nationwide as compared to 22,124 enrolled in government schools, but in 1920, the public schools claimed 30,858 Indian students with 25,396 in government schools.[19] Clearly, the trend toward public education as well as changing labor requirements put an end to the government boarding schools. In 1933, the State of Michigan assumed ownership of the Mt. Pleasant school in exchange for agreeing to educate Indian children in the public school system. The Mt. Pleasant school became a children's reformatory; unfortunately, few modifications were needed.

Indian Land and American Law

If the process of land allotment as outlined in the treaties of La Pointe (1854) and Detroit (July 31, 1855, and August 2, 1855) had proceeded as expected, within a decade Michigan Ottawa and Ojibwa Indians would have been settled on family farms that they owned outright. As envisioned, they would have owned hundreds of thousands of acres and would be viable producers in the country's economy, soon to be completely assimilated into American society. This idealistic vision was not to be.

In fact, George Manypenny, the chief architect of the allotment idea, admitted thirty years later in 1885 that the system was an abject failure. Speaking of the many allotment treaties he wrote during his tenure as Commissioner of Indian Affairs he said, "Had I known then, as I now know, what would result from these treaties I would be compelled to admit that I had committed a high crime."[20]

The first problem was simply bureaucratic delay. Lists of eligible Indians had to be drawn up, and the land selected by each individual from land set aside for that purpose had to be described and registered with the Indian Bureau's Washington office. Certificates or temporary deeds had to be sent back and selections recorded with the local county. After the appropriate period of time had lapsed, permanent patents (initial deeds from the U.S. government) needed to be issued. This required the cooperation of the Indian agent, the Bureau of Indian Affairs, the General Land Office, State Land Receivers, and county Registrars of Deeds. The process was complex and created a huge margin for error. Of course, the disruption of the Civil War also accounts for some of the delays and confusion. However, the most common problem was the different spellings of the name of the same Indian person, a fatal flaw on a legal document. As it turned out, the Ottawa did not receive certification of ownership on their selections until 1870, for the Saginaw Ojibwa it was 1872, and 1875 for the Ojibwa of Lake Superior. Periodic delivery of patents continued for the next twenty-five years or more. A process that was to have taken ten years took four times that long in some cases.

These delays resulted not only in questions about the legal status of the ownership of Indian land selections, but soon produced a clamor from whites who were waiting anxiously to buy unselected lands that, in some cases, were to be returned to the open market. This latter problem was not so critical for the Lake Superior Ojibwa or for the Saginaw Ojibwa because their selections were to be made within bounded reservations over which the government could exercise some control. The Ottawa and Ojibwa of western Lower Michigan and the eastern Upper Peninsula had no such protection.

In an attempt to placate the settlers and to give Indians land who did not qualify under the July 31, 1855 treaty, for example, widows and people who had become twenty-one years of age since the treaty, Congress passed a special Indian Homestead Act in 1872 (*U.S. Statutes at Large,* 18:516). Under the provisions of this act, the Ottawa and Ojibwa had six months to select up to 160 acres of government land. This they had to improve and occupy for five years and, after these conditions had been met, a patent would be issued. Of course, the idea of "homesteads" was totally alien to the Indian understanding of land tenure, which required seasonal movement, and most did not know what was meant by "improvements." Nonetheless, at the urging of the agents, some Indians claimed land under the act, which actually functioned to open more land for white settlement.

In the meantime, several other problems arose to complicate the land ownership issue, the most important being the ambiguous status of Indians under the law and as citizens of Michigan. The practical

Charlotte *Kawbawgam*

In 1845 *Madjigizik* (First Light of the Day), a member of the Carp River band of the Lake Superior Ojibwa, led an American exploring party to a huge iron deposit near modern Negaunee, Michigan. In return for his services he received a slip of paper promising a small share in the Jackson Iron Company, which mined the ore. *Madjigizik* never pressed his claim, but when he died his daughter, Charlotte, went to court to establish her interest in the company. By this time, 1864, Charlotte was married to Charlie *Kawbawgam,* the first citizen of the town that was to become Marquette. Charlotte's case took many years to litigate and went to the Michigan Supreme Court three times before it was settled in 1889. Although she eventually won recognition of the legitimacy of her claim, she was never able to collect a monetary award from the now bankrupt corporation she so tenaciously fought.

Charlotte's otherwise rather obscure claim under Michigan law had two further impacts, one legal and the other literary; neither, unfortunately, of much benefit to Charlotte, who was now living in near poverty and growing blind at Presque Isle, the Indian town on the outskirts of Marquette. From a legal standpoint, her case established an important precedent.

One of the key issues raised by the *Kawbawgam* case was whether or not Charlotte was the legitimate legal heir of *Madjigizik.* The Jackson Iron Company insisted that, since her father had two wives, Charlotte, as the daughter of the second wife, was not a legitimate heir because her father had not formally divorced the first wife before marrying Charlotte's mother, Susan. Charlotte, now joined in her suit by the son and granddaughter of *Madjigizik*'s first wife, *Odonebequa,* argued that, under traditional Indian marriage practices, all of the children of polygynous marriages had equal standing.

In its final decision, the Michigan Supreme Court sided with Charlotte. Indian tribes, they said, were not governed by the laws of Michigan, because treaties recognized tribes as sovereign entities capable of regulating their own social relationships, including forms of legitimate marriage and inheritance. The court also pointed out that treaties explicitly recognize that the rights of treaties survive the generations through inheritance within the Indian system. Thus, Charlotte *Kawbawgam* forced the recognition by state courts of the legitimacy of customary marriage and the full legal rights of the offspring of such

Charlotte *Kawbawgam* and her daughter Mary. Marquette, Michigan, circa 1875. (Photograph courtesy of the State of Michigan Archives.)

marriages. Charlotte remained true to her own beliefs and sense of justice. She did not give in to the power of a huge corporation and was not intimidated by the judicial system of Michigan. She persevered and, in the end, she won not only her point but established a legal precedent important in American law.

Charlotte did not win true fame until long after her death in 1904. In 1965, Robert Traver (John D. Voelker) published the story of her legal struggle. His book, *Laughing Whitefish,* though considerably romanticizing Charlotte and the events of her life, is a fascinating account of early Marquette and the case of *Kawbawgam v. Jackson Iron Company* (49 Michigan 39; 50 Michigan 578; 76 Michigan 498). It is recommended as a good piece of historical fiction and Michigan literature.

and important application of this question related to the ability of local government to tax Indian land holdings. In 1850, the new Michigan Constitution provided a citizenship option for "civilized Indians" who wished to renounce their tribal status. The treaty of 1854 and the two treaties at Detroit in 1855, in fact, all contained clauses dissolving tribal organization. The chiefs had absolutely no problem with this provision when it was suggested by the government because the tribal organizations had been a fiction of the federal government from the beginning.

The question of the jurisdiction of the state and federal governments over Indians became increasingly controversial. For example, Congress passed many laws trying to protect Indians from being exploited by traders and whiskey vendors who preyed on Indians by controlling commerce in "Indian country." The definition of "Indian country" has been modified over the years, but, as early as 1856, the Michigan Supreme Court rejected the notion that unsold ceded land within the boundaries of the state was "Indian country."[21] This effectively confined federal jurisdiction to the land inside reservations or over allotted Indians outside them. The federal government did declare that Indians were not eligible for the draft nor did they have to abide by state hunting and fishing laws because they were not citizens of the state. Michigan, anxious to claim Indians as citizens, cited the state constitution of 1850 as providing the opportunity for "civilized" Indians to become citizens by renouncing tribal allegiance. As a practical matter, after the Civil War, most Indians did consider themselves to be members of Indian bands as well as Michigan citizens and many voted without opposition from local or state authorities.

In 1871, Congress ceased to deal with native Americans on a government-to-government basis, treaty making was suspended (*U.S. Statutes at Large*, 16:566), and Indians were officially regarded as "domestic and dependent nations." In fact, the Indians of Michigan, like those in the rest of the United States, were protected by no consistent body of law or clear authority. In 1877, Congress provided Indian police to keep order, but did not extend federal jurisdiction for serious crimes until 1885, when the Major Crime Act mandated trial in federal court in cases of murder, rape, assault, arson, burglary, and larceny by Indians (*U.S. Statutes at Large*, 23:385). As a further complication of citizenship and legal status,

Ojibwa camp near Marquette, 1864. (Photograph courtesy of the State of Michigan Archives.)

section 6 of the General Allotment Act of 1887 made all allottees U.S. citizens "without prejudice to tribal status."

In this confusion it was to the clear advantage of local governments and local citizens to extend citizenship so that Indian land could be taxed, and this was done, often despite assurances given by agents that the Indian land owners did not have to pay taxes. At the same time, Michigan strictly enforced the occupancy and improvement conditions of the Homestead Act.

The combination of the ambiguity of citizenship, the lack of legal protection, the corruption and incompetence of agents, limited English literacy, and the fact that Indians had no meaningful access to the courts proved a disaster. American citizens took the opportunity to defraud hundreds if not thousands of Indians of their allotments and homesteads. Agent George Betts, a former Methodist preacher, was at the center of one scheme of timber and real estate fraud that resulted in the loss of thousands of acres of Indian land on the Isa-

bella Reservation. Though he was eventually discharged and prosecuted, the most valuable land was lost and distrust for officialdom
was imprinted on the minds of the Saginaw Ojibwa. Likewise, in the
western part of the state, L. H. Jennings, the son of the receiver of
the U.S. Land Office at Ionia, was involved in several schemes to
defraud Indians. His father was dismissed, but the Jennings were
never prosecuted.[22]

It should not be inferred that the government always stood idly
by as Indians were exploited. Bett's replacement, George Lee, was
a decent man who tried his best to protect his Indian charges. Unfortunately, during the mid-1870s, the entire Indian Bureau was rid-
dled with corruption.[23] Little help was forthcoming from Washington, but Special Agent E. J. Brooks, a clerk in the General Land
Office, was assigned to investigate charges of land fraud in Michigan.
Together, these two men documented what was certainly one of the
most despicable episodes in Michigan history. Their records show
how Michigan's Ottawa and Ojibwa were cheated from tens of thousands of acres of land, millions of dollars' worth of pine timber, and
a chance for a decent future.[24]

Among the many techniques used to separate Indians from their
land was the collateral scam. Cheap sewing machines or parlor or-
gans might be sold to Indians on credit, using their land as collateral.
When payments were not forthcoming, the goods were repossessed
and the land seized for payment. Loan sharking, in which land was
held as collateral against a repayment schedule, was particularly
common because Indian homesteaders were often desperate for cash
to make the required improvements. One man in Mason County,
Michigan, got an entire township, thirty-six square miles, by foreclos-
ing on twenty-dollar loans.[25]

Indians were often taxed off their land in schemes that involved
collusion between real estate "investors" and public officials. In
1877, in the Little Traverse region, Indians were taxed at the rate
of $32.85 on each unimproved eighty acres, twice the amount levied
on non-Indians. A local official in Emmet County promised that the
rate would keep increasing until the community had "relieved itself
of the presence of Indians."[26] If taxes were not paid, which they
frequently were not on the advice of agents, notice would be given
in an English-language newspaper and the land put on the market
for back taxes.

Another method of land fraud was to invalidate Indian homestead claims by alleging that the residence or improvement requirements were not met. This was nearly a foolproof way of getting land, because Indians did not know how to acquire the protection of the law and could not afford attorney fees if they did. The case of Lucy *Penaseway*, an Ottawa widow with four children, serves as an example. Having filed a homestead claim at the Traverse City Land Office, Mrs. *Penaseway* cleared a field and garden, planted fruit trees and strawberries, and built a house and an outhouse. In the summer of 1876, she and her children left their farm to pick blueberries, which they would sell door to door in Traverse City. This was one of the few sources of cash income available to Indian women and vital to the operation of her homestead. While she was away, William Thompson bribed a land office clerk to advertise the property as abandoned, and, when she did not enter a formal objection, Thompson claimed her property as a homestead himself. When Mrs. *Penaseway* and her children returned they found their garden and orchard plowed and all proof of their improvements destroyed.[27] Agent Lee protested vehemently about this case, but the government did nothing. Thompson stripped the *Penaseway* homestead of pine timber and abandoned it five years later.

William Gribb, a cultural geographer, has made a parcel-by-parcel investigation of the fate of land allotments made under the Treaty of July 31, 1855, in Leelanau County. Of the six townships set aside for Indian selections, about 30 percent was unavailable because it was either claimed by the federal government as school sections or by the State of Michigan under the Swamplands Act. When selections were made in 1856 and 1857, 93, or 12 percent, had to eventually be reentered because of administrative mistakes. As a result of these and other problems, certificates of Indian selections were not issued until 1864. President Grant did not sign the patents for the Grand Traverse Band until July, 1872, when 304 patents were issued for over twenty thousand acres, or about 32 percent of the land available for selection. On the average, Indian allottees were able to retain their land for an average of only 6.3 years. In fact, almost 7 percent of the land was sold within the first six months. Within twenty years, Indians of the Grand Traverse band held less than one hundred acres, most located around the small community of Peshawbestown on Suttons Bay. Although some of the original twenty thousand acres passed to whites for back taxes, the vast majority was sold on warranty or quit claim sale. Many of these sales involved fraud, one indication being the price paid per acre. On the average, where land transferred from Indians to whites, $4.50 was paid per acre while the average was $6.95 per acre when the sale involved whites only. Gribb found that most of the allotted lands eventually went to sixteen individuals either for their own use or for timber and real estate speculation. Prominent among these were two members of the Grand Traverse band, Frances Blackman and John *Ahgosa*. These men on their own or, more frequently, representing Chicago land speculators were able to "acquire" most of the allotments that went to widows, the elderly, and disabled Indians who were desperate for cash.[28]

The case of land loss among Indians of the Grand Traverse bands is typical of other areas of the Great Lakes region. The net result was that the Indians were often without property and they began to concentrate and form villages on the few lands that they still retained. Often, these were lands purchased in common or by chiefs or missionaries for the collective use of a group. As they moved to these small refuges, band integrity began to break down; the identity that remained was tribal and community centered. Thus, people would have said they were Ottawa from Middle Village or Ojibwa from Nahma.

Fortunately, the last several decades of the nineteenth century and the first decade of the twentieth century were times of high demand for labor. In the north, Indian men became skillful lumbermen and were also employed extensively in the fishing industry. In the south, wage work in agriculture was available. In the tradition of reciprocal exchange, wages and other resources continued to flow freely between kin. This was so often the case that some agents, such as J. Mahon at the Red Cliff reservation near Bayfield, Wisconsin, paid Indians doing government work on the reservation in goods, since he believed cash payments encouraged the ambitious to support the lazy and goods were less easily transferred than cash.[29]

At the turn of the century, the natural resources of northern Michigan were almost depleted and complex machinery was already reducing labor requirements in mining and agriculture. Indians were ill-prepared to compete with whites in this diminishing labor market. Lack of language skills, little formal training in the use of mechanical

Indians fishing for whitefish at *Bowating*, the rapids of the St. Marys River, Sault Ste. Marie, Michigan, circa 1890. (Photograph courtesy of the State of Michigan Archives.)

equipment, and their nonaggressive demeanor were practical disadvantages. But more depressing was the fact that Indian students returning from boarding schools with training and skills had to face intense hostility and racial prejudice from the competing white majority. As never before, Indians were forced even farther to the margins of the American economy. About the only positions open were as domestics or very unskilled laborers.

Some unique avenues for earning income, however, did remain open. Indians collected berries, particularly blueberries, that were sold door to door. Likewise, a considerable market existed for game and fish that could be sold to the restaurant trade. Indian women also began to produce handicrafts for both the commercial and tourist markets. Berry baskets, clothes hampers, corn husk mats, utility baskets of split ash, and souvenir boxes beautifully trimmed with sweetgrass or dyed porcupine quills as well as bead work became very important sources of income. Unfortunately, the skill and artistry needed to produce these "curios" was not rewarded in terms of the time spent to make them. An Indian woman producing these items would have to work for pennies per hour. While this may also have been true of hand produced products in other industries at the turn of the century, handicraft Indian items did not become really profitable until the development of a market in Indian art in the 1960s.

Late in the nineteenth century, the railroads developed a huge summer resort industry in northern Michigan and Indians found themselves part of the local "color." Henry Longfellow's adaptation of Henry Schoolcraft's rendering of the Ojibwa *Nanabojo* stories as the very popular "Song of Hiawatha" added immensely to the romance of the north woods and provided the grist for pageants. The most famous of these was held at *Wayagamug* or Round Lake between Petoskey and Harbor Springs. Staged by the Grand Rapids and Indiana Railroad, the pageant ran for many years and employed Indian actors. For most of the parts in the production the railroad went to Canada to hire "real" Indians despite the fact that the pageant was located in one of the areas with the highest Indian population in the state. The lead role of Minnehaha was first played, however, by the beautiful and talented Ella Petoskey, granddaughter of Chief Petoskey. Her picture appeared on countless postcards that were sent all over the world by enthusiastic tourists.

Pow Wows, which had formerly been occasions for the reunions of Indian families and an opportunity to teach children tribal dances and ceremonies, were reoriented to appeal to tourists. They, of course, featured what the tourist expected of Indians: feather war bonnets, war dances, and Indian princess contests. Of course, they also provided a wonderful opportunity for the sale of handicrafts.

These were stopgap measures. In fact, at the turn of the century, Indians were desperately poor and the vast majority lived under conditions of deplorable poverty. When they most needed help from the government, the government decided that federal aid was a barrier to their march toward real assimilation. Commissioner of Indian

Traverse City merchant and Indian basket maker, circa 1920. (Photograph courtesy of the State of Michigan Archives.)

Josie Joe dressed for the Hiawatha pageant at Round Lake, Petoskey, Michigan, circa 1908. (Photograph courtesy of the Little Traverse Bay Bands of Odawa Indians.)

Affairs William Jones said in 1901 that 240 million dollars had been spent on 180,000 Indians in federal subsidies over the last thirty-three years, sufficient on a per capita basis to build and furnish a home and farm for each family. "Certainly," he said, "it is time to make a move toward terminating the guardianship which has so long been exercised over the Indians and putting them upon equal footing with the white man so far as their relations with the government are concerned."[30]

Indeed, the government did withdraw much of its support, leaving Michigan Indians in limbo, lost on the white man's road. An early indication was the refusal of the federal government to back Indians in conflict with state powers. When Michigan and the other Great Lakes states began enforcing their hunting and fishing laws in the 1880s, the federal government, which had always protected treaty guarantees of hunting and fishing in ceded territory, now began to advise Indians that they had to abide by the laws of the states. Likewise, Indians were often charged with crimes such as child abandonment because state officials did not understand that relatives often raised each other's children, particularly in hard times. Traditional marriages, particularly polygamous marriages that often led to Indian men being charged with "fornication," and customary modes of inheritance were often not compatible with state laws. The dignity of Indians was ravaged by game wardens who searched their homes with impunity, by officials who rounded up their children for long stints in distant boarding schools, and by whiskey vendors who set up shop in their communities.

Not only did the federal government contend that most Indians were citizens of their states and, therefore, subject to state civil laws, but the field staff was sharply curtailed. Agency farmers or "dispersing agents" often found themselves representing the United States in complex and distressing situations; Indians learned that they could expect little help from the "Great Father," but they did not quit trying.

In addition, a crisis in leadership was taking place. As band identity crumbled so did the authority of headmen and chiefs. Never great to begin with, the authority of traditional "hereditary" leaders waned, in part, due to the protestations of educated young people who were frustrated by a "system of government" that was without clear authority or a formal way to resolve competing claims of succession. Most communications to the government were petitions of the whole, containing hundreds of names, many accompanied by an inked thumbprint, the twentieth century equivalent to "touching the pen." On reservations, in the scattered rural Indian communities, and in the "Indian towns" attached to white cities, disease, poverty, drunkenness, and almost total unemployment became a way of life.

To be sure, this was not the case for all families, and there are some remarkable success stories, but they were not the rule. Indians became true refugees with no help and none on the horizon.[31]

NOTES

1. Prucha 1986, 77.
2. *Annual Report of the Commissioner of Indian Affairs, 1856–1857* (New York: AMS Press, 1976).
3. Report of the Secretary of Interior for 1860, J. Thompson, Executive Documents of the Senate of the United States, 36th Cong., 2d sess.
4. Leach to Commissioner of Indian Affairs, National Archives Microforms, series M234, reel 407:539–40.
5. J. Knight to E. S. Parker, October 12, 1870, National Archives Microforms, series M234, reel 394.
6. Deed to Chiefs by F. Baraga, 1863, Houghton County Register of Deeds, Liber 6:178–80.
7. Smith to Commissioner of Indian Affairs, October 30, 1865, *Annual Report to the Commissioner of Indian Affairs, 1865* (New York: AMS Press, 1976).
8. Moore 1897, 447.
9. D. C. Leach, *Annual Report to the Commissioner of Indian Affairs, 1864* (New York: AMS Press, 1976).
10. Proceedings of a Council with Chippewas and Ottawas of Michigan held at the City of Detroit, by the Hon. George W. Manypenny and Henry G. Gilbert, Commissioners of the United States, July 25, 1855, National Archives Microforms, series T497, reel 123:57.
11. Rubenstein 1974, 58.
12. Quoted in Prucha 1973, 18.
13. Quoted in Prucha 1973, 203.
14. See Littlefield 1992.
15. Paul Prucha (1979) offers a study of the role of churches in the operations of Indian schools during the period from 1888 to 1912, with particular emphasis on the competition between the Catholics and Protestants for government support.

16. See Littlefield 1989.
17. Hoxie 1984, 196.
18. Littlefield 1989, 439.
19. Bolt 1987, 227.
20. Quoted in Priest 1942, 178.
21. *Compiled Laws of the State of Michigan,* 1:352.
22. Rubenstein 1974, 118.
23. Prucha 1986, 191.
24. E. Brooks to Commissioner of Indian Affairs, January 12, 1878, National Archives Microforms, series M234, reel 413; G. Lee to Commissioner of Indian Affairs, September 20, 1877, National Archives Microforms, series M234, reel 412.
25. Rubenstein 1974, 116.
26. Rubenstein 1974, 117.
27. Rubenstein 1974, 118.
28. See Gribb 1982.
29. J. Mahan to E. P. Smith, October 12, 1875, National Archives Microforms, series M234, reel 396:340.
30. Prucha 1985, 49 and 1990, 201.
31. R. White n.d., 136.

Chapter 8

From Yesterday to Tomorrow

Daebaudjimowim

Among Indian people, elders are not just elderly but those older people who are respected for their wisdom. These are the keepers of *daebaudjimowim,* the stories of experience, oral tradition. Today's elders, those born in the first two decades of the twentieth century, have seen a transition in their own lives and in Indian culture that is more profound than perhaps any period of history. As children, many of these men and women accompanied their parents on seasonal rounds, deer hunting in the winter, making sugar in the spring, and visiting ricing or fishing camps in the fall. These elders knew people who spoke no English and are today the only generation still fluent in their tribal dialects. As children they heard the songs of the *Midé-wi-win* priests and perhaps the voices of the *jessakkid.* Some may have apprenticed as herbalists or learned the spells to protect themselves from the evil bear walker. They alone in today's world know the ancient place names and historic events that transform geography into living history.

These same elders have another side; they were the first of their people to completely master English and to teach it to their children as a first language. They were the first generation to make their living working for wages in factories and stores. They proudly served their country in the armed services and became warriors in Germany, the South Pacific, and Korea. Today's elders were also the first Indians who could legally buy intoxicating beverages and they were the first to become citizens of the United States.

Indian elders form a bridge between the worlds of yesterday and tomorrow. Most are staunch Christians who also firmly believe in the *manidog* that inhabit the places and living things of our world. To these spirits, they offer a pinch of tobacco when collecting plants. These elders know the herbal cures prescribed by the medicine men of old and place their trust in their powers, but they also use the hospitals and visit the offices of men and women skilled in modern medicine. In the summer powwows, these elders offer the blessings, in the language of the *manidogs,* that are carried skyward on plumes of sweetgrass incense, they display their warrior feathers earned on the Rhine and on Guadalcanal, and they teach the young ones the traditions of ancient times.

For young people, the elders are more than sources of information about the past. They also provide stability in the community and are everyone's treasured grandparents. What kinds of advice and knowledge might they give?

Many people believe that this little town is called Bay Shore, after all it says so on the road sign. We old Ottawa people know its real name is *Basho,* which means "near." It has always been called that because as you came up Lake Michigan on the way to the end of Little Traverse Bay you knew by the time you got here that you were very nearby. When the white people came and asked what we called this place they thought when we said *Basho* that we were saying "Bay Shore." Not many people know this anymore. Those of us that do always smile when we go by.

—Foster Otto of Petoskey[1]

My mother taught me to make baskets and she was taught by her mother. She taught me to take my time and to always do my best work. When you make a basket it is much more than a basket; when you make a basket you are practicing your worth.

—Harriet Shedawin of Sault Ste. Marie[2]

For many years the government and the missionaries tried every way possible to get us lake Indians to clear farms. They told us we could get a good living with the plow. We knew it was too cold to grow much. My dad told me how to make a living. "Bill," he said, "four hundred feet of gill net will give you more food than forty acres." That's still good advice today.

—Doc Bill Cameron of Sault Ste. Marie[3]

Susie Shagonaby teaches her son Robert how to identify and collect sweet grass. (Photograph courtesy of the State of Michigan Archives.)

Reform and Self-Determination

The deplorable conditions on Great Lakes Indian reservations and in Indian communities during the several decades before and after the turn of the twentieth century were due to both benign neglect on the part of the federal government and the administrative problems created by the process of land allotment. Since allottees were classified as wards of the federal government by provision of the General Allotment Act of 1887, the Indian Bureau not only had to deal with the tribes on a government-to-government basis but also to supervise the personal affairs of tens of thousands of individuals. Rather than promoting the self-sufficiency and assimilation that were the goals of allotment, it created dependency and resentment. The government controlled almost every aspect of the lives of Indians, a total welfare state. Filth, disease, starvation, and crushing poverty afflicted life in almost every Indian settlement.

These conditions did not go totally unnoticed by the public. In 1881, Indian reformer Helen Hunt Jackson published an influential exposé of government dealings with native Americans in a book called *A Century of Dishonor*. This book, along with articles in the popular press, gave rise to the Women's National Indian Association, the National Indian Defense Association, and the Indian Rights Association, as well as to other organizations devoted to bettering the lot of Indians. Most were supported by eastern liberals and advocated Christianization and civilization policies. Such organizations lobbied the Bureau of Indian Affairs and Congress for reforms that they believed would not only relieve poverty but turn Indians into "self-reliant and independent workers."[4] This meant, however, that many Indian customs and traditions had to be repressed as contrary to this more "enlightened objective." Indians receiving government services were required to cut their long hair, and agents did their best to discourage ceremonies and dances, including (in the Great Lakes) the curing rituals of the *Midé-wi-win*. The failure of these reforms and dissatisfaction both within and outside of the Indian community continued to grow. Partially to escape poverty and partially to support the nation of which they increasingly felt a part, many Indian men joined the army and fought in Europe during World War I. In acknowledgment of their loyalty, Congress offered veterans citizenship and finally, in 1924, authorized the Secretary of the Interior to issue certificates of U.S. citizenship to all native Americans without prejudice to their tribal membership (*U.S. Statutes at Large,* 43:253). It should be remembered, however, that it was not until August, 1953, that Congress extended to Indians the full rights of citizenship, including the right to purchase alcoholic beverages, to own firearms, and to be entitled to equal protection under American law.

These formal measures of change did little to help Indians to enter the American mainstream. Indeed they were still locked in a struggle for mere survival. The people of the Bay Mills reservation near Brimley, Michigan, were starving during the winter of 1930 and petitioned the government for help. Their superintendent, E. W. Jermark, located 325 miles away in Lac du Flambeau, Wisconsin, supported their efforts when he pointed out some of their difficulties to the Commissioner of Indian Affairs. He wrote that the Bay Mills situation was desperate. Because the people had been advised that they had to abide by state game laws, they could not fish without a ten-dollar license, which none could afford. Neither was there work in the woods: the pine timber had been stripped from the sandy plains south of the reservation. To make matters worse, the State and National Forest had purchased this area and now prohibited burning. Because fire is necessary to rejuvenate the blueberry crop, Indians were now denied this one source of cash income. Superintendent Jermark observed that, in 1908, Bay Mills people had picked 2,000 crates of berries on the plains at two dollars per crate. Now, he said, this cash income denied, Chippewa county was forced to pay aid to keep the Bay Mills people from starving to death.[5] In 1930, Indians were kept alive on aid of ten dollars per family per month, none of it coming from the federal government.

Among the most vocal of the critics of Indian policy in the 1920s was John Collier, founder of the American Indian Defense Association, who strongly objected to the government's assault on Indian culture and was angered by the apparent failure of the assimilation policy. The Bureau finally responded to the clamor for reform by commissioning an independent study of Indian policies and programs and the conditions of North American Indian peoples. The report issued in 1928, often referred to as the "Meriam Report" after its author Lewis Meriam, shocked the American people and Congress. The result was a radical shift in Indian policy during the 1930s.

Much of the change came about at the hands of President Franklin Roosevelt's new Commissioner of Indian Affairs, John Collier. The so-called Indian New Deal featured job programs for Indians as well as efforts to provide religious freedom for Indians. Among the most successful job programs was the establishment of arts and crafts cooperatives and Works Projects Administration Arts and Crafts projects. One of the most notable of these was the Michigan Indian Handicraft Project, cosponsored by the Michigan Department of Conservation and various Michigan counties, particularly Emmet County. In 1938, the Cross Village workshop hired local Ottawa, mostly men, to produce traditional items such as bentwood ladles, bows, baskets, and snowshoes, and also rustic furniture, picnic tables, foot stools, and other cabin furniture for the tourist trade. By its own goals, that is, teaching Indians the workings of the supply and demand market and promoting economic self-sufficiency, the project failed, yet it did help to keep Indian artists and craftsmen in the public eye and to provide badly needed dollars at the height of the Great Depression.[6]

The real keystone to change in the 1930s and the law that today governs the relationship between Indian tribes and the United States was the Wheeler-Howard Act, which became law in June, 1934 (*U.S. Statutes at Large*, 48:984–88). This act, known as the Indian Reorganization Act or the IRA, was based on the idea that Indians were capable of governing themselves and conducting their own business. To promote these ends, the IRA provided a corporate model that enabled the tribes that so desired to establish government-to-government relationships with the United States. To accomplish this, groups of Indians had to submit a draft charter and bylaws for the approval of the Secretary of the Interior as a basis of "acknowledgment" or "recognition." These documents specified the mechanism of government, which was usually by means of an elected tribal council and officers, including a tribal chairperson. Also required were rules of defining membership and enrollment, which usually specified proof of quarter-degree Indian blood or ancestry from a preexisting tribal roll. Soon, various bands and tribes were petitioning the government for recognition, a process that is still continuing today. The Wheeler-Howard Act also ended the allotment of land, and, in fact, the government began to purchase land that it took into trust for newly acknowledged tribes.

Although many tribes made enormous strides under the IRA, corporate principles and majority votes did not jibe well with the traditional consensus method of decision making nor with the influential roles of traditional chiefs and spiritual leaders. The government's insistence on reserving the right to approve all major decisions and its control of tribal budgets made the new mode of government less than ideal in the eyes of many tribes.

In fact, most of Michigan's historical bands did not initially apply for federal acknowledgment. The Bay Mills and Hannahville communities, the Saginaw Chippewa, and the Keweenaw Bay people applied and were acknowledged in the 1930s. The Sault Ste. Marie Chippewa and Grand Traverse Ottawa and Chippewa were not acknowledged until the late 1970s, and the Lac Vieux Desert band of Lake Superior Chippewa was only recognized as recently as 1986. Other bands are in the process of seeking official federal recognition.

Historically, gaining federal recognition was not always an easy matter. The Ottawa provide a good case study in this regard.[7] Thanks to the work of several turn-of-the-century Ottawa chiefs such as Simon *Keshigobenese, Miscogen,* John *Kewaygeshik,* and Thomas Petoskey, who all visited Washington on several occasions and wrote to the Bureau and Congress in support of treaty claims, it was discovered that the Ottawa and Ojibwa descendants of the Treaty of Detroit in 1855 had money due from a government investment.[8] To get the money, they were forced to sue the United States, since the government regarded the Ottawa as a small group of assimilated mixed bloods. After winning a court judgment against the United States, the government was in turn forced to renew their relationship and deal with the Ottawa and Chippewa of western Michigan and the eastern Upper Peninsula so that the award could be distributed. Horace Durant was sent to make a list of the descendants of the signers of the 1855 treaty, work that he finished in 1908. The Durant roll lists the names of all known descendents as well as their ages and degree of Indian blood. To the surprise of federal officials, the roll contained the names of thousands of individuals, most with a high degree of Indian ancestry.

During the 1920s and 1930s, Ottawa chiefs Paul Daybird, Albert *Shananaquet,* Jacob *Cobmosa,* and Sampson Robinson continued to agitate in Washington on behalf of their people. In 1932, they founded the Michigan Indian Organization to work for reservation land and the right to hunt and fish on public land. With the passage of the IRA, they asked for federal acknowledgment but were denied. Commissioner of Indian Affairs Collier favored the recognition of small, traditional groups rather than newly created statewide organizations. The Ottawa thus became victims of their own political progress.[9]

With the encouragement of their parish priest in Petoskey, Father Aubert, the Ottawa and Ojibwa of northwestern Lower Michigan founded the Michigan Indian Defense Association in 1934. When Father Aubert learned the federal government would not recognize this group for the same reasons it turned down the Michigan Indian Organization, he preached against the whole idea of federal recognition. So much suspicion and negative opinion was raised in this predominantly Catholic community that a petition for federal recognition could not be successfully organized. In the meantime, there were other attempts to seek redress from the federal government. In 1934, Robert and Waunetta Dominic of Petoskey and others formed the Northern Michigan Ottawa Association in order to pursue treaty claims against the government. In fact, the Northern Michigan Ottawa Association, with its eleven units representing the bands of the 1836 Treaty of Washington, succeeded in winning a $10 million award through the Indian Claims Commission, which was established to hear such cases in 1949. This award, made in 1971, has not been distributed because of the lack of a fair mechanism for per capita distribution; today, interest on the original award has pushed the balance of this account to over $50 million.

In 1975, the Northern Michigan Ottawa Association leadership pressed the federal government to recognize it as a tribal government under the IRA. Intense disagreement within the Ottawa community over the wisdom of this move, much of it originating from the feuds of earlier generations, split the community. The Ottawa of the Northern Michigan Ottawa Association decided against federal acknowledgment. Thus, for the second time, the Ottawa of western Lower Michigan decided to go their own way. Despite the recognition of the Grand Traverse Ottawa/Chippewa tribe in 1978, there are still about fifteen thousand Ottawa Indians who are not eligible to receive assistance from the Bureau of Indian Affairs or the benefits of treaty rights because they lack the formal government-to-government relationship the United States demands.

City Life and Termination

The emergence of industries in the cities of southern Michigan in the early decades of the twentieth century drew large numbers of workers from rural populations. Many Michigan Indians as well as Indians from other areas of North America found good-paying jobs in the auto industries of Detroit, Flint, Saginaw, and Lansing as well as the furniture industry at Grand Rapids. The Indians who immigrated to these cities lived with relatives or in homes nearby, so that Indian neighborhoods soon formed in these urban settings. Despite the Great Depression of the 1930s, this urban migration has been a long-term trend. Perhaps it would surprise some to learn that, today, about 80 percent of Michigan's 62,000 Indians live in cities. It should be quickly added, however, that urban Indians are unique among city dwellers because of the very strong emotional and physical ties they maintain with their rural bands and tribes. It is very common for Indians with jobs in cities to return regularly to rural and reservation areas in the north to renew bonds with family and friends. This goes far beyond the usual visit home; among Michigan Indians, the visitors maintain kin obligations and hunting and fishing partnerships, and establish rights to continuing access to community resources. Thus, during the depression of the 1930s and again as recently as the deep recession of the early 1980s, the Indian populations of northern communities increased dramatically as unemployed workers returned to seek the support of their kin. Similarly, money earned in good times often finds its way home to help support the rural partners. This "teeter-totter economy" is an adaptation of long standing and great advantage to Great Lakes Indians. It is also true that many, many Indian workers return home after they retire, bringing their skills with them.

The urban movement solved some important problems for Indians, but it also created others. Federal programs are geared to provide services to Indians who are enrolled members of acknowledged tribes and live on or near reservations. The vast majority of Indians in Michigan have no access to these services because they reside hundreds of miles away in southern Michigan cities. They are thus disenfranchised by geography, and the Bureau of Indian Affairs serves less than 20 percent of the state's Indian population.

The picture is still more complicated because many Indians from other states and regions reside in Michigan cities. There are more people who claim Indian ancestry through Cherokee relatives than there are Potawatomi in Michigan. The Michigan Department of Social Services has tried to provide for urban Indians through its Urban Indian Affairs program, but, without some means of identifying a legitimate clientele, its meager resources are soon expended without much effect.

The problems for Indians in coping with urban life were and are immense. Disassociation from family and friends and exposure to pressures of the city environment have often led to alcoholism and family dysfunction. Many Indians have been aided in these situations by Indian organizations that provide economic, political, and emotional support for urban Indians. Since the founding of the Detroit American Indian Center in 1940, other Indian centers have sprung up in most major cities. Some examples include the Genesee Valley Indian Center in Flint, the Grand Rapids Inter-Tribal Council, and the Lansing North American Indian Center. Recently, the Michigan Urban Indian Consortium has been formed to coordinate these programs. There is also a wide variety of organizations devoted to special purposes, such as the Great Lakes Indian Artists Association, the Michigan Indian Press, Michigan Indian Employment and Training Service, and the American Indian Business Development Consortium. Among the almost four dozen Indian organizations of Michigan are also several educational groups, including Bay Mills Community College and the Nokomis Learning Center of Okemos. Most colleges and universities have native American student organizations to help Indian students cope with the special problems of college life. The Michigan Commission on Indian Affairs maintains an up-to-date list of these organizations in the state.

After World War II, specifically during the Eisenhower administration, there was a strong movement to "emancipate" native Americans from federal guardianship. House Concurrent Resolution 180, passed in 1953, declared it to be national policy "to make Indians within the territorial limits of the United States subject to the same laws and entitled to the same privileges and responsibilities as are applicable to other citizens of the United States and to end their status of the United States ... " (*U.S. Statutes at Large*, 67:B132). Even in the best cases, this policy was an abject failure. The Menominee tribe of Wisconsin offers an example.

The Menominee, organized as a tribe under the Indian Reorganization Act, had prospered during the late 1930s through the early 1950s. Thanks to a long and vigorous defense by their chiefs and by the Bureau of Indian Affairs, the Menominee had been able to maintain an unallotted reservation of almost a quarter million acres near Keshena, Wisconsin. Two hundred thousand acres of this land was prime forest that the Menominee skillfully managed for timber. A tribal sawmill and forestland employment permitted full employment and prosperity to the five thousand or so tribal members. The Menominee were so successful that they drew the attention of the federal government, which now wanted to end federal stewardship over Indians. The Menominee seemed to provide an excellent test case, since they had obviously "made it" as market competitors.[10] In 1954, the tribe was terminated by act of Congress and their reservation became Menominee County, Wisconsin.

The presumption that the Menominee could fend for themselves without government assistance was almost immediately proven false. The imposition of state and federal taxes and other business difficulties befell Menominee Enterprises, Inc., which now ran the Menominee industry. Layoffs forced a huge number of people to turn to public assistance, and a prosperous community was transformed into a welfare burden for the state of Wisconsin. To make matters worse, Menominee Enterprises, in a desperate effort to succeed, was forced to enter into a partnership with outside interests in the "Legend Lakes" development. This joint venture permitted hundreds of non-Indians to build expensive vacation homes on the reservation lands that had been so tenaciously defended since the early nineteenth century. In 1969, violent protests by antidevelopment Menominee broke out and eventually this movement led to efforts to restore the reservation. In 1973, after years of struggle, Congress passed and President Nixon signed the Menominee Restoration Act, which provided a process to return Menominee land to trust status and recognized tribal members as American Indians. In April, 1975, the Secretary of the Interior and Ada Deer, head of the Menominee Restoration Committee, signed a deed conveying Menominee tribal land back into trust.[11]

Although relatively few tribes were terminated, it was realized that the grand ideal of "emancipating" Indians from their special status was neither desirable to Indians nor beneficial to their welfare.

The Kennedy administration repudiated the termination idea, and the 1960s saw an effort to improve health, welfare, and rights of Indians. Most important was the beginning of an effort to give Indian tribes the responsibility of managing their own affairs. In the 1970s and 1980s, Congress greatly strengthened the self-determination movement by passing numerous pieces of legislation that provided funding for the protection of tribal sovereignty, economic development, education, housing, and health care.[12] Unfortunately, the full development of local tribal management was impeded by the huge, remote, and often inept bureaucracy of the Bureau of Indian Affairs. Despite the appearance of a vocal and active "red power" movement, the Bureau controlled Indian affairs because it controlled funding.

During the Carter administration, the federally recognized tribes of the Great Lakes underwent a miraculous transformation. This was due to the coalescence of the self-determination policy, increased federal funding through the various programs put in place through the 1970s, and a new generation of educated young Indians returning to their local communities. In Michigan, the tribes began to acquire trust lands, to form corporations for the construction and management of new housing and health care facilities, to charter business enterprises, and to assert their civil and treaty rights in court.

The Mar Shunk neighborhood of the City of Sault Ste. Marie provides an example. In 1975, this neighborhood was typical of the "Indian towns," really rural slums on the peripheries of many northern cities. Living conditions for the hundred families who resided in the neighborhood were deplorable.[13] More than 80 percent of the residents were Indian. Although Mar Shunk is within the corporate limits of the city, little money had ever been spent to provide services. There were no paved streets, water lines were inadequate, there were no street lights, parks, playgrounds, or sewers. In the spring, water from the city's storm sewers flushed into Mar Shunk and the streets became quagmires. Homes burned because fire trucks could not negotiate the streets, and children had to walk through the mud and sewage to reach paved streets where they would meet their school busses. These conditions had drastic consequences, because poor sanitation produced sickness that led, in turn, to poor work records and school attendance for Mar Shunk residents. Extremely high unemployment and school dropout rates were part of the conse-

Joseph Lumsden

The largest and certainly most successful of Michigan Indian tribes is the Sault Ste. Marie tribe of Chippewa. Since its modern political establishment did not come until 1975, it is also one of the newest. Much of the tribe's success, the benefits that its members enjoy, and the new standing of Indians in northern Michigan is attributable to Joe Lumsden, who became Chairman of the tribe soon after its formation and held the position until his death in September, 1987.

Joe's early years were fairly typical of many Indian young people of his era. After his mother's death, Joe and his brothers were taken in and raised by his extended family, which included, at various times, his grandmother and his uncle. Joe's family has a long history at the rapids of the St. Marys and included fishermen, canoeists, and, later, dredgemen among its members. Although of mixed Ojibwa, French, and Irish descent, the family was strictly Indian in culture. Its members spoke both Ojibwa and French in the eighteenth and nineteenth centuries, and Joe, in the twentieth-century generation, grew up fluent in Ojibwa as well as English. He learned Ojibwa culture informally through stories told around the family table.

Although a good student in school, Joe was undisciplined and was expelled from Catholic school in sixth grade for truancy. He went by himself to enroll in public school, and, although he was often absent and dropped out on several occasions, he did maintain good grades when he attended. As was Indian custom, his family did not insist on actions that did not meet with the agreement of the child. They encouraged school but did not insist that he attend. Thanks to his interests in high school sports, Joe stayed in high school long enough to graduate.

After returning from a tour in the U.S. Marine Corps, Joe came to realize the importance of education and decided to attend Northern Michigan University on the G.I. Bill. At college he was interested in education, anthropology, and Indian history and eventually earned a B.S. degree and teaching certificate in 1967. By that time he had also married his wife, Susie, and two of his four children had been born.

Returning to Sault Ste. Marie in the late 1960s, Joe was able to see his hometown with a new perception. He was struck hard by the desperate plight of his people, the effects of prejudice, and the lack of self-esteem borne of generations of poverty. He saw himself as a boy

Joe Lumsden, chairman of the Sault Ste. Marie Tribe of Chippewa Indians, 1976–87. (Photograph courtesy of the *Evening News,* Sault Ste. Marie, Michigan.)

in the children playing in the filthy streets of the Mar Shunk neighborhood and most upsetting was that the same future likely awaited his own small children. Joe was angry. He knew that something must be done and that his own fight for a better life had little meaning while his people continued to suffer.

With other Indian men and women of influence in the community, Joe realized the importance of federal acknowledgment for establishing an independent Indian power base in Sault Ste. Marie. As one of the few educated Indians in the area, Joe could write and speak the language of American officialdom, and he was able to use his skills to organize the effort that eventually won political sovereignty for the tribe in 1976.

As Joe put it later, "Recognition has helped us. Most of all we became visible. Often people perceive us negatively but at least they see us. We are here. There are Indian people here. You cannot ignore us any longer. We have power and you are going to have to deal with us whether you like it or not. This is a big change. Most of all in the past whites have tried to keep us invisible so they could ignore us to death. We are not trying to cause trouble but we are going to stand up for ourselves. We are not going to be pushed around. I hope in time the controversies will pass and people will recognize our legitimacy."

For the next eighteen years Joe Lumsden led the Sault tribe from battle to battle. A reservation was established, and decent health care, new housing, paved streets, the right to fish, and the right to work good jobs were the result. He, of course, did not accomplish all of this alone, but he had a vision of the future and the persistence to fight for a better life for his people. Joe Lumsden died a young man and he no doubt had dreams unfulfilled. He did live to know that his children and the children of future generations of the Sault tribe would get a fair chance for a decent, prosperous life and to be Indians, too.

quence. The Indians of the Mar Shunk neighborhood were caught in a grinding cycle of poverty, a downward cycle with no apparent end.[14]

In the mid-1970s, the City of Sault Ste. Marie was successful in obtaining a large Community Development Block Grant from the U.S. Department of Housing and Urban Development to improve city services. As the city had done many times before, it planned to use these funds to improve existing facilities, which meant it would not be spent to provide even the most basic needs of the Mar Shunk neighborhood. Tribal Chairman Joseph Lumsden was incensed, and he engaged attorney Jim Jannetta to force the city to deal with the problem. Jannetta used the same strategy that civil rights lawyers were employing at this time to overcome similar problems in black neighborhoods in the Deep South. With the support of the U.S. Commission on Civil Rights, which investigated the situation, and technical help from the Lawyers' Committee for Civil Rights Under Law, Jannetta filed a lawsuit, *Perry v. the City of Sault Ste. Marie,* in U.S. District Court. In 1979, this case resulted in a consent judgment in which the city agreed to spend almost $6 million in the Mar Shunk neighborhood. Streets were paved, sidewalks and street lights were installed, the water supply was improved, and drains and sewers were provided. In 1980, for the first time in their lives, people in this Indian neighborhood had the advantages that had long been an accepted part of life in much of the rest of America.

Similarly aggressive steps were taken in other Indian communities and reservations, so that housing developments, extended care facilities, recreation centers, and tribally owned stores and gas stations made their appearance beside new tribal headquarters buildings. Indians began to regain their pride and to face the future with new optimism.

The Right to Fish

Big Abe Le Blanc was a man with a very strong presence. Not only was he big at six foot, five inches and 400 pounds, but on the Bay Mills reservation near Brimley he was a mover, an Indian entrepreneur. Commercial and subsistence fishing had long been important to Bay Mills people, and, for several generations, they had been forced to buy commercial licenses from the state despite a firm belief that their ancestors had reserved fishing and hunting rights in the 1836 treaty. When, in 1970, conservation officers began to confiscate nets and boats and arrest the community's fishermen, Big Abe had had enough. He arranged to get himself arrested for fishing with an illegal device, that is, a gill net, and for fishing without a license from the State of Michigan.

The arrests of Bay Mills fishermen and Indian fishermen, hunters, and trappers on the waters and in the forests of the Great Lakes region did not commence in the 1970s. In fact, as early as the 1880s Michigan, Wisconsin, Minnesota, and Ontario began to enforce hunting and fishing laws aimed at conserving game and fish species for sportsmen. These policies conflicted with the use of these resources as an important aspect of Indian subsistence as well as the treaties that guaranteed access to fish and game. Clearly, the treaty framers, both white and Indian, knew that it would be impossible for large groups of Indians to concentrate on small reservations without some means to feed themselves. The system worked for many decades. Then, in the 1880s, it became apparent that non-Indian hunters and commercial fishers were grossly overharvesting to supply distant urban restaurants. Indians bore most of the brunt of the crackdown. State wardens entered reservations and searched homes for meat and hides, traps and guns were confiscated, and Indians were fined and jailed. Their protests to agents, the Commissioner of Indian Affairs, and their congressional representatives went unheeded. Federal officials agreed with the contention of the states that allotted Indians were citizens of their respective states and would therefore have to abide by state law. The federal government was only willing to protect Indian treaty rights on the few parcels of allotted land still in Indian hands. Starvation now stalked many Indian families.

Big Abe lost his case in Michigan district court and appealed. In the meantime, several other criminal fishing cases were also making their way through the system, including *People v. Jondreau,* involving the right of Keweenaw Bay fishermen to fish without state supervision in the bay adjacent to their reservation under the treaty of 1842.

In the late 1960s and early 1970s, Americans were awakening to the plight of underprivileged people in society. As part of the civil rights movement there was again interest in fair treatment of native peoples and, as a part of it all, the federal government rekindled an

Grand Traverse Band conservation officers check commercial license of Indian fisherman on Grand Traverse Bay. (Photograph courtesy of *Win Awenen Nisitotung*, the tribal newspaper of the Sault Ste. Marie Tribe.)

interest in treaty rights. In Michigan, this interest was at the instigation of the three federally recognized tribes that were political successors to the tribes that signed the Treaty of Washington in 1836.[15] It was decided by the tribes and the federal government that the claim to treaty fishing rights should be resolved once and for all. A case was filed in the federal court for the western district of Michigan in which the United States, joined eventually by Bay Mills, the Sault Ste. Marie Tribe of Chippewa, and the Grand Traverse Tribe of Ottawa and Chippewa, sought to prevent the State of Michigan from interfering with treaty fishing. Bruce Greene of the Native American Rights Fund, a brilliant legal strategist, orchestrated the complex legal, historical, and political dimensions of this landmark case.

The State of Michigan, joined by the powerful Michigan United Conservation Clubs and other sportsmen's groups, presented its case through the cooperative efforts of the Department of Natural Resources (DNR) and the Attorney General's office. From the beginning, they took the most conservative and unyielding position. The Indians, they contended, acquired the art of gill net fishing from the

French. These nets they used for subsistence purposes only and, in the event that they may have made use of such nets in 1836, Indians had only reserved the right to use nets of bark fiber and other primitive technology. *If* such rights were reserved in 1836, said the state, then they were most certainly signed away in the Treaty of July 31, 1855 because the Indian signers agreed to renounce their tribal membership and, hence, their rights to hunt and fish.

To the Michigan DNR, Indian fishermen posed a serious threat to their efforts to restore the Great Lakes to ecological good health and to build an internationally famous sports fishing industry. To understand the state's zeal one has to understand something of the ecological and social history of the Great Lakes themselves.

By 1940, the stocks of native fish species, especially whitefish and lake trout, had been decimated by non-Indian commercial fishermen licensed by the state. The parasitic sea lamprey, which entered the Great Lakes by way of the Welland Canal around Niagara Falls, had attacked and largely exterminated lake trout in Lakes Huron and Michigan and severely depressed the whitefish population. Uncontrolled by predators, alewives, another exotic species, multiplied and, along with smelt, made up the vast bulk of the biofauna of the lakes. Annual die-offs left tons of these fish rotting on the beaches. To control this plague, fisheries biologist Howard Tanner suggested stocking Pacific salmon in the lakes, which, in combination with the development of an effective lamprey larvacide, produced dramatic results. Through the 1960s, the Great Lakes were gripped by "fish fever" as sportsmen flocked to Michigan ports to catch Coho and Chinook salmon. The fishermen, in turn, filled motels and restaurants and sports fishing was suddenly worth many millions of dollars.

The DNR, with the cooperation of the federal government, also decided to try to rehabilitate the lake trout, an effort that met with tremendous problems. First, the trout stocks used were not native to Lakes Michigan and Huron. The fry that were stocked faced predation by salmon, and, if they reached breeding age, predation of the spawn by huge populations of bottom-feeding sculpin made for long odds against the eggs even hatching. Perhaps worst of all, the fry were often planted near shore where they would be most accessible to fishermen when they returned to spawn as adults. These were not often places that gave the best chance of breeding success. There was, of course, the other obvious problem, mortality. This came from two sources: sports angling and commercial gill nets. Because of the combination of many or all of these factors, lake trout reestablishment was a total failure. Millions of stocked fish and not a single nonstocked adult fish was ever found.

In order to control mortality of adult lake trout, the DNR set out to eliminate gill nets and, with them, commercial fishing. They accomplished this by requiring the commercial fishermen they licensed to fish less and less efficiently, until commercial gill net users were forced out of business—regulated to extinction. The state now turned its attention to Indian commercial fishermen and began to confiscate their nets and boats, intent on driving them from the lakes as well.

In the spring of 1974, the tribes began to prepare their case for trial in federal court. Their case was simple. The Ottawa and Ojibwa of western Lower Michigan and the eastern Upper Peninsula had been gill net fishermen since A.D. 800. With the arrival of Europeans, they had caught and sold fish as a commercial enterprise to supply the needs of traders and soldiers on the frontier. As the Americans replaced the British, Indian fishermen acquired more sophisticated gear and new means to fish for the market as well as for their own subsistence. At the time of the treaty of 1836, Ottawa and Ojibwa fishermen were active in the fishing business and, in fact, requested, in the treaty itself, barrels and salt for the purpose of shipping fish to market. The tribes also believed that these rights to fish survived the treaty of 1855.

Unlike most Americans, Indians knew that treaty rights were not granted by the United States but were rights held by Indians to begin with. Many Indians could not understand why the state would interfere in an agreement between their forefathers and the federal government, when the government agreed with them on what the treaty reserved. Finally, it seemed that the supremacy clause of the U.S. Constitution should give treaties precedence over state law.

As in other treaty rights cases that had come before U.S. courts over the years, the interpretation of the treaties of 1836 and 1855, which were at issue in *U.S. v. Michigan,* was bound by an established set of precedents in American law. These precedents, called the canons of treaty construction, are based upon the recognition that the original treaty-making process gave an inherent advantage to the United States. Since the treaties were initiated by the United States, controlled by skilled American negotiators, written in English, and explained to Indians through interpreters hired by the United States, the courts had decided to give special consideration to these conditions in interpreting treaties. The canons, therefore, require that ambiguities in meaning be interpreted in favor of Indians, and that the language of treaties not be read technically, but in the simple language of common usage. Most important, the courts are required to interpret treaties as they would have been understood by their Indian signers.[16]

The canons of treaty construction meant that much of the testimony in *U.S. v. Michigan* revolved around historical questions and the testimony of anthropologists and ethnohistorians.[17] Key questions to be answered included: what kind of fishing right did the treaty signers reserve in the treaty of 1836, did this right involve using gill nets, were the Ottawa and Ojibwa fishing commercially in 1836, and did the treaty of July 31, 1855, revoke fishing rights that may have been reserved in the 1836 treaty? Besides these, there were many other questions relating to how a tribal fishery would be controlled and managed and how the state and the tribes would cooperate. Judge Noel Fox decided to hear the case in several parts, first the treaty rights issues and later the more practical matters, should the tribes prevail.

No sooner did the two sides and their respective experts join the battle than the Michigan United Conservation Clubs and personnel from the Department of Natural Resources began a vicious publicity campaign against Indian fishermen. Outdoor writers and television hosts warned the public that "blue-eyed Indians" were raping the lakes with "killer" gill nets. Incredibly, the DNR tried to blame the failure of their lake trout reestablishment efforts on Indian fishermen. Indian fishermen were consequently subject to attack by angry mobs of "sportsmen" who took it upon themselves to destroy their nets, boats, and trucks; they were also constantly harassed by conservation officers. This campaign, aimed at casting Indians in the role of environmental despoilers, had its worst effect on Indian schoolchildren, who were not able to handle the pressure as well as their parents. These children were constantly taunted in school as "gill netters" and were humiliated by shouts of "Save a lake trout—scalp an Indian."

At one point in the legal process the attorney for the Michigan United Conservation Clubs tried to present Judge Fox with petitions bearing thousands of signatures from sportsmen opposed to Indian treaty rights. The result was a severe tongue lashing by Judge Fox, who reminded everyone present that the basic function of our court system was to provide a forum free from political pressure, a place where the powerless could be heard on an equal footing with the powerful and the poor with a voice as loud as the rich.

By 1976, the arguments in *U.S. v. Michigan* were about to proceed when the Michigan Supreme Court issued a surprising ruling in *People v. Le Blanc*. The court had decided that Big Abe did, indeed, have a right to fish under the treaty of 1836 and that, as an Indian fisherman, he had a perfect right to do so with a gill net. The case did not, however, decide the matter on a civil basis, so the United States and the tribes pursued the case with new determination.

The long, involved, historical arguments heard in Judge Fox's courtroom in Grand Rapids were finally concluded and, in May, 1979, he issued his decision affirming the rights of Indian fishermen to exercise the prerogatives reserved by their ancestors under the treaty of 1836. The state appealed and simultaneously unleashed another salvo in the propaganda campaign. The decision, they said, was a plot by the federal government to take control of the Great Lakes; soon, Japanese fishing trawlers would be sailing under the Mackinac Bridge. The decision, it was claimed, gave Indians the right to fish unregulated.

In fact, the Fox decision directed the tribes to develop their own regulations, management, and enforcement mechanisms in cooperation with the U.S. Department of the Interior. This was done in 1979, and, in 1980, the new regulations were judged adequate by the courts to protect the fishery resources of the upper Great Lakes. In July, 1981, the U.S. Court of Appeals affirmed the decision in *U.S. v. Michigan,* and, in December, the U.S. Supreme Court refused to review the case, making the Court of Appeals decision final. The state was at last forced to deal with treaty fishing, but they did not do so in the spirit of cooperation. While wrapping itself in the mantle of the conservationists, the state permitted the few remaining licensed commercial fishermen to catch far more whitefish than permissible to maintain a healthy whitefish population, thereby forcing the tribes to obtain court-imposed closure orders to protect their fishery interests.

Finally, by the spring of 1984, Judge Richard Enslin, who took over the case upon the retirement of Judge Fox, appointed a Special Master to attempt to negotiate an equitable plan for the joint use and management of the lakes. Ultimately, a scheme emerged that divided the treaty waters of the three upper Great Lakes into management zones. These could be dedicated to different uses, fishing techniques, and catch levels. Through a process of give and take, the tribes, the state, and the U.S. Department of the Interior eventually agreed to a joint management plan that became the basis for the consent order entered by the court in 1985.

The management plan, which is good until the turn of the century when a new agreement will have to be reached, has been largely successful. In exchange for exclusive control of the commercial fishery, the tribes agreed to relinquish their claims to some areas of the lakes and to withdraw from other areas that are prime locations for sports angling. Likewise, the tribes agreed to begin fishing with trap nets in some places so that sports species could be released alive, an option not available with the gill net. Both the state and the tribes agreed to ban all fishing in several lake trout rehabilitation areas in the hope of reestablishing this species, which is important to both sportsmen and commercial fishermen.

This agreement has not completely ended all problems, but it does make the tribes, through their Chippewa-Ottawa Treaty Fishing Management Authority, a full partner in the upper Great Lakes fishery. Today, Indian fishermen catch about one-third of all the whitefish that enters the U.S. market and the income produced is vital to the economy of these people who work at a hard and risky job.

The case of *U.S. v. Michigan* was just the first of several treaty rights hunting and fishing cases that have been won in the federal courts of the Great Lakes region. The *Lac Courte Oreille v. Wisconsin,* or the Voight case, won the Lake Superior Chippewa bands of northern Wisconsin the right to hunt and fish over the lands and waters ceded in the treaties of 1837 and 1842 as long as these areas are in public ownership. The newly established right to hunt and fish over much of northern Wisconsin created a tremendous political backlash among the non-Indian citizens of the region, who particularly objected to the Ojibwa spearing walleyes during the spring spawning season. Huge, ugly riots marred the ability of these fishermen to exercise their court-mandated treaty rights. In 1991, however, the State of Wisconsin and the Lake Superior Chippewa agreed on a management plan that will, it is hoped, end this strife.

Much of the public outcry against treaty rights is based upon a common perception that such rights give an unfair advantage to Indians and that those advantages are based on antiquated, nineteenth-century agreements. As a matter of fact, Indians, as aboriginal inhabitants, have reserved rights that do provide them with a special status under American law. There is nothing inherently unfair in this, since American law protects the special rights of many classes of citizens. What perhaps really lies behind the resentment is that the treaty cases give Indians not just political muscle but social reality.[18]

As long as Americans could relegate the reality of Indians to the historical past they were no threat, except perhaps to the conscience. These court decisions made the Indian tribes real players in issues with real importance and, in this way, gave Indians a viable context in modern political life. Before the court decisions, average citizens would react with surprise to hear that there were still Indians around. Now they know.

Michigan Indians Today

It is difficult to calculate exactly how many people of Indian descent live in Michigan. The 1990 federal census lists 55,638 based upon self-identification, but the Michigan Commission on Indian Affairs believes this to be an undercount and suggests that a figure of 62,000 would be more accurate. At any rate, Indians represent only about 0.6 percent of Michigan's total population. While the 80.0 percent of the Indian population that resides in the urban areas of the Lower Peninsula seems invisible by virtue of their relatively small numbers, the 20.0 percent who reside in the north are a more noticeable segment of the population. In St. Ignace and Sault Ste. Marie, people of Indian descent make up 15.0 to 20.0 percent of the population. In many areas of the state, Indians have long-established, local communities either in rural areas or as neighborhoods in towns. Some examples include Harbor Springs, Cross Village, Dowagiac, Wilson, Hartford, Manistee, and Watersmeet, but there are many others.

Michigan also has seven federally recognized tribes with a total of 20,244 enrolled members. Other bands, including at least the

Michigan Indian reservations of today. (Drawing by B. Nemeth.)

Little Traverse Bay, Burt Lake, and Little River Ottawa as well as the Pokagon Potawatomi, are in the process of seeking federal recognition. Gaining federal acknowledgment is a long and difficult procedure in which a group of Indians must demonstrate the historic existence of the band or tribe, show a continuing political relationship with the United States, and, finally, show that the applicants are the legitimate political successors of that tribe or band. Since all federal benefits are channeled through recognized tribes, there are decided advantages to this status; however, some Indians find the very concept demeaning. They argue that, because the bands existed before the United States, they should not have to "prove up" to the newcomers. Be this as it may, most Indians believe acknowledgment to be the only practical means to deal with other American political entities on a government-to-government basis. In Michigan, there are currently no acknowledged Potawatomi bands in lower Michigan and only one group of Ottawa. The Ojibwa are, however, well represented among the seven federally recognized tribes, which are as follows.[19]

1. The *Bay Mills Indian Community* is an Ojibwa community that was established in 1854 on the Lake Superior shore near Brimley, thirty miles west of Sault Ste. Marie. There are presently 915 enrolled members with perhaps another 250 actually eligible for enrollment. This is a community that primarily depends upon commercial fishing, a pursuit that employs at least 60 percent of the work force. The reservation was established by act of Congress in June, 1860 (*U.S. Statutes at Large*, 12:58) and their constitution and bylaws were approved under the Indian Reorganization Act in 1937. The Bay Mills reservation consists of approximately 2,209 acres. Membership is by quarter-blood quantum and the legislative body is the General Tribal Council, which consists of all enrolled members over eighteen years of age. This latter feature is unusual, because most tribal legislatures consist of elected tribal councils. The Bay Mills executive is the tribal chairman, vice chair, secretary, and treasurer, all elected by popular vote. The judiciary is vested in a tribal court with a chief judge and three appeals judges.

2. *The Grand Traverse Band of Ottawa/Chippewa Indians* is located on the eastern shore of the Leelanau Peninsula near Traverse City. Although the community was established at about the time of the Treaty of 1836, it was not federally recognized until 1978. The 1,702 enrolled members are mostly scattered along the Lake Michigan shore from Charlevoix to Manistee. The center of community life is at Peshawbestown, where tribal buildings are located, including a flourishing casino that, along with fishing and the tourism industry, provides employment for band members. Today, the Grand Traverse Band holds 375 acres of land.

3. The *Hannahville Indian Community* is a Potawatomi community located twenty-six miles west of Escanaba, near the Wis-

consin border. There are presently 408 enrolled members, most of whom live on the reservation of 4,025 acres. Many are employed in lumbering and transportation, but the largest employer is the band itself, which provides jobs through its various programs and its gaming enterprises. The Hannahville community was established by act of Congress in June, 1913 (*U.S. Statutes at Large*, 33:102), and its constitution was approved under the Indian Reorganization Act on July 23, 1936. The community is governed by a tribal council of twelve members elected annually.

4. At the end of Keweenaw Bay in the western Upper Peninsula is the *Keweenaw Bay Indian Community*, which was established on a reservation set aside in the treaty of 1854. The 412 enrolled members and approximately 800 eligible for enrollment are descendents from the L'Anse, Baraga, and Ontonagon bands. The reservation today consists of 15,114 acres, with a reservation boundary established by treaty to encompass three townships. As allotments passed from Indian ownership, the reservation became a checkerboard of Indian and non-Indian ownership. Many of the Keweenaw Bay community are employed in logging and fishing, but the tribe provides most employment through a modern casino, motel, and restaurant complex. The tribal constitution and bylaws were approved under the Indian Reorganization Act in December, 1936, and provide for governance through a council of twelve members elected to three-year terms.

5. The *Lac Vieux Desert Band of Lake Superior Chippewa* was historically closely allied with the Keweenaw Bay bands, but resided near Watersmeet in Gogebic County. In 1988, the band gained federal recognition with 75 acres of trust land. The reservation was established by Public Law 100–420 (*U.S. Statutes at Large*, 102:1577) and the temporary tribal constitution provides for a nine member council, to expire when a new constitution is ratified by the 215 enrolled members. Tribal gaming operations provide most of the employment for band members.

6. The most southern federally recognized tribe is the *Saginaw Chippewa Tribe of Michigan,* who currently have 1,702 enrolled members who are descended from the Black River, Swan Creek, and Saginaw bands of Chippewa. Consolidated near Mt. Pleasant by the treaty of July 31, 1955, these bands were provided with a reservation in the treaty of 1864 to consist of six adjoining townships. Today, only about 1,400 acres of land are held by the tribe within their reservation. The tribe also holds another 70 acres of land at Standish on Saginaw Bay. The tribal council has ten members elected biennially.

7. By far the largest Michigan tribe is the *Sault Ste. Marie Tribe of Chippewa Indians* with 14,870 enrolled members. In effect the Sault tribe is a collectivity of the Ojibwa bands of the eastern Upper Peninsula. The tribe holds small parcels of land in Sault Ste. Marie, St. Ignace, Cedarville-Hessel, Manistique, Munising, Marquette, and Escanaba, together comprising about 400 acres. The Sault tribe is a viable economic force in northern Michigan and particularly in Chippewa County, where it is one of the largest employers. A government budget and various grants for housing and health care, as well as a casino and other profitable businesses give the Sault tribe a multimillion dollar annual budget. Formally recognized in December, 1974, by proclamation of the Secretary of the Interior, the tribe's bylaws and constitution were approved in November, 1975. A board of ten directors, elected for four-year terms, directs the activities of the tribe.

These federally recognized tribes articulate with the Bureau of Indian Affairs through the offices of the Michigan agency in Sault Ste. Marie and the district office of the Bureau in Minneapolis. Within the state, the tribes coordinate their various goals through the Intertribal Council of Michigan, which sponsors an annual Grand Assembly of the tribes.

Federal Indian reservations are unique in many ways, since jurisdiction is mainly determined by federal rather than state law. Since reservations are not state property, state taxes are not collected on Indian-owned property and sales of goods and services from Indian-owned reservation businesses. Tribal governments may license hunting and fishing of its members as well as issue automobile licenses. Likewise nearly all reservations operate some type of gaming. Gambling is regulated under the Indian Gaming Regulatory Act of October, 1988 (*U.S. Statutes at Large,* 102:2467–69, 2472, 2476), which recognizes certain classes of gaming and permits tribes in states where gambling is conducted to negotiate tribal-state compacts to govern the conduct of gaming.

Civil and criminal jurisdiction on Indian reservations is also confusing to many people. Essentially, tribal or federal authorities have jurisdiction over Indians on reservations, while the state may exercise such authority over non-Indians on reservations and Indians who commit crimes off reservations. Some of the confusion arises because tribal police and conservation officers are often also cross-deputizedly county sheriffs and, in that capacity, may issue citations to non-Indians for local district courts. Otherwise, tribes have no criminal authority over non-Indians, though the question of the authority of the tribe to protect its welfare and the health and safety of its members within reservation boundaries is constantly contended in the courts.

Tribal courts hear most civil problems involving member Indians including marriage, divorce, child custody, and probate. Major crimes such as murder, rape, larceny, assault, or arson that are committed by Indians on reservations are investigated by the FBI and prosecuted in federal district court. Legal authority for this procedure is given under the Major Crimes Act of March 3, 1855, and its several amendments, including the Indian Crimes Act of 1976 (*U.S. Statutes at Large,* 90:585–86). Tribes do exercise some limited authority over tribal members in off-reservation situations. Under the Indian Child Welfare Act of November 8, 1978 (*U.S. Statutes at Large,* 92: 3069, 3071–73, 3075–76), for example, the tribe has a voice in the dissolution of Indian families and the court's placement of dependent children.

The administration of federally recognized tribes is perhaps one of the most difficult management tasks. The chairperson is first responsible to a tribal council that is often beset by deep political divisions, some involving long-standing family alignments or religious grounds. Not only does the tribal administrator face built-in opposition, he or she is often pressured by relatives and supporters for tribal jobs, a temptation hard for tribal politicians to resist, given the lack of other employment opportunities in many reservation areas. In addition, the chairperson must be responsible to the Bureau of Indian Affairs, whose often nonsensical procedures and vast inefficiency make it one of the least competent of federal bureaucracies. Because of its control over budgets, the Bureau is indirectly involved in many tribal and intertribal decisions. The tribal chairman must also represent the tribe in dealings with other governments—state, county, municipal, and tribal—and most tribes have complex ongoing dealings with these other governments. Intertribal relationships are always difficult. From the outside it would seem that all tribes ought to have common goals, while, in fact, they often have very different viewpoints and political agendas. The problem is that within the Bureau of Indian Affairs the tribes are all competing against each other for limited resources. Despite this fact, the federally recognized tribes have developed some excellent, cooperatively administered units, for example the Ottawa/Chippewa Treaty Fishing Management Authority and the Great Lakes Indian Fish and Wildlife Commission. They have also developed a whole range of joint political positions in dealing with state government and cooperative business ventures.

Perhaps because of the inherent difficulties of tribal management, Michigan Indian tribes have produced some men and women of outstanding administrative skills. Many, but not all, are college educated; all are well-schooled in the complex legal, fiscal, and political realities of managing multimillion dollar governments.

The majority of Indians in Michigan, perhaps 35,000, either do not belong to one of the state's three historic tribes—the Ojibwa, Ottawa, or Potawatomi—or have not yet become enrolled members. Many claim descent as Blackfoot, Navajo, Cheyenne, Cree, or Cherokee, while others identify culturally with one or another of the historic tribes but have not documented their genealogical descent. Others have done so but may lack the quarter-blood quantum that is the key to qualifying for many Indian programs. Unfortunately, it is these disenfranchised Indians who are often most desperately in need of help.

Despite advances made since the late 1970s, by any objective measure one might apply, native Americans are on the bottom rung of Michigan's socioeconomic ladder. Per capita income is lower and infant mortality, unemployment, and school dropout rates are all

Spirit houses over graves on Garden Island, 1973. (Photograph courtesy of the Michigan State University Museum.)

higher for Michigan Indian citizens than for other racially or culturally based groups. For whatever historical causes, and they are complex, Michigan and the nation have not shared economic abundance equally among its citizens, particularly with its native peoples.

To some degree, federally recognized tribes are able to take care of their own. This is often not possible in the case of people who belong to unrecognized Michigan bands or Indians of other tribes who reside in Michigan cities. The various urban Indian centers, which are always poorly funded and survive from one grant to another, are the first line of defense against urban poverty and its effects. Organizations such as the Confederate Historic Tribes Inc. and the Native American Institute at Michigan State University provide expertise and technical assistance to these centers and other local organizations to obtain grants for operations and to provide badly needed services to Indian clients. The Michigan Commission on Indian Affairs also provides coordination and direction for current federal programs and organizations.

The Michigan Indian Commission, as it is commonly called, was founded in 1964 to provide advice to the governor's office in regard to Michigan Indian affairs.[20] In 1977, the commission was formalized by the legislature, when it created the modern commission by passing Public Act 195 of 1972. Administered through the Office of Management and Budget, the commission is composed of eleven appointed members. Two come from the federally recognized tribes, two from the largest cities, five from various geographic areas, and two are appointed at large. Unfortunately, the state Indian commission has never been very effective in dealing with the problems of Indians. Despite able leaders, the commission suffers from the lack of any real political power and from a pitifully small annual budget. Even given these limitations, the commission does manage to keep Indian problems in the public eye and to provide information about Indians to state government and the public. One very notable success is the Indian tuition waiver program administered through the commission. Under this program, any North American Indian of at least quarter Indian blood who has resided in Michigan for twelve months may receive full tuition at one of the state's public colleges or universities. In 1991, nearly 1,800 Indian college students benefited from this program. Lake Superior State University alone awarded bachelor's degrees to thirty-nine Indian residents.

Future Prospects

In the early decades of the twenty-first century there will be more Indians in Michigan than there are today, and they will undoubtedly constitute a higher proportion of the general population. This is due to the fact that birth rates among Indians are four times the Michigan average. It is also expected that substantial progress will be made in economic development, which, in turn, will lead to better family income and health and higher levels of educational achievement. This progress will depend on bringing more Indians into federal programs, a more liberal policy of tribal fiscal management on the part of the Bureau of Indian Affairs, and more entrepreneurial activities on the part of the tribes themselves. It will also depend on solving the problem of getting services to the state's nonrecognized and geographically disenfranchised urban population through the development of new state programs.

Prospects have brightened for the federally recognized tribes since the advent of gaming in the late 1980s. For the first time in their histories these tribal governments have had cash to invest in tribal programs as well as in outside business ventures. Of course, some have chosen to criticize an economy based upon gambling, but, considering the unemployment and poverty that gambling is eradicating, it seems a wonderful alternative to most Indians. This is also an opinion shared by the non-Indian business owners in towns located near reservations.

Among the most troublesome questions Indians will have to face in the near future are: who is an Indian, and who will share in the benefits available to Indian people? This is an old and difficult question, one that was faced first by nineteenth-century chiefs as they were forced to decide how their "halfblood" relatives would share in treaty benefits. The question has become more critical as passing generations have married non-Indians. Logic would indicate, as the failed assimilation policy of the early twentieth century predicted, that Indians would simply be absorbed into the American mainstream. This has not happened because Indianness is not simply a biological phenomenon, but a cultural one as well. The idea of blood quantum, though based upon the scientific racism of the early nineteenth century, provides an objective measure of ancestry and is thus reassuring. Because a person has one "full-blooded" Indian grandparent or its proportional equivalent does not mean that person is more or less Indian in cultural identity as opposed to persons of more or less Indian "blood." Obviously, it is an advantage of vested Indian groups, such as acknowledged tribes, to discourage the recognition of more bands or the inclusion of more people in the "Indian" category. Again, Indians are placed in a dilemma. They may not increase their political clout without diluting the already limited funds available for programs. They cannot help other Indians gain rights without diminishing the value of their own hard-won advantages.

The definition problem is not academic by any means; it is at the core of the future of Indians and Indian culture. It is so difficult that a $10 million award to the Ottawa and Ojibwa from the 1836 treaty area that was obtained decades ago has not been distributed for lack

A young dance contestant waits for her turn at the Sault Tribe Pow Wow, 1990. (Photograph courtesy of *Win Awenen Nisitotung,* the tribal newspaper of the Sault Ste. Marie Tribe.)

of a solution to the problem. On the bright side, interest has by now pushed the balance to over $50 million; the incentive keeps mounting and with it the pressure for resolution.

Another problem for Indians as well as the general public is to find a way to heal the ugly scars of poverty. Alcoholism, dietary disorders with the associated curses of obesity and diabetes, family dysfunction, suicide, and low self-esteem continue to plague Michigan Indian communities. With such small numbers it is seldom possible for Indians to muster the political pressure to help solve these problems on either the state or national level. It is perhaps worth noting that most of these and other problems were created as Indian tribes were conquered and then progressively pushed to the margins of American society. It seems clear that the lesson of the past is that curing the cause is much cheaper than treating the disease.

Michigan Indians, like the other native people of the Great Lakes region, have withstood and survived a biological and cultural assault that has now lasted for eight generations. The scourge of smallpox, generations of intense warfare, the total disruption of communities, alcohol and drunkenness, poverty, and the loss of their land and many cultural traditions have come upon them without their choosing. It is almost beyond belief that they have endured at all, let alone thrived as a people who are proud of their traditions and enthused about the future. It is perhaps in their distinctiveness and in the beliefs that make them unique that others could find values worth emulating.

NOTES

1. Foster Otto was for years a tailor in Petoskey, a skill he learned while a student at the Mt. Pleasant Indian School and at the Carlisle Indian School in Pennsylvania, where he played football on the same team as the great Olympic champion, Jim Thorpe. Mr. Otto's son Simon has recently published a book of Ottawa stories called *Walk in Peace* (1990); many of the stories come from his father.
2. Mrs. Shedawin and her husband, Charlie, were renowned for their beautifully crafted split-ash baskets. The quote given here came in the context of preparing a video on basketmaking, made for the Museum of Ojibwa Culture and History in St. Ignace. This museum provides an excellent introduction to the Indian cultures of northern Michigan.

3. Doc Bill Cameron, a member of the very prominent Cameron family of Sault Ste. Marie, was called "Doc" because he was believed to be a "blood stopper." This European belief was based on the notion that some people were born with the power to stanch the flow of blood. Doc Bill was a popular figure around the Sault for many years. He had a great sense of humor and a way with a story. The book *Kahwamdameh* by Jean Frazier (1989) details some of the history of the Cameron family, particularly Herman, a Bay Mills Ojibwa and the longtime, distinguished director of the State Commission on Indian Affairs.

4. Prucha 1986, 226.

5. Jermark to Commissioner of Indian Affairs, February 19, 1931, Office of Indian Affairs, Central Classified Files, Lac du Flambeau, 62592, National Archives.

6. See Dyer 1990.

7. See McClurken 1991.

8. McClurken 1991, 63.

9. McClurken 1991, 67.

10. Fixico 1986, 95

11. Deer 1983, 113–18.

12. Protection of individual and tribal rights, increased fiscal support, and more local autonomy were made possible by the following Acts of Congress: Civil Rights Act of 1968, Titles II and VII (*U.S. Statutes at Large*, 82:77–81); Indian Education Act of 1972 (*U.S. Statutes at Large*, 86:335, 339–43); Indian Financing Act of 1974 (*U.S. Statutes at Large*, 88:77–79); Indian Self-Determination Act of 1975 (*U.S. Statutes at Large*, 88:2203–14); Indian Health Care Improvement Act of 1976 (*U.S. Statutes at Large*, 90:1400–1407, 1410–12); American Indian Religious Freedom Act of 1978 (*U.S. Statutes at Large*, 92:469–70); Indian Child Welfare Act of 1978 (*U.S. Statutes at Large*, 92:3069, 3071–73); Tribally Controlled Schools Act of 1988 (*U.S. Statutes at Large*, 102:385–87); Indian Gaming Regulation Act of 1988 (*U.S. Statutes at Large*, 102:2467; 69:2472–76); and the Native American Graves Protection and Repatriation Act of 1991 (*U.S. Statutes at Large*, 104:3048–58).

13. Anonymous 1976, 81.

14. Mar Shunk was typical of many rural Indian communities in the State of Michigan at that time. The Governor's Commission on Indian Affairs contracted with Touche Ross Inc. to study the condition of Indians on a statewide basis in 1970. Touche Ross collected data from 383 Indian households in both urban and rural areas (see Anonymous 1971).

15. There are several nonrecognized Indian bands that have a legitimate claim to treaty rights under the Treaty of 1836, including, at least, the

Burt Lake, Little Traverse, Little River, and Grand River bands. Since the courts have taken the position that treaty rights are vested in the tribe or band rather than with the individual, the responsibility to regulate treaty rights also belongs with the tribal entity. When tribes are not acknowledged, the federal government contends it has no formal mechanism to deal with the tribe and, therefore, no means to oversee the treaty benefits of individuals.

16. The canons of treaty construction are based upon several key legal precedents.

   a) Language of treaties must be interpreted as Indians understood them. See Jones v. Meehan, 175 U.S. 1, 10–11 (1899); U.S. v. Shoshone Tribe, 304 U.S. 111, 116 (1938); Choctaw Nation v. U.S., 138 U.S. 423, 431–32 (1943); People v. Jondreau, 384 Mich. 539, 185 NW 2d 375 (1971).

   b) Doubtful expression is to be resolved in favor of Indian parties. See Winters v. U.S., 207 U.S. 564, 576–77 (1908); Carpenter v. Shaw, 208 U.S. 263, 267 (1930); Standing Rock Sioux Tribe v. U.S., 182 Ct.Cl. 813, 820 (1968).

   c) Treaties should be construed literally in favor of the Indians. See Choctaw Nation v. U.S., 139 U.S. 423, 431–32 (1943); Antonine v. Washington, 420 U.S. 194, 200 (1975).

   General references to the canons of treaty construction also appear in Washington v. Washington State Commercial Passenger Fishing Vessel Association, 443 U.S. 658 (1979) and U.S. v. Michigan, 471 F. Supp. 192 (Western District of Michigan 1979).

17. Great credit for the successful outcome of *U.S. v. Michigan* should go to ethnohistorian Dr. Helen Tanner, who skillfully marshaled volumes of documents to build and support the case of the tribes. Supporting expert testimony was also presented by Dr. Charles E. Cleland and Dr. James Clifton.

18. See C. Cleland 1991c.

19. The information on the federally recognized tribes is taken from Anonymous 1990. Data on trust lands was provided by the Real Estate Division of the Michigan Agency of the Bureau of Indian Affairs.

20. See Hilman 1981.

Bibliography

Adams, Arthur T., ed.
1961   The Explorations of Pierre Esprit Radisson. Minneapolis: Ross and Haines.

Adney, E. T., and H. I. Chapelle.
1964   The Bark Canoes and Skin Boats of North America. Smithsonian Institution Bulletin 230. Washington D.C.: U.S. Government Printing Office.

Ahearn, Phyllis, and R. E. Bailey.
1980   Pollen Record from Chippewa Bay, Lapeer County, Michigan. Michigan Academician 12 (3): 297–308.

Allen, Robert S.
1988   His Majesty's Indian Allies: Native Peoples, the British Crown and the War of 1812. Michigan Historical Review 14:3–24.

Anderson, Dean.
1991   Variability in Trade at Eighteenth-Century Outposts. In French Colonial Archaeology: The Illinois Country and the Western Great Lakes, ed. John Walthalle. Urbana: University of Illinois Press.

Anderson, John.
N.d.   A Short History of the Life of John Anderson. University of Michigan Archives, Clements Library, G 35168, Ann Arbor. Typescript.

Anonymous.
1812   The Capitulation of a History of the Expedition Conducted by William Hull. In War on the Detroit, ed. Milo Quaife. 1940. Chicago: Lake Side Press.

Anonymous.
1971   A Study of the Socio-Economic Status of Michigan Indians. Lansing: Governor's Commission on Indian Affairs.

301

Anonymous.
1976   Civil Rights and the Housing and Community Development Act
       of 1974, vol. 3, The Chippewa People of Sault Ste. Marie. Lan-
       sing: Michigan Advisory Committee to the United States Commis-
       sion on Civil Rights.
Anonymous.
1990   Michigan Indian Communities. Sault Ste. Marie: Second Grand
       Assembly of Michigan Tribes, Michigan Intertribal Council.
Armour, David, ed.
1971   Attack at Michilimackinac. Mackinac Island: Mackinac Island
       State Park Commission.
Avery, Charles P.
1866   The Treaty of Saginaw of 1819. In Indian and Pioneer History
       of the Saginaw Valley and Pioneer Directory and Business Advi-
       tizer for 1866–68. Compiled by Thomas and A. E. Galatin. Sagi-
       naw: Thomas and Galatin.
Baraga, F.
1973   A Dictionary of the Otchipwe Language. Reprinted from 1878
       edition. Minneapolis: Ross and Haines.
Barnouw, Victor.
1977   Wisconsin Chippewa Myths and Tales. Madison: University of
       Wisconsin Press.
Bearrs, R. E., and R. O. Kapp.
1987   Vegetation Associated with Heisler Mastodon Site, Calhoun
       County, Michigan. Michigan Academician 19 (1): 133–40.
Berger, J.
1971   Animal World. New Society, 25 November, 1042–43.
Berkhofer, Robert F.
1972   Salvation and the Savage: An Analysis of Protestant Missions and
       American Indian Response, 1787–1862. New York: Atheneum
       Books.
Bettarel, Robert L., and H. G. Smith.
1973   The Moccasin Bluff Site and the Woodland Cultures of South-
       western Michigan. Anthropological Papers, no. 49. Ann Arbor:
       University of Michigan Museum of Anthropology.
Binford, Lewis R.
1963   The Hodges Site: A Late Archaic Burial Station. In Miscellaneous
       Studies in Typology and Classification. Anthropological Papers,
       no. 19. Ann Arbor: University of Michigan Museum of Anthropol-
       ogy.

Birk, Douglas A.
  1989   *John Sayer's Snake River Journal, 1804–5*. Minneapolis: Institute for Minnesota Archaeology.
Bishop, Charles A.
  1989   The Question of Ojibwa Clans. In *Actes du Vingtieme Congres Des Algonquinistes*, ed. William Cowan. Ottawa: Carleton University Press.
Blackbird, Andrew J.
  1887   *History of the Ottawa and Chippewa Indians of Michigan*. Ypsilanti: The Ypsilantian Printing House. Facsimile printed by Little Traverse Regional Historical Society, Petoskey, Michigan.
Blair, Emma H.
  1911   *The Indian Tribes of the Upper Mississippi Valley and the Region of the Great Lakes*. 2 vols. Cleveland: Arthur H. Clark.
Bliss, Eugene, ed.
  1885   *Diary of David Zeisberger, a Moravian Missionary Among the Indians of Ohio*. Cincinnati: Robert Clark and Co.
Bolt, Christine.
  1987   *American Indian Policy and American Reform*. London: Unwin Hyman.
Branstner, Susan.
  1991   Decision-making in a Culture Contact Context: An Historical and Archaeological Perspective of the Tionontate Huron of St. Ignace, Michigan. In *Entering the 90s: The North American Experience*, ed. T. E. Schirer. Sault Ste. Marie: Lake Superior State University Press.
Brashler, Janet G.
  1981   *Early Late Woodland Boundaries and Interaction: Indian Ceramics of Southern Lower Michigan*. The Museum, Michigan State University Anthropological Series, vol. 3, no. 3. East Lansing: Michigan State University.
Brose, David S.
  1970   *The Archaeology of Summer Island: Changing Settlement Systems in Northern Lake Michigan*. Anthropological Papers, no. 41. Ann Arbor: University of Michigan Museum of Anthropology.
Brose, David S., ed.
  1976   *The Late Prehistory of the Lake Erie Drainage Basin: A 1972 Symposium Revised*. Cleveland: Scientific Publications of the Cleveland Museum of Natural History.

Brown, James, and R. Vierra.
  1983   What Happened in the Middle Archaic: An Introduction to an
          Ecological Approach to Koster Site Archaeology. In *Archaic
          Hunters and Gatherers in the American Midwest*, ed. J. L. Philips
          and J. A. Brown. New York: Academic Press.
Brown, Jennifer, and Robert Brightman.
  1988   *"The Orders of the Dreamed" George Nelson on Cree and North-
          ern Ojibwa Religion and Myth, 1823*. St. Paul: Minnesota Histori-
          cal Society Press.
Buckmaster, M. M., and J. R. Paquette.
  1988   The Gorto Site: Preliminary Report on a Late Paleo-Indian Site
          in Marquette County, Michigan. *Wisconsin Archaeologist* 69 (3):
          101–24.
Burton, M. Agnes, ed.
  1912   (Navarre's) *Journal of Pontiac's Conspiracy 1763*, trans. Clyde
          Ford. Detroit: Speaker Hines Printing.
Caldwell, Helen N.
  1894   Indian Reminiscences. *Michigan Pioneer and Historical Collec-
          tions* 21:297–313.
Callender, Charles.
  1978   Great Lakes–Riverine Sociopolitical Organization. In *Handbook
          of North American Indians*, vol. 15, *Northeast*, ed. B. Trigger.
          Washington, D.C.: Smithsonian Institution.
Calloway, Collin G.
  1987   *Crown and Calumet British Indian Relations, 1783–1815*. Nor-
          man: University of Oklahoma Press.
Campeau, Lucien, S.J.
  1987   *La Mision des Jusuits chez Les Hurons, 1634–1650*. Montreal:
          Editions Bellarmine.
Champlain, Samuel de.
  1902   *The Voyages and Explorations of Samuel de Champlain*. New
          York: Allerton.
Claspy, Everett.
  1966   *The Potawatomi Indians of Southwestern Michigan*. Dowagiac:
          Braun and Brumfield.
Cleland, Charles E.
  1965   Barren Ground Caribou *Rangifer arcticus* from an Early Man Site
          in Southeastern Michigan. *American Antiquity* 30 (3): 350–51.
  1966   *The Prehistoric Animal Ecology and Ethnozoology of the Upper
          Great Lakes Region*. Anthropological Papers, no. 29. Ann Arbor:
          University of Michigan Museum of Anthropology.

1973   The Pi-wan-go-ning Prehistoric District at Norwood, Michigan. *Geology and the Environment.* Lansing, Mich.: Basin Geological Society.

1982   The Inland Shore Fishery of the Northern Great Lakes: Its Development and Importance in Prehistory. *American Antiquity* 47 (4): 761–84.

1985   Comments on "A Reconsideration of Aboriginal Fishing Strategies in the Northern Great Lakes Region" by Susan R. Martin. *American Antiquity* 54 (3): 605–9.

1991a   Cass, Sassaba, and Ozhawguscodaywaquay: History, Ethnohistory, and Historical Reality. In *Entering the Nineties: The North American Experience,* ed. Thomas Schirer. Sault Ste. Marie: Lake Superior State University Press.

1991b   From Ethnohistory to Archaeology: Ottawa and Ojibwa Band Territories of the Northern Great Lakes. In *Text-Aided Archaeology,* ed. Barbara Little. Caldwell, N.J.: Telford Press.

1991c   Indian Treaties and American Myths. *Native Studies Review* (University of Saskatchewan) 6 (2): 79–85.

N.d.   Economic and Adaptive Change Among the Lake Superior Chippewa of the Nineteenth Century. In *Approaches to Culture Contact: Ethnohistorical and Archaeological Perspectives on Change,* ed. J. D. Rodgers and S. M. Wilson. New York: Plenum Press.

Cleland, Charles E., and Susan S. Branstner.

N.d.   The Historic Period. In *Michigan Archaeology,* ed. John Halsey. Birmingham, Mich.: Cranbrook Institute Press.

Cleland, Nancy N.

1989   Analysis of the Botanical Remains and Paleo-Environment of the Weber I Site. In *Archaeological Cultural Resource Investigation Series,* vol. 1, *Archaeological Investigations at the Weber I and Weber II Sites,* ed. William A. Lovis. Lansing: Michigan Department of State.

Clifton, James A.

1975   *A Place of Refuge for All Time: Migration of the American Potawatomi into Upper Canada, 1830 to 1850.* Canadian Ethnology Service Paper, no. 26. Ottawa: National Museum of Man Mercury Series.

1977   *The Prairie People.* Lawrence: Regents Press of Kansas.

1983   The Reemergent Wyandot: A Study in Ethnogenesis on the Detroit River Borderland, 1747. In *The Western District,* ed. K. G. Pryke and L. L. Kulisek. Windsor, Ontario: Essex County Historical Society.

1984 *The Pokagons, 1683–1983.* New York: University Press of America.

1986 The Potawatomi. In *People of the Three Fires* by J. A. Clifton, G. L. Cornell, and J. M. McClurken. Grand Rapids: Grand Rapids Intertribal Council.

1989 *Being and Becoming Indian: Biographical Studies of North American Frontiers.* Chicago: Dorsey Press.

Cochran, Thomas, ed.

1972 *The New American State Papers.* Indian Affairs, vol. 4, Northwest. Wilmington, Delaware: Scholarly Resources.

Cohen, David W.

1989 The Undefining of Oral Tradition. *Ethnohistory* 36 (1): 9–18.

Coleman, Sister B., E. Frogner, and E. Eich.

1961 *Ojibwa Myths and Legends.* Minneapolis: Ross and Haines.

Conway, Thor A.

1979 Heartland of the Ojibway. In *Collected Archaeological Papers, Archaeological Research Report 13,* ed. David Melvin. Toronto: Ontario Ministry of Culture and Recreation.

Cunningham, V. M.

1948 A Study of the Glacial Kame Culture. In *Occasional Contributions from the Museum of Anthropology,* no. 12. Ann Arbor: University of Michigan.

Deer, Robert E.

1983 A Menominee Perspective. In *The Great Lakes Forests: An Environmental and Social History,* ed. Susan Flader. Minneapolis: University of Minnesota Press.

Denke, Christian F.

1990 The Diaries of Christian Denke on the Sydenham River, 1804–1805. Trans. Irmgard Jamnik. *KEWA,* Newsletter of the London Chapter of the Ontario Archaeological Society (London), September 1990, 3–21.

Densmore, Frances.

1970 *Chippewa Customs.* Reprint. Minneapolis: Ross and Haines.

Dewdney, Selwyn.

1975 *The Sacred Scrolls of the Southern Ojibwa.* Toronto: University of Toronto Press.

Dowd, Gregory E.

1990 The French King Wakes Up in Detroit: "Pontiac's War" in Rumor and History. *Ethnohistory* 37 (3): 254–78.

Dunbar, Willis.

1965 *Michigan: A History of the Wolverine State.* Grand Rapids: Eerdmans.

Dunning, R. W.
  1959   *Social and Economic Change Among the Northern Ojibwa.*
         Toronto: University of Toronto Press.
Dustin, Fred.
  1919   *The Saginaw Treaty of 1819.* Saginaw: Saginaw Publishing Com-
         pany.
Dyer, Patricia.
  1990   W.P.A. Arts and Crafts Project: The Impact and Errors of a Fed-
         eral Economic Development Project. Paper presented at the an-
         nual meeting of the Michigan Academy of Science, Arts, and
         Letters, Albion College.
Eccles, William J.
  1988   The Fur Trade in the Colonial Northeast. In *History of Indian-
         White Relations,* ed. W. E. Washburn. Handbook of North
         American Indians, vol. 4. Washington, D.C.: Smithsonian Institu-
         tion.
Eckert, Allan W.
  1970   *The Conquerors.* New York: Little, Brown.
Edmunds, David R.
  1978   *The Potawatomis, Keepers of the Fire.* Norman: University of
         Oklahoma Press.
  1983   *The Shawnee Prophet.* Lincoln: University of Nebraska Press.
Eggan, Fred.
  1966   *The American Indian: Perspective for the Study of Social Change.*
         Cambridge: Cambridge University Press.
Eklund, Cox.
  1991   *Chippewa (Ojibwa) Language Book.* Privately printed by the
         author. New York: The Equitable Tower, 787 Seventh Ave.
Ely, Edmond F.
  N.d.   Journal, Ms E52. Typescript of originals in the Houghton Library,
         Harvard University. St. Paul: Minnesota Historical Society.
Feest, Johanna, and C. F. Feest.
  1978   Ottawa. In *The Handbook of North American Indians,* vol. 15,
         ed. B. Trigger. Washington, D.C.: The Smithsonian Institution.
Ferris, Neal.
  1989   Continuity Within Change: Settlement-Subsistence Strategies
         and Artifact Patterns of the Southwestern Ontario Ojibwa, A.D.
         1780–1861. M.A. thesis, York University, Toronto.
Finlayson, William D.
  1989   "A Sedimental Journey": Twenty Years of Archaeological Re-
         search in the Crawford Lake Area. *Palisade Post* (London, On-
         tario) 10 (4): 2–8.

Fischer, D. C.
1984   Mastodon Butchery by North American Paleo-Indians. *Nature* 308:271–72.

Fitting, James E.
1963   The Hi-Lo Site: A Late Paleo Indian Site in Western Michigan. *Wisconsin Archaeologist* 44 (2): 87–96.
1965   *Late Woodland Cultures of Southeastern Michigan*. Anthropological Papers, no. 24. Ann Arbor: University of Michigan Museum of Anthropology.
1970   *The Archaeology of Michigan*. New York: Natural History Press.
1972   *The Schultz Site at Green Point*. Memoirs of the Museum of Anthropology, no. 4. Ann Arbor: University of Michigan.

Fitting, James E., J. Devisscher, and E. Wahla.
1966   *The Paleo-Indian Occupation of the Holcomb Beach*. Anthropological Papers, no. 27. Ann Arbor: University of Michigan Museum of Anthropology.

Fitting, James E., D. S. Brose, H. T. Wright, and J. Dinerstein.
1969   The Goodwin-Gresham Site (20IA8), Iosco County, Michigan. *Wisconsin Archaeologist* 50 (3): 125–83.

Fixico, Donald L.
1986   *Termination and Relocation Federal Indian Policy, 1945–1960*. Albuquerque: University of New Mexico Press.

Flanders, Richard E.
1969   Hopewell Materials From Crockery Creek. *Michigan Academician* 1 (1–2): 147–51.
1977   Some Observations on the Goodall Focus. In *For the Director: Research Essays in Honor of James B. Griffin*, ed. Charles E. Cleland. Anthropological Papers, no. 61. Ann Arbor: University of Michigan Museum of Anthropology.

Fogel, I. L.
1963   The Dispersal of Copper Artifacts in the Late Archaic Period of Prehistoric North America. *Wisconsin Archaeologist* 44 (3): 129–80.

Fogelson, Raymond D.
1989   The Ethnohistory of Events and Nonevents. *Ethnohistory* 36 (2): 133–47.

Foote, Edward A.
1891   Historical Sketch of the Early Days of Eaton County. *Michigan Pioneer and Historical Collections* 3:379–81.

Ford, Henry A.
1888   The Old Moravian Mission at Mt. Clemens. *Michigan Pioneer and Historical Collections* 10:107–15.

Ford, Richard I.
    1981   Gardening and Farming Before A.D. 1000: Patterns of Prehistoric
            Cultivation North of Mexico. *Journal of Ethnobiology* 1 (1): 6–27.
Frazier, Jean.
    1989   *Kahwamdameh* (We See Each Other). Grand Ledge: Herman E.
            Cameron Memorial Foundation.
Garland, Elizabeth, ed.
    1984   *Archaeological Investigations in the Lower St. Joseph River Val-
            ley, Berrien County, Michigan.* Kalamazoo: Western Michigan
            University Department of Anthropology.
Garland, E., and J. Cogswell.
    1985   The Powers Mastodon Site. *Michigan Archaeologist* 31 (1–2): 3–39.
Gibbon, Guy.
    1986   The Mississippian Tradition: Oneota Culture. *Wisconsin Archae-
            ologist* 67 (3–4): 314–38.
Gilman, Rhoda R.
    1974   The Fur Trade in the Upper Mississippi Valley, 1630–1850. *Wis-
            consin Magazine of History* 58:3–18.
Gilpin, Alec R.
    1958   *The War of 1812 in the Old Northwest.* East Lansing: Michigan
            State University Press.
Gould, Stephen J.
    1981   *The Mismeasure of Man.* New York: Norton.
Greenberg, A. M., and J. Morrison.
    1982   Group Identities in the Boreal Forest: The Origin of the Northern
            Ojibwa. *Ethnohistory* 29 (2): 75–102.
Greenman, Emerson F.
    1937   *The Younge Site: An Archaeological Record from Michigan.* Mu-
            seum of Anthropology Occasional Contributions, no. 6. Ann Ar-
            bor: University of Michigan.
Gribb, William J.
    1982   The Grand Traverse Band's Land Base: A Cultural Historical
            Study of Land Transfer in Michigan. Ph.D. diss., Michigan State
            University.
Griffin, James B., ed.
    1961   *Lake Superior Copper and the Indians: Miscellaneous Studies of
            Great Lakes Prehistory.* Anthropological Papers, no. 17. Ann Ar-
            bor: University of Michigan Museum of Anthropology.
Griffin, James B., R. E. Flanders, and P. F. Titterington.
    1970   *The Burial Complexes of the Knight and Norton Mounds in Illi-
            nois and Michigan.* Memoirs of the Museum of Anthropology, no.
            2. Ann Arbor: University of Michigan.

Grignon, Augustin.
    1904   Seventy-two Years' Recollections of Wisconsin, ed. Lyman C.
           Draper. *Collections of the State Historical Society of Wisconsin*
           3:197– 295.
Grim, John A.
    1983   *The Shaman.* Norman: University of Oklahoma Press.
Grim, John A., and D. P. St. John.
    1989   The Northeast Woodlands. In *Native American Religions: North
           America,* ed. L. E. Sullivan. New York: Macmillan.
Gringhuis, Dirk.
    1970   *Lore of the Great Turtle.* Lansing: Mackinac Island State Park
           Commission.
Harris, R. Cole, and G. J. Matthews, eds.
    N.d.   *Historical Atlas of Canada,* vol. 1. Toronto: University of Toronto
           Press.
Harrison, Sidney.
    1966   The Schmidt Site (20SA192) Saginaw County, Michigan. *Michi-
           gan Archaeologist* 12:49–70.
Heidenreich, Conrad.
    1971   *Huronia: A History and Geography of the Huron Indians, 1600–
           1650.* Toronto: McClelland and Stewart.
    1978   The Huron. In *Handbook of North American Indians,* vol. 15,
           The Northeast, ed. B. Trigger. Washington, D.C.: Smithsonian
           Institution.
    1990   The Iroquois Wars to 1660: A Search for Causes. Paper delivered
           at the conference of the Society for Ethnohistory, Toronto.
Henry, Alexander.
    1969   *Travels and Adventures in Canada and the Indian Territories,
           1760–1776.* Edmonton: M. G. Hurtig.
Hickerson, Harold.
    1970   *The Chippewa and Their Neighbors.* Rev. ed. Prospect Heights,
           Ill.: Waveland Press.
Hill, Edward E.
    1967   *The Office of Indian Affairs, 1824–1880: Historical Sketches.*
           New York: Clearwater Publishing.
    1981   *Guide to the Records in the National Archives of the United
           States Relating to American Indians.* Washington, D.C.: National
           Archives and Records Service.
Hilman, James R.
    1981   Development of the Michigan Commission on Indian Affairs: The
           Study Commission. State of Michigan Library. Photocopy of
           typescript.

Hoffman, Walter J.
1891 The Mide-wi-win or Grand Medicine Society of the Ojibwa. In
U.S. Bureau of American Ethnology Seventh Annual Report,
1885–1886. Washington, D.C.: U.S. Government Printing
Office.

Holman, Margaret B.
1984 Pine River Ware: Evidence for in situ Development of the Late
Woodland in the Straits of Mackinac Region. Wisconsin Archaeologist 65 (1): 32–48.

Holman, J. A., D. C. Fisher, and R. O. Kapp.
1986 Recent Discoveries of Fossil Vertebrates in the Lower Peninsula
of Michigan. Michigan Academician 18 (3): 43–63.

Horsman, Reginald.
1963 The Role of the Indian in the War. In After Tippecanoe: Some
Aspects of the War of 1812, ed. Philip Mason. East Lansing:
Michigan State University Press.

Hoxie, Frederick E.
1984 A Final Promise: The Campaign to Assimilate the Indians, 1880–
1920. Cambridge: Cambridge University Press.

Hruska, Robert.
1967 The Riverside Site: A Late Archaic Manifestation in Michigan.
Wisconsin Archaeologist 48 (3): 145–259.

Humins, John.
1983 Furs, Astor and Indians: The American Fur Company in the Old
Northwest Territory. Michigan History, March/April, 24–31.

Hunt, George T.
1940 The Wars of the Iroquois. Madison: University of Wisconsin
Press.

Ingold, T., ed.
1988 What Is an Animal? London: Unwin Hyman.

Jacobs, Wilbur R.
1950 Diplomacy and Indian Gifts: Anglo-French Rivalry Along the
Ohio and Northwest Frontiers, 1748–1763. Stanford, Calif.: Stanford University Press.

Jameson, Ann.
1970 Winter Studies and Summer Rambles in Canada. 3 vols. Facsimile edition. Toronto: Coles Publishing. Originally published in
1838 in London by Saunders and Otley.

Janzen, Donald E.
1968 The Naomikong Point Site and the Dimensions of Laurel in the
Lake Superior Region. Anthropological Papers, no. 36. Ann Arbor: University of Michigan Museum of Anthropology.

Jenness, Diamond.
  1935 *The Ojibwa Indians of Parry Island: Their Social and Religious Life.* National Museum of Canada Bulletin 78, Anthropological Series 17. Ottawa: Department of Mines.
Jennings, Jesse D.
  1968 *Prehistory of North America.* New York: McGraw-Hill.
Johnson, Ida A.
  1971 *The Michigan Fur Trade.* Grand Rapids: Black Letter Press.
Johnston, Basil.
  1981 *Tales the Elders Told: Ojibway Legends.* Toronto: Royal Ontario Museum.
  1982 *Ojibway Ceremonies.* Toronto: McClelland and Stewart.
Jones, William.
  1916 Ojibwa Tales From the North Shore of Lake Superior. *Journal of American Folklore* 29:368–91.
Kapp, R. O.
  1977 Late Pleistocene and Postglacial Plant Communities of the Great Lakes Region. In *Geobotany,* ed. R. C. Romans. New York: Plenum Publishing.
Kappler, Charles J., ed.
  1904 *Indian Affairs: Laws and Treaties,* vol. 2, *Treaties.* Washington, D.C.: U.S. Government Printing Office.
Karrow P. F., and P. E. Calkins, eds.
  1985 *Quarternary Evolution of the Great Lakes.* Special Paper 30. Ottawa: Geological Association of Canada.
Kellogg, Louise P.
  1917 *Early Narratives of the Northwest, 1634–1699.* Original Narratives of Early American History. New York: Charles Scribner's Sons.
  1925 *The French Regime in Wisconsin and the Northwest.* Madison: State Historical Society of Wisconsin.
  1935 *The British Regime in Wisconsin and the Northwest.* Madison: State Historical Society of Wisconsin.
Killaly, Charlotte E.
  N.d. History of John Johnston of Sault Ste. Marie, Michigan, USA. George Johnston Papers, Bayliss Library, Sault Ste. Marie. Typescript.
Kingsley, Robert G.
  1981 Hopewell Middle Woodland Settlement Systems and Cultural Dynamics in Southern Michigan. *Midcontinental Journal of Archaeology* 6 (2): 132–78.

Kinietz, Vernon W.
1940   The Indians of the Western Great Lakes, 1615–1760. Occasional Contributions from the Museum of Anthropology, no. 10. Ann Arbor: University of Michigan Press.
Kirkland, Joseph.
1893   The Chicago Massacre of 1812. Chicago: Dibble Publishing.
Kobawgam, Charles.
N.d.   Ojibwa Myths and Half-Breed Tales Related by Charles and Charlotte Kobawgam and Jacques le Pique to Homer H. Kidder. American Philosophical Society, Philadelphia. Typescript.
Kohl, Johann G.
1985   Kitchi-Gami: Life Among the Lake Superior Chippewa. St. Paul: Minnesota Historical Society Press.
Landes, Ruth.
1971   The Ojibwa Woman. New York: Norton.
Larsen, Curtis E.
1987   Geological History of Glacial Lake Algonquian and the Upper Great Lakes. U.S. Geological Survey Bulletin 1801. Washington, D.C.: U.S. Government Printing Office.
Leeson, M. A.
1881   History of Saginaw County, Michigan. Chicago: Blakely, Brown, and Marsh.
Levi-Strauss, C.
1964   Totemism. London: Merlin.
Littlefield, Alice.
1989   The B. I. A. Boarding School: Theories of Resistance and Social Reproduction. Humanity and Society 13 (4): 428–41.
1992   Learning to Labor: Native American Education in the United States, 1880–1930. In Political Economy of Native Americans, ed. J. Moore and V. Tishkov. Norman: University of Oklahoma Press.
Lovis, William A., ed.
1989   Archaeological Investigations at the Weber I and Weber II Sites, Frankenmuth Township Saginaw County, Michigan. Michigan Cultural Resources Investigation Series, vol. 1. Lansing: Michigan Department of State.
Lovis, William A., and J. A. Robertson.
1989   Rethinking the Archaic Chronology of the Saginaw Valley, Michigan. Midcontinental Journal of Archaeology 14 (2): 226–60.
Lowrie, W., and W. Franklin, eds.
1834   American State Papers: Documents, Legislative and Executive of

the Congress of the United States. Washington, D.C.: Gales and Seaton.

Lurie, Nancy O.
1978 Winnebago. In *The Handbook of North American Indians,* vol. 15, ed. B. Trigger. Washington, D.C.: Smithsonian Institution.

McClurken, James M.
1988 We Wish to Be Civilized: Ottawa-American Political Contest on the Michigan Frontier. Ph.D. diss., Michigan State University.
1989 Augustin Hamlin, Jr.: Ottawa Identity and the Politics of Persistence. In *Being and Becoming Indian,* ed. James A. Clifton. Chicago: Dorsey Press.
1991 *Gah-Jhagwah-buk* (The Way It Happened). East Lansing: Michigan State University Press.

McKinney, Thomas.
1959 *Sketches of a Tour to the Lakes.* Minneapolis: Ross and Haines.

McPherron, Alan L.
1967 *The Juntunen Site and the Late Woodland Prehistory of the Upper Great Lakes Area.* Anthropological Papers, no. 30. Ann Arbor: University of Michigan Museum of Anthropology.

Martin, Calvin.
1978 *Keepers of the Game: Indian Animal Relationships and the Fur Trade.* Berkeley: University of California Press.

Martin, Susan R.
1989 A Reconsideration of Aboriginal Fishing Strategies in the Northern Great Lakes Region. *American Antiquity* 54 (3): 594–604.

Mason, Carol I.
1986 The Historic Period in Wisconsin Archaeology. *Wisconsin Archaeologist* 67 (3–4): 370–92.

Mason, Ronald.
1981 *Great Lakes Archaeology.* New York: Academic Press.
1986a The Paleo-Indian Tradition. *Wisconsin Archaeologist* 67 (3–4): 181–206.
1986b *Rock Island: Historical Indian Archaeology in the Northern Lake Michigan Basin.* Midcontinental Journal of Archaeology Special Paper 6. Kent, Ohio: Kent State University Press.

Mason, R., and C. Irwin.
1960 An Eden-Scotts Bluff Burial in Northeastern Wisconsin. *American Antiquity* 26 (1): 43–57.

Mead, Barbara, and R. G. Kingsley.
1985 20IS46, A Late Archaic Cemetery in Iosco County, Michigan. *Michigan Archaeologist* 31:67–81.

Mills, James C.
  1918   *History of Saginaw County, Michigan.* Saginaw: Seemann and
         Peters.
Miquelon, Dale.
  1987   *New France, 1701–1744.* Toronto: McClelland and Stewart.
Monfort, Margaret.
  1990   Ethnic and Tribal Identity Among the Saginaw Chippewa of
         Nineteenth-Century Michigan. M.A. thesis, Michigan State Uni-
         versity.
Moore, Charles.
  1897   The Days of Fife and Drum. *Michigan Historical and Pioneer
         Collections* 28:437–53.
Morton, Samuel.
  1839   *Crania Americana; or, A Comparative View of the Skulls of Vari-
         ous Aboriginal Nations of North and South America.* Philadelphia:
         John Pennington.
Murphy, Carl, and N. Ferris.
  1990   The Late Woodland Western Basin Tradition in Southwest On-
         tario. In *The Archaeology of Southern Ontario to A.D. 1650,* ed.
         C. J. Ellis and N. Ferris. Occasional Paper of the London Chapter
         of the Ontario Archaeological Society, no. 5. London.
Nelson, Paul D.
  1985   *Anthony Wayne: Soldier of the Early Republic.* Bloomington: In-
         diana University Press.
O'Connor, Catherine A.
  1990   The Fishing Rights Controversy in Michigan: Federal Treaty In-
         terpretation, Backlash, and Fishery Depletion. Senior paper, Uni-
         versity of Michigan–Flint.
Otto, Simon.
  1990   *Walk in Peace: Legends and Stories of the Michigan Indians.*
         Grand Rapids: Michigan Indian Press, Grand Rapids Inter-Tribal
         Council.
Ourada, Patricia K.
  1979   *The Menominee Indians.* Norman: University of Oklahoma Press.
Ozker, Doreen.
  1982   *An Early Woodland Community at the Schultz Site in the Saginaw
         Valley and the Nature of the Early Woodland Adaptation in the
         Great Lakes Region.* Anthropological Papers, no. 70. Ann Arbor:
         University of Michigan Museum of Anthropology.
Papworth, Mark L.
  1967   *Cultural Traditions in the Lake Forest Region During the Late*

Highwater Stages of the Post-Glacial Great Lakes. Ph.D. diss.,
University of Michigan.

Parachini, Kathryn.
1984   Botanical Remains from the Eidson Site. In *Archaeological Investigations in the Lower St. Joseph Valley, Berrien County, Michigan,* ed. Elizabeth Garland. Kalamazoo: Western Michigan University Department of Anthropology.

Parker, John, ed.
1976   *The Journals of Jonathan Carver and Related Documents, 1766–1770.* St. Paul: Minnesota Historical Society Press.

Parkman, Francis.
1883   *The Conspiracy of Pontiac.* Boston: Little, Brown.

Peckham, Howard H.
1947   *Pontiac and the Indian Uprising.* New York: Russell and Russell.

Peters, Bernard C.
1981   The Origin of Some Stream Names Along Michigan's Lake Superior Shoreline. *Inland Seas* 37 (Spring): 44–55.

1985   The Origin and Meaning of Chippewa and French Place Names Along the Shoreline of the Keweenaw Peninsula. *Michigan Academician* 17 (2): 195–211.

Pioneer and Historical Society of Michigan. *Historical Collections.* Lansing: Thorp and Godfred.

Prahl, Earl J.
1966   The Muskegon River Survey: 1965 and 1966. *Michigan Archaeologist* 12 (4): 183–212.

1991   The Mounds of the Muskegon. In *Pilot of the Grand,* Papers in Honor of R. E. Flanders, Part 2, ed. T. J. Martin and C. E. Cleland. *Michigan Archaeologist* 37 (2): 59–125.

Priest, Loring B.
1942   *Uncle Sam's Stepchildren: The Reformation of United States Indian Policy, 1865–1887.* New Brunswick: Rutgers University Press.

Prucha, Francis Paul.
1979   *The Churches and the Indian Schools, 1888–1912.* Lincoln: University of Nebraska Press.

1985   *The Indians in American Society from the Revolutionary War to the Present.* Berkeley: University of California Press.

1986   *The Great Father the United States Government and the American Indians.* Lincoln: University of Nebraska Press.

1990   *Documents of United States Indian Policy.* Lincoln: University of Nebraska Press.

Prucha, Francis Paul, ed.

1973   *Americanizing the American Indians: Writings by the Friends of the Indians, 1880–1900.* Lincoln: University of Nebraska Press.

Quaife, Milo M.

1962   *The Western Country in the Seventeenth Century: The Memoirs of Antoine Lamothe Cadillac and Pierre Liette.* New York: Citadel Press.

Quimby, George I.

1941   The Goodall Focus: An Analysis of Ten Hopewellian Components in Michigan and Indiana. *Indiana Historical Society, Prehistoric Research Series* 2:61–161.

1962   A Year with a Chippewa Family, 1763–1764. *Ethnohistory* 9 (3): 217–39.

1966   The Dumaw Creek Site: A Seventeenth-Century Prehistoric Indian Village and Cemetery in Oceana County, Michigan. *Fieldiana Anthropology* 56 (1): 1–91.

Radin, Paul.

1956   *The Trickster: A Study in American Indian Mythology.* New York: Philosophical Library.

Ritzenthaler, R. E., and G. I. Quimby.

1962   The Red Ochre Culture of the Upper Great Lakes and Adjacent Areas. *Fieldiana Anthropology* 36:243–75.

Ritzenthaler, Robert E.

1978   Southwestern Chippewa. In *Handbook of North American Indians,* vol. 15, ed. B. Trigger. Washington, D.C.: Smithsonian Institution.

Rodgers, E. S.

1978   Southeastern Ojibwa. In *Handbook of North American Indians,* vol. 15, ed. B. Trigger. Washington, D.C.: Smithsonian Institution.

Roosa, William B.

1977   Fluted Points from the Parkhill, Ontario Site. In *For the Director: Research Essays in Honor of James B. Griffin,* ed. Charles E. Cleland. Anthropological Papers, no. 61. Ann Arbor: University of Michigan Museum of Anthropology.

Rubenstein, Bruce A.

1974   Justice Denied: An Analysis of American Indian–White Relations in Michigan, 1855–1889. Ph.D. diss., Michigan State University.

Russell, Nelson V.

1939   *The British Regime in Michigan and the Old Northwest, 1760–1796.* Northfield, Minn.: Carleton College.

Sahlins, Marshall.
1968   *Tribesmen.* Englewood Cliffs, N.J.: Prentice-Hall.
1972   *Stone Age Economics.* Chicago: Aldine Publishing.
1981   *Historical Metaphors and Mythical Realities.* Association for Social Anthropology in Oceania, Special Publication no. 1. Ann Arbor: University of Michigan Press.

Sauer, Carl O.
1980   *Seventeenth-Century North America.* Berkeley, Calif.: Turtle Island Foundation.

Schoolcraft, Henry R.
1839   *Algic Researches.* New York: Harper and Brothers.

Schneider, David M.
1980   *American Kinship: A Cultural Account.* Chicago: University of Chicago Press.

Schultz, George.
1972   *An Indian Canaan: Isaac McCoy and the Vision of an Indian State.* Norman: University of Oklahoma Press.

Service, Elman.
1971   *Primitive Social Organization.* 2d ed. New York: Random House.

Simmons, Donald, M. J. Shott, and H. T. Wright.
1984   The Gainey Site: Variability in a Great Lakes Paleo-Indian Assemblage. *Archaeology of Eastern North America* 12:266–79.

Skinner, Alanson.
1924   The Mascoutens or Prairie Potawatomi Indians, Part 1: Social Life and Ceremonies. *Bulletin of the Public Museum of the City of Milwaukee* 6 (1): 1–262.

Smith, Beverley A.
1989   Analysis of the Faunal Remains from the Weber I Site. In *Archaeological Cultural Resource Investigation Series*, vol. 1, *Archaeological Investigations at the Weber I and Weber II Sites*, ed. W. A. Lovis. Lansing: Michigan Department of State.

Sosin, Jack M.
1975   Britain and the Ohio Valley, 1760–1775: The Search for Alternatives in a Revolutionary Era. In *Contest for Empire, 1500–1775*, ed. John B. Elliott. Indianapolis: Indiana Historical Society.

Spindler, Louise S.
1978   Menominee. In *The Handbook of North American Indians*, vol. 15, ed. B. Trigger. Washington, D.C.: Smithsonian Institution.

Spry, Irene, ed.
1968   *The Papers of the Palliser Expedition, 1857–1860.* Toronto: Champlain Society.

Stoltman, James B.
  1986   The Archaic Tradition. *Wisconsin Archaeologist* 67 (3–4): 207–38.
Sword, Wiley.
  1985   *President Washington's Indian War: The Struggle for the Old
         Northwest, 1790–1795.* Norman: University of Oklahoma Press.
Taggart, David W.
  1967   Seasonal Patterns in Settlement, Subsistence, and Industries in
         the Saginaw Late Archaic. *Michigan Archaeologist* 13:153–70.
Tanner, Helen H.
  1974   Report of *United States of America v. State of Michigan.* Bentley
         Historical Collections, Clements Library, University of Michigan,
         Ann Arbor. Typescript.
  1987   *Atlas of Great Lakes Indian History.* Norman: University of Okla-
         homa Press.
Tanner, John.
  1956   *A Narrative of the Captivity and Adventures of John Tanner Dur-
         ing Thirty Years Residence Among the Indians,* ed. Edwin James.
         Minneapolis: Ross and Haines.
Tapper, Richard.
  1988   Animality, Humanity, Morality, Society. In *What Is an Animal?*
         ed. T. Ingold. London: Unwin Hyman.
Thwaites, Ruben Gold, ed.
  1899   *The Jesuit Relations and Allied Documents.* 73 vols. Cleveland:
         Burrows.
  1904   *Early Western Travels, 1748–1846,* vol. 2, *Voyages and Travels
         of an Indian Interpreter and Trader—John Long.* Cleveland:
         Arthur H. Clark.
  1905   *New Voyages to North America* by Barron de Lahontan. Chicago:
         A. C. McClurg.
  1910   A Wisconsin Fur-Trader's Journal, 1804–1805 by Francois V.
         Malhoit. *Collections of the State Historical Society of Wisconsin*
         19:163–233.
  1911   A Wisconsin Fur-Trader's Journal, 1803–1804 by Michael Curot.
         Collections of the State Historical Society of Wisconsin 20:396–
         471.
Tooker, Elizabeth.
  1964   *An Ethnography of the Huron Indians, 1615–1649.* Smithsonian
         Institution, Bureau of American Ethnology Bulletin, no. 190.
         Washington, D.C.: Smithsonian Institution.
Trigger, Bruce.
  1969   *The Huron Farmers of the North.* New York: Holt, Rinehart and
         Winston.

1976   *The Children of Aataentsic*. Montreal: McGill–Queens University Press.

1984   The Road to Affluence: A Reassessment of Early Huron Responses to European Contact. In *Affluence and Cultural Survival*, ed. R. F. Salisbury and E. Tooker. 1981 Proceedings of the American Ethnological Society. Washington, D.C.: American Ethnological Society.

Trigger, Bruce, ed.

1978   *Handbook of North American Indians*, vol. 15, *Northeast*. Washington, D.C.: Smithsonian Institution.

Vansina, Jan.

1985   *Oral Tradition as History*. Madison: University of Wisconsin Press.

Vercheres, Thomas.

1940   The Chronicle of Thomas Vercheres de Boucherville. In *War on the Detroit*, ed. Milo M. Quaife. Chicago: Lakeside Press.

Verwyst, Chrysostom.

1892   Tchissakiwin or Indian Jugglery. State Historical Society of Wisconsin. Typescript.

Viola, Herman.

1981   *Diplomats in Buckskins: A History of Indian Delegations in Washington City*. Washington, D.C.: Smithsonian Institution Press.

Voelker, Donald W.

1990   Robert Stuart, A Man Who Meant Business. *Michigan History Magazine*, September/October, 12–19.

Vogel, Virgil J.

1986   *Indian Names in Michigan*. Ann Arbor: University of Michigan Press.

Voss, J. E.

1977   The Barnes Site: Functional and Stylistic Variability in a Small Paleo-Indian Assemblage. *Midcontinental Journal of Archaeology* 2:253–305.

Waddell, Jack O.

1985   Malhoit's Journal: An Ethnohistoric Assessment of Chippewa Alcohol Behavior in the Early Nineteenth Century. *Ethnohistory* 32 (3): 246–68.

Walker, Louise J.

1959   *Legends of Green Sky Hill*. Grand Rapids: Eerdmans.

Walsh, Martin W.

1982   The Condemnation of Carnival in the *Jesuit Relations*. *Michigan Academician* 15 (1): 13–26.

Warren, William W.
　1984　*History of the Ojibwa People.* St. Paul: Minnesota Historical Society Press.

White, Bruce M.
　1982　Give Us a Little Milk. *Minnesota History,* Summer, 60–71.
　1987　A Skilled Game of Exchange: Ojibwa Fur Trade Protocol. *Minnesota History,* Summer, 229–40.

White, Richard.
　N.d.　*Ethnohistorical Report on the Grand Traverse Ottawas.* Prepared for the Grand Traverse Tribe of Ottawa and Chippewa Indians. Manuscript.

Williams, Ephraim S.
　1886a　A Certificate of Statement Made by Chippewa Chiefs, Signers of the Treaty of 1819. *Michigan Pioneer and Historical Collections* 7:140–44.
　1886b　The Treaty of Saginaw in the Year 1819. *Michigan Pioneer and Historical Collections* 7:262–71.

Williams, Mentor L., ed.
　1953　*Narrative Journal of Travels Through the Northwestern Regions of the United States Extending from Detroit Through the Great Chain of American Lakes to the Source of the Mississippi River in the Year 1820 by Henry Schoolcraft.* East Lansing: Michigan State College Press.

Wilson, R. L.
　1967　The Pleistocene Vertebrates of Michigan. *Papers of the Michigan Academy of Science, Arts, and Letters* 52:197–257.

Wittry, W. L., and R. E. Ritzenthaler.
　1957　The Old Copper Complex: An Archaic Manifestation in Wisconsin. *Wisconsin Archaeologist* 38:311–20.

Wolf, Eric.
　1982　*Europe and the People Without History.* Berkeley: University of California Press.

Wright, Henry T.
　1964　A Transitional Archaic Campsite at Green Point (20SA1). *Michigan Archaeologist* 10 (1): 17–22.

Wright, H. T., and R. E. Morlan.
　1964　The Hart Site: A Dustin Complex Fishing Camp on the Shiawassee Empayment. *Michigan Archaeologist* 10:49–53.

Wright, H. T., and W. B. Roosa.
　1966　The Barnes Site: A Fluted Point Assemblage from the Great Lakes Region. *American Antiquity* 31 (6): 850–60.

Wright, James V.
  1966   *The Ontario Iroquois Tradition.* Bulletin 210. Ottawa: National
         Museum of Canada.
  1967   *The Laurel Tradition and the Middle Woodland Period.* Bulletin
         217. Ottawa: National Museum of Canada.
  1972   *The Shield Archaic.* Publications in Archaeology, no. 3. Ottawa:
         National Museum of Man.
Yarnell, Richard A.
  1964   *Aboriginal Relationships between Culture and Plant Life in the
         Upper Great Lakes Region.* Anthropological Papers, no. 23. Ann
         Arbor: University of Michigan Museum of Anthropology.

Index